PROPHECY
OF LOVE

By

T. SATTERFIELD

ISBN: 978-1-7377862-0-7 (paperback)

Tamiko Press, an imprint of Attention to Living, LLC

DEDICATION

These pages, collected and bound, are whole-heartedly dedicated to Tim.

ACKNOWLEDGMENTS

I wrote this love story for you my dears, my greatest loves. My twinkle, twinkle little stars. My moon in the great green room. My strawberry snatchers. That is, I wrote it for you after your father inspired me with decades of his patience and devotion.

Perhaps it is quite possible I've always, infinitely even, been writing this for him. Scribbling down our moments together, lifetimes spanning vast spectrums of space and time. Tucking the expectant words behind my ear where the little heart-to-hearts whispered into my hippocampus, weaving into sentences and paragraphs, plotting love's course.

But!

No, never but—always and—And!

And still I wrote this story for the two of you. Nevermind, my Diddywopps, my Keeffers, that you both grew up before I ever started to finish.

And then there's Cathy. All her brilliant notes scrawling the margins, marked shyly in dull pencil. The hours and hours spent side by side editing at the kitchen table.

And Charlie. Yes. Always, Charlie. Charlie.

INTRODUCTION

For centuries, love has been possibly our most misunderstood experience. Some of our greatest human suffering arises from this pervasive misconception and the manipulation of love's profound power. Yet love is the experience we credit with the greatest meaning. We devote our life to its pursuit.

So...what *is* love? Is it an emotion, a sensation, an experience? Is it of our bodies or our minds? Are there degrees, or kinds of love? Can it be bad?

What if love is more about imagination and sub-atomic particles? Would you travel backwards through all your memories, perceptions, and beliefs to change your brain and acquire love and the sense of purpose it provides?

Prophecy of Love, written in the genre of magical realism, is a romantic adventure of self-discovery packed with historic, scientific, and cultural information. It promises to demystify love while providing readers with a solid foundation for building healthy, loving relationships that still embrace the mystical.

1

"I'm gonna need someone to help me. I'm gonna need somebody's hand."
Singing along, pretending Nathaniel Rateliff and I were a couple of salty bikers in leather jackets, I sat at my desk with more swagger than self-awareness. Imagining our fat wallets clipped and chained. Both of us worked up. Clapping and stomping, rocking and rolling to a soul revivalist's pitch. Preparing to break out of some godforsaken prison.

Nothing made my job at The Law Offices of Dumas, McPhail & Cox easier than plugging in with the volume high enough that somebody standing nearby could hear the gospel of I-don't-give-a-damn.

Belting out, I sang from a bottomless pit of regret. With eyes closed, I conjured myself yanking at my tie, unbuttoning the first button. Maybe the second. "Son of a bitch! Give me a drink. One more night, this can't be me. Son of a bitch, if I can't get clean, I'm gonna drink my life away."

I crooned, exaggerating my pain, lifting my chin high toward some imagined golden rays of light, some forgiving lord. And just as I was about to feel the salvation of a new day dawning, my boss called out. "Gabe!" Her voice was sharp, and she had the eyebrows to match.

She'd cracked open the door just enough for her head to float in. I pulled out my earbuds. She flashed me a perfunctory smile. "We're meeting at four-thirty now."

"Today?" I eyeballed the clock. It was just past four. I sighed, having hoped I could've snuck out by five.

"Them's the breaks, kiddo. Gotta be worth your salt 'round here." She pointed her hand as if it were a gun and made a double-clacking sound. "Keep an eye on the time." She tapped her watch. "Don't want you late."

Sighing again, I ran my hand through my messy curls. "I won't be." I'd made other mistakes, but tardiness wasn't one of them.

She faked another smile. "Four-thirty." She tapped her watch again and closed the door. As she passed by the glass wall of my office, her head bobbed atop her overpriced pantsuit. The Persian floor runners absorbed the clatter of her heels.

Figures. Shaking my head, I balled up my earbuds and shoved them into the top drawer where I spied a blister pack of Pepto-Bismol. No sooner had I popped two than the dangerous sound of Amy Winehouse announced a call from My Ex. "I told you I was trouble, you know I'm no good."

I groaned, sliding to the edge of my chair, clearing my throat. "Hello," I said, feigning total disinterest. After all, it'd been a year of nonsense since the break-up.

She was casual. "Hey, I can't make it tonight." I heard windshield wipers.

"Seriously? This is the third time. Do you want your stuff or not?"

She spoke as if I were a child, enunciating each word. "Gabe, we are two adults," she said, like that explained something.

"No! No!" I shot up off the desk and onto my feet. "As usual, you flaked! And *two* adults? You're kidding, right?"

"Oh, get your control-freak head examined! You're like, so attached. You can't let anything go. You're a big baby, and I'm not your mother, Gabe. I've got a life, and it doesn't include dragging you around at the tit."

I jumped out from behind my desk. "After three years with you, I oughta have my head examined! And the expression is teat, and if you think I'll just go on being decent—"

She cut me off, laughing. "You're hardly a boy scout. Grow up, Gabe. Have another beer."

"Seriously? You're saying *I'm* not decent?" I paced in front of the glass wall, almost shouting.

"Gabe." She drew out my name like it was a sedative. "Settle down." I heard her kill the engine. I knew she'd pulled into a 7-Eleven and was likely checking herself in the rearview mirror. Sounding as if she was applying lipstick, she blathered on about what was best.

"Oh, is that right? Look who sounds attached now that you want something. Well, check this out. I changed the locks, and—"

"You changed the locks? My shit's in there!" She reeled, then caught herself. "Listen. I don't want to fight. Let's get along. Okay?"

"Oh, sure. Yeah, let's be civil *now*, shall we?" Now sitting on the edge of my desk, I noticed a passerby giving me the side-eye. "Uh-huh." I lowered my voice, transferring the phone to my other ear while she babbled. I heard her oversized keyring jangle and the car door open. I imagined one of her spiked-heel boots already on the ground. She was getting antsy for her Big Gulp.

"Gabe, you've become so cynical."

"Oh! You feel like I'm sarcastic, do you?" I stood again. "I'm so sorry. I don't mean to be caustic. I mean, why would I be bitter or humorless?" I was louder than was in my best interest. "The only problem is, as usual, you've forgotten about your little—"

The car door slammed. She talked low into the phone. "Listen, Gabe," she hissed, "and listen good. He has nothing to do with this, and I'm sick of you belly-aching about it." Bells rang, and I knew she'd yanked open the convenience store door.

"Oh," I said, slapping my leg, "so if I hadn't been snowboarding, that wouldn't have happened? Oh, that's right!" Spit flew. "It's all because *I'm* not honest and never say how I feel."

She was screaming, probably right in the middle of the store. I couldn't make out her words but recognized the sentiment.

"No! No! No! I'm not exploding. I'm saying how I feel, and you don't—No, it's not at all—"

"Look," I finally hollered over her, "here's the deal. You want your stuff? Come by at seven. I won't be there. Just like you asked."

It was quiet. Then she whined. "He can't help me tonight."

I closed my eyes, clenched my jaw and I bottled up my fury. "I gotta go. Get your crap tonight, or it all goes to the curb." I smashed the phone down onto my desk, realizing a moment too late that I'd shattered the screen. My stomach lurched, and another familiar ringtone announced a text. Before I knew it, I'd swiped a finger across the busted screen, deleting my mom's message, then headed to the men's room.

Planting my hands on the cold marble vanity, I studied my reflection. "When are you gonna get it? You're the walking dead. Pa-the-tic," I said, then spat for emphasis. Cranking the faucet, I slapped my face with cold water, then watched while it dripped from my closely trimmed beard and splattered my shirt. Captivated by the dark spots that bled and bloomed, I felt a moment's peace; that's when I noticed my suit jacket didn't match my trousers. *God almighty.* I closed my eyes and remembered dressing from a week's worth of discarded work clothes piled on my bedroom chair. I groaned.

"Hey, everything okay?" one of the second-year associates asked, coming through the door dressed to the nines in a starched, white shirt and finely knotted navy tie. "You know, it looks like you might've—" he started, but I pushed past him, wiping my hands on my pants before flinging open the door.

"Well, there you are, Gabriel Mendes!" Fanny, the receptionist said, backing up, cycling her arms and shuffling her feet like a train. "Can you do me a favor, muscles?"

I blushed. "Sure." I said, figuring the watercooler was empty again.

"Hey." She tugged on my lapel, then motioned to my pants. "I've always thought of you as a trendsetter." She leaned close. "Not to worry. I almost came in wearing two different navy shoes. Uniform hazard. Know what I mean?" She pretended to elbow me. "Listen, this might be the seventh circle of hell, but these sharks are too self-absorbed to notice much past someone's Rolex. Honey boy, you just sit those sugar britches down real fast, and, sweetie, nobody'll be the wiser." She winked, then sashayed off, calling back, "Thanks for the muscle, handsome!"

Shedding my jacket and throwing it over my arm, I hurried to the water cooler to change out the five-gallon jug, grumbling about My Ex and work the entire time. Once finished, I raced down the hall, brooding, hoping the thick carpet absorbed my frantic footfall. All I've ever wanted was to feel loved. "Like I matter to somebody. Anybody!" I said, tossing my hands.

Catching my breath outside the conference room, I tucked in my shirt and straightened my tie. I cleared my throat, and with great care, rearranged my suit coat over my arm. Sighing, I stepped inside.

The partners hadn't yet arrived, but the place was still spooky: dark, with only the eerie spotlights over every chair. Finding my place at the long, lacquered table, I hurried into the leather and chrome chair. Except for a few hushed conversations, most of my colleagues scrolled their phones. Perspiration ran down my back and from my pits, soaking my discount dress shirt. I snatched the closest crystal carafe. Water splattered. Blushing, I swiped at the puddle with a sweaty palm and then my sleeve, but the wet beads defied my efforts and remained glistening on the polished table.

Slumped back in my chair, I stewed over how I'd dump My Ex's things on the stoop before heading to the pub tonight. It'd be good to have her out. Maybe I could finally breathe. But something about her driving off with the last of her stuff made me feel like a real loser. Totally alone and dead inside. Whatever.

I gazed out the window. The sun had already set. It was the solstice. "Darkest day of the year," I muttered, playing with the provided weighted black pen, tastefully inscribed and detailed with gold fastenings. I ran my hand through my hair.

You're gonna need more than the cycle ride home tonight, Mendes.

"Yeah, maybe a long, long, loonnggg run."

"Excuse me?" the woman beside me asked with a sour face.

"Oh, nothing." Catching a whiff of my stress sweat, I shifted in the chair, adjusting my wet shirt and pants, hoping I didn't stink. I shrugged. "Just reminding myself to go for a run when I get home." I gave her a quick nod, trying to appear normal, but it was too late. She'd already spotted the spilled water. She flashed a forced smile, but averted her eyes.

See Mendes, everybody knows you're a mess.

"What difference does it make?" I mumbled, shaking my head, "I can't do this." I stood. People looked up from their phones. "Uh, I have an emergency," I lied. "Okay?" I asked, nodding, backing away from their stares and hurrying for the door.

"Gabe," someone said, pointing to my suit jacket.

"Oh, right," I said, backstepping, hoping my pants would go unnoticed. Then making a break for the door, I shoved it hard at the same moment Mr. Dumas stepped right into its advancing trajectory. The door struck him square in the nose. A collective gasp rose from the room. Blood gushed from his flared nostrils, staining his perfectly pressed lapel and crisp white shirt.

Approaching home on my bike, I squinted in the dark to make out my neighbor seated on my front stoop. As soon as I dismounted, the single mother stood and her two noisy kids jumped off the cement steps and flew at me, throwing their arms around my legs.

"Hey, girls," I said brushing past, not even looking at them.

"Bubbles, Mushkin," my neighbor called to her girls, "leave Gabe be." Then to me she said, "Sorry Gabe," and nodded toward my wide-open front door. "I wasn't comfortable just shutting it, so we waited for you." She made a sorry-for-you smile.

"Thanks," I said nodding, trying to seem like it wasn't a big deal.

"Girls? Bath time. Say goodbye to Gabe," their mom said.

"Bye, Gabe!" Bubbles and Mushkin shouted as their mom took them by the hand to cross the street and head back home. With my back to them, I flashed an open palm in a half-hearted wave as I headed to the door.

Inside my house the kitchen window screen lie on the floor. My Ex's things were finally gone. All she'd left was a message scrawled in red lipstick across the refrigerator. It read, *Happy now you dead zombie?* An icy breeze blew through the house. My phone rang. I shoved it between my ear and shoulder, answering. "Yeah?" I barked before slamming the window shut.

"Oh! What was that? Is everything alright? You never answered my text."

"No, Mom. Everything's not alright. I'm missing something, or something's missing in me."

2

A week later, planted in my La-Z-Boy, I reclined but still stumbled around inside my head. Revelry and celebration? "Not tonight," I said, numb but not too numb to remember the New Year's resolution *not* to grow drunker as the night went on.

Exchanging one distraction for another, I put down the beer and plugged-in to Ornette Coleman. The saxophone blasted. I closed my eyes and transported to the familiar house of broken mirrors. Feeling lifeless and lost, I half-enjoyed the imagined sensations of tripping down long hallways and bumping into screeching confrontations of myself. My Ex and I having sex in the back of the car. Saying nothing when she stole a bag of Skittles from the checkout and boldly consumed the candies before we were even out the door. On the lookout while she pulled a nip from her bag and spiked her drink at Pronto Pizza. Truth be told, I'd been among the walking dead for a while.

Oh, don't misunderstand. I did faithfully roll out of bed five days a week and bike in to work as an overqualified paralegal. At home, I paid my bills, vacuumed, cleaned the toilets. Sometimes I even bought groceries before the cupboards went bare. I exercised. Stood in seas of others to witness rites of passage at weddings and funerals. To a stranger, it probably looked like I had a life outside my small, bleak mind. Maybe, it even looked as if I were loved. Maybe.

But this New Year's Eve, I'd promised myself liberation from my own restless brooding twin. That night, I ditched the whole intellectualization that there is no way and surrendered. I cut Coleman and let Chet Baker's velvet trumpet envelop me, his mellow voice singing, "I fall in love too easily. I fall in love too fast." Keeping four-quarters time and soft-shoeing in my seat, I didn't raise a bottle to

Coleman's higher math. I didn't hunker down in my loneliness and desperation. I didn't relish the familiar urgency and paranoia of a rat in a maze.

Finished with the constipated struggle of making myself into a pretzel, the confines of my self-imposed straitjacket, I took off my headphones and chugged the last of my rich, malty beer. Setting the bottle in line with too many others, I climbed out of the easy chair. This was the night that all my previous years of wrestling myself to the ground would amount to something more than swearing I'd be different tomorrow. This was the night I would pin myself down to more than a renewed commitment to my job or my love life. This night, when I flipped open my thin, sliver laptop, the room illuminated. This was the night I found a way out.

Taking a deep breath, I cracked my knuckles and lengthened my spine. "Okay," I said and typed into the Google search bar:

Finding happiness

I scrolled through the many options: ten tips; two key steps; seven fast fixes; three simple ways; five truths. Go vegan. Swim in the Ganges River. Retreat to the desert. Drink green juice. Visit Peru. Take up bonsai. Volunteer at a soup kitchen. Hike the Camino de Santiago. Build a labyrinth. Raise chickens.

Sighing, I sank into the chair, chewing a fingernail. I'd heard it all before. I'd even once tried making a labyrinth, and I didn't believe chickens were the answer. I mean, I got the back to nature and collecting fresh eggs thing, but I don't know. I guess that's my problem: I don't know! My brows creased. My chest weakened at its center. Here we go! It was only a matter of time before I returned to that desolate place inside my mind. "Argh!" I growled through clenched teeth, plowing my hand through my thick hair. Mustering all my determination, I threatened myself and some god. "I am not giving up. Not this time. At the very least, I deserve some happiness." Doesn't everybody?

Startled, Cat pulled her ears back and shot me a dirty look. Lowering my voice, I whispered, "Sorry, old girl. Didn't mean to wake you." Petting her, I smoothed her hackles and kissed her head.

Beyond the window, the flower boxes overflowed with ghosts of last year's calibrachoa. Dried leaves and skeleton stems replaced the millions of bell-like flowers. The full moon unveiled a frigid winter landscape. The naked Japanese maple stood lonely over the brittle lawn. The garden pond would have frozen over if not for its heater, yet the waterfall only trickled. A stiff gust stirred the copper whirligig My Ex had given me. And the tall brown reeds, all that remained of the ornamental grasses, bent to the winter wind. Everything else holed up in the frozen earth, waiting for spring.

I imagined the promise of my summer garden. How a warm breeze would make the bee balm stems wave, their rose-colored heads bobbing, while the purple coneflowers with their hardy stems stood strong, barely influenced by the current. I leaned closer to the window. Two raccoons scampered up the gigantic ash tree. I'd seen a family of them late last summer scavenging grapes from my neighbor's arbor. Maybe there was a natural order to things that was easy, even abundant.

My mind drifted, traveling backward, way before law school, long before My Ex, all the way back to the prettiest girl in the sixth grade. I'd secretly loved her, even pretended she was mine while we stood side-by-side at our lockers. I'd even planned to ask her to the school dance. But Theo Winner beat me to it—asked her right there in front of me, at our lockers!

Dude! Seriously. Come on. The sixth grade does NOT sum up the natural order of things.

"Focus, Mendes," I told myself. I nodded, closed my eyes, laid my fingers on the keyboard, and then typed: *What is love?*

The search netted similar results, only with tips and truths about what love is not, Cher lyrics, and ads for dating apps. Except with one deviation.

Lost looking for love in all the wrong places? The Oracle of Delphi https:// www.PythiaOracleofDelphi.com/where-is-love-how-do-you-find-love

Join the quest for answers to the questions of love. Let Pythia, mystic and high priestess, take you through the umbilicus and into the sacred spring known as love. Be prepared to sacrifice your black ram.

I scratched my beard, then the back of my neck. Umbilicus? High priestess? I sat back with my legs crossed, my lips twisted with skepticism. How big of a sucker did they think I was? "Be prepared to sacrifice your black ram?" I read aloud before scoffing. Leaning in, I scrutinized the listing. I shook my head. "What a racket." How many sure fools before me had fallen for the tricks of these hucksters? I scanned the entry. "Sacred spring. Huh? Everything does bloom in the spring."

Cat stood to stretch her tuxedoed body. I ran my hand along her bony spine, holding her tail as she pulled it through my fist; it was our game. She jumped from the desk. "Hey!" I called. "You're gonna miss The Oracle of Delphi!" I laughed. "Honestly! What impudence." I shook my head. "Ridiculous," I said under my breath, and before I knew it, I'd clicked.

The site opened to an alluring woman. Mature. Fiftyish. Standing before a bubbling brook at the edge of a forest. Detailed bangles and large gemmed cuffs wrapped her arms from wrist to elbow. Her long, wavy auburn hair spilled from under a thin gold crown and flowed over her breasts, clad in the soft green silk of her gown. A skeleton key threaded on a gold chain hung at her lovely neck alongside an impressive faceted blue stone set in an intricately carved bezel. Both dangled near her cleavage.

Through the screen she looked right smack at me, as if she'd known me all my life. I could see she was a woman of great opinion. Her bright blue eyes were kind but frank, holding me to a reflection of myself more honest than comfortable. If not for her striking beauty, I would have turned away. She made no sound. The only discernable movements were the blinking of her uncompromising eyes and the rise and fall of her full breasts.

The image rippled and beckoned me. A mirage that lapped at my fevered brain, lulled and stilled the chaotic chatter that usually flooded my head. Then, cruelly, she faded away. For some minutes, I sat staring wide-eyed at the empty webpage, waiting. Thinking it was a marketing ruse, I checked my connections, refreshed the browser, but the screen remained blank.

I hit the return key. Nothing. I hit it again, searching the nothingness for some clue. It crossed my mind I'd been played for a fool. I glanced out the dark window and then over my shoulder. I'd made myself an easy target searching the internet for advice. I ought to have been embarrassed. But she'd looked sincere, I couldn't help believing I was meant to have more. I bit my bottom lip too hard. My tongue dashed out, darting back and forth to soothe the harm I'd done.

I shrugged, then placed my fingers on the keys again. What did I have to lose? *Where did you go?* I typed.

I'd barely finished when letters, kerned and shaped like those of a typewriter, formed the words, *I am here*, across the bottom of the page. Though the screen remained vacant of her beauty, I jumped to my feet. "Yes!" I raised my arms in victory with an enthusiasm usually reserved for the Chicago Cubs. Then sounding like a spy arranging a rendezvous, her hushed voice came through the computer.

"The time is getting late. Meet me at the hour of cockcrow," she said.

3

I didn't sleep that night and was up before dawn, busy in my dim but tidy kitchen. Tidy, that is, except for the message still scribbled on my refrigerator, now pink and ghosting from soap and elbow grease. Ignoring it, I also turned a blind eye to the worn cupboards and places on the counter where, for decades, sandwiches had been sliced. This morning, I only wanted to feel bright.

My house sat on a steep incline at the foothills of the Rockies across from the university. Originally a gold-miner shack, only modest improvements had been made over the years. The living room faced the front of the house and spilled into the kitchen at the back, the two rooms notably divided by the change in flooring from a green carpet to gold linoleum. Two bedrooms and a full bath accounted for the square footage upstairs while the backdoor led from the kitchen to my beloved garden and the front door into a diverse neighborhood of graduate students, young families, some old-timers, and me.

Digging around the cabinet that no longer latched, I finally extracted an old box of peppermint tea—an unappreciated gift from my mom to, "perk me up and start the day fresh." Still in its cellophane wrapper, I fumbled to open it while gazing from the kitchen through the living room and out the big picture window. Usually I would drink coffee, the number of cups matching the number of beers I'd consumed the night before. But this morning, I wanted The Oracle of Delphi to see me prepared. I wanted her to know I was ready and willing.

Upstairs, I eyeballed the computer. Perched at the edge of my chair sawing my lip with my teeth, I waited to see her. Light-headed, my brow and palms sweated. What if she's not real? Maybe I'd invented the whole thing. Or worse, I'd been catfished. But steadfast to the possibilities of a new horizon, not even my wild imagination nor Cat rubbing up against me wanting affection could distract me from the computer.

Then out the window, a golden aura rose in the east as words, on cue, streamed at the bottom of the computer screen, otherwise blank. "Good morning!" She sounded clear as a bell, albeit disembodied.

"Oh, thank God." I sighed. "Good morning!" I tried my best to match her polished tone. "Oh," I said, realizing she couldn't hear me and typed out the salutation with an exclamation point that I immediately fretted was too eager.

"Very well," she said, her tone an official-sounding affectation that inspired my greatest attention. Though I wished I could see her, I imagined her head held high. "I am, as promised, Pythia, mystic, and high priestess. Here to answer all your questions, but first, we must agree to terms. The information I am about to share with you shall be dispensed succinctly over sixteen days. These sixteen days shall be held in five, three-day increments over the next six months, beginning on the third Sunday of every month and ending on the third Tuesday. On our sixteenth meeting, we shall meet solely on the third Sunday." Her voice was cool and smooth as glass.

Lost in the song of her, I realized the need for pen and paper and cursed myself for not having the foresight regarding the essential materials for such a life-changing encounter. Despite my opening and closing of desk drawers as I rummaged for a working pen, stopping frequently to scribble until I finally happened upon one hidden under a stash of Pepto-Bismol packets, she rambled on.

"You shall take today and the following time to arrange for our tutelage and secure a cone of laurel leaf incense. On the third Sunday of this month, and for the next five months following, we will meet from sunup to sundown for three days. If this is agreeable to you, and you keep your word…" she paused, and while I couldn't see her, I imagined her cocking her head and arching a brow. "…I will impart to you the key to the multiverse, with one requirement. In return for this key, you shall be charged as a steward and provide pilgrimage to others who seek the prophecy of love. Said tutelage will be in the form of the written *and* spoken word. Make no mistake, unlocking the cellular memory of love will require you to become lord of your own castle. It will change your life, and you shall be responsible for the conscious creation of your own reality. Expanding your vibration is the nature of things. It is the frequency of love. Can you agree?"

Yes, I can! I typed and without a thought used another exclamation point due to wondering what was meant by the term multiverse. At the same time,

I imagined myself seated on a throne, cloaked in a red velvet robe and leopard trimmed crown, entertained by a polar bear riding a unicycle. *Wait. What about teaching?* Overwhelmed and realizing I had no idea what I'd just agreed to, I ran my hand through my hair. "Whatever," I told myself, hoping she'd see my punctuation as a sign of my earnest commitment.

"Does anything about the path we are about to embark on cause you consternation?" she asked.

I frowned at the implication and worried that she'd disapproved of the exclamation points. It certainly would be easier if I could see her, but I typed, *No*, shaking my head and striking the period key with great intention.

"Very well. Until the third Sunday sunrise of this lunar phase, yes?"

"Yes," I said and typed, *YES!* Striking the exclamation key with purpose, deciding now was as good a time as any for enthusiasm. And then, I remembered my boss.

4

I had two weeks of vacation coming. But considering it was only the first of January, I would use nearly all my time by the second quarter's close. I weighed such an investment and concluded it made little difference; after all, I mostly used my time off in dribs and drabs for days I couldn't bear heading in.

From her spacious and well-furnished but monochromatic office, my boss harped about my commitment to Dumas, McPhail & Cox. Sitting in a chair that looked far more comfortable than it was, I explained that an unexpected opportunity had availed itself concerning the multiverse. Having researched the word, I said it with authority, but then couldn't help myself and further explained. "Of course, I'm sure you know that our solar system is only one of an infinite collection of parallel universes that comprise reality." She looked at me from over the top of her reading glasses, and I saw her concern regarding my ability to work under pressure. So, referencing my last review, I elaborated (exaggerated, really) that instruction from this well-established and reliable entity would improve my organizational skills and balance my keen attention to detail.

Her mouth twitched and her eyes bugged. She closed her eyes, bowed her head, and nodded. I suspected she may have been conceding to some inevitable outcome of my employment, something she'd hoped to avoid since my stepfather was an old colleague, but "Okay," was all she said.

After work, I biked to Paper and Pens and found felt-tip pens and a journal featuring a kaleidoscope design. I flipped the notebook over and, seeing the small print, squinted to read: Passage—The Divine Rite to The Corridor, *by Rusty Caldron. In the natural phenomena of the multiverse, patterns are pervasive organized expressions that reveal life as vibrational resonances taking geometric forms. From the incalculably minute to the stellar, this metaphysical gestalt pervades the natural order.*

Exalted and unbounded shapes that tirelessly encircle the circles that make life, reminding us of our sacred beginning in oneness.

"Huh." My eyebrows knitted. Noting the use of "multiverse," I smiled, then re-read the description. My brow furrowed again. Maybe my patterns aren't taking form in a natural order. I wondered if I had forgotten my sacred beginning. I shook my head. What in the world am I getting myself into? But remembering the way Pythia had looked at me, I tossed the tablet into the basket and headed to the register.

At the check-out, I asked the heavily inked cashier the whereabouts for securing incense. "Try Incense Is Us," he said. "They're emissaries aligning the human breath with the frequency of the divine vibration of love." He passed me my change. "It's across the street." He pointed through the shop window.

"Oh. Wow." My mouth hung open as I spotted prayer flags waving in the winter wind from the eaves of a red and gold storefront. "Where did that come from. I mean, when—how?" I shrugged. "I guess I've just never noticed it before."

He bowed his head. "Your every wish is my command, dude."

"Thank you," I said, looking at him sideways, taking my package.

How had I never noticed this place, I wondered as I approached the gigantic wooden door. It was red and intricately carved. I paused considering the weight of it, then pushed hard only to find it light as a feather. It flew wide open and sucked me into the dim space. I stumbled right up to the counter, a smooth slab of exotic wood with live edges. Apothecary jars lined the wall behind the register. Stacked on shelves from floor to ceiling, they were mostly filled with dried herbs, though some contained teeth, bones, and slippery things that floated in fluids. While scrutinizing the jars, an old woman appeared out of the shadows.

"Oh! You surprised me. I didn't see you."

"Cone of laurel leaf incense?" she asked as she took down a jar labeled *Bridge Broker* and screwed off its lid. "Well, you asked, didn't you?"

"I don't think so," I said and frowned. Then, distracted by a curious, sweet scent, I found my fingers burnishing a well-worn spot in the wooden counter. "What's a Bridge Broker?" I drummed my fingers.

"It's what you want." She scooped out the single cone and slid it into a small brown paper bag before folding its top over. "That'll be seventy-nine cents, please." She smiled and handed me the bag as I fumbled through the loose change from my pants pocket, then handed over three quarters and four pennies.

"This is a dime," she said and passed back a penny.

"Oh." I reached again into my pocket.

"No worries." She slid a penny from a little dish with a sign that read: *Love is like a magic penny; give it away, and there is always more!* She said something that sounded friendly and turned away.

"Pardon me?"

She spun around with her neck craned forward. "You heard me right," she said, scolding me, "Enjoy life!" My eyes widened and she took a step toward me. "You're an agent for consciousness now, unlocking the cellular memory of love. Don't just stand there looking dazed." She pointed to the exit. "Go on. Get on living already." She nodded to the door. I turned, only to hesitate. "This sounds crazy," I said, with my back to her, "but I'm embarking on a quest for the truth of love, and I just bought this notebook." I pulled it from the bag and scanning its back cover, I asked, "Would you happen to know if the metaphysical standard of oneness is the interconnected consciousness?" But when I looked up, she'd vanished.

At home I tossed my keys on the kitchen table. Still wearing my jacket, I took the stairs two at a time directly to my desk. I checked the computer screen and refreshed the page. Satisfied that my internet connection was secure and Pythia hadn't left a message, I scrolled past Ornette Coleman and clicked on "Brand New Day."

"How many of you people out there have been hurt in some kind of love affair? And how many times do you swear that you'll never love again?" Sting asked.

I sang along as I arranged my purchases on my desk, entered the meeting dates into my calendar, and then called Pronto Pizza to order delivery of a large, spicy Kitchen Sink.

That night with a full belly, I couldn't sit still in the La-Z-Boy so I headed to my bedroom early. I pulled the blinds and dressed in the old sweatpants and *Spider-Man* T-shirt that had lain on the floor just the way I'd discarded them that morning. Then I climbed between the sheets and under the comforter before switching off the bedside lamp. I closed my eyes and folded my hands over my chest. I lay there waiting to sink down into sleep but after about five seconds, I opened my eyes. I was wide awake.

First I thought about Pythia, then the clerk at Paper and Pens, but how about that old woman?

Pretty serendipitous, dude.

And the notebook?

That's just weird, Mendes.

I thought over the conversation with my boss. I bet she thinks I'm crackers. "What if the multiverse is a real thing?" I asked. "What if I could be happy?" I whispered to myself and wondered if I could feel whole? Alive? Like I mattered?

I pictured myself in the future, climbing out of bed in the morning clear-headed. I envisioned myself at work, focused but relaxed, sitting at my desk with the door open. I'd wave to a colleague. "See you tomorrow," I'd say with a genuine smile.

On my back, still in bed, I interlaced my hands behind my head. "Answers to the questions of love," I said out loud and grinned. "Finally. It's about time." I closed my eyes.

She'll be smart and pretty with a sense of humor. Sometimes bold, but shy in unexpected ways. I dreamed up talks we'd have where she'd have my back. She'll be reliable. I conjured cute petty arguments and then bigger ones. "She's passion-ate." I opened my eyes, still relishing the thoughts of her until the old stain on the ceiling came into focus. How many nights had I lain wide awake contemplating reproach? What if nothing's different? I closed my eyes. What if there really is something missing in me? My thoughts drifted to My Ex.

We'd met online. She'd been late to the expensive steak house, the place she'd picked because she said she liked the cocktail lounge, as she called it, but later it turned out to be more about the bartender. That night I stood waiting, not know-ing then about all the other times I'd wait for her to show. But that night, I'd been seduced. Me, checking my watch, trying to look casual. Eyeing the door, nursing a warm beer at the crowded bar. Her, sneaking up from behind me, pressing her lively body up against the back of mine. Making me feel alive with her hot breath at my ear, the potent scent of patchouli.

"I am awful sorry I'm late," she'd whispered with deliberation, her words like soft pillows absorbing the din of the room. She grabbed my hand and I followed.

She spoke again, this time sounding like we were kids, "Let's get out of here." She took my bottle from me and handed it to the hostess as she hurried toward the front door pulling me along. She wasn't wearing a coat, and outside in the cold she smiled at me and pulled lip balm from her cleavage. In the streetlight, her dress clung to her in all the right places. "I should tell you," she'd said all matter-of-fact while generously applying the balm, "you make me feel really alive."

5

O n the third Sunday of January, before the break of dawn, I stared at the
computer with the impatience of a boy waiting for Santa. Except for the
frozen words of our last exchange, the screen was blank. My tongue poked at my
raw lip while I streamed highlights from the Pioneers versus Kansas State game.
Cat flicked her tail.

Then, in increments, mostly unnoticed, the purple night gave way to a pink,
rosy light. "Good morning!" Pythia said in such a bright voice, and I remembered
her nearly symmetrical face with its broad straight nose and soft arching brows.

"Good morning," I said as I typed the same salutation. I tried not to feel dis-
heartened that the screen remained empty except for the stream of words running across the bottom. Would I never see her again?

"Please conduct a thorough internet search using the keywords 'true' and
'love.' Allow the results to inform your conclusion concerning love." She articulated and lilted her words, making each one seem like a dancer, but the only thing
I saw was a parade of no-nonsense letters forming up words and sentences that
would apparently (and disappointingly) serve as our mode of communication.

"Now?" I asked and typed as my brows furrowed into a unibrow at the realization that there was no poetry in what she'd said. We'd only just exchanged
morning salutations, and already her instructions seemed a little, I don't know,
dispassionate? Besides, wasn't *she* supposed to tell me what love was? Not to
mention the fact, I'd already searched for love online. I ran my hand through my
hair and scratched the back of my head.

"Yes, now. Make a full inquiry and be prepared to discuss your findings at
high noon."

At high noon? I typed, more to bide time than for clarity.

"Yes, high noon. Until then, yes?"

I nodded and typed, *Yes*. Then, staring at the blank screen, I brought my ear close. Was Pythia gone? I sighed, sinking into the chair, and narrowed my eyes. I'd fancied myself sitting spellbound by her beauty, lost in the rhythm of her lyrical voice as she divulged the enigmas of love and changed my life forevermore.

"Whatever." But what if I'd been wrong to trust that things could be different? "No such thing as a free lunch. Everything comes with a price." I grumbled, then drew in deeply and blew the breath out from my cheeks before I cracked my knuckles. "Alright, Cat." Cat hunkered on the desk, stalking a magpie in the window box. "Let's do this thing. It won't do any good to give in before I even get started."

The search took me through the usual five-hundred-word, three-point-sentence self-help articles meant for direct application to daily life.

I clicked on each, wanting to be thorough, and made notes in my new journal, analyzing the articles for commonalities. They mainly focused on the hows of successful interpersonal interactions. While the articles were applicable (and efficient), their purpose seemed merely a palatable dose of anti-anxiety meant to calm the age-old fear of dying alone and misunderstood. Bringing my nose closer to the screen, inspecting the words, and clicking through the pages, I noticed something else. "Hmm. Humans appear to be inherently skeptical." What could account for such pervasive distrust? Well, My Ex certainly gave me a good reason! But it wasn't just her; I am even suspicious of my own mom. Shouldn't love between a child and parent feel safe?

"True love fear," I said, typing into the search bar.

The page loaded, and I combed the YouTube songs, Bible quotes, literary works, and movie clips interspersed with self-help articles. "Ah-ha! Stories! Myths, legends, histories. That's it, Cat." I poked her as she now lazed in a patch of the morning sun. "Handed down from generation to generation. Our human narrative. Look at them." I gestured to the computer and stood to emphasize the importance of my discovery. "Stories are spoon-feeding us cautionary lessons about love." Cat chattered and flicked her tail. The bird had returned, this time in the ash tree.

The tree's bare boughs cradled snow at the elbows where they divided themselves into off-shoots of limbs and branches that finally tapered into sprigs. The crisscross of their pattern dissected the clear sky into blue pieces. Beneath the winter ground, I envisioned the tree's roots and how they mirrored the crown, cutting the earth into similar fractals. Comprised of never-ending intricate patterns, the world was geometry that foretold the natural marvels of the world. Tales that romanced and lulled us into trusting that every little part contributes to a larger infinity.

"Yep." I smiled, sitting to ruffle the top of Cat's head. "It's the stories."

That morning, I consumed three large bowls of Honey Nut Cheerios and now gobbled a cheese sandwich made from stale bread ends along with half a bag of pretzels. I downed a beer, cataloging love stories into my journal. "The Love Song of Shu-Sin," headed the list, dating to second-millennium Mesopotamia.

Something that ancient must contain at least one forgotten truth of love. But the poem only devoted itself to the consummation of marriage for fertility and prosperity. From where I sat, attempting to conclude the truth of love through conjugal acts fell short. After all, I lived in a culture abundant with information regarding sexual experiences. As far as I could tell, it had done little for me or my fellow humans' understanding of love.

From there, the research took me to "Song of Solomon," 965 BCE, then skipped ahead to 1594 to Shakespeare's *Romeo and Juliet*. After that, I found centuries of doomed themes of forbidden love, a fair share of tragic unrequited love, some love triangles and a handful of love lost and mourned. All calling love as a losing game, a fool's errand. That is, save two.

First, Jane Austen's *Pride and Prejudice*. The early nineteenth-century tale of Elizabeth Bennett and Mr. Darcy, two characters who braved traditional gender and class norms in favor of marrying for love. Second, the late nineteenth-century true and unconventional love story of Marie and Pierre Curie. Two groundbreaking Nobel Prize-winning physicists who were faithful partners in love and vocation.

At noon, I related this in a long and thoughtfully worded document that was probably too long and too thoughtful, given the simple conclusion. Our present-day understanding of love isn't much different from 2,000 years ago.

"Hmm, yes." She seemed unimpressed.

You knew this? I typed.

"Yes. Love is possibly the most misunderstood experience." She sounded weary. I nodded, as much in agreement as for encouragement. I worried I'd already become tiresome, or that maybe she wasn't all that wise. Perhaps she knew no more about love than the man in the moon. In that instance, I wondered, would I be out eight vacation days if the ad had touted the moon as prophesier? "Love…" she let the word linger like she was drifting into a dream, making it sound tempting, and I heard her slide her pendant on its chain.

In my mind's eye, I saw her pleasant oval-shaped face. Its cleft chin and strong jaw, her heavy-lidded eyes now compelling instead of only softening her no-nonsense approach. I pictured her straight yet flexible spine rounding, her head hanging. I imagined her wistful for something other than the stone and key she bore around her neck. I was afraid she wished she was somewhere else. Maybe My Ex was right. Maybe I am depressing. I bit my lip before my tongue could intervene.

"We believe love to be a deep secret, profound mystery, and yet, it is the experience credited with the greatest meaning." Her bracelets jangled as she spoke, and then it sounded like she held something between her teeth. Was she putting up her lovely tresses? I remembered the sound of My Ex's voice when she spoke with hair fashions in her mouth while gathering up her hair. I wished I could see Pythia. "As you noted," Pythia continued, "love has been the focus of inquiry from the beginning of recorded time. Even so, it remains misunderstood. Mysterious." The last part sounded clear again, and I suspected she'd stacked her hair sexy-like on her head with loose strands straying, framing the sides of her face.

"Is your hair really red?" I blurted. Then scrambling to gather my thoughts, I stammered, "Well, what I mean is—what I meant to say was that your hair was very pretty when I saw it. And of course, I'm sure it still is, but I can't see it, so—" Then remembering she couldn't hear me, I typed: *You have beautiful red hair, and it's so striking with your blue eyes.*

"Yes, well, thank you." She sounded gracious, and finding myself giddy with relief, I fantasized that her cheeks took on a pink tint as she modestly tucked a loose lock behind her ear. "It is unusual, the red with the blue. You were right to notice."

Well, it's quite nice, and you are quite welcome, I typed, beaming a fool's grin, unable to save myself from behaving like a half-wit.

"Thank you again. But enough flirtations, hmm? Very well, now." On the screen, a red glass lamp with a bronze rabbit-foot pedestal appeared. Its shade was embroidered with gold thread.

"Oh!" I typed: *I have a lamp just like that.*

"Yes, I know."

"You do?"

"Yes."

"Oh, of course," I mumbled red-faced, "I see now. That *is* my lamp on my bedside table."

"Please retrieve the shade."

Now? I typed.

"Yes, please."

I hesitated for no good reason, then headed to the bedroom. My bed was a mess, my sweatpants and *Spider-Man* T-shirt lay on the floor. I shoved them beneath a pillow and wondered if it mattered which lamp, as there was one on each bedside table, both identical. I considered returning to my desk and asking, but settled on the one nearest the side where I slept. The lamps were by far the nicest furnishings in my house, purchased at a craft fair. My Ex had been shamelessly gregarious; flirting with the artist right in front of me. So, unsure if she was playing the other guy or me, I bought the lamps. It was the only thing I could think to do. I sighed, unscrewing the finial, and carried the embroidered shade to my desk.

"Perfect! The shape and basket-weave pattern is stupendous." Then, as if these accolades weren't enough, she added, "Fine job!" and I worried she thought I'd constructed the shade myself.

"Um, just to be clear," I said, holding the shade to the screen as if she lived in the computer. Then remembering, I set it down and typed: *I didn't make this.*

"Of course not! It's artisanal." She laughed. "Now, by 1,400 BCE, the two white eagles flying at the same speed determined Delphi the center of the multiverse. One flew from the east and one from the west, and when they met smack dab in the middle on Mount Parnassus near the Gulf of Corinth, Delphi was that spot."

I sat with my ear turned to the screen, listening and worrying, hoping to understand her point.

"Zeus, the God of sky and thunder, marked the spot with a dome-shaped stone carved with a crisscrossed pattern of woven vines. Zeus referred to the marker as the navel of the universe and called it the omphalos. Delphi became the heart of intellectual and artistic inquiry and the place to settle disputes. Zeus built a sanctuary there over the Castalian Spring, a place known to emit hypnotic ethers, and the omphalos became a conduit for prophecy." Then Pythia deepened her voice. She slowed her speech. "It is I, Pythia, the high priestess appointed by Apollo, son of Zeus, the God of prophecy and healing, who traveled and does travel the fifth dimension to guide seekers to their futures. I am the oracle of the greatest temple in all of Greece. Those seeking my prophecy must bring offerings and sacrifice."

Captivated and wide-eyed, my heart raced. *The black ram?* I typed.

"Yes," she said, flat as a closed book. "But fear not your sacrifice. It shall come in due time, and you can trust that by that time, you will relinquish it with ease." I swallowed hard, reminded of how often I felt like I wasn't enough of a man. Times when my grandfather chided me for not hitting it out of the park, or My Ex saying the equivalent.

"Some thought the omphalos housed the angels. Some thought it was the vessel from which all terrestrial life sprang. Still, some believed it translated the spirit of humankind into a life-everlasting flame, but all of that was untrue."

Then sounding like herself again, Pythia said, "The omphalos allows for direct communication with the gods through the three holy portals of heaven." Still a bit mesmerized, I imagined such a journey. The cooing of white doves, the soft fanning of angel wings, the smell of rain while I traveled on a fluffy marshmallow cloud.

"Are you ready?"

"Ready?" I asked, muttering to myself. "Ready for…the holy portals, communicating with God?" I paused. "No," I said, shaking my head, "I mean, how would that even—" My heart went savage, merciless in its need to escape. I struggled to breathe. "No," I said, "I'm not sure—this is not—argh!" I groaned, then typed. *Not now. This is not a good time for me.* I pulled away and slid back from the desk. "I can't do this," I mumbled to myself.

"Of course, you can. You have an omphalos, haven't you?" she asked.

"Ahh? No. No!" Then, making it sound like an apology, I said, "Oh. No," and with confidence typed, *No, I am sorry, I don't have an omphalos.* Thank God, I thought, laughing a little. How silly. Of course, it would require an omphalos! Besides, the whole thing was ridiculous.

"What's that in your hand?"

I looked at the lampshade.

"You are all set then. Tomorrow, yes?"

"Uhh," I said while typing, *Where exactly are we going???* and added two ex-tra question marks to convey that I hadn't completely abandoned all rational thought.

"We are going to the round table. I want you to meet those before you who have committed and contributed to the prophecy of love." On the screen, a very long list appeared, the font so small it was nearly illegible. "As you can see…" she said scrolling through the infinite list. Nearly cross-eyed I brought my nose to the screen to make out the first name. "…It begins in Greece with Socrates. Where never before or since has there been such a thorough inquiry into love. Regardless, the others have made fine contributions from all corners of the world. Please note that the list is disproportionate in its representation of men over women. Hmm?" This "hmm" sounded more irritable and less provocative than her other "hmms," and I wondered if she arched her eyebrows in judgment.

"Yeah, I see what you mean," I said and then grumbled at the need for typ-ing. *I guess that's history in its making. You know, the way of the world and all.* Then I quickly added, *It's not right, of course,* wanting her to know I sympathized with the plight of women, that I was a modern man.

"Yes. Where are all the women and people of color in this discussion? They are there, but for better or worse, you live in a western world where history has been recorded most carefully from the Anglo-Saxon male perspective. While it is skewed, it does, nonetheless, inform your beliefs today. Does it not?"

Well, not mine. I mean, I'd like to believe I think differently than that, but I suppose you have a point. Like it or not, we're all a product of our time. I typed, finally satisfied with the communication groove we'd found.

"Precisely."

Glad we agreed on something potentially prickly and wanting to further build solidarity my fingers tapped out, *There's this old saying. Behind every great man, there is a great woman.*

"Oh, my!" She laughed. "Are they still saying that?"

Yes, they are. People say it, print it on T-shirts and mugs, and on the internet, on something called memes. It's very popular. Sitting back in the chair, I grinned. Completely engaged in our conversation I let my hands relax on my thighs.

"That's mine! I said that!" I heard her bracelets jangle and thought she might be leaning in toward me. "I told it to Zeus," she said, the way people name-drop celebrities. "I told him he'd be nothing without Leda. Everyone knew that. Zeus knew it, too, but he could be an ass without even trying."

I guess you probably ran into a lot of inflated egos back then. Smiling at her trash-talking, my fingers flew at the keys.

"Oh, don't you know it!" She laughed again, then composed herself and returned to her business-like manner. "Anyway, I've digressed. The list is by no means complete, but your research will give you an idea of how these people have contributed to the current understanding of love. Take the rest of today to research the philosophers, activists, psychologists, and religious leaders listed. Understand the historical contribution of each and how they've shaped the conversation of love. Tomorrow you shall don your omphalos and transport to the circle of knowledge. There you'll meet some of the world's greatest teachers."

6

Chewing a thumbnail perusing Pythia's long list, I sat in my den at the ancient lawyer's desk. Once the property of my unforgiving grandfather, today the massive hunk of old oak claimed an entire wall below a bank of windows that offered a decent view of my garden. Alongside the La-Z-Boy, the two dominated the cozy room where I spent most evenings searching the net or plugged into jazz.

Cat stood and stretched, awakened from her favorite spot on the desk. Traipsing over the new notebook, she maneuvered around the salsa jar full of new felt-tips and stopped to sniff the Rubik's Cube. She eyed the printer before making her way around my laptop and butted her head against my chin.

"This is an absurd amount of research," I said scratching my head. "Isn't this exactly the kind of thing she's supposed to impart to me?" I mumbled. But then I remembered the way she'd looked that first night and the intrigue of her voice. I weighed my options. Secure the key to the multiverse and understand the great mystery of love. Or die alone and misunderstood. "Yeah," I said and got busy.

Much later, I flipped on the lights and stretched my neck. I'd typed pages and pages that literally covered the map, traveling from 470 BCE Middle East to 20th-century America. "Is this what she wants? Because I can do hours of mindless and meaningless research at work." In my head, I rehearsed dumping the research and sounding dull, droning on and on while the poor priestess's eyes glazed over before she begged me to stop.

"This won't work. It's way too hard to digest." I rubbed my grumbling belly and examined the long compilation for long enough that the awaited moment of brilliance announced itself. "Ah-ha!" I rifled through the desk, collecting scissors, string, and tape.

At the sound of the printer, Cat raced toward it before slinking, her slender body crouched low, her eyes wide as if the machine were spitting prey. But before she could paw at the pages, I shoved the desk chair and La-Z-Boy to the wall to make room on the floor. Cat jumped and raced out with the commotion. Leaving me to sit alone in the middle of the floor, making a mess, cutting and taping late into the night.

When I finished, the floor was a sea of paper. A mosaic of like-minded words connected by a string that indicated chronology and influence. I stood, barely noticing my aching back and knees, appreciating the gigantic link diagram. Cat strolled by and plopped down onto the paper labeled "Descartes." She beat her tail on the floor.

"I think I found a pattern, Cat." Not taking my eyes off the life-size chart, I pointed. "In the western hemisphere, the Greeks philosophized that love is beauty inspired by the divine. Then, after the Romans conquered Greece, St. Augustine appropriated the Greek ideology of love. *But*, and the but is essential, Cat. This guy added a Christian twist. He makes love moral, preaching that charitable acts inspire God's salvation and reward us with God's love. And then you know what happened, old girl?"

I swept my hand over the diagram that sprawled across most of the beat-up wooden floor. "Cat, it's like a bomb went off. I've got entry after entry inspired by the conflict between religion and a social movement called Free Love. Check it out."

I squatted, studying the details. "It started in the Middle East and celebrated both celibacy and free sex. Mushroomed to North Africa where they renounced marriage. And in Persia, there's opposition to slavery and divisions of wealth." I pointed to each. "Then there's a switch in focus, and we got an Afghani dude named Ahmed ibn Sahl al-Balkhi who claimed lovesickness is an idealization. He warned it led to obsessions and the inability to distinguish truth from infantile fantasy."

Something prickly stirred in me, but I ignored it.

Standing, I mumbled "Okay," and focused on the next century where the Free Love movement swelled into Europe. "Check out this bawdy troupe, Cat. This coarse caravan of risqué actors sang and danced, drawing common crowds; denouncing religious obligation, moral prohibition, and gender inequalities for three hundred years!"

Suddenly, flushed with embarrassment, I could hear their heckles and roars of laughter, all over again. Feeling the shame like it was yesterday, when in fact I'd been a freshman in college. My friends had warned me. Like spies, they'd reported back sightings of my girlfriend disheveled, slipping in and out of dorm rooms while I was in class. She wasn't even enrolled at my school. But she was the "love of my life," the "one I'd marry." Humiliated, I did nothing. "I don't own her," I'd reasoned. "Pussywhipped," they'd said. And then the crushing blow. She hitched a ride to California and left a note stating my pathetic middle-class life had suffocated her spirit. Apparently, living in my room rent-free and eating on my meal plan was bourgeoisie. I'd thought I'd die. The facts brought me to my knees. I'd begged her to stay. I'd have dropped out of school, lived in a tent on the beach with her, but it was too late. Afterward, I'd noticed a guy wearing a collection of Modest Mouse concert T-shirts that were suspiciously familiar. Turns out, she'd been selling my things all over campus. Even then, I'd defended her.

My stomach growled, and happy for the distraction, I hurried to the kitchen. Plucking a box from the shelf, I devoured chocolate chip cookies while pulling a beer from the fridge and overlooking the traces of the big question and foreboding declaration that still loomed on its door. I drank in swills and swiped crumbs from my shirt while I waited on the coffee.

What a fool I was. Lovesickness. Free love. What am I, SpongeBob SquarePants at a frat party? I pounded the rest of the beer. A draft blew through the old window over the sink. Outside the black glass, there was nothing. Not even the moon. It had all but disappeared from the winter sky. Even its shadows were missing. How do you ensure benevolence if love is free? The coffeemaker beeped. I grabbed the pot and poured a cup. Distracted by the wafting, sharp scent, I grabbed another beer.

Upstairs I stood over the Sufi mystic, Jalaluddin Rumi, slurping hot coffee and gobbling cookies. Chocolate crumbles littered the paper marked *13th-century Turkey: Your task is not to seek for love, but merely to seek and find all the barriers within yourself that you have built against it.*

An unexpected sharp, acid slurry bubbled. Indigestion burned through my chest and I choked it back down. Would I mark time this way forever? Would that day always be the beginning of the end? Tired of referencing that day as the before and the after on my life's timeline, I parked myself in the chair and stared down the Rubik's cube on the desk.

My Ex had already left her third job in not as many years, and I'd secretly suspected that there was something wrong with her beyond her ever-changing hair color. But how do you tell someone that? Instead, I'd harped, saying, "Maybe you should go back to school." Or I'd send her job postings and articles about honing her resume.

But that day, I couldn't get out of the stale and dreary state buildings fast enough. I had my fill of the courthouse drama. Fresh out of law school, and inexperienced at managing the demands of clerking for a judge, case after case weighed on me. The harm people inflicted upon each other; the injustice of the system. The downright ugliness of it all had sucked the life right out of me, and yet I thought it meant there was something wrong with me.

"That's stupid," My Ex said when I got home.

"No, it's not," I snapped as I loosened the hold my tie had on me.

"Well, aren't you the privileged one? Didn't your mommy ever tell you the world is unfair? Grow up, Gabe."

"Grow up? You won't even talk about having children."

"I never said I didn't want kids."

"Oh, don't make that face at me. You said, and I quote, 'They're no fun, they cry like babies, and eventually they resent you and only want your car.' I never said it before, but your description of kids? Well, it pretty much describes *you*."

"Wow! Astounding. You've clearly been harboring that for a while. What else haven't you been honest about? Besides, just about everything. You never say how you really feel."

"Oh, that's rich. What else haven't *I* been honest about? Hmm, let me think...." I put a finger to my chin, striking a scholarly pose.

"You don't need to be sarcastic," she said through clenched teeth. Her eyes were two slits. "At least I don't keep secrets."

"No, you're just a liar. But let me tell you some of my secrets, like how I lie awake at night wondering how not to be embarrassed by your hair. Look at it! You look like a clown. Who has bright orange hair except for Carrot Top? I'll tell you who, you! So, if you're wondering what's wrong with me, well, I'll tell you. Intimacy's more than sex, and I'd like to feel attracted to my girlfriend deep down inside." I thumped my heart. "And by the way, not even sex can keep me from feeling afraid you're turning into Ronald McDonald!" I pointed to her flaming hair.

"Oh. My. God! I never recall you turning sex down, Gabe, and don't make it my fault that sex is the only way you feel alive. And hair? Well, it looks like you never comb yours. Do I complain that it might host a family of weasels?"

"My hair!" I spat, "Is naturally curly. That's hardly the same. I can't help my hair."

"I'm just sayin', you're not everything you think you are." She shrugged. "But maybe there's another reason you can't measure up to your own expectation of hero. And maybe it is more about how you let yourself down than the way the rest of us have failed you." Her nostrils flared as she stared me down. Then grabbing her ginormous purse, she was already reaching for the doorknob.

"So now you're leaving? Your favorite MO." Feeling desperate, I added, "Whenever it gets tough, you always get going."

She halted with her hand on the knob. "I am *so* done with this scene." She seethed and swung the door open, slammed it shut, and was gone.

Yeah, not my best moment. I grabbed the Rubik's Cube and belched.

"Yep, that was the beginning of the end," I said, putting my feet up on the desk, pretending I didn't care. I'd tried what Rumi suggested: to break free from the prison I, myself, had constructed. I was honest that day, and what did it get me? "Nothing but misery. Another year clerking and—" Coleman's screeching sax loomed at the edges of my mind, just waiting for an invitation. Whatever. I fidgeted with the puzzle; then, catching sight of something at the window, I set the cube aside and sat up. The image of a man met me in the midnight glass. My eyes widened, then I chuckled recognizing his wild hair, deep-set eyes, and determined jaw. I leaned forward, trying to see myself as if I were the strange voyeur peeping in. At first, my reflection appeared intent but curious, as if he'd just seen me, too. I snatched the cube as a ruse, trying to catch sight of him before he could mimic me.

Busying my hands, I worked a row of squares while slyly lifting my gaze, but by the time I caught sight of him, he was already looking at me. I shook my head and ran my hand through my hair. He did the same. I laughed, and he laughed. I stared at him, and he at me until I turned from my reflection and set the cube aside. Something vaguely familiar nagged but eluded me. Move on, Mendes. I balled up the dirty napkin and slam-dunked the garbage into the wastepaper can.

"Game on." I swiveled the chair toward the chart. "Looks like Rumi might have opened up the playing field for philosophers, Cat. But it takes four hundred years." Grabbing my beer, I took a good swig, wondering how long it'd take me.

Still staking claim to Rene Descartes, Cat stubbornly swatted me while I slid him out from beneath her. "Sorry, old girl, but Descartes is pretty influential." I gestured to the wealth of paper squares descending below his. *17th-century Netherlands: Descartes married the Greek and Christian ideals, concluding that love is self-love created through the union of body and soul.*

"He's a game-changer, alright. And look, a hundred some years later, the tension heats back up." I pointed to Mary Wollstonecraft. "Unpopular, she beat the drum for love free of duty and inclusive of mutual equality and respect." I visualized her standing up to the status quo, her frank dark eyes, unyielding as she set the spark that fired-up feminism. "That takes guts," I whispered.

Wandering through the papers and string, I perused the congestion. "Look. It's about to blow-up in the 19th century. People are banding together and crossing lines."

Squatting inside the maze, I showed Cat. "We got Soren Kierkegaard peddling love as the charitable duty of every Christian. Here's Elizabeth Barrett Browning poetically promoting love as Christian salvation. But Karl Marx, he fought for equality." I raised a revolutionary fist. "Social-economic productivity cannot evoke love. Only love begets love!" I lowered my fist and steadied myself on my haunches. Had I expected lawyering to be love?

You did think it would make you loveable, dude.

"Did I?" I lowered myself to the floor. I'd hoped the law would liberate some worthy version of me. I closed my eyes, running a hand through my hair. But instead, I'd only felt exposed. "Am I a fraud?"

Dude, it's pretty tough to feel alive when you're terrified your natural nature is unlovable.

I stood and paced. Cat's ears flattened. Her eyes became green saucers. "But hold on. No, no! I did what Rumi said. I opened the door of my cage and—"

But did you come out, dude?

"Well, My Ex didn't make it easy."

Dude! Get real. You're your own worst enemy.

"What the hell time is it? I can't stand here arguing with myself all night. Look! I've still got Tolstoy, Nietzsche, and Freud for God's sake!" I pointed to the chart. "Move on!" I commanded.

Okay, okay.

I frowned and focused on Russia. "Alright. Leo Tolstoy echoed Marx, cautioning love is not a transactional commodity. In Germany, Friedrich Nietzsche reasoned that friendship saved love from inequality, while Sigmund Freud defined love as an unconscious maladjustment of sexual desire." I shuddered. Please, no more rabbit holes. Dead tired and longing to be between my sheets, sloppy and jumbled under the old comforter, I snatched the malty ale and emptied the last warm dregs.

"You're almost done," I said to myself. "Okay. Next stop, 20th-century Paris. Feminism's in full swing. Simone de Beauvoir argued love must promote freedom of self-expression. While Luce Irigaray advocated it required unconditional respect and awe for the irreducible difference between partners.

"In Switzerland, Carl Jung bundled his deep Christian roots with psychology. He enlightened us to the collective consciousness and claimed it supported love as a journey through the inner and outer self. Then the action shifts from Europe to America. Where Erich Fromm contended that love is the fruit of personal development that values loving one's neighbor and therefore, is a rare occurrence." I scratched my beard. Rare, really? "Leave it." No sideshows, remember.

I blew through the Brits with C. S. Lewis and his best-seller popularizing love as the Christian relationship with God. And I'd had every intention of doing the same with U.S. Ayn Rand, who disagreed with the likes of Lewis in massive volumes, except I halted.

"Wait. What? That can't be right." I reread it: *Selfless love contradicts self-preservation; others exist for one's own self-promotion; and without self-value, there is no valuing others.*

Easy, Mendes. This could be a bullet to the heart.

My Ex, my boss, even that second-year associate, certainly my grandfather... how could they possibly exist for my own self-promotion? They've only ever exposed me for the colossal loser I am. "I mean... it's not that I think I'm a loser. They think I'm a loser and then make me believe it. Right?"

No.

"No?"

No.

I sighed, running my hands through my hair, then lowered myself to the floor.

The ceiling light cast the room in a thick yellow. A soft felt of gray dust covered the baseboards. Around one of the desk-legs, something had puddled and dried sticky. It hosted several hairs, a sequin, a plethora of dust particles, and something red that on closer examination turned out to be a Skittle. I looked around. Did I value myself, and if I didn't, who would? I pitched the candy in the trash.

Was it possible others saw good in me, but I only saw them seeing me broken? I shook my heavy head. "Is this what Pythia wanted? To bring me to my knees?"

Dude, you're doing it again.

"Oh, mother of God! What the hell!" My hand went for my hair. "Argh!"

Focus.

Bushwhacked, I staggered and brushed off the floor-grime. I eyed the labyrinth. Only three squares remained.

The first was the 1960s New York City Sexual Revolution with its long-haired men and braless women. These passionate and brave youth organized and marched, championing polygamy, homosexuality, and gender equality while challenging both the traditional and Judeo-Christian values of sex and marriage. Divorce, blended families, and domestic partnerships became more commonplace and heartily opposed by Christianity and the Republican political party.

Finding my groove, I signaled to Joseph Campbell. Twenty years later, America tuned in to how this guy leveled up Jung's ideas. Campbell summoned us to act as the lead in our own story. I smiled. "See, Cat. It's like I said, it's the stories." I lifted Campbell just far enough off the floor that the string snaked between him and Jung. "This guy says if we play out the myth of the hero's gentle and noble heart, we can create a distinctive Western consciousness of self-love. He claims this will exalt the individual over all other sovereignties."

Cat caught the movement, and with her hard-wired instincts, she readied herself for an ambush. Low to the ground, she inched forward, then froze. With her eyes fixed on the string, she positioned her haunches and rushed. In one powerful thrust, she lunged and pounced. Entangled with the imagined snake, she wrestled. Papers flew. Most became casualties.

"Hey, hey, hey!" I scrambled in laughing. She raced through the diagram, mad if not comical, chasing the moving strings and killing the papers. In no time, she destroyed the whole thing. Only Alan Watts had survived. *Love is a spectrum of energy in which all expressions, from spiritual to animalistic, are the same and, when nurtured, blossoms according to its nature.*

"Oh, Cat." I sighed, blowing out my cheeks, and reached for my coffee, but the mug was stone-cold. I checked the time; it was after midnight. I rubbed my eyes and scooted into the chair to root through the bottom desk drawer. Finding an old box of resume paper, I reproduced the diagram. Cat took her usual place on the desk, teasing me with her tail. "You're a troublemaker," I said while enjoying the soft sensations of her fur. "What else?" I asked, scrutinizing the chart. Digging through the top drawer, I found the colored pencils hidden beneath several copies of the same Greek take-out menu.

"She'll be pleased." But just to be sure, I practiced. "Well, you see, Pythia, while Socrates started the conversation of love as beauty, our contemporary definition ultimately takes root in centuries of a moral tug-a-war. A battle between love as redemptive and for the deserving; or as natural and free. It's a crusade all the way into the 20th century." I smiled. "I got this," I said nodding.

And then, I saw Pythia. Sharp and precise as a laser, she'd point to the chart. "Yes, so it is, but presently we are in the 21st century, are we not?"

I groaned. Exhausted and blurry-eyed I checked the time again. "Oh, twelve-thirty. I gotta get some sleep." I surveyed the chart. I thought about perusing the pages of research again. "What more does she want from me?" The list hadn't even included the 21st century. I closed my eyes.

Get real, Mendes. This whole thing's a joke. Go to bed already.

I drummed my fingers. I paused. Then typed *contemporary ideas about love* and slid to the chair's edge. The listings mostly concerned themselves with heterosexual, homosexual, bisexual, transgender, and queer relationships. As well as *30 Modern Wedding Invitations We Love* by Martha Stewart and *Falling in Love with the Contemporary Bathroom.*

"Hmm." I withdrew from the keyboard. I sunk deep into the chair, then shot up and typed *love and science.* I hit enter. The screen loaded. I brought my face in close, scanning the results. "Nope. Nothing." I scratched my head. "How about 'love and physics'?" I typed. "Bingo! There it is. 'The God Particle.'" Reading the article, I frowned. "Oh, boy. Quantum physics. The Higgs boson?" I sat for a minute, weighing fatigue against curiosity. I thought about the time but decided against checking. Cat rose headlong from her favorite napping spot on the desk and butted her head against my chin. "Yeah, that's what I think, too. But give me fifteen minutes. I think I found what I've been looking for." My poor eyes rallied, darting like well-trained athletes until my fingers took charge and pounded the keys.

"Sweet! Cutting edge science that weds ancient faith." I closed my computer and swiveled in the chair. "If God is an unbiased phenomenon that allows all things to take up space in this world and follow their nature, well, all I can say is that sounds like a kind of love I'd like to learn more about." Cat stood and stretched before walking across the keyboard. The computer stuttered with the striking of too many keys at once. She paid it no mind as she vigorously and repeatedly rubbed the side of her face against mine. "Okay, okay," I said, "Let's go."

7

I woke in the same position I'd fallen asleep despite a faint recollection of a bizarre dream that had left me eager to know more about this Higgs boson. Throwing back the covers, my feet hit the floor, and I hurried into the shower with my toothbrush as a time saver. In front of the mirror, I ran a brush through my wet hair, not even trying to tame it, and trimmed my beard in haste before I hurried downstairs to feed Cat. With a hot mug of peppermint tea in one hand, I grabbed the Honey Nut Cheerios, and tucking it under my arm, took the carton of milk from the fridge. I stacked a bowl and a spoon in the other hand and headed to my desk, taking the steps two at a time.

I wolfed down breakfast, rushing to research the Higgs boson before daybreak. Stretching my neck from side to side, loosening a growing knot, I read and typed until the Higgs boson, like the rest of the research, served as a single soundbite. Lickety-split, I added Higgs boson to the chart, then admiring my work, I beamed. My research would not be a monologue of facts. It was a high-stakes war.

Socrates, Aristotle, and Plato headed it up in white robes and sandals, engaged in scholarly and civil discussions. Sentiments of love as beauty or friendship. Debates of love as carnal or divine.

I looked to St. Augustine, cloaked in his rich, red pontifical vestments, literary and tenacious. Dramatic even, articulating his vision of Christianity in fiery sermons that stirred and captured the masses.

"I get it." I nodded, literally seeing what Pythia had wanted me to appreciate. They all just wanted to understand love but instead ping-ponged across the centuries. Even today, we're polarized in a twenty-five-hundred-year war. One side fighting for love as something earned and the other demanding that it's a natural right.

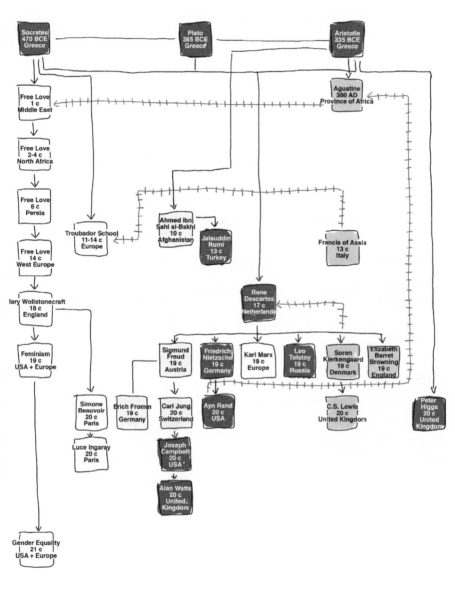

"Good morning!" Pythia chirped.

Good morning. I typed. *I put this diagram together to illustrate the history of love.* I held up the chart. *First, it's an intellectual inquiry of love with the Greeks.* I pointed out the three boxes across the top. *Then, it's a reward for prescribed behavior.* I pointed to St. Augustine. "And boom!" I stood and sent the desk chair sailing off behind me. Cat pressed back her ears and shot me a wide-eyed stare. "This thing blows up and boomerangs across the world. An epic tennis match. Back and forth!" I swung my arms. "Christianity declaring that love requires pious obedience and Free Love claiming it's natural and therefore, available without moral obligation." I brought my face right up to the camera. "And it doesn't let up!"

I imagined she smiled, and I smiled, until I remembered. "Oh!" Grabbing the chair, I sat and went at the keys. *All the inquiries are valuable, but each is only one piece of a larger puzzle. A few warned that love led to liability, countless found it as the purpose for living, some believed it was reverent, others saw it as playful, and many deemed it necessary for personal or humanitarian evolution. There were those who thought love was synonymous with sex, and those who felt sex was the physical expression of love.*

"Excellent work!"

Thank you! I typed, high on adrenaline. *But there's more. I've extended the research into the 21ˢᵗ century, and I think you'll be pretty pleased with what I've discovered.* Grinning like a fool, I copied and pasted my morning's research for Pythia to read: *In 2012, scientists in Switzerland observed a new boson called the Higgs boson. A boson is a group of distinguishable particles that each exclusively serve one of the four fundamental forces of nature for a particular outcome. These forces are electromagnetism, gravitation, the weak interaction, and the strong interaction. The weak interaction facilitates radioactive decay of atoms, and the strong attracts, holds, and binds smaller particles.*

Named after physicist Peter Higgs, the Higgs boson is unique in two ways. It forms an infinite and invisible force field, and will partner with any particle to endow it with mass, allowing it to bind and form atoms. Because atoms compose everything on Earth, the Higgs boson may be the source of our reality and all potential parallel realities. The Higgs boson may be like a god granting us access to any reality simply because we asked. It may be a loving source of all life. It may be the genesis of nature. Maybe even Mother Nature.

"Outstanding! Brilliant work!"

I smiled, hearing, then seeing her two exclamation points as the words streamed across the screen. "Thanks, I worked hard, and I think—" catching myself again, I said a quick, "Oops!" before my fingers worked the keys, *Thanks. I feel—*

"You think what?"

I was saying, I typed, and then something crossed my mind. Checking her streaming dialogue at the bottom of the screen, I scratched my head. "Wait. What do you mean, what do I think?" I said, and then typed, *How did you know I was thinking?* "Can she read my mind?" I wondered aloud, and that's when I heard her laugh.

"Of course not! But I heard you. I can see you, too."

"You can hear me?" I thought of all the typing I'd done. "Why didn't you tell me? Wait, you can see me, too?"

"You never asked, and, yes, typing provides us with a formal record, and I think you'll find it a valuable teaching tool in the future."

"You could have told me, though."

"I'm sorry."

I was curious about her apology, not that I found her unsympathetic, but she was a high priestess, and I was just this guy fumbling with love. My face reddened. Maybe I'm out of my league. My heart sunk. What do I know about anything? The doors of my gloomy mind creaked. I eyed the stupid Rubik's cube. What an idiot, sitting up late, thinking I could come to some profound conclusion about love when, for centuries, wiser minds than mine had failed. Who am I to figure anything out? My brow pressed down on me.

"Do you trust me?"

Disarmed by her directness, I grabbed hold of the computer and searched the empty page. My shoulders encroached upon my ears, and I bit my thumbnail. What if this was all a trick? Was I only seeing what I'd wanted to see? "I wish I could see you again," I mumbled, and the white screen rippled.

Her image appeared like something coming up out of the water, taking shape until the edges sharpened. There she was in her green silk gown with all her bracelets. The blue stone and skeleton key dangled at her cleavage, but for me it was her eyes. They flashed in the sunlight.

"Ahh." The sound escaped from somewhere deep inside me. She smiled and my heart sank. "Oh." I gasped. "You're real." Google-eyed, I blinked feeling almost tearful, my shoulders dropped. Her thick, reddish-brown hair cascaded over her shoulders, but this time I saw hints of gray at her temples and around her ears. Her heavy-lidded eyes seemed dreamy. She was real! And more beautiful than I remembered.

"Funny, huh? What if Mick Jagger was wrong, and you *can* get what you want? But to get what you want, you must ask," she said. "Now, moving on, tell me what you're thinking about love."

"So, I can see you from now on?"

"You may see me from now on. Your every wish is my command." She bowed. "But remember," she narrowed her eyes, "asking is how you shall receive. So be careful. Know what you want before you ask. Hmm?"

I nodded.

"Now, give me the skinny."

"Well," I began, "There have been many proclamations of love throughout history, but few strung the sentiments together, articulating a broader definition. All these stories," I pointed to the squares in the chart, "start with the narrator's perspective of place and time. But love isn't one single story set in one single time. Any expression of love innately conveys an individual's life experiences and what they think and feel about those events. Love's definition includes the accumulation of family stories told through the generations, and cultural ones communicated through songs, books, and movies. It's all the little stories buried inside the bigger one. Love may be an intelligence that was previously beyond our comprehension."

"Bravo!" She clapped, and her gold bracelets jangled as her silk gown shifted with her excitement. "You've nailed it." She smiled, revealing perfect teeth. Imagining she smelled woody and resinous, like a freshly cut Christmas tree, I blushed. Then without a thought, I took a bow, which she returned, and we stood facing each other, two dweebs grinning. "Come on," she said, beckoning me with her hand as old friends do. "Let's go. It's time to meet some masters."

I leaned in as if to climb into the computer to follow her, but then, drew back. "Wait, what?"

8

"I 'm not sure how long I can do this. There's not much room for footing here."
"Not to worry," she said.

Easy for her to say, she wasn't the one straddled over a steaming tub of scalding water, holding a lit cone of incense, while balancing a lampshade on her head. The shade kept threatening to topple into the bath, causing me to quickly right it without losing my equilibrium.

"Now, take my hand," she said from my laptop positioned on the vanity.

"Take your hand?" I shouted, but then it felt like her hand was in mine. I shot a glance to see she was fully embodied on the screen.

"Now bend your knees just a bit," she said. "That's right. Good. Now really hold that incense. That's fine. Perfect! Now, close your eyes tight. Very tight." I closed my eyes till they hurt. "That's right." She encouraged before she asked, "Ready?" I nodded, and suddenly, sounding reverent, she spoke, "We drop our arms to our sides—"

"What? I can't," I protested.

"Shh!" She scolded before continuing with the incantation, "—relinquish our history of losing our shirts in favor of the lapis rings."

What in the world? This is ridiculous!

"I NOW and HERE..." and as she spoke, her voice boomed. Thunderstruck, my eyes popped open, and my heart went wild. What had I gotten myself into? But she went on, "...declare the wheels of motion be set, cracking the steel rim, and taking us into the ditch."

A ditch! But it was too late. Something powerful tugged at my legs and pulled me under. Slipping fast, I fought to steady myself on the ledge of the tub.

"Lay us down the viaduct of vertigo dreams and deep into the slipstream where we come as we are. Summon fish to the dish, chickity China the Chinese chicken. Memoria, memoria, memoria."

"Aah!" I cried. "Oh, nooo!"

The Earth's floor dropped and I screamed, descending into a narrow tunnel where I soared at the speed of light, like something shot from a canon. I opened an eye, peeking. The tub, lampshade, and incense had all vanished. Surrendering to centrifugal force, I blasted through some blazing blue electromagnetic shaft. Golden sparks flashed and fired. With my arms glued to my sides, I squeezed my eyes and fists as hard as I could. I braced against the unknown. Soaring, I moved so fast I feared I would blow apart, and then—pop! The tension in my head burst, and then I floated like a feather, parachuting through brilliant rings of rainbow light until the last one deepened to the color of blood, and I smelled the earthy scent of clay before landing softly, thanks to my bent knees.

When I opened my eyes, the colors were vivid, everything was crisp and clear. Pythia had my hand, and I exhaled a soft, "Oh!" She was pretty, but it was more than that. She was lovely, like summer. I felt the fine structure of her bones, and then her strength, as she pulled me toward a circular opening enclosed by giant redwoods. I followed her to a round pool of steaming water defined by four alabaster columns, each topped with scrolled caps, each marking one of the four cardinal directions. The last beams of an afternoon sun cast the turquoise bath in a golden glow. The water sparkled. On the stone deck of the pool, a woman sat east, and a man west with their robes hiked to their knees, their legs dangling in the glistening water. Pythia motioned for me to take a seat to the south as she took the north.

I watched while she loosened her sandals, slid them off, and cast them aside without regard. I dropped my gaze when she lifted her gown and lowered herself at the water's edge. Following her lead, I removed my own shoes and socks and sat as well.

"Diotima, Socrates, this is my friend," Pythia said looking my way and smiling. "The one on a quest for love. He has researched the matter well, and his conclusions will please you both."

They nodded at me, and I shot to my feet, extending my hand, only to realize how absurd I looked, traveling the distance around the pool with my arm outreached and my hand ready for shaking.

"Please." Socrates raised his hand to stop me. "Be seated. The round bath is a circle of trust. We have no weapons, no hidden agendas." He spat as he spoke and licked spittle from his thick lips.

"Yes, of course." I nodded too many times. Then shook my head, and probably impersonated a stammering nitwit as I rambled, "I didn't mean to imply—I simply—it's just, a handshake is a customary greeting where I come from." Sighing, I retreated to the water's edge and tried to look dignified as I rolled up my pant legs. Socrates watched, his round eyes bulging from his square face, his snub, flat nose twitching.

"Isn't he wonderful?" Pythia asked as she playfully kicked her feet, creating rolling waves that soaked her dress. "So, determined. So genuine." The familiar crimson heat bloomed at my chest, then rose. Unsure if she meant Socrates or me, I turned beet red.

"I see what you mean." Diotima's high cheekbones cast her face in shadow while her eyebrows crawled like caterpillars over her deep-set eyes. Her nose was straight and narrow, a contrast to her full and puckered fish-mouth. She tucked her long black tresses behind her enormous round ears before sizing me up and down with more than a passing interest. It was then that I knew they were talking about me.

"Diotima is from the Peloponnesian city of Mantinea. She is honored by Zeus and deemed the prophetess of love," Pythia explained, arching her brows.

"I am pleased to meet you, your prophetess." Wondering if I was to bow, I looked to Pythia, but she paid me no attention. Diotima faked a smile, and I swallowed hard.

"And this, of course, is Socrates." Pythia gestured graciously toward the bearded man with pensive eyes, his mouth hidden by a prodigious mustache. His resting expression resembled a mug shot. "The enigmatic lover of wisdom and beauty." She eyed me, but this time like a warning, then turned toward Socrates. "It is so very good, as always, to see you," she said as she laid her eyes upon his. He held her gaze for enough time that Diotima and I turned away. Visceral scorn for the man swelled in my head. From the corner of my eye, I saw Pythia lean toward Socrates. They whispered, and I acted interested in the columns and pretended to inspect the moss growing along the edges of the bath.

Get a grip, Mendes. She's not your girlfriend!

Diotima inspected her nails while I watched my ankles turn circles under the warm water. Diotima cleared her throat. I lifted my chin, pretending to be interested in something off in the distance, then sniffing the air, I imitated someone enjoying the pert scent of the redwoods.

"Where's Plato?" Pythia asked, her voice a welcome sound, now no longer low and whisper-flirting with Socrates.

"Oh, he had a thing." Using spittle and forefinger, Diotima rubbed something sticky from the stone. Pythia frowned. Diotima shrugged.

"So, you've brought me a student, have you?" Socrates pulled at his wooly white beard. Then rubbed his hands, eyeing me like I was a steak dinner. "And a fine specimen, indeed." His eyes consumed me, a habit he'd already displayed in the short time I'd spent with him.

Pythia laughed. "We are here to learn of the *Symposium*, Socrates," she said, keeping him on course, and then to me, "Philosophers can be the worst."

"Do tell," Diotima egged her on.

"As if we don't all already know!" Pythia said, and the two women laughed with their heads thrown back and their mouths wide open.

Sounding irritated, Socrates turned his attention to me. "Let's begin, shall we? It is my point to tell you that when humans speak of love, it is, usually…" he hesitated, rubbing his nappy beard, staring me down until I squirmed, and then began again. "When humans speak of love, it is, first, without thoughtful inquiry and, second, from an illusion cast in the smooth glass of a crystal-clear narcissistic lake."

I scratched my beard. Oh, boy!

Pythia rushed to say to me in a hushed voice, "One sees things only from one's own experience. Yes?"

"You are about to hear of the truth of love as was imparted by this exquisite creature." Socrates gestured toward Diotima, who bowed in return, but a rustling sound at the forest's edge grabbed our attention. "Well, well," Socrates said, his eyes gleaming as he gestured to another bearded man, stocky and built like a wrestler, fighting his way through the luscious, evergreen boughs. His struggle released a bright forest scent. "My esteemed student, author of *Symposium*, and the most pivotal figure in all of Western history."

Plato's close-set eyes appeared especially beady aside the big nose on his little face. "Plato," Pythia sang his name and ran to greet him. Her gown dragging behind her, soaked at its hem.

Socrates stepped out of the water. "We were just embarking on the story of love. Do tell, won't you?" Socrates motioned for Plato to take a seat at the pool, but both men remained standing on the large stone slabs alongside the bath. Plato's wispy, thin hair caught the setting sunlight.

"Wise men talk because they have something to say; fools, because they have to say something." Plato laughed, embracing Socrates. "I cannot stay." He frowned. "Though the water looks fine, and it is good to see you well, my brother."

"You've been busy. I hear the web of wisdom has you highly engaged."

"It is true." Plato looked at Pythia. "It is true."

"You've not time to spar with your greatest teacher?" Socrates said and raised his dukes and faked a jab, his feet fancying the footwork of a boxer. Plato raised his fists, and the two jousted in fun until Socrates reached for Plato's head and pulled him in. The men hugged.

"You do me well, Socrates. Love is a noble spirit between God and the mortal."

"Indeed, old man." Socrates wrapped his arm around his friend and walked Plato in my direction. "Meet this fellow who searches for the meaning of love. He is odd but has committed to sacrifice the black ram."

"Impressive." Plato said with his focus on me. I stood drying sweat from my palms on the sides of my trousers before extending my hand out of habit.

Socrates laughed and whispered to Plato. "He fears for weapons."

Plato shook my hand. "Your search is honorable." He leaned in close, my hand still in his, and spoke low. "He who love touches does not walk in darkness." When he pulled back, his eyes met mine, and the cryptic message hung in the air between us. Sounding sincere, he smiled, and said, "I do regret my hasty departure, but you are in excellent hands here." He referred to the others before handing me a scroll of parchment tied with twine and adorned with a bay leaf. "I think this will assist your search." Raising his hand, he backed away. "Be well, my friends. I bid you adieu."

"We bid you farewell," Diotima said.

Pythia blew him a kiss. "My gratitude to you, dear Plato, respectful, and in earnest."

Plato bowed before slipping out of our circle and disappeared into the towering trees, again stirring their ancient, damp scent. The light was dimming as the day leaned into twilight.

"A fine man," Socrates said to no one in particular, making his way to sit at the edge of the bath again. Then addressing us, "My initial caution is worthy of repeating: Open your mind beyond your own experience. An uneducated man can discover the wisdom of a mathematical proof. As wisdom is less a matter of learning than remembering what the soul already knows.

"Plato's *Symposium* is a brilliant story on the nature of love told through seven conjecturing voices, six lost in a single thought. That is, until the seventh, being sage, foresees the thing foretold of love. Diotima, if you please." Socrates rose from his seat and bowed to the prophetess. Torches mystically fired themselves from the four directions, giving us light and causing me awe, but the magic went unnoticed by the rest.

Diotima, still seated, straightened her spine, lifted her chin, and proceeded to speak in a manner meant to command our obedience. "It is true that on that night men deliberated love. One rambled, calling love a god who inspires virtue. The second argued that in the desire for love, even the exchange of flesh could lead to virtuous knowledge." Diotima scoffed. "The third prescribed that love is in the arts and provides for a sound mind and moral character that leads to righteous behavior." Absorbed by her command, I inclined, and my pant cuffs soaked up the spring water. "The fourth told of a time when we were twice the people we are now, born with love inside ourselves and for each other. And how that threatened Zeus." She broke from her orating and, with disgust, said, "Zeus can be such an asshole." Pythia flashed a raised brow my way.

"The fifth," Diotima said rolling her eyes, "let us just say he gave an elaborate, umm, rather heavy-handed discourse praising love as a youthful, brave god, but Socrates stepped forth and challenged the poor boy's argument." She turned to the old man. "How you do love the spotlight, Socrates."

He grinned, and she leaned back onto her elbows and kicked her feet just beneath the water's dim, blue-green surface. The waxing crescent moon barely revealed her large bony feet and painted red toenails. She cocked her head, sure of herself. Emboldened, she leaned toward Socrates and mocked him. "You, the sixth, with your queries, 'Is it love or rather the object of love?' never wanting to proclaim, only provoke."

Socrates laughed. "Well played, well played." He clapped. "But what might we assume of Diotima as she boasts of her superior position that eve?" he asked of us.

"Ask what you will of my vanity, Socrates, but was it not you who invited me to that party of fools?"

"True you are." Socrates nodded and smiled.

"Socrates spoke that night in favor of my wisdom and recounted what I had once imparted to him and gave me the said credit." Diotima rose and stood in the pool holding her robe high above the water, then made her way out to stand above us. "Love." She eyed me. "Is not a god, nor wise, nor beautiful, nor virtuous. No, love is the mediator between us and our desires for wisdom, beauty, and virtue. Love impregnates our souls and bodies with decency that we may create and reproduce respectable thoughts and dreams from the greatest knowledge and the highest virtue. For this, we must strive."

Tall and still, she cast her eyes beyond the giant wooden gods stirring in the light breeze with their soft red trunks and green canopies. She set her gaze beyond the star-studded sky, past the slight, slivered moon, taking in something I couldn't see.

Socrates rose, clapping, paying no mind to the hem of his robe dipping into the aquamarine pool. He spoke, looking in my direction, "Is not the true meaning of love the contemplation of the divine? You may think you love something, but isn't your nature that of a rational creature? Does your mind not naturally gravitate toward the object of whatever you love? And are you not rewarded by your body's emotion as you grasp at the object you think you love? Is this not merely self-promotion? And of what value? What purpose of falling in love with your own reflection? I ask you?"

He waited. Ayn Rand raced through my mind, but Socrates' silence rattled me, and I could only pray he wouldn't single me out while I was still deciphering his questions, posed with too many negatives.

Socrates stepped from the bath and circled around toward me. His sopping robe dragging behind. "Is not the value of love independent of human thought and emotion? Ah, yes. Is the existence of genuine love experienced without thought and emotion and in the marriage of God and mortal?"

Socrates stopped and stood before Diotima. Relieved, I let out a small sound. Taking her hands in his, Socrates looked disheveled and old in her presence, yet she welcomed him. "I look at love in the only way that love is seen," he said, drinking her in. "Only then is love mine to nourish, from whence to become immortal. How is that a life not to regard?"

"It is regarded, dearest Socrates, but you do digress." Diotima smiled and let go of him and his intimacy. "What followed that night, do you recall?" she asked the old man, but turned her attention to Pythia and me, like an attorney engaging with the jury.

Socrates chuckled, his round belly shook. He appeared unruffled and enter-tained. "Drunken dolts that night, yes. But yet, weren't we still poetic in our proc-lamations of love? Is love only measured worthy according to its performance?"

I bit my lip, then chewed my thumbnail. My Ex and I had mostly steered clear of our individual and coupled anxieties and regrets. Let alone considered their roots. Rather than be honest, I'd hid my fears, and she'd put hers on display. If Diotima's answer was yes, we'd been failures at love.

"Forsooth, a question." Diotima acknowledged the inquiry before ignoring it. "And so, Socrates, Pythia, and the seeker before us, I have told you of the tongues that flapped records of love that night, but the truth of the matter I believe to be this: There is no absolute in love, no right love, no wrong love. Circumstances can deem which lover and beloved respectively belong together."

Impassioned, Socrates spoke, "Love first fares in one form and, in due course, in another, and then many. From beautiful bodies to beautiful minds, and in the beauty of laws and institutions, until all beauty is one kindred, beholden only to the everlasting nature of all things. Remember, everyone is not the same in gain-ing wisdom. How can love not be the same?"

My shoulders softened with his words. I'd been holding my breath.

"Yes, it is so," Diotima said. "Describing love, even as the everlasting posses-sion of the good, isolates it to be a particular thing. Such denies the greater under-standing. The contemplation of love is not a discourse in goodness but purifies the heart to behold beauty. A beauty not seen with the eyeball, but with the eye of the mind. Only then will true creations of virtue and wisdom come forth."

"Agreed, agreed," Socrates said, and silence followed before he grinned. "Oh, I am not so inflated as to not know my place. Anyone right of mind can see that Diotima's eyes know beyond that, which puzzles me. I have been a slow learner, but I have moved from outside myself to live inside here." He pointed to his heart.

Pythia stood, then stepped out of the sacred water and joined the others. "Socrates has spoken," she said to me. "Diotima, high prophetess, and seer has revealed the hallowed and lowly. You must see now. Has she not compelled you to reach for new heights?"

My face flushed at such a pointed question, dizzy with their six eyes set upon me. "Well," I stammered, "first, thank you for your time." I bowed. "This has truly been—"

"Seeker!" Diotima barked, "say now what you know of love." My heart surged. My eyes darted among them. "Stand, please," she demanded, directing me with her hand.

Terrified, I stood. My shirt clung to me with sweat. Cold, I shivered and rubbed my palms on the sides of my trousers. My pant legs slid deeper into the water. With my eyes I begged Diotima for forgiveness. Then she smiled and softened.

My shoulders relaxed, and without thinking, I spoke. "Love cannot be contained in any idea. Instead, love inspires. Its nature is naturally inclined to knowledge, beauty, and virtue. Love is resilient, an enduring source of harmony among and between the mortal and divine. Love transcends the body and is not interested in justice, but is everlasting and ever available to the soul and the spirit of humanity." Standing tall and at the center of something profound I looked to Diotima, then Socrates, and finally Pythia. Calm and satisfied, I nodded. The corners of my mouth turned into a broad grin. I shrugged. "Love's the bomb."

"Ay," Pythia said, "and with a touch of love, everyone's a poet."

9

Pythia held my hands loosely in hers at the edge of the forest. "Between now and next we meet, please discover, practice, and document the seven kinds of love as outlined by Plato. Be ready to discuss. I shall see you on the third Dominicus of February for three days." Her eyes danced. "Ready?"

I looked around, but the others had already disappeared. I nodded, and she surprised me by leaning her forehead against mine. "There you go, there you go. In another time, in another place. Home on high, we come as we are." She stopped, looked to the north, and when a fierce wind blew, she shouted over the howling gale, "Memoria, memoria, memoria!" Then, in quick succession, she hollered, "Yada, yada, yada. So be it, so be it, so be it." As the wind gained momentum, she cried, "Close your eyes tight!"

The gust roared and bellowed, scaring the bejeebers out of me. "JUMP!" she yelled, and in the next moment, I was coming up for air in my bathtub.

Seemingly, only moments had passed. The lampshade lay on the floor. My laptop was as I'd left it. Cat sat tall beside the tub. Stunned, but not feeling a bit foolish, I sat soaking in the old pink tub. "Well, hello, old girl!" I said, then shook my head and pulled the plug. I laughed, shivering until the last of the icy water gurgled down the drain, I stood with the weight of my sopping clothes and stripped to shower. Lathering up in the gathering steam, I grinned, recalling Diotima putting old Socrates in his place. It sure was beautiful.

Letting the invigorating spray of hot water beat against my back, I called to mind the earthy aroma of the trees, the soft light spilling through the forest's crown, and the refreshing turquoise water. That's when I remembered feeling jealous of Pythia's attention toward Socrates.

Sitting at my desk, Cat nudged me. I set aside the parchment from Plato and scratched her ear. "You'll never believe what happened. I don't even know if I do, but Cat, I time traveled. Don't ask me how, but I jumped out of this dimension and into another."

Cat lifted her chin, and I scratched.

"And guess who was there?" I asked, "I can barely believe it myself, but I met some of history's greatest minds."

Cat stretched and turned away to look out the window.

"Oh, my defying time and space bores you, does it?" I teased.

Cat chattered at a magpie pecking for bugs in the window box.

"I hear you." I replied, "It won't go to my head. What's important now is how it inspires me and for me to inspire others." I reached for one of the brand-new pens and neatly printed in my ultramodern journal, titling seven pages. Each with a type of Greek love.

Flipping first to agape, I transcribed Plato's definition. *Considered the highest expression of love. Describe as selfless, unconditional, and extending to all living things regardless of any circumstance.*

Seriously? Sounds like a Hallmark card.

But I remained focused and moved to eros. With pen to paper, I scribed: *a sudden, immediate, and potentially dangerous expression of passion.* "What the—" I pulled back and read ahead. "Eros can lead to a loss of rational behavior often driven by the desire of the flesh." I bit my lip. "That's a kind of love?"

See, Mendes? Told you so.

Turn the page, dude. Don't even give it a second thought.

I held my head high and turned up my nose. Putting distance between myself and eros, I swiped my sweaty hands on my pants, then smoothed the book's spine flat to page three. *Ludus is the good-natured, fun-loving affection expressed in lighthearted, provocative speech, jest, and playful touch. It can be a frivolous game or indulgence and may lead to something more.*

I scratched my head. "Maybe that's like flirting?" Thinking of Fanny, I blushed. Then waggled the pen, shook my head, and shrugged.

"Okay, page four, Philautia." Thinking it a funny word, I checked the spelling and satisfied, I copied the definition. *Self-love practiced through self-acceptance and self-extension. It is the amplifier for all other expressions of love and necessary to deepen any expression of love. It enriches life and improves the health of the individual and the community.* My brows arched in respect until they narrowed into a frown. *Narcissism, Philautia's shadow aspect, is an excessive and exclusive preoccupation for self-promotion and perpetuation. It is unhealthy and contrary to any expression of beauty.*

You can be self-absorbed, dude.

"Yeah, well, so could she!" I barked back before I sighed, then cracked my knuckles. "Okay, Philia."

An expression of virtuous and righteous friendship or comradery developed over time by those who've shared challenging or emotionally rich experiences. Often evidenced by generosity and loyalty to the other's health and well-being. "Brotherly love. I get it."

I paged ahead. Seeing there were still two entries left, I blew out my cheeks. "Pragma."

A deep understanding of each partner and the romantic partnership resulting in mutual respect, patience, and acceptance of difference. It requires a test of time and endurance between lovers resulting in a lifelong supportive relationship.

I stared at the words. "For real?" I frowned, wondering where in the world this existed.

Finally, the list was ending. *Storge. The Greek word for natural affection. Referring to the love shared through the familial relationship between parent and child, or people and animals. It requires a dedication to the other's physical, emotional, and mental comfort, safety, and health.*

"Hey, old girl," I said, pointing to the entry, but Cat's interest was still all about the mouthy Magpie out the window. "Look! This one's about us." I quickly scribbled under its header, *With Cat, of course!*

Eager to stash the book, I flicked back through the pages. I didn't even want to think about eros and agape. Was that even a real thing? Steering clear of conjuring Coleman's screeching sax, I imagined the Greeks and the Socratic debate that led to the list. Scholars examining love. Pondering and wrangling out their theories. Theories! No judgments. No consequences of success or failure. They were explorers of something mystical, miraculous maybe. Love was worthy of investigation, accessible to all and owned by none. It was a phenomenon, like the constellations or the seasons. Something to discover. Today, was it even possible to define love without religion or politics?

Cat turned from the window, brushed her lanky body past me, and flopped down on Plato's list. "Careful, that's ancient history," I joked as I slid the document out from under her. As usual, she made no attempt to accommodate my efforts but pawed playfully and grabbed my hand. "Oh, you wanna rough-house, do you?" I asked, ruffling her head and wrestling with her.

The next day, I woke at the crack of dawn. Bright-eyed, I first tackled the load of discarded laundry piled atop the bedroom chair. From the heap, I gathered various dress slacks and their corresponding jackets. Folding the pants lengthwise and squaring the coats' shoulders, I took my time fixing each on a proper suit hanger. I sniffed the remaining shirt pits, folded the clean ones alongside my jeans, stacked everything in drawers, and carried the dirty clothes to the hamper.

Showered and dressed in my favorite suit, I stood at the mirror, brushing lint from my lapel, and tried to tame my hair before heading to the kitchen. My Ex's message still loomed largely on the refrigerator. *Happy now you dead zombie?* "Maybe," I quipped under my breath while I fed Cat, then ate my usual bowl of cold cereal standing beside her. Finished, I slid out of my suit jacket and tucked it and my journal into my backpack. At the door, I called goodbye to Cat, who meowed back, then left locking the door.

Walking my bike from the garage I spotted Bubbles and Mushkin. "Hi, Gabe!" they shouted. Mushkin, the little one, jumped up and down, "Mommy, there's Gabe!" she said pulling on her mom as the woman herded the two into their car seats. "Okay," I heard their mom say as she hurried the girls. Their mom then waved, giving me a cursory smile before sliding into the driver's seat. As I rode into the street the children twisted themselves in their car seats to again wave at me. Blushing, I lifted a palm their direction and pumped hard past them.

Inside Dumas, McPhail & Cox, Fanny waved from the receptionist's desk. "Welcome back, handsome!"

"Thanks, Fanny." And then, daring myself, I added, "It's good to be back."

I nodded good morning to the other early birds and turned the expensive knob to my office. Presuming entry, I proceeded with the full expectation of access, but the door refused. I pushed, then shouldered against it, before shoving hard. When I finally stumbled into the windowless room, I saw how a jam of files, likely having toppled from my desk to the floor, had obstructed the door. The stale, cramped space that was always dark without artificial light confronted me. Two days away might have had me cleaning up my act at home, but it certainly didn't change a thing at work. I sighed, spotting another load of files stacked tall on my desk.

The sum of my work was a growing, relentless daily stack of new, but banal files, each threatening to suck the lifeblood out of me. Stealing my soul by the minute, and over the years with an everyday fresh hell of inane research and filing, I wanted to bolt the moment I stumbled in. But I stepped over the wreck of paper and pulled the notebook from my backpack, hoping for salvation. I searched the headings. *Eros?* "God, no!" I ran my finger over each definition. *Ludus, philautia, philia, pragma, storge?* Nothing. Nada. Zero. "There's no love here," I grumbled and shoved the mountain of files out of my way. Resigned to my place behind the desk, I plugged into good old Nat and opened one of the mind-numbing files, preparing to die—again.

It is what it is, Mendes. This is your life.

Lost in the supreme court case that ruled 'shredded wheat' is not trademarkable, I first recognized Fanny by a single blue fingernail lightly tapping at the top of my computer's screen. She lowered herself until her face met mine. I yanked out the earbuds. "Sorry, sugar britches. I knocked but—" She made a face, then motioned to the jumbled folders scattered all over the floor. "Looks like a tornado ripped through here, huh?" I stood, muttering about the door, but she was already scooping up the mess. I crouched beside her. She smelled spicy. "I bet you can guess why I'm here?" She handed me the files, now stacked and orderly. "Do you mind?" She made a face as if I would. "I just need to borrow your muscles for one minute."

"No, no. Of course not." I shook my head as if we were really talking about something that required convincing. "Anytime. I'm happy to help."

"Anytime?"

I blushed.

"Oh, my! I didn't know men like you still existed." She winked and wiggled out.

I hurried, pulled out my journal, and skipped through the pages until I found the heading. "Ludus," I said, transcribing our interaction.

That Friday, after work, I sat down with a beer and reviewed my love entries.

Storge Experiences:

- *With Cat, of course!*
- *The Cardinals flocking to the feeder outside my window.*
- *Admiring the squirrels' tenacity and agility at the birdfeeder, instead of going crazy thinking of them as annoying pests.*

Ludus Experiences:

- *Fanny saying, "Can I borrow your muscles, handsome?"*

With my pen poised, I concentrated. My eyes darted. I drummed my fingers. There had to be more. I scanned the chart and stared at the bleak entries. "I have to find a bunch of random people." I scratched my beard, then took the last hearty swig from the brown bottle, closed the journal, grabbed my coat and car keys, and headed to the supermarket.

Satisfied, I circled the crowded parking lot. A mother and child sped past me, sloshing through the snow. Hand in hand, they laughed, racing toward their car while I awaited their parking space. The boy packed a snowball and called out to his mother. She raised her eyebrows. She shook her head. "No," she said, laughing. "Yes." The boy challenged before soft balling the threat. His mother ducked. They both laughed and climbed into the car.

Watching from my car, I remembered my mother lifting me, just a little boy, so I could press stones into the packed snow and bring to life the snowman we'd built. I'd had trouble getting the carrot in place, so she'd shifted me to her hip, and with one arm around my waist, she'd helped wiggle the orange root. Together we'd pushed against the icy snow until she became unsteady, and the two of us toppled onto the snowman, bringing him down with us.

I recalled the freezing snow caked to my mittens and hat. The big-eyed upset of being on the ground. My mother laughed. Standing, she brushed the snow from her jeans. "Come on!" She waved me over. "We can fix this."

Somewhere there's a photo of us standing beside that lopsided snowman. I switched off the car's engine. Who'd taken that picture? I had a vague sense of someone I once knew but had long forgotten.

Anyway. I slipped off my gloves to page through the journal. Ludus or storge? To be safe, I noted the parking lot mother and son under both and climbed out of the car.

Pulling on my gloves, I trailed behind an elderly couple. At first, I veered to dodge around the bundled pair intertwined at the elbows but then dropped back. Taking ginger steps on the packed snow, the man leaned into the woman while she pointed strategically to places of bare pavement, steering them both to safer ground. Once inside, he pushed the cart, and she advanced past him. "Get ham," he called to her back. She nodded, making a beeline to the deli. I snuck to the side and made a note under pragma and philia.

Super Food was buzzing with people. Most pushed a cart with great purpose, others rushed about with the plastic basket over their arm, and a few were just obstacles in the aisles. Deciding a cart was a better cover, I headed to the cauliflower. Pretending to inspect several heads, I stole a cursory glance through the produce department. There were plenty of people, but none were engaged in love as far as I could tell. Even young couples were serious about shopping. Overlooking the single shoppers, I scrutinized the others, and that's when I uncovered a father and son by the apples.

The teenager stood. His head hung while his father loaded a plastic bag. "You gotta get in there. We've talked about this before," the man said, twisting a tie around an overfilled bag of handpicked galas. "You were sloppy and slow." He looked at the boy for the first time and I could feel his impatience. "Are you even listening?" He didn't wait for an answer and cast the fruit into the cart. "I can't help you if you don't listen to me." The teen shuffled behind as the man squeezed the cart between shoppers, into the bakery.

I felt for the boy. My grandfather used to humiliate me with exchanges he claimed were motivational, and there was my stepfather with his talks about how to think more and feel less. But ultimately, they all only hurt.

Shamelessly captivated by the family drama, I hurried after them and took cover along a wall of pastries. The man spoke low now. The boy's eyes glistened, and he said something I couldn't make out. Turning my ear, I strained to hear.

"Excuse me." Another shopper reached around me, obliterating my surveillance while she went for a boxed cake.

"I'm sorry," I heard the man say as I bobbed and darted, finally catching up to the father-son scene. "I overreacted. You're right. If basketball's not your thing, it's not your thing. There's no shame in that, and I'm sorry I made you feel like there is. Will you forgive me?" The man lowered his gaze to the teen. The boy nodded. "Come on," the man said with his arm around the kid. "Let's finish up and order pizza." I trailed behind, almost ghoulish, spying until the boy chattered. Animated, he talked with his hands, and the man laughed.

Biting my lip, I ushered the cart over near a display of McCormick's savory pot roast seasonings. I was almost disappointed. I hadn't expected a happy ending. I couldn't remember a time when either my grandfather or stepfather had said they were sorry. Irritated, I opened the journal. Flipping through the mostly blank pages, I ruminated. I hesitated at the page titled, storge, scribbled the father-son encounter, then with a critical eye, scratched through the entire paragraph and began again, shaking my head. I mumbled, trying to find a way around my uncomfortable feelings, "What's the point of this? It's not like I'm searching for a father figure."

Man up, Mendes.

Dude, this is what you signed up for.

"If you're tallying a list of pros and cons, I can tell you I think the McCormick's seasoning is worth the investment."

"What?" I looked up to find a woman standing there. She fingered her earring as she smiled at me from behind her cart.

"Oh, the seasoning," I said. "Yeah, no. I'm just standing out of the way over here. I'm not in the market for seasoning."

"You're not in the market for it?" she quipped, snapping bubble gum. "You look skeptical. What? Not sure?" She cocked her head, and the pom on her loose-fitting beanie flopped. "Hey," she reached out and touched my arm. Her metallic green puffer jacket fell open, revealing her nicely fitted white T-shirt. "I'm just kidding. I didn't mean to make you nervous." She smiled, and I felt very warm. She motioned to my cart. "You're aware you're halfway through the store, and your cart is empty, right?" She gave me a disapproving look. "If you wanna pick up women, at least throw in some veggies." Then walking away in her skinny jeans, she turned back toward me, and said, "Oh, and ditch the notebook. Very uncool."

"Oh. Oh! No, no. I'm not—nothing like that. I'm just doing some research here."

"Uh-huh," and she threw me a dirty look over her shoulder.

I scanned the crowd. Relieved no one was paying me any attention, I dashed into the middle of the busy flow of shoppers, hoping to disappear. I wandered up and down the aisles, brooding enough that I'd forgotten why I'd come in the first place and then loaded up unnecessarily on cat food. "Mothers and fathers. Family." I bellyached, heading down the next aisle. "And women! Go figure that one." Sizing up a cleaning product that claimed *Real Fast, Real Clean, Industrial Strength* results, I chucked it into the cart. Still grumbling, I proceeded to the check-out, where my cart clipped the customer's heels ahead of me.

She turned. I closed my eyes. *God almighty!*

She blew a giant pink bubble from the fat wad she'd otherwise snapped. "How many cats do you have?" she asked. "Or are you partial to small helpings of tuna?"

"Oh, hello, again. Sorry about bumping into you. I was…" I shrugged, "busy thinking and, um, yeah," I nodded, "the food, it was on sale. I'm stocking up."

Her tongue poked the inside of her cheek and she leaned closer. Smelling fresh like soap, she teased me. "You still didn't answer my question." She eyed me, then paid the clerk and left, her athletic figure strutting out the door.

Outside the store, I craned my neck, determined this time to spot the bubble-blowing woman before she surprised me again. Watchful, I exchanged cash with a Girl Scout for an armful of cookies. Then hurried to pass all but one box to a homeless man. That's when I spotted the elderly couple I'd trailed earlier. The man moved in slow motion as the woman helped him into the car. Forgetting my paranoia, I jogged over and helped load their bags into the trunk.

With the cat food stacked in the cupboard and the fridge door at last clean, I sat at my desk wiping the greasy grilled ham and cheese from my mouth and gulped my second beer. Cat brushed the empty bottle, nearly knocking it over before curling up in her favorite spot. I opened the journal, smoothing the spine flat before penning between the fine blue lines.

Storge Experiences:

- *A mother and son running hand in hand, laughing.*
- *A father asking forgiveness from his son and then having fun.*

Pragma Experiences:

- *An elderly couple helping each other.*

Ludus Experiences:

- *A mother and son goading each other in repartee.*
- *The witty gum-snapping woman playfully challenging me.*
- *The absence of ludus in my obtuse and dull responses to said woman.*

My brows leaned into each other in judgment. I buttoned my lips, then coached myself. Not every woman's your Ex. Not every interaction has to be a failure. I nodded. "You're a girl, Cat." I put my feet up on the desk and nudged her. "What do you say? Is there one out there for me?" She rolled onto her back and grabbed hold of my foot, and play-fought before rolling to her side. I gently ran my foot along her spine. She smiled with her eyes before flicking her tail in my direction. "I can't play with you all night," I said, but tugged her tail one last time. "Okay. What else?" I flipped through the pages. "How about…" I said, already writing in the journal.

Agape Experiences:

- *Giving three boxes of cookies to a homeless man.*
- *Helping the elderly couple with their bags.*

Philia Experiences:

- *The elderly woman's patience and commitment to her husband.*

I shrugged and closed the book. "It's a start." But I wished I'd seen something significant, something that would knock Pythia's socks off. Bothered, I opened a sleeve of Toffee-tastics and gobbled one after another, washing the sugary carbs down with the last of the rich ale. When only crumbs were left, I plugged into Ornette Coleman and opened a second sleeve.

The violin strings vibrated in a mournful mood. The foreboding drums percussed. Then with the sound of the whining sax, I panicked and fumbled to close the app. Popping a couple of Pepto Bismol, I decided to stream the basketball game instead. I rubbed my belly, distracted, while Denver powered up the court, fixated and sweating. South Dakota intercepted.

"Oh, no! If the Pioneers keep this up, there'll be no coming back." The announcer's tenor was larger than life. "It sure looks like they're gonna get rolled. They just can't seem to cash in those buckets tonight." I ran my hand through my hair, gulping, fighting back the acidic contents of my stomach while the players pounded the polished floor. Their feet a steady drum, the dribbled ball relentless. I closed my laptop.

"What were you thinking?" Irritated, I flicked the empty bottle. It went down hard, taking other old empties with it. Cat bolted upright, and I snatched Plato's paper, this time reading it with some good old skepticism before casting it aside. I opened my notebook and glared at my neat penmanship. Each letter was a capital, with no loops or curves, primarily straight lines standing tall—a blatant and desperate attempt for self-importance. I pitched the book to the floor. "Examples of love? Really? That's what you're calling these brief encounters with strangers? And at the friggin' grocery store of all places!"

I ran both hands through my curls and thought of My Ex, the day she'd discovered a big ding in her car door. "Ahh," she'd said and shrugged with a crooked smile, "whatever." She rolled her eyes. "It's gonna get dinged, anyway." Her reaction wasn't much different when we finally broke up: "This was gonna happen someday." She had a way of making disappointment sound and look comfortable, natural even.

She was a good time, Mendes.

Dude, she wasn't happy.

I shoved my hands into my hair. "Why couldn't I be happy?" She didn't exactly think things through. She was out of control. Way impulsive!" Wild, really, and right from the get-go. "Eros, that's all that was."

Maybe I like being tied up in knots. Maybe I am a glass-half-empty guy. I picked up the parchment. The paper was thick, but it had no weight. Maybe My Ex wasn't so wild as she was free. What would it be like to feel free? Could I handle that? "I'm not *really* unhappy," I asked myself. "Am I? But I am afraid to venture outside my comfort zone."

Yeah. But dude, look what you've done lately.

I closed my eyes, took a deep breath, and let my mind wander. Does it matter how far or wide a person travels or the significance of the people they encounter? Maybe I could find, even nurture love in the ordinariness of day-to-day living.

10

Over the weeks, I'd made little progress, except for the page labeled storge. There, I'd listed plenty of examples of love for animals. At first glance, ludus looked even better, except that it was a long list of failures. Pragma, philia, and agape had those grocery store examples, but philautia and eros were still blank. The first for lack of example, and the second because I really didn't want to think about it.

"You gotta step it up, Mendes," I told myself on Sunday. "You've got one week until you meet with Pythia. Even if the examples are still only within the context of your unexceptional life, it's time to get some game." So I spent Sunday afternoon scouring how-to-flirt videos on YouTube. That evening I rehearsed a variety of come-hither looks in the mirror: the alluring tucked chin, the playful tilted head, and the inviting lifted brows.

Monday after work, I read and re-read *Short Jokes Anyone Can Remember* and *Small Talk for the Tongue Tied*. Loading the washer with whites, I practiced slowing my vocal cadence and considered the timing of comebacks while dumping detergent and bleach into their respective depositories. I closed the lid, turned the dial, and in my living room, I ran the vacuum. Lulled by the white noise, I envisioned scenarios of chance encounters.

Washing dishes, I practiced running lines from the likes of romcom scenes while I shoved a soapy sponge inside a boatload of bowls and cups. Rinsing and stacking them to dry, I tried out several casual laughs before I returned to the laundry.

"Well, maybe we could—" I practiced making an easy suggestion. "What the—oh my God!" Frantic, I pulled at the heap of pink wet garments that only an hour ago had been white. Searching the washing machine, I discovered the culprit. A never-before-washed red dishtowel my mother had stuffed into last year's Christmas stocking. "Why does this always happen?" I shot my hand through my hair, then sighed, shoving all the rose-colored cotton into the dryer. "I'm trying to get my act together!" I threw my hands up "But something's always against me!" I looked at the ceiling. "What do you want from me? What?!" I slammed the dryer door and kicked the machine. I took my head into my hands and grabbed fists full of hair before I looked. Sure enough, I'd dented the panel.

Tuesday, I woke sullen and a bit resentful, right away noticing the cracked ceiling looming overhead like a dark cloud, so I turned away to pet Cat until she purred. Then dragged myself out of bed and to work, where I spent most of my time holed up in my office, plugged in. At the end of the day, still licking my wounds, I bumped into the second-year associate in the men's room. Remembering something Fanny had told me, I inquired about his new puppy. His face lit up, and I enjoyed looking over his shoulder while he scrolled through pictures on his phone. I even shared shots of Cat. He introduced himself as Josh.

Feeling good after work on Wednesday and loaded up with white undershirts at Macy's, I stood in a long line of customers. The young woman ahead of me turned, and said, "Big sale." Her long-lashed eyes widened, and she doe-blinked. "It's my dad's birthday. What'd ya think?" She held up a baby blue cable-knit sweater.

"Nice."

"Not your style, is it?" She frowned. "Not mine either, but I think he'll like it." She shrugged. "It's hard to shop for men. You probably don't know that, being a man and all."

I nodded.

Loosen up, Mendes.

Dude, tell her a joke.

I cleared my throat. "Hey. The long line and all," I motioned with my head, "well, maybe not so long now, looks like you're next, but I was thinking—"

"What?" She bubbled.

"Um. A joke. You know, pass the time and all. So, do you know what kind of coffee they served on the Titanic?"

"Sanka!" she said like we were on a game show. The clerk waved to her, and she advanced, but turning toward me, asked, "Do you know how men are like coffee?" She grinned from ear to ear and bounced a bit in her knee-high fur-lined boots. "The best ones are rich, hot, and keep you up all night. Kinda naughty, isn't it?" She crinkled her nose.

She's cute, dude.

I laughed, and she laughed, and then a sales associate called to me from another register.

"Bye." She waved. "Maybe we'll bump into each other again." She flashed her lashes.

"I hope your dad likes the sweater," I called to her. Yes! Finally, Ludus! And I killed it!

"She's a firecracker, huh?" the man who lined up behind me said, but I was busy scribbling the encounter into my book.

Thursday, when Fanny popped in and made her usual request, I paused. Feeling brave, I considered the opportunity to again create ludus. Initiating good eye-contact, I rose from behind my desk. I smiled just a little, tucked my chin, and retorted, "Sure, Fanny..." I counted three beats, then raised an eyebrow, "as long as I can borrow yours?"

She burst out laughing. "Are you making a pass at me?"

"Oh, no!" Hurrying toward her, I broke into a cold sweat. Dizzy, I stopped and steadied myself at the desk's edge. "Oh, God. I am so sorry. I didn't mean it the way it sounded." I was breathless.

She cocked her head. "You're the cutest thing. If I was ten years younger. Mmm, mmm!" She stepped forward to pinch my cheek. "Hey, there's this fundraiser Saturday, the Chili Bowl. It's right in your neighborhood. What do you think? Gabe? Are you okay?"

I nodded but worried she was asking me out and wished I'd worn one of the new undershirts because my white dress shirt was now sopping in sweat. Anxious that the pink T-shirt was bleeding through, I grabbed my suit jacket off the side chair, pulled it on, and slipped back behind the desk. "Yeah, sure. Saturday. Right." I buttoned the jacket.

"Day after tomorrow."

"Yeah. No, I eat a lot of chili." I nodded, pulling out my wallet.

"Do you?" she asked, and I set the wallet aside.

"Yeah, of course." I tried to look like I knew what we were talking but was distracted by the sweat pouring down my sides. Wanting to wrap things up I stood and reached into my pants pocket for my wallet. Feeling confused I patted all my pant pockets before ripping through the breast pockets of my jacket. "I just, um, I'm not sure—"

"Here." She handed me my wallet. "Gabe, I'm asking because they're short on volunteers. It's not a date. You can eat for free."

"Oh. Right." I nodded. "No. Yeah, okay. I knew that." I shrugged nodding.

"Good." She wiggled her hips. "Sooo, the cooler?"

Friday, my boss poked her head into my office. "Meeting's canceled. Leave early if you like." She turned away and then popped back in. "Oh, that shredded wheat thing—outstanding. The partners want you to know it didn't go unnoticed." She did the gun thing and winked, making that double-clacking sound before she bobbed past the glass wall. I finished filing and took her up on her offer, heading to the dry cleaners on my way home.

There, the man made a face while searching the revolving rack of laundry, and from across the counter, I surveilled the circling shirts hoping to spot mine. Finally, he called to his wife. She snatched the voucher and pointed out the date. "This is an old ticket," she said.

"Oh, geez. Sorry." I blushed, rooting through my coat pockets until I located the proper receipt. "You're quite the team," I said, practicing courage.

"Only for about thirty-five years!" He boasted.

"Wow." I paid and took my shirts.

"You'll find love," the wife chimed in, "There's a lid for every pot."

"You wanna know the secret to thirty-five years?" he whispered. "She's the boss."

She rolled her eyes and whacked his behind. "Get back to work," she teased.

The bell rang, and we all turned as the next customer stepped in from the cold. "Oh, my God!" the newcomer cried out, recognizing the customer behind me. The two embraced, both overwrought with emotion. "How long has it been?" one asked when they finally pulled apart. Pained, the other struggled to speak. The second grabbed the first and they hugged again. Their bodies shook as they sobbed. "I'd never have gotten out alive if it weren't for you." I heard one say as I slid past them and out the door.

Bothered with emotion myself, I sat in my car, spying on the scene. The two talking with their hands, shaking their heads, laughing or sometimes overcome with emotion looking to the floor or away. When I'd witnessed enough, I opened my notebook and paged through. *Phila: Comradery shared during an emotionally challenging time, now evidenced by generosity and affection.* I switched on the engine and cranked the heat. Had I ever endured anything that afforded me such love with someone despite the distance of space or time? My mother came to mind, and in an instance, the muscles in my face contracted. Why was there only distance between us around the things we'd endured together? My stepfather came to mind, followed by a pang of heartache regarding my real dad.

I thumbed the pages. *Pragma: a romantic partnership that's endured the test of time with mutual respect and patience.* I noted the dry-cleaning couple and engaged the car into reverse. What chance did I have at pragma if my mom had had none? Then, catching sight of myself in the rearview mirror, I braked and parked. My eyes were bloodshot, my face wet from tears. My jaw hung open accommodating my mouth-breathing. I swiped the back of my hand across my runny nose. The heat was finally fired up and blowing hot air. I adjusted the fan and went for the radio knob, knowing full well it didn't work. I snapped it on and off and on and off again, finding the resistance right before the click satisfying.

Was my story doomed as only some continuation of my mother's? Had she been a victim of fate? Was I? I adjusted the mirror. Determined, I looked hard to see past my unruly hair and thick eyebrows, my broken nose. "Am I loveable?" I asked my reflection. The answer came by way of my softening muscles. "Philautia?" I asked, wondering if self-love felt like letting go. But of what?

That night, I tossed and turned. Finally, sitting at the edge of the bed, I coached myself to the kitchen for water. With the glass, I shuffled to the sofa, plopped down, and flipped through the channels.

Michael Douglas's character paced while Glenn Close's stood in her nightgown. "I don't know what you're up to, but it's going to stop now," he bellowed.

"No, it's not," she said, calm and collected. She stepped closer. "I'll not be ignored!!" She roared. Then, she sounded soft. "What're you so afraid of?" She reached for his pants. He strong-armed her. "Don't flatter yourself," he spat, and I pointed the remote, clicking off the drama.

A blue light flickered. Across the street, someone else couldn't sleep. I slid on my coat and escaped to the front stoop like someone stealing a smoke. Parked, I rubbed my hands together while the icy cement numbed my backside. Somebody played guitar in the distance. An infomercial flashed on my neighbor's big screen. I looked away. The air was still but frosty. The stars were millions of brilliant players, while the moon was less than a waning crescent.

Keys jangled. I strained to see a couple crossing the street. "How can you say that?" an outraged woman's voice demanded. "They painted her as a crazed bunny killing home-wrecker, a sexist trope that's still alive and kicking thirty-years later. They were both reckless, using sex to feel alive. The whole thing unleashed monstrous behavior with dire consequences," she preached.

"Oh, yeah. I see what you mean. The rabbit, right?" he said, getting into the car.

"Oh, my God! No." She closed the door.

"Eros," I whispered.

Saturday, I arrived at the pottery studio on time and dressed in the Chili Bowl T-shirt. "I'm looking for…" I asked, reading from the Post-It Note Fanny had provided, "Ah, here it is, Amy. I'm here to volunteer."

"Oh, perfect! And many thanks for helping us out. Amy's right over there."

"Oh." No. Please, God, no. "Do you mean?"

He pointed.

"Not the woman blowing bubble gum?"

11

"Good morning," Pythia said from the computer screen.

"I've met someone!" I blurted from the edge of my chair where I'd been waiting since well before sunrise.

She laughed, sliding the medallion back and forth along its chain.

"Yesterday, I met a woman named Amy. She's beautiful and funny and smart. She's so smart, and she thinks I'm interesting," I said and then rambled having a hard time keeping up with my thoughts. "We both like cats, and art, old movies, and hiking. Her eyes are brown, but light, not like mine. They're pale with flecks of green, and her hair is jet black. It's short. I mean really short, but she has a nicely shaped head. You know how some people's heads need hair? She could be bald and still be a looker. She wears the tiniest piercing on her nose. It's sparkly blue, almost black. A sapphire, I think she said. You don't even notice it at first, but when you do, you think it only makes her seem more interesting than she already is. And her skin is soft and smooth. She smells clean. That's funny to say, I guess, like some kinda sweet mediciny soap. She's so nice, Pythia. And we really hit it off. I know you'd like her. Did I say her eyes sparkle? Like somebody's home, you know, somebody lives inside. And when she speaks, she's so sure of herself, but in an attractive way. I can't believe my luck. A few days ago, I didn't even know about the Chili Bowl. I've never met anyone at all like this in my entire life. Never!"

Pythia listened with great attention. "You've described an attractive person inside and out. Tell me, how do you think this happened? If you consider that you've played a part in this seemingly chance encounter, to what can you attribute such success?"

"Well, at first, when I was looking for love—you know, the homework—and

I worried my life was boring. Not complex or sophisticated enough for a mean-ingful experience of love. But then I realized the complexity depended on my participation. I think it might not matter who you are or where you live, or how much money you make. Or even your level of education. You get from love what you put in. The funny thing is, I'd already met Amy." I stopped. My eyes widened. "Can you believe that? It was a few weeks ago at the supermarket. And when I saw it was her at the Chili Bowl, I almost turned and left. But that was because I'd been so self-absorbed at the market, and I'd thought she thought I was a dufus. But I hadn't been paying attention to a lot of things. Or maybe I'd only paid atten-tion to certain things. Or things that aren't even real." I frowned, wondering how the last part was even possible. "Before this, I was only noticing what I thought was happening, and I made that real. But Amy was paying attention to every-thing. Amy didn't make up a story that already ended before it began."

"Brilliant! Simply brilliant, yes?"

"I know. It's so cool, right? So, Pythia, where do we go from here? I mean, I think I'm finished. You know, end of story. After all, I understand the stories I've been told influence my vision of love. I get it about the seven kinds of love, and most important—I've already met someone! Pythia, thank you. This is more than I ever expected."

"Indeed." She smiled, then paused long enough for me to remember the black ram. I swallowed hard. As if she could read my mind, she cocked her head and smiled again. "We will go from the electromagnetic fields at the Earth's core to the depths of your cells to far-out outer space before we've finished. But first, let's not dismiss what's at hand this very moment. It seems you believe you were, first, supposed to find love. Second, that love would feel a certain way. And third, that for those reasons, you wouldn't miss it when it showed up. Why do you think you thought those things?"

Had I thought those things? But instead, I said, "Good questions," then felt a pang of unexpected irritation. Wasn't it enough that I'd met Amy? Wonderful Amy. Exuberant, talking-with-her-hands, Amy. Coy, fiddling with her earring, Amy. I felt so good about her and about me with her. Digging around in that might wreck it. Part of me wanted the whole love inquiry to be over. I wanted Pythia to gush over my fast study. But instead of being honest, I pretended I was fine. "I suppose, um, well … am I missing something here, Pythia? Because, I don't know—I mean, I feel a little like you want me to admit—divulge," I articulated the word, "some hidden truth about Amy. I like her. I don't want to jinx this."

"Do you feel exposed?"

"Exposed? No. Um, Hmm? Exposed? Well, yeah. Yeah, I do. Like you set me up to feel good, and now you want me to see it's not all that. I'm even embarrassed I feel this way. Actually," I ran my hand through my hair, "I feel betrayed. This is ridiculous. Just moments ago, I was on top of the world, and now I feel—well, like I might cry. I don't even know the last time I cried, for Christ's sake."

Get ahold of yourself, Mendes.

Breathe, dude.

I inhaled deeply.

"That was a lovely thing you just did. Breathing? Letting yourself be alive. Yes?"

"Is it hot in here?" I pulled at my shirt.

"What are you afraid of?"

"Afraid?" My eyebrows snapped together, and I gave her a sideways stare. "No, I'm not afraid." My shoulders lurched to my ears. "Why would I be afraid?" I asked, feeling like I was listening really hard for something far off. "Maybe I am afraid." I frowned.

"Let's just sit with your fear, shall we?"

We sat, and my mind wrangled the quiet, begging me to think, to speak, to intellectualize the fear. But the chatter died. My wild heart eased, and my breath followed. I pulled back and relaxed into the chair. I closed my eyes and rested my hands on my thighs. Moments passed. "Pythia?" I opened one eye and then the other. "I'm afraid everything is a lie. You. Love. Amy. Maybe even me. I don't want this to be a dirty trick. I want love and happiness. I want peace of mind. I wanna feel alive. Something's been missing in my life, and I want it so badly that I'm afraid to admit it's missing. So I pretend everything's okay. That's the lie." My stomach flipped. "What if I don't think I know who I am?" I doubled over in a cold sweat. I moaned. "Maybe I'm not loveable!" I looked to her and she looked right back at me. Then pressing her lips together, she shook her head. "I don't know, Pythia. Sometimes I feel like everything's hanging by a thread, and it's only a matter of time before it all comes undone, and I crash and burn. I don't even know what I'm saying. I can't explain myself."

"The words fall short. They fail you, yes?" She sounded kind. "How can you communicate what you feel if the words are lacking, hmm? Same question, but now a little different. What might you be misunderstanding, misinterpreting, if the words can't capture the essence?"

"I don't know." I shrugged, tossing my hands. "What difference does it make, though? I mean, whether I can communicate what I'm feeling or not doesn't change the fact that love feels threatening. Like it's something I'm supposed to know how to find but never do. Or, if I do, I worry I can't sustain it. I don't know if love is real or even matters." I picked the Rubik's cube up and fidgeted with it for a second before I tossed it aside to slouch in the chair. "Sometimes, I think I'm just a zombie."

"Yes. I know."

We were quiet in the space of nothingness, that place of consideration. "I got scared when you asked questions about me and then about Amy and me. I doubted myself."

"What changed?"

"When you asked the questions?"

"Mm-hmm. You were excited, happy even, and then I asked a question, and you doubted everything that you'd just shared. What changed after I asked the questions?"

"Nothing." I shrugged. "Well, I guess how I felt."

"Why?" she said, creating momentum.

"Because…" I stretched the word, trying to match the pace, my shoulders hedging toward my ears. "Because the questions implied that I had misunderstood something. And I know I did. There's a lot back there, in my past." I pointed behind me. "I don't know if you understand. There are so many things with My Ex, and not only her, other women, too. And my grandfather, my stepfather. My mom, even. The people closest to me. It seems like there are secrets, things I'm supposed to know. Unspoken things. Things I never ask about, but also things I never say. I know there are things my mom doesn't say, and I don't ask, but there are things I never tell, too."

I looked hard at Pythia. Steadfast, she met my gaze. "If it's my fault that love wasn't in my life, that love isn't in my life now, and if I still don't know why. If I don't know what I'm doing wrong. Well, then the future likely holds more of the same."

I looked off and out the window, not seeing the bare window boxes or old ash tree, instead I searched my mind. "Unless there is some magic, some god who will bestow to me the privilege of love and happiness, I'm a goner. A dead man walking."

"Have you seen this before?" A picture appeared on the screen. A painting of a pipe, vernacular, yet scholarly. With its polished walnut wooden bowl and deep ebony mouthpiece, the thing hoovered over the hand-scripted words, *Ceci n'est pas une.*

"Ah, maybe." I searched the archives of my mind. "On a T-shirt or—I think it's a painting, actually by some surrealist painter, right?" I felt the watery way information can surface out of obscurity.

"You are right! French surrealist Rene Magritte. Do you know its title?"

"Nope."

"This is not a pipe."

"No? Looks like a pipe to me."

"No."

"What do you mean? It is a pipe. It's clearly a pipe or whatever the French word for pipe is. Is that what you mean?"

"No." She laughed.

"No? It's not a pipe? It's not a pipe in English, and it's not a pipe in French?"

"That's right."

"Well, at least I'm right about something. But I have no idea the point of saying a pipe is not a pipe."

"Magritte challenges our understanding of the use of symbols, or words, by pointing out that they only describe something. They are mere stand-ins, proxies of sorts for the things they describe. Language, the words and symbols we use to communicate, are only labels. They are not the real things. Things are not always what they seem to be. Instead, they are what they are."

"Ah, the pipe is not a pipe; it's the thing it is."

"Precisely! The pipe is what it is. A thing we call a pipe. Therefore, language is, in and of itself, a lie."

"That seems a little extreme. I guess I get it. But what does this have to do with the questions you posed or how they made me feel?"

"Neuro-linguistic programming."

"Neuro-linguistic programming?"

"Yes, the neurological connections between language and patterns of behavior," she said smiling, her auburn hair framing her face as she nodded. "Humans are programmed through language, and when language is not efficient in capturing the entire essence of the message, it's skewed for both the operator and the receiver. Think about the word love." She paused and I could hear the brook babbling behind her. A cardinal lit on the branch of the big oak in the distance. "You *think* you know what it means," she said in a way meant to draw my attention back to her. "You *think* it looks a certain way. You *think* you'll know it when you see it. You *think* you'll find it. But," she warned arching a brow, "it is only the word you recognize. You understand the word as a pattern of specific behaviors that result in winning or losing. But love is not a word. It's not a head-game."

"It feels like a game. Only I don't know the rules. All I know is it's important to score. Sometimes I just stumble across home plate, the crowd cheers, and I'm a hero. But you're right. I have no idea how to make that happen, and I'm definitely not chomping at the bit to broadcast that insight to the world."

"Yes, I understand. If all you have are the words, and the words are empty, how can you create a good story—a love story in this case? One that you can trust, one that sustains you. One you can believe in. One that's safe to share. One that's real." She paused. "Think about it, hmm? After lunch, yes?"

In the kitchen, I poured the congealed contents of a can of chicken and rice soup into a pan. I stirred the melting glob, waiting for it to become something I could stomach, and wondered about the difference between the word love and the experience of love. How many things had I misunderstood simply by accepting them at their face value? Family, relationships, career. Even pizza and beer, for that matter.

I stood blowing on a spoonful of hot soup, slurping it straight from the pot at the stove. The briny broth with its buttery sheen tasted good despite the mushy diced bits of chicken and carrots floating about the overcooked rice. Maybe things could be different with Amy. I looked out the window. In the bright yellow sunshine, the neighbor girls rolled a big ball of snow around leaving their front yard nearly clean of snow, revealing the green grass. With the pot in hand, I stepped closer to the window to spy on the girls struggling as the enterprising ball grew in girth and weight. Reaching an impasse with the gigantic ball melting, now slick and icy from the sun, the two stopped and the bigger one, Bubbles, placed her hands on her hips to boss her little sister. Mushkin then gave the snowball a good kick before Bubbles climbed atop and surprised them both by obliterating all their hard work in just a few stomps. Stunned they looked at each other and then my direction. I darted back from the window, the hot soup swirling in the pot.

Spring will come, I thought heading back to the kitchen to set the pot aside and retrieve a proper bowl. Then sitting at the table slurping soup, I let my mind wander in the promise of the jonquils pushing through the snow. Afterall, without promise, what is there?

Just before one o'clock, I headed to the stairs, then hesitated to turn an ear. Had Cat inadvertently engaged an app? She'd been known to walk across the keyboard or TV remote, turning things on and off. I listened, climbing the stairs, letting an animated tenor saxophone and back-up drums pull me to the room. Cat smiled. Sitting pretty, her tail kept the beat. "Whaddaya got going here, Cat?" I asked, looking to close the app, which, curiously, was not open.

Instead, the projection of Pythia danced on the screen. Her silky green gown swayed while she moved her hips, snapping her fingers, all jazzed with her eyes closed. Her bracelets jangled and her toe tapped out a groovy beat. "Da da da da da," Pythia sang along, although the song had no words. "Catchy tune, huh?" Her eyes remained closed, allowing the music to transport her to some hip place.

"'My Favorite Things.'" I slid into my chair to appreciate the avant-garde rendition of the show tune.

"Johnny couldn't have told this story if he went by spoken language. Anyone who has something great to share, shares it from their own head, their own heart."

"Are we gonna go see John Coltrane?" I was already rising for the lampshade.

"Easy." She laughed. "You're not ready. You don't know the language yet."

"English?"

"No, silly. *Your* language of love. You can hardly tell a new story without understanding the language of the old one, now can you?" She didn't wait for me to answer. "Of course not. You'd only go on writing the same old story. So, first things first, and then Johnny and Albert."

"Albert?"

"Mm-hmm." She grooved with the music, her head keeping the beat until the song ended. "That's that," she said. "So, we shall head out first thing in the morning. Between then and now, please consider the movies, television programs, and songs that have resonated with you for each stage of your life. Then contemplate the story about love you've been telling yourself and everyone around you. Be ready in the early ante meridiem. Until then, fare thee well." She waved.

"Wait, wait!"

"Yes?"

"More research?" I whined.

"Becoming a steward and providing pilgrimage to others who seek the prophecy of love requires dedication. If you'd like to hold the keys to the universe of love, you must understand love from your cells to the solar system and beyond. Remember, you've been programmed. You have lost sight of the natural order of things," she warned. "Slogging through research might be the easiest part." She eyed me. "Bear in mind, you have agreed to provide tutelage in the form of the written and spoken word. This project requires your competency in creating the experience of love. This will change your life." She looked at me and arched a brow. "I'm sure I needn't remind you of the black ram."

"No, no. I am dedicated. No reminders needed. Well, I am sorry. I just—John Coltrane and…" I trailed off, shaking my head, afraid again that I really didn't understand what I'd agreed to.

"Yes. Of course, it's understandable, and it's not my intention to squelch your enthusiasm. Perhaps…let me check something. Will you please excuse me?" She ducked out of sight.

"Sure," I said, and looked to my fingernails. "Take your—oh, that didn't take long."

She leafed through a workbook. "It is possible for us to shift the bulk of this lesson forward. But be forewarned, this may put you at a disadvantage." She made a face, cocking her head one direction and then the other, shifting her hips weighing something in her mind. "Here's what we'll do. Please consider only the music that has influenced you at various stages of your life. Keep Magritte's pipe handy and mull over the ways these influences have set your stage for love. We'll save the deep contemplation for later. Fair enough?"

I nodded.

The screen went blank, and she was gone. "Well. That's that, I guess." I stood

and stretched. Noticing the sunset, I turned up the thermostat and headed to the
bedroom to throw on a hoodie. This better not be another late-nighter. I sighed,
wishing for some distraction—then seeing exactly that, I climbed onto the mat-
tress. Balancing on wobbly tiptoes I ran my hand along the cracked and stained
ceiling. The plaster was cold but dry and the crack seemed less impressive than it
looked. Taking this as a good sign, I climbed off the bed and grabbed my phone.

Hey, Amy. Gabe here. Would you like to meet me for dinner sometime?

Hi, Gabe. I would.

How about Saturday night?

I'd love to, but I'm busy. What about Saturday afternoon?

She's busy. I stared at the text. "Really? She's busy?"

Do you know the Tea House in the park?

"The Tea House?" Maybe she thinks I'm someone else. I scrolled up to be
sure I'd introduced myself, and she texted again.

I love that place. It's my fave, and they have the best Chai if you're into that.

Great! I typed.

How about 2?

Sounds good. See you then.

Gabe, thanks for asking me. I'm really looking forward to seeing you again.

She's really looking forward to seeing me! *Me too!* I fired off, and then re-
reading our exchange, I added. *I mean, I'm really looking forward to seeing you, as
well.*

I know what you mean!

"Cat! She knows what I mean!" I swiveled in the desk chair until I was dizzy.
Grinning like a fool, feeling too good to sit home alone, I grabbed my jacket and
headed out down the hill.

At the bar, I scanned the place, nursing the beer I'd ordered. A college pub wasn't
really my scene anymore, but it was convenient, just a few blocks away.

A waft of heavy perfume preceded the young woman sidling up to the barstool beside me. "Surprising? Right? Live music on a Sunday night?"

"Yeah." I smiled and took a swig.

"I haven't seen you around. Grad student?" She pointed to my notebook. Her midriff top rose, exposing her little belly.

"No. I'm just—I just wanted to get out and be around people."

"Yeah, I get it." She played with her beer bottle, then picked at the label with her well-manicured nails before she stole a sideways glance and flung her long straight hair over her shoulder. "So, he's kinda good, right? Playing old singles, but not bad. Wanna buy me a beer?" She looked right at me.

"Van Morrison," I said, listening to the song and motioning to the bartender for a couple more beers.

"Oh, I don't think that's his name."

"Um. Yeah, no. Not the musician. He's playing a Van Morrison song, 'Moondance.'" I nodded, not wanting to make it a big deal. "I haven't heard this in ages. My mom hauled a handful of albums from place to place over the years. This is a great song, but when I was a kid, I begged her to play 'Astral Weeks.'"

"And when you come my heart will be waiting to make sure that you're never alone," the singer sang.

"But then, one day, she just wouldn't play it anymore. Bet she's still got it, though." I downed the first beer.

"Weird. Go figure, right?"

"Yeah. She had others, too. Sylvia Telles. You know her?"

"Sorry." She took a good gulp and scanned the bar.

"Oh, you should give it a listen," I said, even though I could see she wasn't interested. "It's that bossa nova sound. My mom really liked it. She'd groove to it while she cooked dinner. Swaying, singing along, pleading like she was begging someone to stay." I smiled.

"Blast from the past, huh?"

"Yeah. Jackson Browne and Bob Seger, too."

"My parents listened to a lot of Queen. Aerosmith, too. You know, that kick-ass sound that makes you wanna shove it into somebody's face." She bobbed her head, sneering while she sang. "Walk this way, walk this way, walk this way. Just gimme a little kiss."

"Huh. Yeah. No. I grew up with a—I don't know—I guess a kinda melancholy, more of a longing sound. Except for the bossa nova."

"Cool," she said, catching my eyes. "To each his own, huh?" She leaned closer, bringing with her a potent musk and vanilla scent. "But I like it when music makes me want to move. Do you like that?" She stroked my curls.

"Not so much for me." I pulled away. "I mean, I liked that Barenaked Ladies song when I was a kid. 'One Week,' you know it?" I laughed. Then singing, I tried to recall the first line. "It's been one week since you looked at me, cocked your head to the side, and said I'm angry."

The guitar player crooned, "And she says baby, it's three a.m. I must be lonely."

"Matchbox Twenty!" I shouted, pointing to the musician, and pounded the second beer. "You want another?" I motioned to the barkeep. "Two beers." I opened my notebook.

She looked over my shoulder. "Are you a musician?"

"No. Just doing some research. It's like a class."

"A music class?"

"No, a class on the meaning of love." I put down the pen. "It's really more of a quest for the answers to the questions of love."

"What are the questions?"

"I don't know. I'm missing something, and my teacher is helping me figure it out."

"With the questions? Or the answers." She looked confused.

"Funny. But no. Seriously, I'm missing something, or something's missing in me. I mean, look at this." Feeling the alcohol, I rambled, poking at the titles of several songs I'd written on the page. "I go from Barenaked Ladies to Nirvana to King Krule! What happened to me?"

"Well, you've got Train in your little chart, and R.E.M. too." She reached across me, thrusting her breasts in front of me. "But what's wrong with Nirvana. The grungy guitar, the steady pounding drumbeat, they make you feel alive. Don't you want to feel alive?" She went for my curls again.

"R.E.M.? That's exactly my point." I raised my voice. The problem was obvious. "And Nirvana? Well, that dangerous sound is the heartbeat of my teenage discontent. I can feel it in my body right now." I ran my hands along my torso. "That friction between desire and rage. The way the two rub up against each other, stirring up wounded courage." I rubbed my chest. "Like that's the only way I can believe in myself."

"I kinda like that," she whispered, rubbing my back. "Let's get out of here."

"No. I gotta get home. I got homework."

"Seriously? Why the hell did you buy me beers?"

"I'm sorry. I just wanted—all I ever want, is to do the right thing. You don't understand, I just want her to see I'm good, so I gotta get home."

"What're you talking about?" Her eyes narrowed. "Do you live with your mother?"

"No, no. I own a house up the hill. I work in a law firm."

"Christ! Do I ever know how to pick 'em. A momma's boy lawyer." She was already climbing off the stool with her beer. "You know what they say about lawyers and sperm? One in 3,000,000 has a chance of becoming a human being." She turned her back, paused, then swung around. "By the way, I think I know what you're missing."

"I'm not a lawyer," I said, as she made her way through the thinning crowd. "Sorry!" I called after her. With her back to me, she shot me the finger. I sighed. Note to self: another calamity in ludus while sidestepping eros.

Outside, I zipped my coat and pulled on my gloves. The crisp air cleared my head, and I wondered about my mom and the Van Morrison album. Did she stop playing it when she re-married? That certainly was a turning point in our relationship, and it was about the time Nirvana became my life's soundtrack.

I remembered hissing at her. "You're a coward. Afraid to stand up to grandfather, your mother, and even that asshole you married. I never want to be like you. NEVER!"

She'd hidden her face and sobbed. "I am a coward. You're right. I'm a coward."

The memory sat heavy on my chest as I huffed up the hill. How many incidents like that would Pythia say it takes to erode storge? Or, for that matter, any kind of love. I hoped my mom had forgiven me. What had I held against her back then? "What am I still holding against her?" I muttered. Picking up my pace and doing my damnedest to get ahead of my shame, I focused on music. All American Rejects, Sum 41, The White Stripes. "Oh, yeah, and TR/ST." Searching for hope amid my post-apocalyptic world view sounds about right.

My heart ached just thinking about the soundtrack of my life. There was a geometric musical pattern that mostly mourned or longed for something. "But I love those kinds of songs," I whispered. Feeling their familiarity, I halted. Halfway up the hill, my gaze went to the sky. The clouds drifted in the night, slowly enveloping the barely waxing moon. The world darkened. "Am I in love with sorrow? Those sensations it stirs in my body?" I asked, trying to feel what was inside me. "What kind of love is that?"

"Philia," someone said wrestling his way out of the bushes and zipping his fly. Alarmed, I backed off the sidewalk. "An aberration of it," he said as a matter of fact, "of course, but none-the-less it sounds as if you've built a sustainable relationship with this music, and it's seen you through some tough times." He stood in front of me in the dim light, clearly dressed in khaki cargo pants and jacket. He saddled a sizeable backpack. "Shall we walk?" He motioned with an open hand, inviting me to continue up the hill. "Take 'Astral Weeks,' for example. Van Morrison?"

Ascertaining that his hands were empty, I nodded and walked beside him but kept a distance.

"A portal for certain. You got started young too, didn't you? Who turned you on to the stuff?"

"My mom," I drew out the words, eyeing him sideways, suspicious but curious where this would lead.

He put his hand to his ear. His stocking hat bulged with what I assumed were dreadlocks he'd piled on top of his head. "Your mom, you say. Yep, this stuff doesn't give a rat's ass who you are. You get hooked, you get hooked good. Once you get an ear for that vibration," he shook his head, and his towering hat wobbled. "You're gonna wanna dance to it for the rest of your life. That is, if you don't pay attention." He leaned into me and pointed ahead into the blackness. "Vibration is everywhere."

I scanned the space.

"No. You gotta feel it. You can't see it, but it's all anything is. Ever was. Ever will be. Don't let the words fool you. Tend to the experiences, what they evoke in your human psyche, in the heart." He thumped his chest. "The sounds you love are beautiful reminders of something you lost, but they aren't you. Rise above the programming, son. A pipe is not a pipe. Create a philia that your heart can beat for, not against." He searched my face before his attention went to the clearing clouds. "Ah, look at her." His gaze went to the slivered moon. "There she is. My beautiful bride." He winked at me. "My ride." He raised his brow smiling, then set off jogging until he became the darkness, and all that was left was the fading sound of his boots.

12

"What are you doing?" Pythia asked, poised from the computer screen the following morning.

"What do you mean, what am I doing?" I was doing my best to balance over a tub of steaming water with a burning stub of incense while holding the lampshade in place and eyeing the computer screen situated on the vanity. Between the steam and smoke, I squinted to make her out. "You said to be ready, and I am ready, but the cone of laurel is running out. I ran into trouble lighting what was left."

She laughed. "You're a good sport."

"What do you mean?" I narrowed my eyes, realizing I probably looked like my mother when I did that. I took the shade off my head and jumped off the tub. "Pythia? What do you mean I'm a good sport?"

"I mean, you are." She made it sound like a compliment. "You, my dear friend, are an outstanding sport." Her eyes were playful.

I took a seat on the lidded toilet, turning the laptop to better see her. "Okay. What exactly makes me a good sport?" I braced myself for some old dig about my inflexibility.

A line appeared between her brows as she contemplated the question. Then they arched. Her eyes rounded, and she clasped her hands. "I have it! It's your willingness, and then, readiness, hmm? Fine qualities, indeed."

"Oh-kay." I angled my chin, still holding doubt. "As long as you're not making fun of me."

"Oh, God, no!" She shot back. "No." She repeated, shaking her head. "I have the greatest respect for you, agape mou. You are a man of immense regard."

"I am?" I blinked.

"Yes you are, agape mou."

"What is it you're calling me? Agape mou?"

"Agape mou." Pythia slid the cross on its chain. Behind her, a cardinal landed in the bare branches of an old oak tree. The brook still bubbled despite its banks being covered in snow. "It means, 'my love,' like between two esteemed friends. Is it okay?"

"Yes. It's nice, actually. Thank you."

"Are you ready? Agape mou?"

Turning toward the tub with the shade, I heard her laugh again. "No, no, no! The portal's secured. The passage is made. The umbilicus is forever accessible now. Hmm? Yes? I see my error. Remember the pinecone?"

"The pinecone? No, I mean, I know what a pinecone is, but I don't recall a discussion."

"My apologies," she said but by that time Pythia had already disappeared. The stream and oak behind swallowed up into a nothingness as well. The screen was blank.

"Wait!" I yelled. "Don't go!"

"Technical difficulties." She spoke disembodied and then a picture appeared. "There. Can you see that now? A human brain with what looks like a pinecone at its center?"

"Yep, got it."

"Very well," she said emerging like a ghost from the image. Then appeared completely whole to stand in front of the diagram. "The umbilicus is an ancient and sacred portal accessed *initially* through the omphalos with a ceremony of pomp and circumstance. Once accessed, the transportation program is downloaded to your pineal gland." She pointed to the pine-cone-shaped gland at the center of the human brain. "Because it has rods and cones, just like your eyeballs, it's called the third eye. It projects images onto the inside of your forehead." She tapped hers. "It's your mind's eye."

"Cool."

"This mechanism allows you ease in traveling through the dimensions. The cone of laurel, the steaming bath, and the lampshade are no longer necessary. You have everything you need. Of course, you always have." She raised a knowing eyebrow, and I wondered what she'd meant. "Now, use your mind's eye and energetically take my hands, but keep your elbows tight to your sides and close your eyes.

After the recitation, I'll count to three. Then, squeeze your eyelids shut and drop down into your body to descend through the portal. Questions?"

Drop down into my body? I closed my eyes and imagined what that might be like. I opened my eyes. "Okay, I'm ready."

"Let us go then." Her tone had changed. Now stern, her face was humorless. "We drop our arms to our sides, and relinquish our history of losing our shirts in favor of the lapis rings. I, NOW and HERE, declare the wheels of motion be set, cracking the steel rim and taking us into the ditch. Lay us down the viaduct of vertigo dreams and deep into the slipstream, where we come as we are. Summon fish to the dish, chickity China the Chinese chicken. Memoria, memoria, memoria. One, two, three!"

And with that, the bottom dropped with a satisfying whoosh before I flew through the blue circles and rainbow lights, finally parachuting down into the blood-red ring with its scent of dirt until I softly landed in the familiar clearing encircled by the ancient trees. An intimate circle of modern furniture set atop a Persian carpet had replaced the Greek bath where Pythia awaited me.

The rug's complex and intricate geometric design, a combination of mostly reds, oranges, and deep pinks contrasted the simple, clean lines of the circular red sofa set with its low channeled back and slender legs. A man sat on the sectional, cast in warm light, with his hands on his knees. His heavy head hung over a walnut coffee table, round with a live edge; like someone chopped a section from a gigantic tree and polished it. An enormous crystal chandelier dangled, the cord seemingly attached to nothing, illuminating the fellow and how apparently lost in his thoughts he appeared. Beyond the sofa, there was a bank of tall shelves stuffed with leather-bound books. When I'd absorbed enough of the scene my eyes were drawn back to the night sky.

"Whoa!" I gasped taking it in. "Is this for real? I mean, it was just morning and now—My God, Pythia! Look at the Milky Way. It's literally dazzling. Makes you think there is a heaven."

"Yes, it is real. Time is divergent in the ethers. Do you see that cluster of stars?" Pythia pointed. "That's the Seven Sisters. They're entangled, all moving in the same direction at the same rate, traveling together across time."

"Pleiades, right?"

"Yes. The constellation inspires the abstract and the divine, opening the intelligence of the mind and the heart." We stood in the Sisters' radiance; our heads tilted to the sky until Pythia reached for my hand. "Come. I have someone I want you to meet."

At our advance, the man stood and stepped in our direction. He was of average height and wore a black cardigan over a white starched shirt. He moved easily and extended his hand. "Hey, man, it's good to meet you." His voice was raspy, his cadence slow but earnest. "John Coltrane. But call me Trane," he said pumping my hand with a firm grip while the muscles of his face remained soft, his jaw loose. He considered me with dark, wide-set eyes. He smelled of sweet sandalwood. Speechless, I shook his hand. "Well," he said gesturing for me to sit on the sprawling sofa, "I am not much of a talker."

Pythia had already tucked her legs beneath her at the far end. "No, I don't talk too much." He laughed. "But Pythia here, she can get me talking. So, if I'm gonna talk, I may as well have somethin' worth listening to." He studied me like he was seeing more of me than anyone had ever bothered to notice. I felt uneasy, and seeming to sense this, he looked to the space between his feet, just the way I'd seen him do earlier. "Well." He looked back at me, smiling like he was about to cut me a big piece of chocolate cake. "I'll tell you, that's quite The Thang you're wantin' to figure. I always say…" he chuckled, "we are here to be the best good we can. That's The Thang, you know, the best good?" He fixed his eyes on me again.

"Well, yes. Yes." I fidgeted.

"So. You see. As far as I can say, the way I've come to understand it, is like this," he started and stopped, allowing his tongue to sweep over his top lip. Then, wiping his mouth with his hand, he leaned across the table toward me. Mirroring him, I leaned in. "People know truth," he said. "In some way or another, people do know truth. And truth has no name. Each of us must see it for ourselves. The truth, and as far as I can see, that's what you are searchin' for, the truth." He beamed, showing me a mouth full of teeth. "Man," he said, like the word was my name, "love is the truth, and the truth is beautiful. And once you've seen the truth, there's no going back. No way out of it." He shook his head and closed his eyes like he saw something inside himself. When he opened them again, he leaned close enough that I could smell his minty-fresh breath over his sandalwood scent, and whispered, "There's no way back. You gotta just keep on goin'.

Keep on expandin'." He pointed to the sky. I followed his finger, thinking about those sister stars traveling together.

"I'll tell you what I know," he said only to halt again and then smile. "Some of it's from studyin'. I've always been a man likes to figure things. And some's from makin' music." He laughed. "That's The Thang for me, music, the ancient science of sound. Probably my greatest teacher, period. How 'bout you? You got a teacher?"

I pointed to Pythia.

"That's a good teacher. That's a real good teacher." He eyed me, making me feel something I didn't know I did. I felt bright inside. I had found my way out. Things were already different. "Well, you see, the world is nothing but vibration, and vibration's a cool cat. You can feel it, you know. It's got repercussion. It'll affect your state of consciousness. That's The Thang here, man. You gotta feel your life, so's you know how you wanna play it. You gotta play it, man, so you can feel it. So, you can feel alive. Anyway, that's how I understand it. That's how I see it. You gotta feel the vibrations, so you know the difference between playin' the music or the music playin' you."

"Tell us, please, about 'My Favorite Things'?" Pythia drew up her knees and wrapped her arms around them.

"'My Favorite Things,' whew! Yeah, I sure do remember that. It was a hit in 1961!" He looked off, reminiscing, before turning my direction and repeating himself. "A hit!" Surprised, like he was still in shock, his eyes popped, and his mouth hung open. "Me and the guys, The Quartet—see, me and the guys took 'My Favorite Things,' that light-hearted, silly song, and grooved it into this whirling, spellbinding Indian thing. Yeah…." He drifted, his eyes fell to the floor. He was silent, then looked directly at me. "It changed everything. Period. It sure did."

I nodded, shy to meet his gaze. "I know it changed the world of jazz."

"Well, see. What it really did was change the way people thought. It gave them permission to understand something they already understood one way in another way. It gave them the chance to see it differently. It liberated them. Free'd 'em. Yeah, anyway, that's the way I understand it. That's the way it happened for me, anyway. Those of us listening? Well, we all woke up. We felt the truth of the vibration, letting ourselves stretch out of the old sleepy interpretations. Anyway, that's how I understand it now. I don't know if I did then." He looked hard at me. "I am not much of a talker, but you got me talking." He smiled shyly, but his eyes were always searching deep into something. He looked to the floor again before looking up. "Whatcha got on the board, Pythia?"

I looked to where Pythia had sat, but she was across the room, pulling a giant blackboard into view and minding her gown from catching under its wheels.

Trane read from the board. "What compares the multiverse to a mechanical clock? Clue: The gears of an appliance operate by the laws of physics; it is exemplary in its tick-tocking and therefore predictable in every way." Then in a low voice, he gave me the answer, "Sir Isaac Newton's theory." He nodded. "Basically, Sir Isaac put it out there, that all things are based on the mechanics of the physical. But that's the thing, right: what *is* a thing? What Sir Isaac proved, and how most of us have come to interpret it, is two different things. First, as far as Sir Isaac concerned himself, a thing has physical properties. Its composition can be observed, like this thing." He pulled a red rubber ball from his jacket pocket. "This little ball is a thing. Things operate under Sir Isaac's three *laws of motion*. Things are obedient to his laws."

He licked his lip and wiped his mouth before rubbing his chin. The irises of his eyes darted while he worked his mind. "The way I understand it is like this. Remember what I was sayin'? You gotta listen to *all* the music, all the sounds, and more, until you know your own language. Let the best good of yourself come up out of the depths. The rules, the laws, they're a good thing, but they are not The Thang. You feel me, man? The Thang is the space between the rules and your own music. The Thang is the muse, man. And if all that concerns you is this little ball, well, the way I see it, you're missin' 99% of what you could be enjoyin.'"

"I get it," I said, feeling at home. "Or I'm starting to anyway. I've spent most my life thinking love is a definitive thing, like the laws of motion. My cognitive brain can slave away all it wants on making words the final say, but it's the body that tunes into the true meaning of language."

"You got it, man. I can see you've wrestled with Sir Isaac, but he's got no skin in this game. It's apples to oranges. Love is 'no thing.' You see, truth, beauty, love, they have no name. They're what you make them. Period." An owl hooted, drawing my attention to the stars. The moon hung as half a halo, only a glint of what it was becoming.

"See?" He held the rubber ball between his forefinger and thumb. "Take this ball." I looked at the little red ball. "No, man. Go ahead. Take the ball. You see, you gotta take the ball first. Okay, now set it on the table. Yeah, sure anywhere, man. Just set it at rest." He held up a finger. "First law, law of inertia, says that a ball, a thing, will remain at rest unless acted on. This ball wouldn't go anywhere without some kinda force." He raised his brow. "And once acted upon, this ball will continue in motion at the same speed, and in the same direction, until acted upon by another force."

"Okay, yeah," I said, remembering high school science, but mostly the sterile lab with its hard, cold surfaces. The chemical scents beneath the smell of something burning. How the subject couldn't diminish my interest in the sweet-smelling girl sitting next to me in her fitted T-shirt.

"Okay. That ball is at rest, period. Now give it a nudge." I pushed the ball, and we all watched the sphere disappear over the table's edge and roll across the fine carpet, stopping at its fringed edge.

I quoted the law. "A thing in motion will continue in motion at the same speed and in the same direction unless acted upon by another force."

Pythia squatted to grab the ball. "At rest." She held the immobilized ball between her thumb and finger. "And now, acted upon, it is in motion." She tossed it my way.

"Unless acted upon by another force," I said, catching it.

"You got it!" Trane said, then to Pythia, "He's got it."

"Indeed. I told you he was bright."

"You sure did. Okay, man. Let's see what you got now. Second law?"

"Okay, second law." I pulled some previously meaningless information from the archives of my education, practically conjuring the spiral-bound notebook from my twelfth-grade physics class, complete with its boxes and eyeballs doodled in the margins, until I spotted the yellow highlight. "The law of force and acceleration. The greater the mass of a thing, the greater the amount of force needed to act upon the thing."

"That's right," Trane said, rising to situate himself on his haunches at one end of the table. Pythia climbed off the sofa and squatted, facing him, at the other end with her hands positioned like a goalie. "You ever play tabletop football?"

"Sure."

"So, you know, the greater the force over the mass, the greater the acceleration." He rose and stepped away. "It's all yours, man."

I took his place and, with deliberation, pinged the ball across the table with the force of my first finger set against my thumb. The ball flew at Pythia, who employed the first law and brought the speeding ball to rest.

"Friction," she said, and I nodded.

"Third law," Trane said, "for every force, there is an equal and opposing force."

Pythia tossed the ball onto the table at about a thirty-degree angle. The ball bounced at about the same angle but in an opposing direction. At that moment, a hand reached and swiped the ball midair. "Life is like riding a bicycle," a man with a heavy German accent spoke. "To keep your balance, you must keep moving."

"Hey-hey! My man!" Trane said, and I turned to see a very recognizable Albert Einstein. "You see, your timing's a beautiful thang, man." Then Trane turned to me. "This cat knows how to move through the multiverse." Trane grabbed Einstein's hand and shook it hard before the two embraced.

Pythia made her way over. "Albert," she said warmly.

Einstein, still holding Trane's hand, turned toward Pythia and, taking her hand, kissed it before coupling it with Trane's. Then, turning toward me and cocking his head at Trane, he said, "This fellow, making quantum leaps with his giant steps. Particles and waves, chords, and continuous chord progressions. He stands on the shoulders of giants." Einstein smiled. "Ah, well." He shrugged. "Yes. Of course. But logic will only get you from A to B. Imagination, my friend…" he took my hand and placed it in Trane's other hand and the four of us stood holding hands. "Imagination will take you everywhere. And what's love if it isn't imaginative, eh? Love is imagining a space for the greatness of life." He swung our circle of hands, his brown eyes sparkling.

"Pythia. A picture of beauty! How are you?" Einstein asked as we made our way to the sofa.

"I am well, Albert. Busy, as we all are these days." Pythia sat next to me, her Christmas scent encircling us.

"Ah, well, the acceleration of the multiverse keeps us on our toes, eh?"

"Someone once told me that evolution reveals itself in the harmony that follows disorder, not in the concerns of mortal actions." Pythia flirted.

"It's reassuring, isn't it?" Einstein chuckled.

"It is," she said and turned toward me, "Albert," she said motioning to me while she looked at him, "this is the man I spoke of. He is brave and determined and desires to learn the language of love. He has agreed to spread forth its word."

I blushed. Pythia put her arm through mine and drew me close. I felt wooden against her delicate bones and smooth skin. She was warm and smelled sharp but smoky, exotic, and spicy like the scent of ritual. I breathed her in, hoping she wouldn't notice. Black licorice and cookies. Ah, yes, that's it, I thought. Sugar and cinnamon, like the freshly baked snickerdoodles my mom made on the first day of school. Or that puppy I wanted as a boy. The room tilted. Wait, what? I felt myself sliding. No, I thought. The rich colored fabrics of the soft sofa and rug weaved and spilled into the black table that funneled now into a hole. Remembering how perfectly chewy those cookies were, the blackboard and the bookshelves slid across the room. The chandelier swung; the crystals cast rainbow prisms that spun around the room. The entire world turned upside down. "No. Wait. No. Where am I? What's happening?" I tried to hold on to Pythia, but she was slipping away. "Are you even real?" I asked, too loud, panicking, grabbing at her.

"Agape mou." She sounded alarmed. I labored to breathe. Albert stood over me, pouring a glass of water from a pitcher that I'd never noticed.

Trane's sympathetic eyes held me. "Exploration, experimentation, and discovery." He hovered. "This is The Thang. That's all. You're in The Thang." The space rolled over, like someone turning a page, taking me deeper into the story but leaving my friends behind.

"I'm slipping!" I shouted, my arms flailed. "Help! Help me!" The three of them floated over me, becoming blurry and muffled as I sank through some thick watery membrane.

"All is well, agape mou. You'll be fine." Pythia encouraged me, articulating the words, speaking in slow motion, raising her eyebrows as if they could draw me out of the deep well I'd fallen into. "Things are not what they seem to be, yes?" she shouted, bobbing her head. "Find the sea of possibility," she called out. "Look for the Sisters." Then waved.

Something towed me further under. The distance between us grew. Trapped beneath some blurry glass force, I couldn't speak. My eyes pleaded with the others. I battled an enemy I couldn't see. Thrusting my arms and legs like a beetle on its back made no difference, the current sucked me down anyway.

Einstein waved his hands, motioning like he was telling a story about a big fish. "It will find you. In the middle of all this difficulty lies opportunity." His eyebrows arched, making a promise. "Look for what is, and not for what you think it is. You see? Don't worry, mensch." He waved his hand, brushing off my desperation. "No problem is solved from the same level of consciousness that created it. You must ascend to find love. Don't worry." He smiled. "You'll see what you've been missing. Look for the boson." And he drew himself back, disappearing.

A murky shadow fell over me that became Trane, his face close to the thing between us. His cadence was measured, speaking the way a parent reassures a frightened child. "It's all good, man." His eyes held mine. "It's The Thang, is all. You'll be fine." Then he ghosted into an indistinct shape.

Pythia lowered her face to the hole. I reached for her, thrashing against my descent, but only sank deeper.

13

Everything went black before it turned blizzard white. The flesh on my face and neck stretched and flapped against the pressure. My body pivoted and soared, blasting off. My ears ached, and I feared my head would explode. I thought of Cat—the sensation of her tail sliding through my hand. I recalled the crack of a baseball bat striking a fastball and a time my mother consoled me. "I love you," she said, pulling me to the comfort of her warm bosom, stroking my hair. I pictured my garden, feeling the feathery tips of the tall grasses against my palms. Then flashes—me opening a window, the fresh scent of rain, My Ex laughing. The speed of travel increased, and my memories became glints. Indiscernible clips turning into warm blocks of color and pricks of emotions.

This is it, I thought; this is how I die. Feeling too spent to resist the inevitable, in my mind, I lay myself down and let go of fighting. And that's when everything slowed, stopped, and went blank as a new beginning. I was emptied of my past and at peace with all possibility. I floated upward, feeling lifted, carried even, toward another glossy membrane. Then making my way through the bubble's thick edge, I climbed out and emerged on the other side of Earth's navy-blue atmosphere.

Outer space stank of spent gunpowder. Weightless and without direction, I drifted and tumbled through the cold pitch and black-forged-metal scents of some ancient garage I knew in my very cells. The dark boundlessness was nothing and everything. Seeming to extend till the end of all time, until its heavy, diesel rank slowly spilled, like water falling from one pool to the next, casting me out into yet another new world.

A sweet scent of sugared waffle cones replaced the greasy oil stench, and I floated along, passing through swirling multi-colored dust clouds. Sparkling stars twinkled greetings from every direction. I drifted through the magic, with its caramel candy bouquet and mosaic of colored lights dazzling the night sky.

Ahead a luminary cluster flashed a Morse code of light. "Pleiades," I said and steered toward the extra-terrestrial message. The stars were dancers, flickering flames atop a phosphorescent helix spiraling in outer space.

"We are the seven daughters of the night."

"Emissaries of electromagnetic radiation."

"Agents on a mission for consciousness."

"Regaling gratitude for each incarnation."

"Aligning the human breath with the frequency of our expanding vibration."

"Unlocking and transmitting the cellular memory of love."

"Bridging the here with the now, through the divine and mortal heart."

They circled, binding me in what I can only describe as a nurturing force. They were sisters, daughters, mothers—women. I shielded my eyes from their brilliance as they shed light and cast me into my own gold star.

"As you think, so shall it be," they chanted. I closed my eyes, and my eyeballs rolled, opening the portal of my mind. Then the familiar down, down, down, followed by the up and out; before the force spat me through another membrane. This time I landed riding an undulating grid of electric blue lines, surfing a tide that had no shore.

From a distance crossing the lattice plane, a figure emerged walking on a sea of blue squares. His gait and aura were familiar.

"Are you the Higgs boson?" I called. "Is this the sea of possibility?" I pointed to the bright blue framework; the beams of light sailing beneath me.

He nodded, smiling, coming closer. "Yes, I am," he said.

His toneless and rather tense voice somehow set my nerves on end, and I hurried to cover my ears. My heart scrambled, frantic to climb into my throat. I thought I'd retch. Weak in the knees and speechless, I shivered, stumbling backward away from the thing, so familiar it was haunting.

"I don't understand." I cowered, quivering on my hands and knees, hanging onto the grid. I panted and licked my lips, trying to keep from hurling as I digested my doppelganger. The awful thing smiled at me with my same nearly straight teeth and square jaw. We stood, all four of our deeply set eyes under the same bushy brows that worried me as a teen. Had they bothered him? He even wore a fitted Henley, untucked with the sleeves pushed up, and skinny jeans with boots.

"Cat got your tongue?" He sounded playful. Astonished at our likeness, I barely nodded. He lowered himself all the while, keeping his eyes on me, not making any sudden movements, as if I might jump. He lingered on his haunches running his hand along the glowing blue bar showing me it was safe. Then maneuvered himself to sit on the beam. The electric transmission bent to his weight while supporting him in a radiant swing. He nodded, indicating for me to do the same.

Keeping my eyes on him, I reached for the incandescent bar, expecting it to be hot, only to notice a chill emanating from the shaft of light. Safely seated, I faced him with my feet dangling through an opening in the grid. His lashes were long like mine, his beard sparse in places. There was a familiar scar on his forehead. I touched the same place on my own head where a chicken pock had left a blemish. I studied him until overcome with curiosity, I reached toward him. He nodded, and I touched the ends of one of his thick, dark curls. He took my hand. He placed my fingers at his neck. I could feel his heartbeat; he was warm. I pulled back.

"I am you, a version of you anyway." He paused. "Can you trust me?" he asked.

Overwhelmed by a metallic taste I tried to relax the intense tension in my face, but I couldn't take my eyes off him. "I—I don't know. I guess. What are you? Are you? Are you the part of me that's missing?"

"Call me Higgs. And no." He smiled and patted my knee, then gestured to the grid and the black space around us. "This is the quantum world, and here things are better understood through sensory experience than by language. Which, of course, you now know is fundamentally false and limited by logic. Here the information of words is conveyed by a series of emotional responses, bodily sensations, and pictures that appear in your mind's eye. This is the subatomic, the quantum realm. It's where all possibility lies. This place is outside of language. Your words are less meaningful here. Here is about the experience you'd like to create."

I looked around. The energetic power of the intersecting beams was palpable. "Here, Newton's laws are ineffectual. Possibility is not limited to cause and effect. Here, outcome is determined by the desire to *cause* an effect." Higgs grabbed hold of one of the bars and challenged its integrity with a shake. The whole grid came alive, buzzing and flashing a storm of electric strobes of blue light.

"Whoa! Are you alright?"

"I am myself. It is my nature. Sometimes I am this." Higgs nodded to the now-still grid, flat and uniform in every way. "Anything characterized as a particle, or a thing has properties of mass and localization." By way of example, and like a magic trick, he revealed the familiar red ball I'd just played with.

"But..." he pointed way out, where the field was still rippling. He stood, and I stood with him. "And sometimes I am that." He nodded to the undulating field of blue bars. "Everything in the multiverse has a dual nature. Anything characterized as a wave has frequency and wavelength. These properties spread out across space." He motioned like a hula girl, and the grid obeyed, rolling until it was nothing but cascading waves. "It matters less what something is and more what you'd like to make it." Then he tossed the ball into the air, but in place of the ball, he caught a pipe, brown and black just like the one Pythia had shown me.

"Things aren't always what they seem to be." He looked pleased. "Consider the pipe, the ball, the waves, the serendipity of seeing Amy at the grocer's and then meeting her at the Chili Bowl. How it was all seemingly random, but then potentially important."

"You know Amy?"

"She was a particle and then a wave, right? Particles and waves are only words describing the same mathematical object."

"What do you mean, mathematical?"

"Determining a thing from The Thang is a mathematical computation and requires a superposition. The position where an object has infinite possible outcomes. It could be anything. But it matters less what something is and more what you'd like to make it. Got it?"

"No, I don't get it." I scratched my head. "I don't understand." I chewed on my poor lower lip and then my thumbnail.

"Look," he said now holding a pipe. "This pipe is like Magritte's painting. It is not a pipe either. It is *this*." He shook the pipe, declaring it a thing. "Get it now?"

"Okay, yes."

"And this thing..." he shook the pipe again the way a teacher might tap the board for emphasis. "It can become The Thang." Then he gestured to something above my head, and I stepped back to see pictures floating in midair. Magritte's painting of a pipe, the word pipe, a wafting curl of smoke, a worn easy chair beside a warm fire, and a tweed jacket with aged leather-patched elbows.

"Nostalgia." I sniffed the air. "Do I smell the sweet scent of cherry wood and—clove? Leather and sweat?"

"Yes. Wonderful! Show me more."

"What do you mean, show you more?"

"Take the pipe and show me more," he repeated, but confused, all I could do was shrug. "Those are yours, you know?" He pointed to the holograms. "Go ahead, give it a go. Imagine the thing. Make it The Thang." He passed the pipe.

I held the oddly shaped, smooth thing. It was light and cool at one end and heavy and warm at the other. Then I remembered sitting on an old man's lap, the warmth of his heartbeat beneath his worn flannel shirt, the distinct smell of his sweat mixed with Old Spice.

"Yes." Higgs pointed at the suspended images I'd generated. "Those are thought-forms. Go on. Show me more."

"Okay." I nodded and remembered when the old man took me to the barbershop, the scent of Barbicide, the soft shaving cream yielding to the barber's razor against the man's loose skin. How the man's kitchen smelled of coffee. The man puttering around in his garage. The hollow sounds, the dank smells of gasoline and old grass clippings. "That's so strange. It's like a movie about this man I once met. I don't specifically remember him, but he seems important, meaningful to me. It's like he's showing me how to be a man. I can't explain it, but it feels real."

"Excellent! You are in The Thang. 'How to be a man' is not about the words; it's about the way it inspires you. The words matter less. What you can create matters more. You see it?" He tapped his forehead. "You feel it." He scanned the front of his body with his open hand. "And now you *know* it." He pointed to both his head and heart.

"I get it." I held up the little pipe. "If I only think of this thing as a pipe, my preconception of it limits my understanding of its multifaceted nature and all the opportunities it can inspire."

"Exactly! In quantum physics, an outcome's probability is not found in a singular understanding but by squaring that understanding infinitely. This mathematical view provides a matrix of never-ending possibilities and explains how things can be in multiple states simultaneously." And with his words, the spaces in the grid began to multiply and stack. Rows and columns stretched up and down and all around us. Soon we stood at the center of an elaborate high rise of endless rooms. Each depicted some tangential version of my experience of the thing called 'pipe.'

My jaw fell open. "This reminds me of a memory. A man on his knees pinning my trousers. I was getting my pants hemmed for something special. Maybe my mom's wedding? I remember how I stood in front of a three-way mirror, making funny faces, trying to catch all the copy-cat versions of myself just before they made the same face. Back then, that boy and that old man went on and on, reflected forever in the looking glass, one fidgeting while the other pinned."

"Ah, but here it's different. There are choices." With his words, the matrix shifted, depicting millions and millions of versions of the boy and the tailor. "There's more than one way to get your pants hemmed."

"That reminds me of that horrible saying, there's more than one way to skin a cat. I don't know why—No, no, no!" I said, shaking my head and hands while the cells shifted. "No!" I yelled, and the blocks' content blurred and disappeared, and the three-dimensional grid collapsed into a flat plane. "Oh, no," I said, astonished. "I didn't mean—I mean—I just—" I turned to Higgs. "I didn't want a cat—I didn't want to know about—I don't want to think about that."

"It's okay." Higgs patted my back. "You can think about anything you want. And, you can change your mind about anything you think. You can create what you *want*."

"That's a relief; I can control the outcome."

"No." The word fell flat between us. Then, silence.

"I don't understand. Aren't you saying I can control my reality?"

"No."

"No?"

"Nope."

"Okay." I shrugged. "I don't get it then."

"There is no control. None. There never was. And there never will be. No control."

"What?" I stopped breathing. Then gasped and exhaled audibly, shaking my head, pinching my face in disagreement, only to seize my breath again before filling my lungs once more.

"Are you attempting to create control by holding your breath? How long do you think you can do that?"

I blew out from my cheeks, feeling a little light-headed. "Okay, I get it. It's a mindset, right?"

"No."

"Well, maybe not a mindset. But it's a good idea to know what you can and can't control. Like you can't control the weather. That's silly. I get that. Some things you have to accept." I nodded, believing we were finally in agreement, but he didn't nod. Instead he stood patient, waiting for me while my frustration grew into exasperation. "What do you mean there is no control?" I protested. "Of course, there is. People have to control themselves all the time. If everyone did whatever they wanted, what kind of world would it be? There has to be control." I spouted, still balanced on the sea of possibility.

He made that "so sorry" smile, the one with the cocked head, and broke the news to me again. "There. Is. No. Control."

"That's ridiculous." I thought I would scream. My shoulders lurched to my ears, hands fisted at my sides. I wanted to stomp my feet. "If that grid," I flung my arm, pointing my hand like it was a weapon ready to fire at the geometric field, "has infinite possibilities, surely, it has at least one for control." I tried to look righteous as I raved. Then crossed my arms. But despite all the bluster, my face reddened with the flashes of people telling me inconceivable things. Things that made me feel lost and wobbly. My Ex justifying her flirting with that bartender on our first date. The high school guidance counselor echoing my stepfather, telling me I'd better focus on my grades because I would never make it in baseball. My boss referring to my values as pie in the sky. Would I always be on the wrong side, always misunderstanding the way things really are?

Higgs ran his hand through his hair, then frowned. "Look, the fact is, the smaller the space you provide an electron, the more frenetic its activity. That's what's happening here. Give yourself some room." He consoled me. "I know this is hard, but you can't create that which has no foundation in the laws of nature. And control, my friend, is a construct of your world's culture. It is only a word."

My eyes moved between two thoughts. "Okay," I said, bargaining, still reasoning to have things my way. "But surely you must agree that, without control, we're aimless, just blowin' in the wind."

He sighed. "Well, first, there is no guarantee of outcome. There never was. But if there was, how different would that be from blowing in the wind? Aren't the two just polarizations of finite outcomes?" We stood staring in a standoff. "Control, or a complete lack of control, provides you with the illusion of certainty. That's not possible. Do you know why?"

"Too many variables."

"Exactly, and every variable has a subset of variables, and every subset… well, you get the picture."

"So, no control and no blowing in the wind. No certainty."

Biting his lip, he nodded. "There is no control. There never was, and there never will be."

The corners of my mouth turned down as I weighed his words, but within seconds, I shrugged. "Okay." I nodded. "Actually, it's sort of a relief."

"That's what most people say. And you know why? Because there's something better: collaboration." He smiled.

"Yeah, I feel like maybe I've known this all along. So, collaboration, huh? Is that The Thang? Is it like love?"

"You," he pointed at me, "are a fast learner. Come on." He waved for me to follow. "In the illusion of control, your actions were most often inspired by fear instead of curiosity. Without curiosity, you couldn't appreciate the many influences directed upon something that may cause that thing to behave in several different ways. So, you couldn't recognize the opportunities either."

We walked out onto the blue checked floor; every square was blank, none holding any future intention. The grid waited like a genie in a bottle. "The prediction of probability supersedes a measurement that will determine a particular outcome. All the while, the thing under consideration remains in an indeterminate state. That state maps to a superposition of all possibilities, each with different probabilities."

"Schrödinger's cat?"

"Exactly. Is the cat in all states of possibility simultaneously?" The grid filled with a variety of cats in various conditions, behaving in a myriad of ways. "Or, is the cat in an assumed state until the state is decided?" All the squares filled with a cat curled sleeping.

I considered his point. "Does it matter?"

"Good question. It might not if you have influence, and the Higgs boson makes that possible. Think of Higgs as the greatest sugar daddy. Anything you want, it'll help you create it. All you've got to do is entangle with it. Make friends. When you partner with Higgs, you've got all the influence you'd ever dream of. You've got the entire multiverse at your beck and call helping you cause the effect you want."

"Ah." I nodded, remembering what Trane had explained. "So, the Higgs boson makes that possible. But I'm confused, are you Higgs, or am I Higgs, or is Higgs something else?"

"Yes."

"To which?"

"All three. Quantum physics is a strange ranger, no doubt. It's humbling even. It'll blow your mind if you can't bend to it. It's only odd by Newtonian standards but makes perfect sense mathematically. It has truth. Ready?"

"Sure."

"An internal reality remains in a superposition, meaning the idea can manifest itself in any number of ways until observed by the external world. By observed, I mean bringing your full attention to it or making friends. When that happens, the superposition collapses into one definitive state."

"So you're saying that my life has the potential to look any number of ways, and I'm free to choose what kind of life I want to live. Is that right?"

"Yep."

"So if I observe my life, bring my attention to living my life, make friends with it, I can participate in its creation. I can collaborate with the outcome. So, there's Higgs, and there's me. And there's Higgs and me. And then there's The Thang, that's me, Higgs, and Higgs and me; all together we create the outcome I want."

"Exactly. The Thang, that mechanism you just described, is the source that entangles two independent things, each with multiple possible outcomes of equal probability. In other words, there is a fifty-fifty chance that, more often than not, your life will be more comfortable or more uncomfortable. When you decide which you'd like, you entangle your life with the prediction of experiencing either more comfortable or more uncomfortable."

"So an idea is a thought, not a Thang. And if I consciously consider that thought, and entangle it with the Higgs boson's help, then together, we can turn a thought into a *Thang* and then turn *The Thang* into a reality. Boy, I wish Trane could hear me!"

"That's pretty good. But I'll take you one better." He pulled out the familiar pipe. "This is not a pipe until it's a pipe." He handed it to me. "Now put that in your pipe and smoke it."

"Things aren't always what they seem to be."

"Indeed." He shook my hand. "It's been a pleasure. I hope I cleared things up by muddying the water some. Sometimes the only way to really see something is in the dark."

"Thank you. This has been real."

"Oh, you don't know how real it's about to get." He turned toward the grid. "It's a blank slate. What do you want it to look like? It's your life," he said.

"Um. I don't know."

"Remember, this is not about cause and effect. It is about causing an effect. Let your imagination run wild. You don't have to work so hard by thinking. Go ahead, free yourself of the fear. No worries about right or wrong. Instead, play with it. What do you want?" He encouraged me.

"Whew." I blew out a big breath and ran my hand through my hair, feeling like a contestant on a game show. "Okay, I want…" I laughed before my tongue rubbed that injured place, and I shrugged. "Oh, what the hell. I want to share my life with a woman."

The squares clicked and clacked as they filled with different stories about myself and a variety of women: one where I cheered as she crossed a finish line, one where I vacuumed while she whistled off-key arranging flowers in a vase, and the last where I waited in coveralls while she donned the same and slaughtered a chicken. "Whoa, whoa, whoa! Wait!" My hands motioned. "Can I see what it would look like with Amy?" The squares clicked as they shifted and flipped. One depicted Amy at the side of the bed, staring out at the rain while I packed a bag. In another, Amy and I were inebriated, smoking cigarettes and laughing while I poured us drinks in a filthy kitchen. "Hmm. Some of these are pretty sad. I don't even smoke," I said, and Higgs shrugged.

In another, a pregnant Amy and I happily posed with three children under the age of five, all of us wearing Santa hats. "That's intimidating." I pointed to the Christmas scene, only then to notice an infinite number of potential family futures: a crying child, me yelling at a crying child, Amy yanking a child by the arm, Amy and the kids tickling me. "Please don't let it be that one!" I laughed, pointing to one where we all wore matching argyle sweaters.

Still, there were more. Amy running terrified from me, Amy running down the front steps yelling obscenities while I stood in my underwear eating cake and yelling back. Yet another where I chased her into the bedroom, and we fell laughing into each other's arms. One where we loaded a kiln. One where we danced to "Haunted Heart," and she whispered into my ear. The possibilities went on and on.

"I like that one," I said to Higgs and pointed like I was choosing from a bakery display case. "The one where Amy and I are talking to each other from across a little table in a noisy restaurant. The one where we're so interested in each other we don't even notice anything else. That's the one!" I watched us laughing, bantering, sometimes sitting in awkward silences, other times stealing looks at the other from behind a raised fork or a glass. "Yeah. That's the story I want to live," I said, and all the different possibilities collapsed into such slight variations of the one I'd chosen they were barely discernable from each other.

"Nice choice. Now, create that reality. Remember, you are the point of reference, and this," he pointed to the cells, "is your destination. Your work now is to create a cellular memory of this in your brain. A neurological pattern or map that helps you come and go from this place."

"How do I do that?"

He checked his watch. Distracted, he answered, "Practice." Then looking like he'd remembered something, he dug in his pocket. "Oh, here. It's from Pythia. Put it in your pocket. It can get windy."

"Windy?" I asked, taking the letter from him right before the bottom dropped and I fell back to Earth.

14

When I came to, I was on my back in the dark.

"Pythia!" I yelled, frantic, and bolted upright. My eyes adjusted enough to make out the basket of clean but unfolded laundry. Cat stood, stretched, turned in a circle, and settled back on her pillow. "Oh, Cat!" Relieved, I relaxed against the headboard. "What the—?" Turning on the shadeless lamp, I shielded my eyes against the glare from the naked bulb and found a paper pinned to my shirt. A series of words raced across the page in hurried dashes and intersecting lines. I squinted hard, trying to decode the atrocious handwriting.

Attention: Fetch and Release Crew. This being resides at 40.0150° N, 105.2705° W. Please see his safe and comfortable arrival. Discontinue the aquatic portal in favor of the bedchamber for this and all future transporta-tions. Pythia, High Priestess, Servant to Apollo

"Ha! Pythia." I snorted, shaking my head laughing. "Thanks for the dry landing." Then remembering, I dug into my pocket. This note, nearly illiterate as well, required viewing at an arms-length. For other passages, I brought it right to my nose. At one point, I even turned the paper upside-down to decipher her scrawl.

From the second month of the Gregorian calendar
Whence the time of Kairos to the time of Chronos

Dearest Suppliant of Love,
Rest today. Between morrow and the next of our encounters, please:

1. *Begin developing a love story with a partner of your choice integrating the seven experiences of love using the principles of quantum mechanics. Harken back to "a pipe is not a pipe" as needed. Mind recreating history.*
2. *Bring a pair of scissors, a pencil, and a piece of red construction paper.*

Fondly Yours,
Pythia, High Priestess
P.S. Call your mother

"Develop a love story." Closing my eyes with what had to be a silly-looking smile, I pictured myself and Amy in a busy but cozy bistro. Flowers and a candle on the white-clothed table. Me leaning in, wholly absorbed as Amy spoke, while we never noticed the wait staff weaving through the crowded tables with plates of food. I saw how neither of us noticed the young man in the white apron and bow tie filling our water glasses, the noisy party of drunken co-workers singing "Happy Birthday" across the way, nor the cold rush of winter wind when the nearby door opened. I imagined a giant, roaring fireplace romancing us with the scent of burning cherrywood. My hands nervously appreciating the fine linen napkin in my lap. How once seduced by her raspy voice, I rested my forearms on the table's edge and wondered about the faint scar above her lip. I watched me watching her hands gesture, noticing how easily she laughed until she realized my avid attention and then blushed, pushing a cranberry out of some sweet red sauce, and then around her plate with her fork.

"How 'bout you? What do you want out of life?" she'd ask, finally setting her fork aside. Then, resting her chin in her hands before poking the inside of her cheek with her tongue, she'd raise her brows, cocking her head, "Tell me, how did you land at Dumas, McPhail & Cox?"

What would I say? The picture scrambled. My eyes popped open. That I was tired of being irrelevant? That I was drowning in personal and professional compromise, or that the concept of justice is slippery? Could I admit I honestly didn't know? Laying there, I spotted the basket of clean white laundry marbled with fading pink T-shirts. "What if all I know is what I don't want?" The dirty ceiling hung overhead. In the yellow artificial light, the stain bloomed, a watercolor painting of browns and ochre yellows.

Cat stretched a paw, waking to the rose-colored dawn. She stood and arched her back. As daylight spilled through the window the stain faded into the celling, the crack now more visible. I grabbed my phone. "It's only Tuesday? I guess I could go to work." I climbed off the bed. Cat rubbed against my legs. "Or—"

Or what, Mendes?

"Or, I could practice." Cat meowed, circling my feet. "You're not too shabby at creating the reality you want, are you, old girl?"

While Cat sat fastidiously cleaning a paw near the bowl she'd just licked clean in the kitchen. I stood gobbling a big helping of Honey Nut Cheerios, and in place of entertaining the idea of creating my own reality, I ruminated. "Career!" I scoffed. "I had a career, and it all went south when things crashed with My Ex." I stuffed my mouth. "*That's* when I ditched my job." I shoved in another spoonful.

Your dream job.

"Yeah, well." I snapped. "It's not my fault it didn't turn out to be what I thought it was." I shoveled more Cheerios.

Like your Ex?

"How was I supposed to know? I'm supposed to know everything!" I snatched the cereal and headed to the table. "I made mistakes, alright. Is it a crime? I thought eros and ludus *were* love." I pulled out a chair and sat re-filling the already half-full bowl. "How was I supposed to build a foundation for pragma?" I asked, my spoon full and hovering midair. "I didn't even know it existed!"

Dude. It's never too late. Self-acceptance is the only true path.

Holy smokes! Self-acceptance is the only true path? Come on, Mendes. Get real.

"No," I muttered shaking my head. "This is real. This is me choosing what I want. I'm crafting my own story. And, I am real."

I tried biting back my anger. But silencing it only maddened the goading fear. Imagined snickers and implications drew out my looming critic. Years of disappointment rose up. I closed my eyes to the long, tall shadow I'd soon cower in. Dark and cold, self-loathing laid itself down, and like an armored tank, it set about to crush me. My breath shortened.

Using the pipe, I grappled for authority. "Self-loathing is not my master." I offered perspective adopting a voice of reason. "Previously, my job and my love life had only been things. I now know how to make them into Thangs."

Get real, Mendes. You're not John Coltrane.

Stubborn and far too antagonized, I rammed in another spoonful. "I can do this." I fought myself. "I have as much right as anybody." I bit back, shaking my head, chomping and grinding, until—I yelped, "Mother of God!" and bolted.

Food spilled from my gaping mouth. I moaned, doubling over. Dancing in pain, my hand went to aid my jaw. My stomach flipped, and my tongue hurried to the scene. Relieved my tooth was fully intact, I took a seat. Cat watched with bat-sharp ears. Her shoulders hunched, green eyes glowing. "I'm okay," I assured her. "Ohhh." I winced, and feeling very alive with pain I drew a deep breath. "Alright." I sat for a moment, collecting myself. Cat padded a beeline to the stairs and sat with her principled eyes fixed on me. I nodded. "Okay, Higgs said to practice, and work's as good a place as any." Massaging my jawbone, I headed to shower. Cat tailed me, always a scrupulous champion.

Josh passed just as I was unlocking my office door.

"Hey! How are you?"

"Good." I nodded, forcing myself to engage. "How 'bout you? Good weekend?"

"Yeah. The weather was perfect."

I nodded. The weekend seemed like a decade ago but I did recall the clear blue sky.

"What're you doing here, anyway? I heard you were out for some class about the metaphysics of law." Something beeped, and his attention darted to his watch. "Oh. Gotta go." He rolled his eyes. "This place and meetings, huh?" he said and hurried off.

Inside my office, I considered the door, first cracking it and then, by degrees deciding to leave it wide open. Resuming my seat, I opened the file that topped the stack and worked until I found myself closing the last manila folder. Looking up, I was surprised to see Josh. "Quitting time," he said, leaning in the doorway. With his briefcase in hand, he waited while I packed up and we walked out together.

The day hadn't been half bad, I thought, sailing out of the parking lot enjoying the crisp, spring, mountain air. I downshifted, making it easier to take the hill. My legs pumped the pedals, and I thought of Pythia. "Call your mother," I said, huffing, trying on the idea.

I shrugged. Why not tell my mom about Amy? "Practice, right?" I asked Cat. She flicked her tail and smiled sitting in her favorite spot on the desk. "Okay, yeah," I said picking up my phone. Out the window, daffodils were replacing the faded crocuses, and early tulips poked through patches of snow that would soon melt, reds and oranges mostly.

"Hey, Mom," I said with the phone on speaker, forcing a casual tone that I immediately recognized would unleash her suspicion. I closed my eyes, hoping she hadn't noticed.

"Hey, honey." She sounded delighted, and then, as predictable as a bomb-sniffing dog, she sounded alarmed. "What's wrong?"

"Nothing." Irritated and already wishing it was easier, I gulped from the freshly opened beer. The cold, bright evanescence burned the back of my throat.

"Okay," she said, the way people do when they don't believe you. I knew she was frowning and had probably adjusted her glasses. She might have stood to pace if she'd been sitting.

"I'm tired, that's all. Everything's fine."

"You're not sleeping well?"

"I'm sleeping fine, Mom." I picked up the Rubik's Cube, then cast it aside. "I just wanted to give you a call. That's all." I closed my eyes and pinched the bridge of my nose.

"Okay. Well. Did you get some snow?" She played along.

"We had some. How 'bout you?"

"Almost seven inches!" I heard the sounds of water running and the clatter of dishes.

"Did that kid shovel?" I asked picking at the label on the bottle.

"What? I can't hear you."

"Mom, did that kid come by?"

"Let me call you back, love. I'm just cleaning up after dinner."

"Put your earbuds in, Mom. I'll wait." I shook my head, suspecting she'd canceled the snow service, I forgot all about Amy.

I heard her open a drawer. The earbuds were likely tucked in a divided tray next to a notepad and an ancient address book. Only a rubber-band ball roamed free.

"These things never stay put," she mumbled. I knew she was pushing her shoulder length curly gray hair behind an ear as she fumbled with the buds. "There." She tried to sound cheerful and composed. "Can you hear me?"

"Did the kid clear the walk and driveway?" I asked, and she launched into an unnecessarily long story that I didn't even listen to and interrupted. "Well, Mom, you can't—no, Mom, you can't wait—Mom!" Impatient, I shot from the chair and raised my voice. "What're you gonna do if you need to get out?"

Indignant, she argued that I'd "insinuated" she couldn't manage her own "affairs" and was "mortified" by my lack of trust in her abilities. I sat and listened while she raved, opening and closing cupboards with too much vigor as she put things away.

Tired of arguing, I gave in. "Okay. So, it all worked out." My tone was weary but maintained a pleasant facade. I was mostly glad the discussion was nearly over.

"Yes, of course it all worked out. I'm not feeble!"

"Okay! I didn't mean anything by it." I ran both hands through my hair, then leaned over and cradled my head in my hands. "I know you know how to take care of yourself." I indulged her, then downed the last of the beer.

"Well, I do! For God's sake, I am an ER nurse, after all." I imagined her brow furrowing and her eyes narrowing.

I rubbed the back of my neck, longing to hurl a blazing ball of fury at Pythia and her ridiculous instructions but instead played my usual part in such drama and tempered my mood. "I know, Mom," I said and zipped my lips.

"Oh, these haven't been cleaned in years!" Her disembodied voice had changed, sounding farther away now, and I surmised she was on a step stool. At five-three and a hundred-thirty-five pounds, I knew she was reaching for a high shelf. Then sounding like she was stretching, she asked, "Did you get the vitamin C I sent?"

"Yeah. Sorry, I should have called. Thank you."

"There's no reason to be sorry. But how else would I know? If you don't say, then I have to ask." I tried not to listen. It seemed all we ever did was defend ourselves from some imagined threat we suspected the other had imposed.

"Take 1,000 mg every night, not in the morning. Do you hear me? Not in the morning." She repeated it like I couldn't be trusted, and somehow that soothed me. "Apparently, they've discovered that taking vitamin C at night improves sleep, decreases anxiety, and is better absorbed. So, the night, not the morning. Okay?"

"Yes, thanks, Mom."

"Well, I better get going if I want to finish these cupboards. Everything will be right as rain as soon as I get this is done. It was good talking to you, honey." I heard the familiar sound of her unwrapping a Werther's candy.

"Wait, Mom?" I should have seen it coming, her signing off after she'd given me my prescription. I knew she always liked ending on a note of advice. "I met somebody."

"A girl?" I pictured her broad smile.

"A woman, yes. I think you'd like her."

"Does she have a job?" I heard her sucking on the caramel.

"Yeah. Amy is a high school English teacher. We met at a chili bowl fundraiser at this pottery studio. She's a potter, Mom." Because my dad was a potter, I honeyed the sound of the last part. The mention of pottery could make my mom wobbly.

"A potter? What were you doing at a pottery studio?"

"I don't know. Volunteering. It's in my neighborhood. I like pottery. I'm trying to get more involved in things." I heard the wooden sound of a chair scraping against the floor, and I knew she was now sitting. "I mean, I wanted to get more involved in things in general. Not specifically pottery. It's complicated, Mom." I thought about opening another beer.

"I doubt serving chili is complicated." My mother was a fan of "Things are easier than you think." Naturally, I would disagree, defending the difficulty ahead of me, and she would set out to convince me otherwise. But this time, I didn't bite.

"You know what I mean. It's hard to explain." I frowned, struggling to leave out Pythia and all that business. "I wanna get more involved in my own life. I wanna create my own reality." The words were barely out of my mouth when I realized I'd only traded one snafu for another.

"What on earth is that supposed to mean?"

"I don't know what it means." I shut my eyes and rested my forehead in my hands. "I don't know why I said it. I just wanted to tell you about Amy." I ran my hand through my hair, then took the phone off speaker and brought it to my ear. "I want you to like Amy."

"Well, I like Amy if you like Amy. Why wouldn't I like Amy?"

"I don't know." Depleted, I threw up a hand. "There's no reason."

"Well, are you talking marriage? Is this why you're so touchy?"

"No." I rolled my eyes. "We've only just met."

"Well, I'm sure she's quite amiable. You tell her I said 'hello' and I look forward to meeting her? Will you?" She sounded happy giving me instructions again, and I heard her unwrap another candy.

Flooded by the safe feeling of a boy being tucked in, kissed on the forehead, and promised sweet dreams, I answered back, "I will. I love you, Mom."

"What's her last name?"

"Mom. Don't look for her on Facebook. Please. That would be weird. If things go well, you'll meet her."

"I don't understand if she has a Facebook page, doesn't she want people to look at her? Is there something I shouldn't see?"

"Please. It would be stalkerish. Okay?"

"Oh, for heaven's sake." I heard the sound of the chair, meaning she was standing. "Take the C tonight," she told me, and before I had a chance to say I would, she added, "Tonight, not the morning." I could see her face in my mind, studying me to be sure I understood. Her eyes keenly taking my temperature. Her curly gray hair, thick and coarse softening the intensity of her skeptical nature.

"I will." Feeling like a survivor, I ended the call blowing out a big breath and wondered if it'd always been like this. "Well, maybe it doesn't have to be." I shrugged.

15

D espite arriving promptly on Saturday for our official first date, I still cut through the park and hurried over the footbridge. Buskers filled the park playing a variety of instruments while skaters circled on the outdoor rink. I raced past it all, following the creek path, barely noting a couple of ducks floating on the frigid water. The Tea House sat just at the park's edge beside the art museum. Curious little shops banked both, and food carts dotted the lawn.

Taking the steps two at a time, I hurried in and immediately spotted Amy. Sunshine spilled from the lofty sky-lit ceiling and haloed in those golden rays, she sat smack dab in the middle of the room glowing beside the restaurant's main attraction, the impressive koi pond. But to my disappointment way too many people lingered with enthusiasm for the fish, and the water amplified their conversations. I sighed. Then hiding my disappointment, I made my way over.

"I'm sorry," I spoke over the din, sliding into the chair. "I hope you haven't been waiting long."

"Not at all." She made a "no big deal" face. "But I must admit I arrived early. I love it near the pond." Then almost apologetic, she gestured to a teapot and plate of biscotti. "I hope you don't mind. I ordered us my favorite, Full Moon Spice. It's kind of caramelly and nutty. I hope you like it." Then quickly added, "Of course, feel free to order, too."

"Thanks," I said, making eye contact. "Sounds good. I'd like to try it." Amy filled my cup, and I unfolded my napkin.

As if on cue, two women chased a precocious, runny-nosed toddler wobbling up to the water. The three hovered behind my chair. The child squealed, slapping the water, splashing me while her mother knocked me in the head with her enormous diaper bag.

"Oh, I'm so sorry," the grandmother said. "Are you on a first date?" She lingered. "It seems like just yesterday my daughter was dating. And now, here we are. Out with a baby! Where does the time go?"

"Tell the fishies bye-bye," the child's mother said, and the toddler wailed. In a flash, Grandma spun on her heels, promising ice cream, but the child screeched in defiance. Her shrieks echoed off the hard-tiled surfaces and magnified in the lofty space.

"Someone is discovering that parting *is* sweet sorrow. That or a cat is being bathed." I mouthed, feeling witty.

Amy leaned across the table to be heard. "It's not a cat, and I can't blame her. In fact, I should let you know that I might cause a similar scene on departing." She pushed her tongue against the inside of her cheek while resisting a smile.

I searched for a funny comeback but, at a loss for words, only chuckled. "Yes, well, thank you for telling me in advance," I shouted over the top of the steady *shhhhh* from the massive waterfall. Scowling at myself, wishing for wit, I reached for a biscotti.

Amy tilted her head and raised an eyebrow. "Forewarned is forearmed." She teased, trying to draw me out.

"Noted," I said and bit into the hard cookie. The Casablanca-style ceiling fans whirred and stirred a humid breeze while the sun played off the water in the pond. "Yum. These are—" but the pleasure of the taste was suddenly overpowered by pain from my back left molar, "ahhh. ohhhhhoo." My hand flew to my jaw to apply pressure.

"Oh!" She leaned in. "Are you okay?"

"Ahhhh, yes. Yes. Just a little pain." My tongue poked around my molar.

Alarmed, her tongued copied mine. "Is it your tooth?" she asked still mirroring me.

"No, no. It's a, it's fine. Just a little surprise." My eyes watered.

"Oh, my gosh. You're crying." She reached for my hand.

"No. No, I am not crying." Without thinking, I drew back.

"Oh! I should have waited to order. Sometimes I just get carried away."

"No, no, no, no, no." I countered. "It's nothing. Really. Nothing at all. Please don't worry. See? I am fine," I said, raising my cup, and when the hot tea inflamed my tooth again, I pretended it didn't.

"I really enjoyed this," Amy said, cleaning up the last of the crumbs. I thought she might lick the plate. "I mean the afternoon with you, not just the biscotti." She grinned and quickly added. "And I am so sorry about your tooth. I feel awful."

"It's fine, really."

"Gabe, I can see it hurts. You're favoring the left side. You should get it looked at." She leaned in, scrutinizing my mouth. "Are you sure it's not broken?" Her tongue poked again at her own tooth.

"It's fine."

She studied me. "Well," she said, looking at her phone, "I've got to get going soon, but would you walk out with me?"

"Of course." I tried not to sound disappointed while wondering if her leaving had anything to do with the slack way I was holding the side of my face. "Keep the change," I said to the server before joining Amy, who was already wearing her coat.

Outside, she nodded north. "I'm this way. How 'bout you?"

"That way." I nodded south.

"Ah." Her single syllable hung in the air between us and she stayed put. "I love it here." She indicated the park with its massive trees peppering the lawn perfect for escaping the summer sun. The expanse of green with the creek path running along its edge. "It's the center of everything." Turning my direction, she added, "In the summer, the gardens are spectacular. I love roses. Do you?"

"I do." I nodded. "I like gardening."

"Really?" She sounded impressed.

"Well, I wouldn't call myself a gardener, but I like gardening."

"Do you skate?"

"Not at all."

"Me neither. That's another thing we have in common."

"Our fear of skating?"

"No. Our good sense to guard against falling down."

I laughed.

"I like you." She played with her earring. This one a dangly little peace sign that sparkled when the sun lit its tiny blue stones.

"I like you, too." I looked down, tasting the sharp, metallic edges of anxiety mingling with the copper tinge of blood from my tooth, hoping she wasn't playing me.

"How 'bout dinner tomorrow night? Maybe Thai?"

"Well, it's a school night," I said, hoping to be funny. "But I guess by your look, your curfew is later than mine." She smiled, looking so sure of herself, and of me.

"It's a date then?" Her eyes dared me.

"Can I kiss you?" I asked, and she advanced my way, projecting a bashful but flirtatious air. Beneath the pungent scent of soap, she smelled of dark honey, bold and almost medicinal. I reached for her and ran my fingertips along her jawbone. Her skin was silky-smooth. I felt for the nape of her neck and finding the gentle slope at the back of her head, I slid my hand into her short black hair. She yielded to my advance. Her lips were warm and plump. Our bodies swayed.

She drew back. With her eyes locked on mine, she tugged for me to follow.

"You've got to get going?"

"I do." But she didn't, and we strolled into the park.

"Do you think our meeting was synchronicity? Or just coincidence?" She stopped and turned toward me. I saw how her body shifted while her mind dug deeper into the subject. "I mean," she narrowed her eyes as she articulated herself, "do you think we have a destiny, or is it all just happenstance? All this, the band-shell, the rink, the tea house; somebody designed this. They imagined us here. And here we are." She smiled.

"Only you're supposed to be somewhere else?"

"I know! That's exactly what I'm saying. Isn't it amazing? Maybe I'm really supposed to be here? I mean, is life fated? Will we end up where we're supposed to no matter what? Or maybe it matters. Maybe we have a choice." She looked hard at me. "Do you ever wonder who's writing this story? You know what I mean? Am I writing my own story, or is the story writing me?" She searched my face like she was uncovering a secret. "What if," she asked indicating to the space between us and then the space around us, "this is a superposition?"

"You know about the superposition?"

"Of course." She made it sound like the only answer. I studied her sincerity, and in return, her eyes questioned mine, beckoning some answer from deep within me. Strangely, despite the shining sun, a light snow fell from the sky, dotting Amy in big flakes that disappeared almost as fast as they landed. She lifted herself onto her tiptoes and kissed me with slow deliberation. I anticipated her soft lips before they even met mine, wet with a honeyed-melon taste. Aroused, titillating sensations rose from my loins and heated my belly. My stomach exploded with excitement that fired into my heart. Awe and joy burst across my chest and down my arms. My hands trembled. My legs weakened to the alive feelings inside my body.

"Wow," I whispered, once we'd drawn apart.

"Snowbow!" someone shouted, pointing to the east where the full spectrum of colored light hung in an arc. Amy stepped away, walking backward from me. "Seven o'clock? And you can be home by ten." She waved.

"Okay, but let's meet at Amour's."

"Amour's?" Her brows arched, and then with a big grin, she nodded and said, "Alright. See you at seven."

16

A fter we ordered, Amy reached across the table, taking my hands. "So, is this your reality?"

I looked around. The wait staff bustled in the low-lit room. A purple orchid with its graceful stem bowed over candles centered on the white-clothed table set with china and goblets. I nodded, taking in the crowd of boisterous people, and smiled. "Yeah, this is the reality I wanted to create with you."

"It's romantically hip," she whispered, bringing her elbow onto the table and letting the heel of her hand support her chin. "Great music, too. I think music is an essential backdrop to life. You know? Like, it's always playing, referencing our current and past cultural and personal experiences, until finally, we each have our own scores. Mine includes this smoky, soulful sound that's sassy, even edgy sometimes." She pointed to the airwaves. "Like Madeleine Peyroux. You'd think she's a hundred years old the way she sounds. Smoothing out such honest heartache, making it feel like the pain's worth it." She bubbled as she eyed the place. "It's really fun here. Thanks for bringing me."

"I'm glad you like it." I sat back and enjoyed her enthusiasm.

"Oh! Listen. I love it when she sings in French." Amy sang along in a low, lovely voice, looking like she loved to sing. "Et dès que je t'aperçois, alors je sens dans moi mon cœur qui bat. La la, la la, la la." She absently fingered the little silver heart that dangled from her earring while again checking out the restaurant. "This is great," she said to no one in particular and touched the stem of the orchid. "So, talk to me," she whispered, moving the flower aside before crossing her forearms onto the table, "I am all ears." She looked right at me.

"Well, first, I gotta ask. Do you know what the words mean? And second, what do you know about the four fundamental forces of nature?"

Raising an eyebrow, she cocked her head and lifted her chin. "Yes, I know what the words mean. And, you're speaking of the gravitational, electromagnetic, strong nuclear, and weak nuclear forces. The forces responsible for growth, decay, and transformation of the physical world."

"Impressive." Bewildered and intrigued by the way things intersected when we were together, I studied her with the eyes of an optimist. We sat for a moment, taking each other in before I broke the silence. "And what do the words mean?" I asked, suspecting the evening held great promise.

"Ah, the French words, oui?" She sipped water from the stemmed glass. The candlelight caught her healthy sun-kissed skin "They mean something like," she began, then shrugged shyly, "as soon as I see him, I feel alive with my heart beating," then looked away, messing with the earring before looking back at me. "So," she said, regaining her confidence, "can you speculate beyond the four forces?" She played me with her eyes, her lips slightly parted.

"I can," I answered, believing we might already be entangling particles.

"Higgs boson?" she baited, raising her chin and revealing her slender neck.

"The one and only." Feeling loose, I flashed my own smug smile, wondering if she could be seduced by my thick-lashed brown eyes.

"Alright." She studied me before scooting the plate of bread. When did someone bring that? Resting her arms again on the table, she leaned in. "Okay." She confided. "So, I used to think love was the result of the weak nuclear force," but then paused to cut into her filet, which was when I noticed dinner had been served. "You know, all the other forces hold things together." She took a bite and chewed. "But the weak nuclear force takes things apart. Breaks them down, and then with the help of the electromagnetic force, the two reorganize the broken-down stuff into something else. So, I wonder, what if the answer to a greater understanding of love lies in the science of beta decay? I know that sounds weird. But, like how stars are birthed out of gigantic gas clouds that collapse into themselves then heat up under the force of their own gravity, until," she gestured with her hand, "poof! Twinkle, twinkle, little star. When I learned that, I thought, that's what love is." She took another bite. "Or at least," she shrugged, "that's what I wish it was."

"Where there is love, there is life." I dipped a bite of duck into the raspberry sauce.

"Exactly! Mahatma Gandhi. I can't believe you said that! That's one of my favorite quotes!"

Dropping my knife and fork, I leaned back into the chair to get a better look at her. "So, you said you like cats?"

"I love cats." She smiled. Her teeth were almost straight. "What's not to like about cats? They are so self-assured." She shrugged but then looked distressed. "You don't mean to eat, though, right? Because I don't eat cats." She laughed.

Captivated by her charm, I barely noticed her teasing. "We do have so much in common." I sat forward to more easily look into her eyes. "It's refreshing to be with someone so honest."

"Well, thank you." She took another bite and talked with a mouthful. "I mean, don't you agree that if we don't confront our deep-rooted, elusive, and mystic beliefs about love, we can't possibly create something as brilliant and lasting as the stars?" She spoke with her hands. Adept, almost athletic, they danced before me, showing off her ringless long fingers, the ends spoon-shaped with plain nails trimmed short and rounded. "What if love does make the world go around? Does that refer to Earth turning on its axis, or is it an esoteric reference to how love is paid forward to ensure our evolution?"

"Umm," I grunted, agreeing with a mouthful. "I get it." Swallowing, I brought the napkin to my mouth. "So, you said, that's what you used to think, but—"

"So," Amy nodded while cutting herself another bite, "when science recognized the Higgs boson as the mechanism that couples the electromagnetic field to the weak nuclear force field, that was inspirational, right? I mean, don't you think that implies some consciousness or intelligence. What if that's love?"

"What if the Higgs boson is love?"

"Or the mechanism that initiates it. Higgs facilitates that never-ending pattern of birth, growth, death—evolution. The whole thing circles for eons and eons, around and around. It's what projects us forward. That sounds like love, but that's not my point." She frowned. "My point," she articulated the word while still holding her steak knife and gathering her thoughts. "My point is not to prove the existence of love, but more to shake up the way we think about love. So, what if you and I, and all of them," she motioned toward the other diners, "opened our minds to greater considerations about the meaning and the power of love?" Finally, she exhaled. "I don't know." Her eyes searched inward until she found what she'd been looking for. "Nietzsche!" She lurched toward me. "He said, something like, who amongst us will know the kind of love that gives way to lust in favor of a shared thirst for a higher ideal? That's the kind of love I want to experience."

"Now this is going to sound sentimental," I said, "but hear me out. What if love is a recipe or a mechanism for creating a rainbow? Not the rainbow itself, but the instruction, or the actual creation." It was my turn to lean in. "White light passes through a prism. It is refracted and then reflected into a spectrum of colored light." She grinned, nodding, and I nodded. "What if love favors evolution?" I asked. "What if it advances the nature of things the way the prism disrupts the white light and casts a rainbow of color."

"I get it. Similar to the weak force, it breaks the white light into seven rays of color. Like the seven kinds of love!"

"Are you kidding me? You know about the seven?"

"Gabe, you way underestimate me."

"Sorry." I blushed. "This is all new to me, and there's this synergy between us and, I don't know…." Feeling warm, I looked away. She waved it off and craned her neck to catch my eyes. "And then the prism facilitates a magnetic attraction between the seven rays."

"Exactly!"

"The electromagnetic force organizes the seven rays."

"Correct. The strong force binds the attraction."

"And gravity pulls the whole thing into planet earth!"

Her mouth fell open, her fork hung in midair. "Wow!" She shuttered, blinking and mirroring my surprise, then set her fork aside. "That is, excuse my French, fucking brilliant."

We sat silent, digesting the idea. Time slowed with the gravity of our attention. We methodically picked up our utensils, our meals mostly uneaten. As I ate, it came to me how the rich flavored duck contrasted with the fresh, sweet sauce. Its tart-rosy undertones made me salivate. I wanted more.

"You know." She broke the trance. "The Higgs boson is always available and exists infinitely, but only reveals itself when particles call on it to connect and create something new. Higgs is like some noble, sacred—"

"Generous god?"

"Yeah. Generous god."

We nodded like metronomes keeping time.

"That's what I want to create," I said gazing into her pale blue eyes.

"Me too," she said. "That's love. You know? The whole shebang. I want a rainbow of all seven kinds. I want the white light kind of love."

I wasn't even cold, nor did anything feel uphill about the ascent home against the winter weather. With my breath visible, I shoved my hands into my pockets and passed the closed corner grocer. The streets were dark, but the city night sky was clear, making it easier to see my way through the March landscape. Bending to the steady incline, I faced the long hill and fell deep into my thoughts. Wondering as much about Higgs and love as I was contemplating developing this love story, I stargazed. The sickle-shaped moon was waxing. "Can I really participate in the complex interplay of the Higgs mechanism, the thing that provides all of us with not only our physical reality but our experience of it?" I wondered out loud.

"That's The Thang, you know, my dear fellow human." Startled by the scratchy voice, I stopped in my tracks. Captivated in the eerie blue storefront light of 7-Eleven, a gruff woman and her dog sat wrapped in an old wool blanket on the cold sidewalk. "Not the moon, mind you, but the experience of the moon," she said.

"Right?" I nodded to our shared intelligence. Then with a hop in my step, impersonating some long-haired metalhead, I fired back, "It's f'ing brilliant, alright!" and moved on like this was my everyday world.

"True dat, my friend," she called after me. "True dat."

17

I t was hard to keep my mind on work after my date with Amy. At work behind my desk with my neat stack of files and my new open-door-policy all I could think about was when I'd see her next. I even noticed a pang of resentment over giving up the coming Sunday to Pythia. But at the same time looking forward to it, I cast aside the file I'd been struggling to open in favor of rifling through my backpack. Then with my journal in hand, I opened it to the most recent entry and smoothed the spine flat.

1. *Improving at ludus.*
2. *Dabbling with eros.*

I tapped the pen against the paper. Was I practicing greater self-acceptance? I frowned. "How do you even do that?" I sat stumped. Philia? No. No comradery. No challenging or emotionally rich experiences. *Not yet,* I penned. Pragma? I thought of the old couple at the grocery store and the one at the dry cleaners and hoped the story I was creating with Amy was headed in that same direction. Storge? "Oh yeah!" I checked it off thinking of Cat. Satisfied, I underlined it several times, and then my thoughts turned to my mom. At first I scowled but softened, thinking of her chances for pragma. "I'm not alone. I have you," she'd always said. A warm, familiar sadness washed over me. Why had she stopped playing that Van Morrison album? I should call more often.

Yeah, dude. Let her know how things are going.

What're you afraid of, Mendes? She's just your mom.

I frowned and grabbed the file. Words jumped off the page. Moral claims. Fairness. Just rewards. Increased innovation. Economic growth. I rubbed my temples and exhaled loudly. Another ugly intellectual property suit. I surveyed my office. A neat but growing stack of manila folders sat again at the corner of my desk. Knowing I should hunker down into the tedious research, I alternatively considered fine-tuning the database but instead found myself headed down the hall.

Josh gathered files from his desk and the credenza behind him. "Off to a meeting?" I asked at the door of his office.

He rolled his eyes. "Don't get me wrong, I love this job. I just wish I could spend more time doing the part I love. So, maybe I don't love this job." He laughed. "How's the world of research?"

"In a word, unimaginative. Deadly dull." I leaned against the door jamb.

"I think that's three words."

"I guess it's more interesting than I thought." I snorted. "Glad I stopped by."

"Hey. What can I say? I'm that guy."

"Alright, 'that guy,' do you ever wonder how we can honestly stake a claim as the sole creator of anything? I mean, this whole idea of intellectual ownership? It negates the obvious."

"And what would that be?"

"There are no original ideas. Everything's recycled, broken down, taken apart, and put back together. Wasn't it Mark Twain who said it's all shards of glass in an ever-turning kaleidoscope?"

"You sound like my girlfriend."

"And what would you tell her?"

"I don't *tell* her anything." He arched his brow, passing through the door.

18

That Saturday, I headed to the park and the center of my body came alive just thinking of Amy. The way she laughed. Her lips. Her hips! I hustled along the creek path, and by the time I reached the ice rink, she was waiting.

"Hey." She smiled, her eyes sparkling. Our lips met, and my hand remembered the place at the back of her neck where my fingertips fit perfectly. After, our gaze went to the ice. "Check them out," she said pointing to an elderly couple skating like pros.

I nodded but spotted a boy about eight years old, wobbling as his mother skated backward in front of him, coaxing him to let go of the sidewall. "I don't want to," the boy said.

"It'll be fun. I promise." His mother extended her hands, encouraging him.

"That's me." I indicated to the boy, reminded of my own mother's prodding over the years.

"What about them?" She pointed to a squad of rambunctious boys skating fast, cutting in close to each other.

"Never," I said, confident.

"Oh, look." Amy frowned.

"Are you mad at me now? It's too slippery. I don't like skating. Help me," The boy with his mother whined to her back as she headed to exit the ice. Boy, I remember that. The worry that I'd let my mom down, that I was just one more disappointment in her life.

"I'm not mad." The mother turned to help him off the ice. "I just wanted you to have fun, that's all."

"All a mother ever wants is for her child to be happy," Amy said, sounding jaded, and we stepped away to stroll along the path. "Family right? Everybody's got one." She pulled an orange from her coat pocket.

The last snow was melting along the wooded riverbank, making the paths down to the water muddy. But the creek, not yet raging with the spring mountain runoff, was low and exposed a rocky beach. Cairns from earlier in the year still stood in the shallows. A couple of kids skipped rocks across the creek water.

She peeled the orange. "I have a brother two years younger than me. He's married with kids." She offered me a section. I bit into the warm fruit, steering it clear of my bad tooth. "I wish I was better at staying in touch." She didn't look at me, but I nodded, hoping to find a respectful balance between engaging with her and giving her space.

The path narrowed, and we drew in closer. Amy shrugged, slowed her pace, and then stepped in front of me. The orange was still whole except for the segment she'd shared. "So that's my brother and you already know me." She searched my eyes, then turned away and proceeded. This time lengthening her stride, stepping on the fault lines of the sidewalk squares.

Some of the trees hosted the first blooming buds. Little green baby hands burst forth against the blue sky. "So, just you and your brother?" I wondered if her family was as messed up as mine.

"Nope." She stopped and eyed me again. A bicyclist sped by, causing me to step into the slushy snow. "I have a sister four years older than me. She lives with my mom. She has autism."

I met her hard eyes, but she turned away, her long-legged walking put more and more distance between us until I had to jog to catch up.

"Hey!" I called after her. "I'm only a child." I saddled up beside her. Craning around to better see her, my words boomeranged and echoed in my head. "Argh! I mean, I *am* an *only child*. I don't have any brothers and sisters." I waited. Then took a risk. "My dad died. I was only a few years old." I grimaced. "My mom remarried, but that didn't work out either." The words felt too heavy and I feared I should have kept them to myself when she said nothing and kicked a stone.

The wind picked up, and a cloud covered the sun. "My dad died, too," she finally said and sounded very small.

An unusual popping noise echoed off the banks. Cries followed and a desperation filled the air. Panic-stricken people scattered everywhere. Some charged right at us, and I began deciphering the hubbub around us. Somebody moved fast through the water below. From behind, the earth vibrated with the beating hooves of police on horseback. "Take cover away from the creek! Active shooter! Active shooter," they shouted as they flew past, leaving us in a dust cloud. Sirens blasted.

I grabbed Amy's hand. "Keep your head down!" I yelled as we ran low to the ground. More shots rang out, then somebody yelled something and fired back. Afraid of losing Amy in the swarm, I tightened my hold on her sweaty hand, already slipping away.

The little park was crawling with police in riot gear, beating their way to the creek, screaming, "Get down! Get down! Shooter on the creek!" A chill ran through me. There was nowhere to hide. The park was nothing but singular trees planted for picnics. The band shelter was too far. With no other choice, I pulled Amy behind a tree. I unzipped my coat, threw it over us, and we huddled beneath it. My legs and hands trembled. I licked my lips scanning the scene, and that's when I saw a hysterical mob shoving into The Tea House. They would never all fit. I licked my lips. The inside of my mouth was so hot and dry. "We gotta get to the art museum," I said.

Amy struggled, wheezing.

"Are you okay?" I asked.

She whirred, making awful rasping sounds.

"Amy?" But I already knew the lining of her airway was swelling, her throat was constricting. My stepfather had worked himself into plenty of asthma attacks, so I also knew her oxygen intake was diminishing fast. It was only a matter of seconds before she'd fight to breathe.

"Drop the gun!" someone shouted, "Put your hands in the air!" Two more shots were fired, a pop, pop followed, and then a struggle in the water. Hunkered under my jacket, I heard Amy only taking in half-breaths. I ransacked her bag, feeling for an inhaler while her breathing became a high-pitched whistle. Blind and frantic, I made out her wallet. I deciphered a tampon and several wrapped pieces of bubble gum. Then, finally finding it, I fumbled for her hand, shoved the inhaler into her palm, and when I heard the familiar aerosol hiss, her drawing in the dose, I exhaled. She dosed again. This time drawing in more deeply, she made a little gasp and a cry. Relieved, I rubbed her back, and outside sounds returned.

Splashing. More of a struggle. A thud. And then the drama heading up the bank. I clenched my jaw and pinched the bridge of my nose before lifting the jacket enough to see Amy. Her eyes were wide with fright, her face damp with sweat. "We gotta get out of here."

"I know." She snatched my hand and, with her other, grabbed an edge of the jacket.

Seeing how pale she was, I tightened my grip on her. "Ready?" She nodded and squeezed my hand hard. Please, don't let me let her down, I begged myself and some god.

We took off racing across the lawn—only, exhausted from the asthma attack, Amy couldn't keep up. Another round of shots rang out and I dragged her until she reeled forward and fell. I crawled back to grab her as several horses stampeded by, kicking dirt up into our faces. I tugged her to her feet, and we took off again, making it up the museum steps where I panicked, knowing we were now in plain sight. I didn't dare look out for fear of what fate I might see. Frantic, we each yanked at a door, but nothing yielded. We banged and kicked. Enraged, I pounded and Amy wailed, "Help us! Please, help us!" Finally, someone from inside hurried into sight, unlocked the door, flung it open, and pulled us in before slamming it shut and locking it again.

We staggered into a crowd of about one-hundred people huddled against the back wall. While some cried, most were silent. More shots sounded from outside. People gasped. Then nothing. Amy leaned into me. Resting her head on my chest, she placed a hand on my heart while the other tugged at my back-belt loop. I wrapped an arm around her and pulled her close. It was as if we'd known each other forever, as if we'd been running from something for a long time.

The start-stop sound of a police siren called out to then be followed by a cold quiet that crept through the gallery, heightening the collective tension of everyone in the room. A policewoman appeared before the glass door and whoosh of relief exhaled as everyone collectively sighed. A staff member hurried to let her in. "Is anyone hurt?" the policewoman called out as she entered, one hand on her holstered gun and scanning our blank faces. "Is everyone okay?" she asked, and like a spell had been broken, we all mumbled, "Yes." People hugged. Others spoke to each other, but many called out questions of when and what and how.

"Listen!" the officer held up both hands, commanding our attention. "A shooter's been apprehended. We're searching the area to ascertain they did indeed act alone as we suspect. Please remain inside. A police officer will return when it is safe to exit the building."

Relieved, we all disbanded and Amy and I found a new spot on the floor. With our backs against the wall and legs outstretched, the gallery came into focus. "Do you like art?" Amy asked as we both scanned the walls of art. "Wow, there's sure a lot of paintings of pipes here," she said, "Reminds me of Magritte. Do you know Magritte's work?"

19

"Outstanding!" Pythia beamed from the computer screen only to then crinkle her pleasant face into a frown. "Of course, not the part about the shooting. Very frightening. I am glad you and Amy are safe."

Awakened by Pythia's voice, Cat's ears perked. She stood, stretched her back legs, and then passed between me and the screen. "Well, hello, Cat!" Pythia waved and Cat purred, rubbing her chin against the camera.

Pythia laughed at my efforts to get between Cat and the camera. "We're old friends, aren't we, Cat?" Pythia said, virtually rubbing noses with my beloved friend. Finally, having had her fill, Cat returned to her patch of sun on the desk and swatted her tail in my direction.

"Where were we now?" Pythia asked, all smiles. "Yes, of course. You've described all four kinds of intimacy: physical, intellectual, emotional, and experiential intimacy. Astounding! It's brilliant, unexpected, and way ahead of schedule. You're making excellent progress, agape mou."

"So, four kinds of intimacy, huh?" I tugged Cat's tail, and she swatted me before she rolled over to face the window. Outside, the brilliant spring flowers inspired exaltation in the rising sun. I could almost smell the soon-to-come sweet damp spring air. Soon the neighborhood would be filled with the bah-aaaaa of lawnmowers and the scent of freshly mown grass.

"One minute, please," Pythia chirped as she popped out of view to then return just as quickly leafing through the same workbook she'd previously consulted. "Here it is." She pointed to a page. "Our discussion on intimacy is, in fact, weeks away." She arched a brow and flashed an approving smile, but then twisted her lips, appearing worried while she paged ahead.

"Is that okay?"

"Of course!" She grinned, but the troubled look returned. "Your story is progressing faster than expected, and if we're to fit in an appointment with Dr. Jacoby today—"

"From Twin Peaks?"

"No, of course not. Your tooth?" She pointed to my mouth before sticking her nose into the book and ripping through pages. Remembering, I rubbed the side of my face. "There's much to be accomplished," she muttered. "I fear we may best be served not looking a gift horse in the mouth." She eyed me, knitting her brows again.

"Okay." This time I frowned. "Is it okay? Because it sounds like it's a problem." My tongue, an attentive nurse, gingerly checked my tooth. A sharp electrical pulse fired, and I flinched.

She eyed me. "Do you still remain interested in creating a cellular to solar experience of love that is grounded in the natural order of things? You do realize this will change your life?"

"Yes." I said, exchanging the pain for the black ram. At the same time, I scowled with the usual confusion around exactly what it was we were doing. "I mean, I wanna figure out what's missing in me so I can have love in my life." Then thinking she might be duly impressed, I added, "Like rainbow love."

"Then, we shall proceed with intimacy," she said paying my brilliant simile no mind what-so-ever, and simply carried on. "Which, by the way, happens everywhere and can happen even in isolated interactions. But a pattern built over time provides a closeness between people that qualifies their relationship as meaningful."

"Like in pragma."

"Exactly. Let's begin with physical intimacy." A picture of lamp appeared, taking up the full screen.

"Hey. That's—How did you?"

She poked her head from behind the image and stood in front of it, reminding me of the weather forecaster on Channel 7. "Agape mou." She pulled her lips into a tight line as if my question was disappointing. "This," she indicated the picture of Amy and I kissing in the park, "was always a choice on the infinite grid of possibility."

"Oh. Right. But—"

"Rest assured. No one here is interested in all the details of your love life. Ready?" I nodded, and she continued. "Physical intimacy can be expressed through touch between friends or between a parent and child."

"Storge."

"There you go. You are doing a fine job of understanding the many themes of a good love story. And which of the seven terms comes to mind when I extend the discussion of physical intimacy to sexual copulation?"

"Eros, but I want you to know I'm developing a story with Amy that includes a healthy dose of eros. Not the usual sexual drama." I blushed. "Sorry, but I don't want you to think—I mean, what Amy and I have is nothing like eros." I'd barely uttered the words when the screen flashed a single sentence: *Physical intimacy is a personalized sensual expression created consensually through shared sensory activities for pleasure and joy.* "Yes!" I exclaimed. "Exactly. That's what I want."

"Yes, physical intimacy, even sexual intimacy is more than sex."

"I agree."

"Of course you do. Now, moving right along, let's take a look at intellectual intimacy. I'll venture it's your favorite."

A lively clip of Amy talking appeared. "What if love does make the world go around?" she asked again. "Does that refer to Earth turning on its axis, or is it an esoteric reference to how love is paid forward to ensure our evolution?"

I saw my former self leaning forward, eager to hear Amy, then asking, "What if the Higgs boson is love?" I then observed the passionate discourse that had erupted. A rhythm of thought and speech as sexy as the way our bodies might fit together playing out until it concluded in our mutual revelation about rainbow love. Then the picture faded.

"And you thought I wasn't listening." Pythia said all smug as she materialized again. Her wavy red hair cascading down her shoulders up and as always, wearing the same green gown. The cattails behind her bent in the breeze. "That," she said with emphasis, "is intellectual intimacy at its best. The open exchange of similarities and differences in thoughts for the purpose of advanced discovery. Practiced regularly, intellectual intimacy creates a safe space for managing problems and reaching mutually beneficial solutions."

I sat with a fool's grin, dazed by the invigorating memory.

Pythia leaned in. "Hellooo!" She tapped at the screen. "Are we frozen?" she asked someone out of sight.

"No. Sorry. I'm here," I said, catching my daft expression. Gathering my composure, I cleared my throat and put on a more engaged face. The thought of who might be off camera shot through my mind but I continued with another thought instead. "So, as I'm considering the clips, I realize that intimacy leads to philautia. You know, self-love."

"Absolutely. Intimacy leads to self-trust, which in turn provides for self-love. Very astute." She looked impressed and swayed her hips. The skirt of gown swayed as she tucked a loose strand of hair behind her ear.

"And self-love is the amplifier to all the other experiences of love, right?"

"That's correct. Without self-love, all other experiences are reduced from what they could be. Some would even say they can't truly exist at all without self-love. Now, let's take a peek at emotional intimacy, shall we?" She widened her eyes. "Very well. Emotional intimacy involves a deeper trust of oneself, of the other, and the place for sharing. It often includes dialogue for processing information that remains emotionally charged and is considered protected information."

She pointed, and the screen flashed to a guarded Amy walking on the trail. I saw myself beside her, cautious but committed, patiently drawing out information about her family. The picture faded, and Pythia appeared again. I rubbed my aching head. "I wish I would have touched her. Sitting here now, that's what I want to do."

"Empathy, compassion, and physical touch are key to all intimacy."

"Even though it was sad, I do think it provided us a foundation to not only survive the shooting, but to thrive as a couple afterward. Brief as that was, it built trust."

"You are a fast study, and while you're correct about trust, that topic is definitely for a later date. But do hold it in consideration as you develop your love story. Now that brings us to experiential intimacy." The screen engaged, and I witnessed myself rummaging almost violently through Amy's purse. Though she wasn't in the picture, the sound of her struggling to breathe was overwhelming. It was almost deafening.

My feet went cold and numb. I shuffled them under the desk. My heart surged, and I closed my eyes.

"Oh, that's awful." Pythia gulped. I opened my eyes, and the image was gone.

Pythia stood, twisting one of her rings. "Now it is me who wishes I could touch you. Put a hand on your shoulder." She looked worried.

"I didn't even know she had asthma," I said, feeling guilty about something.

"How could you know? Life only reveals itself to us through experience. Yes?"

"I suppose."

"Yes." Her face softened and she held my gaze. "Shall we?" I nodded, taking a deep breath. "Very well. Experiential intimacy can occur within any group: from the setting of a bird-watching expedition to the experience you and Amy shared." She paused with concern. "I am sorry." She searched my face.

"Thanks."

"When the boundaries of an experience are narrowed," she read aloud, already turned and pointing to the paragraph now displayed on the screen, "meaning the topic and setting are clearly defined, it is easier to experience a specific type of intimacy. Conversely, mundane things such as shared caretaking, daily housekeeping tasks, and financial responsibilities can create experiential intimacy that supports long-range mutually agreed goals and a general sense of trust." She flashed me a smile. "So, how has your programming influenced such experiences?"

"Wait ..." I was still digesting the text, "programming?" My brow creased. "Oh. Neurolinguistic programming? The pipe?" I pictured the pipe, the gentle curve of its slope, the black mouthpiece.

"Yes. You're certainly integrating all the necessary concepts for a love story rich with intimacy and facets of, as you say, rainbow love or the seven kinds. So," she smiled, "how has your programming influenced this developing story?"

"Umm, I don't know. But what's coming up is a realization of how important intellectual and emotional intimacy are to me. Which is funny, because, in the past, I avoided that kind of honesty. I was more concerned with what I was supposed to do or be. But intimacy is really a meeting of minds and hearts, like our conversations. And the ones with Amy."

"You are describing consciousness around the life you'd like to create. Realizing now what you do like and now wanting to craft *that* story. Programming is the antithesis. So, I shall ask again. How has your programming influenced these experiences of deep intimacy?" Strumming her pendant against its gold chain, the sound amplified her expectation as she peered at me through the screen, her head tilted, eyes expectant.

"Ah, I don't know." My pits dampened with the anxiety her question prompted.

"You researched the influence of music at each stage of your life?"

"I did."

"What did you conclude?"

"Well," I paused, "it was the weirdest thing. I guess I can't say it was the weirdest thing because there have been many weird things recently—"

"Agape mou." Her brows were arched.

"Right. So I was thinking about music and wondered out loud if I was in love with being sad. And then this guy—"

"Raphael."

"Um. I didn't get his name. He wore boots and talked about the moon. But he knew how music could mess up love."

"Raphael." She smiled.

"You know him?"

"The multiverse loves you, agape mou. Your teachers are everywhere."

"Oh, okay. Well, anyway, we talked, and I realized how mindlessly attracted I am to the way sad songs make me feel. Raphael pointed out that I may have fallen deeply in love with the sensations of longing and mourning, mistaking that attachment for love."

"And the pipe?"

"The pipe?" My eyes darted. "Oh! I get it. A song is not a song."

"Bravo! Now, how do you think your programming influenced these recent experiences of intimacy?"

"Honestly," I shook my head, "I didn't. I've never known such intimacy. This was new to me. No yearning. No craving. Just satisfaction. Enjoyment, even."

"So?"

"So, I created something outside of my programming. Something new. I was engaged. You know, Pythia, Amy's a powerful person. My Ex, and well, my mom too. They're all different, but they're also all strong for sure. I guess sometimes strong might've felt pushy to me. But something changed, and I feel like I can take charge, too. Like both people in a relationship can make decisions. I even picked Amour's for dinner after Amy'd said, Thai."

Pythia clasped her hands. "What progress! So what did your mother say?"

"Excuse me?"

"When you called her? What did she say?"

"Um, well. She was happy for me." I frowned, still confused about the point of the call.

"Do you believe your mother has no business in your love life?"

I laughed. "I guess I do. I mean, not like, 'She has no business!'" I mocked anger and even wagged my finger. "But I don't think about my mom when I think about falling in love."

"Why not?"

"Well, because—she's my mother," I said, louder than was necessary.

"I see." She twisted one the rings she wore, a braided gold band with a purple stone, around and around her finger. "Did you bring scissors, pencil, and paper?"

I showed her I had, and she flashed me a cursory smile. "Very good." She seemed curt, and I endured the feeling that I'd disappointed her. "Yes, let me think for a minute." Her eyebrows knitted while she fingered another ring. This one silver, the band thick and intricately carved with a very large turquoise. "Love is a powerful phenomenon. It's complex, complicated—mysterious." Her tone was cautious, and I dropped back into the chair. "All those things, and it may even provide for our very existence."

"But not everyone comes into the world out of love." I sat up. "You know that, right?"

"Yes, well...." She rolled her eyes, took a deep breath, and held it before closing her eyes. Opening them, she looked at me and said, "Hold that thought. For now, can you please indulge my argument? We've so much to cover."

"Sure." I crossed my arms on the desk and wondered if she knew she'd rolled her eyes.

"Thank you." She smiled politely, then grabbed a fist full of her wavy copper-colored hair, wrapped it around her hand, and piling it on top of her head, worked a pencil through the loose messy bun. "Your progress is superior, but the nuances of your success are critical to repeat such success. We are managing a growing body of content that gives context to what you will create. Your consciousness is paramount."

I nodded, but with a skeptical eye.

"You are in over your head, you know?" She studied me. "The point here is to go deep down. Sitting at the bottom of the gene pool is our work. But I shan't let you run out of breath. Trust me when I say that we will push off with our toes from the depths of such inquiries. We shall break through the surface and rejoice in the next, deep inhale."

I nodded with reserve, but she didn't seem to notice.

Instead, she didn't even look at me and launched into a speech. "Words, conjectures about love, are charged with power and judgment, but they can't come close to articulating love's natural energetic power. We are creatures who process to the simplest denomination. Whether that be the influence of Socrates, Newton, or Higgs, it doesn't really matter," she shrugged and I couldn't figure out if she was angry or tired. "What matters is recognizing that we do reduce things down to their simplest understanding. If, in fact, love is complex, complicated, and mysterious, and we have no organized system for understanding the breadth and depth of it or all its nuances, then what would be the simplest way of understanding it?"

"The simplest way?" I said, surprised that she was addressing me directly.

"Fold the paper in half," her tone was matter-of-fact.

"This paper?" I showed her the red sheet hoping to feel more connected again. "Yes."

"Said paper, now folded."

"Now, on the fold, draw half of a heart. When you are satisfied, cut along the line."

"Ah, a valentine." I scissored. "The simplest understanding of the word love." I revealed the heart.

"Indeed. Despite the Greeks' discourse on love, the laws of physics, the discovery of the Higgs field, or the four kinds of intimacy, most of us are introduced to a concrete understanding of the idea of love through crafting a paper heart. That, alongside a child's earliest experiences of adults who are usually the child's…?"

"Ah, mother," I said, filling in the blank, wanting to please her. Then added, "Well, parents."

But she was already nodding, saying, "Our first impression of our parents, and particularly our primary caretaker, is that they are our gods."

"Hmm?" I imagined my mother vacuuming, tossing her keys after a long day's work, or sifting through bills. Of course, there were times when she sat on the edge of my bed and spoke in a soft voice. But there'd also been times when I shot her daggers, snapped hurtful things, and swung my backpack over my shoulder only to have her block the doorway.

"I don't know, Pythia." I looked away, then at her again and was glad to see she seemed interested despite the absence of her usual engaging smile. "Maybe some might consider their parents to be like gods, but my mom was a single parent, and my stepfather—well, let's just say that if he were a god…." I made a face, then scratched my head.

"What are you itching to say?" Pythia's voice was gentle, her eyes patient.

"Haha," I said but the tension between wanting to say something and keeping it unsaid stymied me. I searched Pythia's face. "There's something I know about my real dad," I said. "Something buried so deep I can't remember it. But a part of me knows." I paused, then narrowed my eyes. "But the man who promised to be my father, the guy who had a choice? I can still hear him," I said triggered by the memory. In my head, I heard his whiskey-soaked voice, gravelly from years of single malt scotch and cigarettes. "'He's soft! He can't cut it!' he'd shout at my mom about me. Then holler back at my pleading mother. 'That's a load of crap,' he'd say, 'It's time he got over that!'" Not meaning to, I yelled imitating him right there, sitting in front of the computer.

In my mind, the sight of him staggering sloppily across the room, slurring his words made my heart race. "I worried he'd hurt her," I said short of breath, "so I'd step out from where I'd been eavesdropping and say, 'Mom, it's time to go,' and boy, oh boy! He'd explode. 'Go ahead!' he'd yell, 'Take your momma's boy!' He'd become incoherent, wailing profanities as we'd hurry to the car."

I let the memory fade. The old blue Chevy Impala, my mother's independence, slowly replaced by the sight of Pythia.

"I am so sorry," she said, her face communicating concern.

"Thanks. Yeah, me too. I guess there are all kinds of gods. I mean, Zeus is an asshole, right?"

She half-smiled, indicating she wished it wasn't true.

"So," I sighed, feeling hungover from sadness, "tell me about gods and babies."

"Hungry?"

"Maybe."

"Would you like company?"

"Do you mean—? What do you mean? I mean, yes. Of course, especially if you mean, lunch with you? But how?" Cat sat up, stretched, yawned until her eyes crossed, then jumped from the desk.

"Yes," Pythia said tilting her head, amused.

"Sure. Yeah! That'd be cool," I said, suddenly nervous with anticipation.

"Perfect."

"You don't mean here?" I gestured to the space around me. "You mean we'll each get our lunch and meet back here?" I motioned to the camera, but she was gone. I looked around the room, unsure if she might appear out of thin air. I checked the bathroom. "Pythia?" I pulled back the shower curtain. Poised in the hallway, Cat watched me search. "Pythia?" I called out, returning to the computer, but she wasn't there either.

The doorbell rang, and Cat darted and hightailed it down the stairs. "Coming!" I called, wondering who'd rung while I scanned the house looking for ways Pythia might manifest for lunch. Making my way toward the door, I popped my head into the broom closet, then the refrigerator. "As if anybody would be in there," I said, relieved that it contained only its proper contents.

"Coming," I shouted, annoyed. Muttering, I glanced around before opening the door. The last thing I wanted was for Pythia to appear like magic in front of some busybody but to my surprise, Pythia stepped in and passed right by me. Her green gown sailed behind her, carrying the sweet woody aroma that hinted of anise and a dash of almond. Cat jumped from the window ledge and trotted, trailing Pythia. The perfumed air lingered.

"Now, I don't cook, agape mou. At least not well," Pythia said, over her shoulder. I watched wide-eyed as she cruised to the fridge. "But I can make a couple of birds in a nest." She pulled out eggs, butter, and bread. "Now, Cat," she said bending over, "Where is the frying pan?" Cat rubbed against her legs and then swished by the exact cupboard. "Thank you, Cat."

"Sit." Pythia gestured to a chair as she grabbed the cooking utensils and necessary ingredients. "Oh, but first, please set the table." I noted both her shiny hair and soft dress swaying while she cracked eggs and buttered bread and looked away.

"Smells delicious," I said, focusing only on the sizzling sounds and buttery scents. Doing my best not to gape.

"Here's to love." She slid the open-faced sandwiches onto our plates. "Bon appétit!" she said, and then cutting hers into bite-sized pieces, continued as if we'd never left off. "Not able to recognize the boundaries that separate our bodies from the physical world, as newborns, we are unable to distinguish ourselves from our mothers. We *are* the soup of the entire multiverse, and the soup is us. And in the soup, all our needs are met." She took a bite. "Yum. Fresh eggs?"

"Yeah. Fanny, the receptionist has chickens."

She brought a napkin to her mouth. "The yolks are almost orange, deliciously rich. Your friend cares well for them."

I laughed. "She does love them. She has pictures of them on her desk. I think she's even named them."

"She is a good mama hen." Pythia mopped up the extra yolk with bread crust and ate it. "In a short time after birth, this idea that we and the multiverse are one plays out as we experience our mothers as energetic forces that come and go in service to us. But here's the question. What kind of service? The Four Seasons or the Bates Motel? Hmm? Yes? You see what I mean?" Glancing my way, she licked the sticky egg from around her mouth. "Yum. So very good!" Her pink tongue poked around the corners of her mouth, searching for more. "Without any further education in the subject of love, our understandings of love are first and primarily programmed by our earliest familial experiences, and then supported by the coding that exists from previous generations."

Setting her fork aside, she asked, "Can you appreciate how powerful that is? Our ancestral history informs our cells about love and everything else! Alongside that first experience of love, our lineage plays a role in programming our central nervous system, cognition, emotional expression, and physiological response. Even Sunday school, or the likes of it, will do little to alter that paper heart." Behind her the light from the big living room window was so bright the edges of her body glowed.

"So you're saying, any religious, moral, or spiritual instruction is secondary to understanding God because that's already been informed by our parents' behaviors and our families' histories?"

"Exactly. Did you grow up with forgiving parents who accepted you as you are? Or were you raised among humans who stumbled in and out of holes of disappointment that impaired their perspective or, worse, threw you into said hole and used you as leverage to pull themselves out?" She consumed another healthy forkful then relaxed into the chair. "I like eggs, do you?"

She was funny, one-minute professing the pedagogy of love and the next immersed in the pleasure food. But she gave me no chance to answer. "Until you reach the age of twenty-five," she continued, "all the preaching, all the instruction, even good examples about the purity of love will mean little. Without the capacity to step out of your child's perspective, and into one that is favored by executive functioning," she tapped her forehead, "the final piece of the brainpower puzzle. Without it," she shook her head, "you can't challenge that previous download. And you can't upload a new operating system either. But it's not just the programming handed down from your parents.

"Remember the power of story. It's not just your parents' story or their parents or those before them. World history and popular culture are programmers, too. Think of those sad songs. Or the ongoing battle between the Free Love Movement and religion. Stories! They're all stories. Just as you suspected." She paused. "But with thoughtful inquiry, all that programming can get an update and forever change the gene pool for future generations to come." She leaned in. "You never said, do you like eggs?" She folded her arms on the table. Cat stirred from the far end of the table.

I smiled. "I do." I used the edge of my fork to scoop the remaining yolk from the plate. "Sometimes, I make an omelet for dinner."

"With bacon?" Her eyes rounded. Cat stretched to sit.

"Yes." I laughed. "With bacon."

"Priestesses are discouraged from eating meat," she whispered, "but I did once try bacon." She breathed in deeply through her nose and closed her eyes. "It was magnificent! The smoked applewood scent. The savory followed by a sweet molasses finish. And I like mine crispy. Well, the one time I did. Omelets, though, too much work." She wrinkled her nose. "So, agape mou, take the remainder of the day and consider the stories most meaningful to you: familial, cultural, and experiential. Questions?"

Sitting tall, Cat looked patient.

"No. No questions."

Pythia stood and put her hand on my shoulder. Cat jumped to the floor and stood attentive beside Pythia. "Do take care. This is a bit of a ride from here out. Which reminds me, I am sorry for my impatience earlier. Forgive me?" she asked.

"Of course," I said but still wondered what had provoked her.

"Thank you." She gave me an appreciative smile. "Sometimes I get lost in the details."

I laughed. "Me, too. It's actually helpful to see that it happens to you."

"Oh! You don't know the half of it, but speaking of details, here's Dr. Jacoby's card. The appointment is for later this afternoon."

I pointed to a notation she'd made. "Is—that a—three?"

"Um-huh." She nodded, seeming clueless about her penmanship. "See you tomorrow, bright and early." With Cat at her heels, she headed to the door, then bent to balance on her haunches and scratch Cat's ears. "Hum? Agreed?" I heard her whisper. Cat stretched her neck to rub against Pythia's jaw. "Very good then." Pythia stood and waved to me. "Toodles!" she said and was gone.

20

"Hello!"

I was fifteen minutes early for my appointment with Dr. Jacoby but there was no one to be seen. The empty, bold-colored waiting room stunk of a familiar sweet scent. Maybe vanilla wafers? "Must be a pediatric dentist," I mumbled as I spotted a wall of shelves filled with antique toys, wooden toys, and vintage games. As I sat back in one of the bubbly-colored chairs, Mystery Date and The Game of Life caught my eye just as the slick, rubbery upholstery gave way and the chair flatulated. Instinctively, I shot up, embarrassed, surveying the vacant room. I chuckled, shaking my head, and inspected the gaseous seat. Tossing out the hidden whoopee cushion and grabbing the only magazine in sight, I kicked back. Thumbing through *The Journal of Nonodontogenic Pain: Ancient Remedies for Modern Dentistry*, I discovered a dog-eared page.

The article was entitled, "Maybe it is your mother's fault, but your father is to blame, too," and its author was none other than Dr. Jan Jacoby. Huh, Jan? I pictured a big teddy-bear of a man. Burly and dark-haired, packing a few extra pounds, stooped with age, grinning at the children's antics. My tongue darted to my tooth as I imagined his thick fingers clumsy in my mouth.

Glancing past the illustration of a baby swaddled in a DNA strand, I scanned the article: *trans-generational epigenetics inheritance, gene modifications, one generation's trauma becomes the legacy of the next.*

I sat up.

A parent's thoughts, emotional experiences, and daily habits influence a baby's gene expression well before conception. Without consciousness, these parental behavioral patterns can determine a trip to the dentist's office, not to mention our future understanding of love, how alive we feel, or even the meaning of life.

"What is this?" I flipped to the cover. *The Journal of Nonodontogenic Pain: Ancient Remedies for Modern Dentistry.*

"Hello, Gabe."

I was surprised by a striking, big boned woman. Her lion's mane of kinky black hair, large beaming wide-set eyes, and luscious full lips all conveyed unyielding confidence. "I'm Dr. Jacoby," she said as I stood to shake her extended warm hand. Her appeal was only increased by her thick Jamaican accent. "You know, Gabe," she said, pointing to the magazine, "there was a time when you would have come here, and I might have suggested the healing powers of a live frog held loosely in your mouth." My brow furrowed, but her big brown eyes sparkled, and her face enlivened. "Oh, don't worry! Now is not that time," she teased before flashing me a mouthful of disastrously crooked and badly stained teeth.

My jaw dropped. I pulled back, anticipating a putrid cloud of halitosis; I almost drew my hand to my face. But when I imagined that squirming frog, I shut my mouth.

"Gotcha!" She bellowed and doubled over, laughing. "That's a dead wid laugh it is. You should've seen the look on your face, man!" She removed the bridge of rotten teeth. "Well, I bet your tooth is the least of your worries now! Please, right this way." Her muscular calves indicated her athletic prowess despite the high heels, pencil skirt, and lab coat. Still giggling, she motioned me through a door and into another bright room. The four walls were muraled with a baseball diamond, complete with fans and a scoreboard. Adjusting her headlight, she pointed to the familiar dentistry chair, now made to look like the Cub's team mascot, and invited me to sit in the bear's lap.

"So, you like working with children?"

"What makes you say that?" She clipped a bib that resembled Ernie Banks's baseball jersey to my shirt.

I cocked my head. "Well, the teeth, the silly chair, and now this room. It's all for kids, right?"

"Oh?" She stuck out her lower lip like she was really considering something. "I guess I'd say I am the dentist for the child within." She smiled, revealing a perfect set of brilliant choppers, and pulled on her gloves and mask, then passed me a ridiculous pair of giant blue sunglasses. The arms were baseball bats.

"Seriously?"

"To protect your eyes. The light is very bright." She tapped her headlight, and her own eyes widened as if to encourage me.

I hesitated and scanned the room.

"Go ahead. We've no time to waste."

I slid on the glasses and sunk into the chair. A hot blush covered my face, and I broke into a sweat.

"Open wide, please." She lifted her brows, then leaning in uncomfortably close to my face, she poked around my mouth, holding my tongue captive in a piece of gauze.

I squirmed like a frog myself. Then raised my hands, shaking my head. "Ah oh ike iss. Am ine. Illy. Ih illy uhsnt urt."

"Oh, I know. No one likes this, Gabe. And of course, you're fine." She pacified me while shoving things in my mouth. "And I'm glad you say it doesn't really hurt." Then she leaned in and whispered, "I know it does, though." Her breath was hot, and then, I heard the whir of a drill.

"Ait, ait!" I said, gagging. "Aut e uh ewing?"

She pulled down her mask and met my frantic eyes. "Your tooth is badly cracked. You're going to need a root canal and crown. I'll proceed with the root canal and install a temporary crown. Then you'll come back for the permanent one."

"Ill it urt?"

"Aren't you sweet. No, it won't hurt me one bit." She smiled kindly.

I shook my head. "Ot ew! Ehh!" I poked at my chest.

"Oh! Will it hurt you? Oh, I see." She laughed. "My mistake. I thought when you'd said it didn't really hurt that you weren't one of those scared little mice."

"Ahat?" I spat out all the contraptions in my mouth. "I'm sorry. This is not what I expected!" I pulled off the bib. "This place, and calling me a scared little mouse." I struggled to sit up. Seeing the mural again, I pointed to it. "This is all for kids." My hand shot through my hair. "I'm not a child!"

"Did you read the article?"

"In the waiting room?"

"Yes."

"No. I mean, some of it, but what difference does that make?"

"Well, it does make a difference. The article was published in *The Journal of Nonodontogenic Pain.*"

"So?"

"So!" she snapped, "if you'd read the article on epigenetic inheritance, you'd know that the baby mice of parents exposed to one stimulation while subjected to electric shock came to associate the first stimulation with pain, even without the electric shock. Those parents genetically passed their intense fear on to their un-born babies. Those little pups lacked the experience of electrical shock but were still fearful when introduced to the first stimulation."

"Okay. This is banana shenanigans crazy now!"

Her nostrils flared. "No, it's not! The mice were pre-conditioned and there-fore programmed for fear before they ever had a chance to decide what they wanted to feel. It's the same for descendants of the survivors of the holocaust or even the children of 911 victims."

I went to speak, but she blasted right over the top of me. "I was under the impression that *you* are a diligent student and serious steward of the prophecy of love! As such, I expected you to have read the suggested article. It *was* dog-eared!" Breathless, she ranted. "I took your earlier comment about pain to mean that your roots of resilience had not been compromised before you were born, and that you were, therefore, not afraid. The article," she took a breath but remained visibly enraged, "helps people understand their fear of dentistry may not be fully based on their own experience. Therefore, most people begin to feel greater confidence in overcoming their fear. You are afraid of love, right?"

"Maybe." I eyed her, weighing what she'd said in the context of my work with Pythia. "Okay, yes. I think so. I mean, I'm new at this. You called me a little mouse and, well, I don't think I need to explain that any further. I'm sorry. I overreacted."

"Apology accepted. Truth be told, I'm new at this, too," she confessed. "In fact, I, too can become, let's say, spirited on matters. I'd appreciate it if you'd give me an-other chance." I looked at her sideways, weighing things. "Given how popular you are, it might be held against me." She looked like she might cry. "Please." But then, sounding defensive, she spouted off again. "This is not entirely my fault. You've not been honest about who you are. Your reviews mention a sense of humor."

"What?"

"Well, everyone has genes, you know? I have genes, too. My people have a long history of fighting to survive. We're a tenacious clan," she said as if that ex-plained something. "What? Humor is essential."

"Okay. But—"

She growled. "Okay, have it your way. So sometimes I can get a little overzealous. Is that what you want to hear?" She stared me down.

"I'm sorry. I don't know what you're talking about."

"Oh, you're gonna make me spell it out, are you? Okay, fine. I can get a bit scrappy, and maybe today I took the humor bit too far. But a sense of humor is important, Gabe. It brings balance to our suffering. It gives us perspective so we can interrupt our genetic programming."

"No, no." I waved my hands.

"Yes, yes, Gabe." She got up in my face looking very determined.

"Yes, of course." I said, putting up my hands. "Yes, yes, I see what you're saying about all that. But what do you mean by my reviews?"

"Really? In all I've said, that's what interests you? Fine! Surely, you know that everyone's given you five stars. Everyone loves you." She mocked, sounding resentful. "Even Socrates."

I sank back in the chair. "I didn't—So, is this—are we—?"

"Yes! I've been charged with supplying you an understanding of epigenetics."

"Are you even a dentist?"

"Of course!!" She turned away. "What a thing to ask." She pretended to busy herself with the dental instruments.

"Hey, look. I'm sorry. I should have known better. Of course, you're a dentist. I can see that." She still gave me the cold shoulder. "This is my fault," I continued, "I should have read the article. Like you said, it was dog-eared." I nodded, even though her back was to me. "I think I might have arrived late." I lied. "If I'd been on time, I would have finished the article, and none of this would have happened. It's really all my fault. I should have expected something like this."

She blew her nose. "Well, you should always be early for your medicals. There's often paperwork, you know."

"You're right."

She sniffled. "You know a little self-awareness goes a long way, and by the way, Gabe, too much is self-absorption. Everyone's jumping through hoops for you. Pythia, bless her heart, I don't know how she's keeping up with you." She blew her nose again, this time making a loud, honking ruckus. "Why are you making that face?"

Caught off guard, I shrugged and stammered.

"I'm here on a Sunday. Did you think about that? No," she said, with her hands flying everywhere. "You can't travel through the portal with a bum tooth. Nor can you miss the unit on trans-generational epigenetic inheritance. Honestly!" Exasperated, she dropped into her native dialect. "Mi nuh not why yuh rankin. You bein charmin an funny, mi raas. Rhaatid!" She rolled her eyes. "Yuh know seh yuh a real battyhole?"

"Okay, I don't know what any of that means, but obviously, I've offended you."

"Work me a work, anuh chicken me a jerk!"

I shrugged. "Again, I'm sorry. Please, can we—"

"Mercy me. Talk and taste your tongue, man." She eyed me down. "The feet of your ancestors certainly have plodded a path of misunderstanding where love is concerned, and I might add, a well-paved path!"

"Okay, okay. Let's not—You know what? Just tell me what you want me to learn."

"You'll listen? Oh, really, will you now? Mister I don't trust anyone, Mister Waa Waa nobody loves me?"

I closed my eyes and took a breath before I reopened them. "There's no reason for name-calling. I am sorry. Yes, I want to hear what you have to say."

"Really?" She rolled her eyes. "Cause I'm not just speakin' to hear my own words."

"Yes, really."

She cleared her throat. "Well," she said, taking the stool and rolling up to me. "The beliefs you have about love: Love hurts. Love is sacrifice. Love is elusive. These are the beliefs of your ancestors. Your mom, your dad, your grandparents, and their parents. As well as the ones you have formed based on your education and personal experiences."

"My real dad is dead. I don't know anything, really, about him, and honestly, I don't really know what my mom thinks about love either." I chuckled, shaking my head, remembering how I'd thought my love life had nothing to do with my mom.

"Their choices don't have to predict yours, and just because you don't think you know your dad, you do. He gave you his emotional download at insemination. And your mother automatically fed you hers alongside vital nutrition, and an ongoing host of emotional hormones, all the way up until your birth. Don't let them and that fetal hothouse impose your adult brain today. Break the pattern, man. Morph into something new and brilliant. Change your mind. Change your life. Change the world."

I nodded, thinking.

"Don't let those multi-generation transactions activate specific receptor proteins in your cells and trigger a cascade of physiologic, metabolic, and behavioral changes that create a reality where love is to be feared but longed for like some sad heartache song. You *can* change these complex and historic biological transactions that underlie your DNA programming of love."

I searched her face.

"You make too many assumptions. That's your programming. Like the little baby mice. Why do you make that face?"

"I'm sorry. I guess it's the baby mouse thing."

"Oh, you're too big of a man to be a mouse? A big man knows the baby mouse inside himself."

"Okay." I hesitated, worried she'd fire up again, but despite that, I said, "You know, no offense, but, well, you're not what I expected."

"I never am," she said like it was a truth that made her mad. "Please?" Her voice was sweet-tempered as she led me by the elbow to recline in the chair. I obliged, admiring her beauty while she re-pinned the childish bib. "And I know you know what's it like to feel as if you never meet other's expectations. But how much of that did you learn, and how much of is honest genetics. Now that's the question. Isn't it?" Looking down at me she pulled on gloves and a mask.

21

In the elevator watching the doors close, something bubbled in my brain while my tongue busied itself obsessing over the changes. Did I have a tendency to absorb responsibility for things that weren't mine, making them about me when they weren't? The numbered buttons above my head illuminated my descent, and when the elevator stopped, I waited for the ding and the doors to open.

Outside, I unlocked my bike and climbed on, thinking a little self-awareness probably did go a long way. I could also see my propensity for too much and how it did lead to self-absorption. Balancing on the bike without thinking, my legs pushed against the pedals propelling me toward home while my mind cranked its own wheel. Up in my head, passing through the little town, I paid no attention to the people out and about on a Sunday. Could it be I was comfortable feeling guilty? Did making it my fault provide me a false illusion of control?

Dude, you do have a way of making yourself special like that. Why not focus on the fact they're all pulling for you. Even Socrates.

I frowned, never appreciating the lack of traffic.

Yeah, well, Mendes, you being a real darling won't change what's wrong with you.

Fighting myself, pushing through the burn, I searched the archives of my mind. Why would I feel at home as a victim? Flipping through memories, I scanned for some ancestral bedrock of failure? Fear? Inferiority? Unlucky in love?

Growling, I huffed up the hill past Dot's Dinner and Half Fast Subs, sweating against the forces of gravity, fighting the familiar doubt already blooming in my stomach. How many of my ancestors had been afraid of intimacy and given up on love? How doomed was I? I don't wanna die alone, misunderstood, and unloved.

I shook my head, battling the old desire to give in, and flew past the retail stores: Meow, Meow, Albums on the Hill, and A Little Piece of My Heart. I stood to pump the pedals while beating down the destructive possibilities of such an ancient underpinning. Certainly, someone before me had dared to love and be loved.

Yeah, and then they died. Get real, Mendes, love's not your game.

I rode the bike hard, straight up the hill, while my mind furiously ransacked the past. A flash of My Ex and I, standing with a thick dead zone between us. "You're a drag," she'd scream. You're impulsive and unreliable, I'd think. But I'd only curl my lip.

A girl in college, Eva, Ava? How she'd sit on the edge of the bed, hopeful. Her back to me, waiting, wanting me to ask her to stay. But I'd only roll to face the wall until the bed shifted when she'd stood. Silent with my back to her. I'd listened for the sound of her gathering her clothes from the cold floor, then the door carefully closing. Relieved she was gone, I'd roll over.

My legs burned. My mind reeled. Why was I afraid to be honest? Even with myself?

Don't be a baby, Mendes. Get real and grow up.

Refusing to downshift, I plowed through the shame and headed toward the front range. The mountains, the wall of granite always there to the west. Always before me. "Arghhh," I roared, and a hot tide slapped my brain, walloping me, it washed out everything. Leaving only the bones of my own love beliefs. The very marrow of my love genes. My parent's story.

Eight years old, fidgeting in the doorway of my mom's bedroom while she made the bed, I waited until she'd turned her back. "How did you meet dad?" I asked with downcast eyes. She hesitated, then turned with pursed lips and pointed to the floral bedspread. I joined her and together we carried it toward the headboard, folded it back before pulling the quilt over the top of the pillows, and tucked the excess beneath them. She smoothed out the wrinkles, then patted the bed. "Come here." I sat near but not next to her, pinching and twisting a tuft of the spread.

"Well, when I was a girl, I dreamed of the mountains. You see, where I'm from, the earth stretches for miles, flat as the palm of my hand," she'd said, showing me, forgetting I'd once lived there too. "It's funny how stuck a person can feel in nothing but space. But I did. I felt trapped smack dab at the center of dusty cornfields and the stench of manure." Then she'd looked off and I followed her gaze. That's when, right there in front of me, she turned into the girl she once was and I could see the twelve-year-old girl. Leggy, her curly, chestnut-brown hair tamed by a headband. The side of her bed shoved up against a wall with a window. But unlike in the old photo in my grandparent's albums, this time, in my mind I saw her longing. Her elbows resting on the wide, white-framed windowsill, supporting her chin while she looked past the farms and dreamed how mountains could disrupt the same old thing that seemed to go on forever.

I'd wondered, *Was I a mountain to her, or the unforgiving prairie?* I remembered I'd wished I'd never asked about my dad, wanting to pull at her hand, to drag her away before she disappeared into a place I didn't exist.

But then she'd smiled. "Me and my girlfriend, we couldn't wait to get out," she'd said, and it scared me that she meant it. "Right after graduation, we drove all the way across the country. One of us sleeping while the other drove, taking turns driving for three days." My mom's eyes softened, then she smiled just a little at first until she was grinning and chuckled. She'd looked so happy, and I'd wanted to be in that happiness, too. But it only belonged to her, and the more she told the story, the farther she got from me.

"I fell in love with those mountains," she'd said, taking my chin, her thumb at its cleft, she lifted my gaze to meet hers. "And your daddy! Well, I was head over heels for him. He was a good man." She'd forced a smile over her pain and let me go. "And then, you came along!" She'd kissed the top of my head, the story over. She hadn't told me what I'd wanted to hear, but I knew she was done, and she'd seemed happy, and I didn't want to spoil that. "Go on now," she said smiling like my mother, "little boys should be outside."

As I hopped off my bike to walk it into the garage my tongue played near my tooth. My mother had told me a child's version of the truth. Even then, I knew she was hiding a secret. Something that didn't live up to the mountains, or worse, something they'd devoured instead. "Those mountains," she'd said, worshiping them, as if all the answers were buried deep in the rock.

I took off my helmet and hung it on the handlebars. Was my mother afraid of love? Maybe she couldn't measure up to her beloved mountains. What then? Did she give up? Do I give up on love? Amy popped into my mind. My stomach dropped, my hands went icy. Was it only a matter of time before I checked out? Stopped being alive and pretended I was me, instead of being me?

"No," I whispered. "I won't do that." Besides, I laughed, my mom never gave up on anything! Then I frowned. "Did she?" How could I understand so little about my own mother?

Closing the garage door, my thoughts shifted. This time, I sat in the backseat of my mom's prized Chevy Impala throwing a ball into my stiff new leather glove, sorting out my thoughts as we traveled north with the front range at our side. It was a beautiful day; the sky was as blue as it's ever been, and the man who'd eventually marry my mom was meeting us at my little league game. It was the first time anyone besides her would come just to see me play, and I wished it would rain.

My mom sang along with the radio, her head bobbing as she belted out, "And I'm here to remind you of the mess you left when you went away," and when she finished with the, "You, you, you oughta know" part, I spoke up.

"Did my dad like baseball?"

Eyeing me in the rearview mirror, she turned off the radio. "Yes. Yes, he did." Her whole body nodded. The road wide open before us.

"What was his favorite team?" I challenged.

She made that face she'd make when something stumped her. "Umm, I don't know, love." She tried to make it sound upbeat.

"How do you know he liked it, then?" I asked, pleased I'd caught her in a lie.

"Well, everybody likes baseball, and he probably followed the Buffalos." She looked at me in the rearview mirror. Her head bobbing as she agreed with herself.

"The Buffalos aren't in the Majors, Mom. How did you meet him, anyway?"

"Your dad?" Her reflection eyed me. "Well…."

"I already know all that about the mountains. I want to know *how* you met him."

She looked at me through the mirror again, this time studying me. I could tell she was weighing something. "That's what I am gonna tell you. You gotta be patient. Sometimes stories have more to them than you think they do. Okay?" She waited for me to agree, but I didn't. I wasn't going to give up the advantage I had.

Looking at the road again, she slowed down a just a little. I focused on the predictable white dashes painted on the pavement, consistent and tidy. "So," she began again, "I was working at a breakfast diner, and your daddy came in first thing every morning." She checked me again in the rearview mirror, her eyes framed in its glass.

"Mom," I snapped, "Watch the road!" even though the empty highway stretched out forever in front of us.

"I am. I'm just making sure you're listening." But then she paused as she followed the bend, we headed east into the high plains where soon a creek would snake through the land around stands of scrub trees, the lone cottonwoods would follow. In no time, the mountains would completely disappear.

"I'm listening. Go on." I said, annoyed and impatient, searching the brown dirt and grasses out the window to spot prairie dogs.

"So," she said, "your daddy came in every day and ordered two scrambled eggs, whole-wheat toast, bacon, and a cup of coffee. He was always my first customer." While I couldn't see her watchful eyes, they still made the hair on the back of my neck stand on end and I shivered, feeling prickly.

"Stop looking at me!" I said, pinching my face into a frustrated ball. Then looked away, refusing to see the hurt look on her face.

"Well, after a few weeks of waiting on him, I asked him, 'Aren't you bored of scrambled eggs and bacon every day? Don't you wanna try something else?'" She pretended like she was really asking him as if he were really there. "But he shook his head with all those dusky curls. Your dad had a beautiful head of hair, just like you." I hoped she wasn't looking at me but knew she probably was. I made a mad face and turned my whole body to the window. Behind us, the mountains were getting smaller, fading into the distance. Ahead everything was dull from lack of rain, the creek bed bone dry.

"Well…" and she drew the word out, making it sound friendly, trying to placate me. "Your daddy smiled. He was very handsome, your dad, with his brown eyes and a killer smile. Well, he said, 'Nope.' Just like that, 'Nope.'" She made the word sound like it accounted for everything anyone ever needed to know. "So, I said, 'Well, you could make scrambled eggs at home,' and he said, 'I can't do that.' And I said, 'You can't make scrambled eggs?' And he said, 'I don't come here for the eggs. The eggs are just the way I get to see you.'"

Crossing to the backdoor, the early tulips waved in my yard, brave for growing out of the frozen earth, the sun having only just crossed the celestial equator. They sure didn't have the favor of nature like the daisies would come summer, but still, they bloomed. Their heavy heads burdened their slender stems, yet the brazen flowers swayed in the spring breeze. What intelligence inspires such boldness, such bravery? What kind of god? Why couldn't I have inherited my dad's courage? The world dimmed, and I looked to the sky. Clouds covered the sun.

The musty scent of the old house met me as I unlocked the door. Without the sun, the place was gloomy. What's kept me skeptical of love? Tossing my keys and jacket on the kitchen table, I spotted the heart-shaped crystal from Amy. In my mind I could see her stretching, her T-shirt riding up revealing her soft flesh while she hung it on an old hook. "See," she'd said just a few days ago, "it was always meant to hang here." And with the thought of Amy, the clouds parted. A late afternoon sunbeam shone through the window and cast rainbows around the room.

Cat meowed, rubbing against my legs. "Hey, old girl." I said and squatted as much to scratch her ears as to further improve my own mood. She purred, then satisfied, sat tall with her tail curled at her feet, squinting at me. I guess not all my propensities for love are accumulated from ancestral fear.

I plugged the kitchen sink and ran the faucet. With a squeeze of soap, I swished the water. Maybe it's just my turn to play the tragic hero in a generational saga of love lost. I shrugged and began dropping dirty dishes into the sink, soap suds flying and water splashing. I snatched the tall mug before realizing it was the one Amy had made me, and then with care, I emptied the cold, stale coffee. Was it even possible to divert from such a storyline? Washing the mug, I spied the heart carved inside at the bottom. I imagined Amy's skilled hands throwing the mug on the wheel. Had she told others it was for me? I smiled just enough to feel it.

I called Amy from my desk while I toyed with the Rubik's Cube.

"So, you don't really know what happened?" Amy asked, then mumbled, "Well, I'm one to talk. I don't really know what happened to my dad."

"She's always been vague. He died in a car accident." I shrugged, studying the puzzle until I found myself shifting squares.

"An accident." Amy sounded disgusted. "Why don't they tell us the truth?"

"Right? She's always been guarded about it. As a child and even an adult, I've trusted it was for the best. It was our unspoken agreement."

"Family secrets."

"Family secrets for sure. But one time in college, she took me to this fancy place to tell me something. It was weird. Everything was red: the carpet, the chairs, even the dishes. They played whale music. You know, those mournful recordings, beautiful and haunting. And right in the middle of the place was this aquarium-sized circular tank of jellyfish. Those peaceful transparent, saucer-shaped membranes, just floated in blue, flashing fluorescent colors."

"Where was this? It sounds like a dream."

"I know. The chairs were these giant cocoons of thick foam suspended from the ceiling. Filled with pillows."

"Do you think it was a dream?"

"No, it wasn't a dream. I vividly remember it!"

"Okay. It just sounds a little, I don't know, fantastical?"

"That's because it was. Look, I don't even know why I'm telling you this."

"Don't get upset."

"I'm not upset. I'm just, you know, Amy, a little self-awareness goes a long way. I'm telling you something I've never told anyone. I haven't even told you the most important part, and you're, I don't know, insinuating that I'm delusional! How am I supposed to trust you?"

"I never said that! And it hurts to think you'd wonder if you can trust me. I mean, really? A little self-awareness does go a long way, but too much, Gabe, is self-absorption."

"Ahhh. Wow! And I know that."

"Yeah, well, wow and right back at you. You're not the only person here feeling vulnerable. I don't always know the right thing to say."

My brow furrowed as I imagined her feeling afraid and not knowing what to say, but I said nothing.

"Gabe?"

"Amy." I sighed. "I feel awful."

"Me, too. I'm sorry. I don't think you're delusional. You're right. I was thoughtless."

"No. I was too sensitive." My heart fluttered, but I pushed myself. "Forgive me?"

"Of course. Will you forgive me?"

"I forgive you."

"Thanks. I really do want to hear what you have to say."

I nodded, even though she couldn't see me. "My mom ended up bawling her eyes out," I said, feeling small. "All she could say was, 'It was my fault. It was my fault.' I finally ended up crawling into her chair and cradling her." Blinking back tears, my eyes stung as I told the story. "The two of us, deep inside some weird opening. We just hugged, rocking in this plush den of thick foam. Everything, soft and red. It still feels surreal, but it *was* real."

"What did she mean?"

"I don't know. She tried to tell me something but then looked lost like she needed my help. I was bewildered, scared even. She was so fragile. So much regret. Something about my dad, but I couldn't bear to press her for more."

"The unspoken agreement, again."

"I guess. But what could I do? She was completely undone. Maybe whatever she's hiding is what I'm missing."

Silence fell between us. "Have you ever wondered what it was like to be alive inside your mother's womb?" Amy asked.

"Nooowa!"

"Geez. Let me finish. I mean, that was the time when the two of you were as close as you'll ever be? I wonder what secrets, agreements you shared then that you don't know or even remember? You know, babies are far more intelligent than we've given them credit."

"I know. The article talked about that. But if that's true, how come I don't know if my dad loved me? Shouldn't I know that?" Choked up, I still drove down the unexpected emotion.

"Even though I knew my dad, sometimes it's still hard to believe he loved me given what he did. It doesn't make sense. Why would he die, that way, if he'd really loved me?"

"I know what you mean."

We were quiet. I could hear the wind pick up. Through the window a boy with a backpack strapped to his back leaned into the stiff gust and held on to his baseball cap.

"I'm sorry, Gabe." Then sounding shy, she said, "Gabe?"

"Yeah?"

"*I* love you."

I blinked, then held my breath. "I love you, too," and my voice cracked. "Is that okay?"

"Yeah. It's okay for sure."

The steady rise and fall of Cat's sleep-breathing sedated me until my attention drifted to the backyard. Out the window, the bare boughs of the ash tree reached for the sky. A pair of squirrels scurried about its many branches and then down the trunk. The birdfeeder swung, likely empty. Its contents stolen.

There was an arborist a few years back. The old man limped while he'd pointed. "Whoever chopped that main branch back to a stub did one of the worst things anybody coulda done for this here tree. You see them seeping wounds? This here tree's having a devil of a time healing itself."

Shielding my eyes to the sun, I'd looked into the tree's crown. "I'm sure whoever lobbed off that limb meant the tree no harm. Can you fix it?" I'd asked.

"Welp, it don't matter much now what was meant. Nope, the proof's in the puddin'. But I got a mind to agree. I think the fella didn't know better. But no use crying over spilled milk. What's done is done. Let's get the deadwood outta here now before she starts budding out. Give her some room to breathe." The sixty-something man took out a rope and prepared to climb the hundred-year-old ash.

Cat's twitching whiskers drew me back. Sound asleep she flinched an ear. I stroked her warm body and she purred. "What do you say, Cat?" I asked, lightly tugged one of her legs, "Think I can change the tragic ending of a long-running love story?"

22

Waking well before dawn, I lay in bed with the gentle strumming of Van Morrison's acoustic guitar, and his soulful voice stuck in my head. "To be born again," I whisper-sang in the dark, remembering the boy I once was. How I'd begged my mother to play the album. Humming the poetic song, I flipped on my bedside lamp. The familiar stain appeared, yellow and sprawling across the ceiling. I cocked my head. Peter Rabbit? Chocolate rabbits. Easter.

I sat up. "Storytellers," I said, testing the word. "We're the storytellers!" Cat opened an eye, then the other. She stretched one paw out before the other, then stood and arched her back. "The familial, the cultural, and the experiential. It's all stories; humans learn through metaphor!" I swung out of bed. Cat jumped to the floor. I peed at the pink toilet in the dim light. She sat in the doorway. Her tail curled around her feet, waiting.

"Don't you see?" I'd asked as if she'd answer. "Just as our collective history of stories pervade and saturate our collective understanding of love, so does our personal. And it becomes *our* story. The story *we* tell. I mean, it's what we believe." I finished up at the toilet. "Oh, this is a big breakthrough, Cat," I said, fixing myself. "Though I should have seen it coming." I hurried to wash my hands. "It's been right there in front of me all this time. Romeo and Juliet. Politics and religion. Music. Movies! Television, even. My parent's story." I rushed out of the room. Cat darted past me and was half-way downstairs before she realized I'd headed to my computer.

"These stories are playing on a cellular loop, generation after generation. Songs on the jukebox of life." I grabbed my notebook and ripped through the pages. "Ah, yes, here it is. Oh, that's right!" I laughed, remembering the time in the bar with that grad student who shot me the finger and equated my worth with a bad lawyer joke. I shook my head. "Just a bit self-absorbed," I whispered to myself, blushing. Maybe a lot. Perusing the double-page spread, I examined the rudimentary tables I'd made that night. One entry was underlined, starred, and circled. Van Morrison.

But what makes some stories more important than others? My mind was blank, but my stomach was sick with wistful yearning. I cracked my knuckles, but the nostalgic homesick sadness only prospered. I wrinkled my nose.

"Van Morrison." I stared hard at the two words. "What am I missing?" I muttered, picking up the cube. "My parent's story is really just an anecdote." I palmed the puzzle, feeling its weight. "Something I lost but never had?" I exhaled, blowing out my cheeks. "So the thing I'm missing is something I never had?!"

Frustrated, I wrestled the ancient urge to give up, the kind that had defeated me before I'd met Pythia. But even so, in an instant, I'd slammed the book shut and shoved it just as Cat leaped onto the desk. She dodged it like an athlete, and the book sailed onto the floor. She shot me a look. "Sorry. I know." I bent for the book. "You're right. Pythia will be here soon." I said, but Cat was already pounding down the stairs for the kitchen.

"The scattershot origins of epigenetics." Pythia said, tilting her head, looking concerned and interested at the same time. "Is it the parent cell memory of past emotional states influencing cellular regulation of its offspring's genes? Or is it the collective cultural memory?"

"Or both? And then there's the narrative we bring to the combined two, which is a whole other story."

"Hmm. It's a rabbit hole for sure."

"Yeah."

"What are you thinking?"

"I get stuck, Pythia. Trapped inside some story in my head. All uppity and righteous."

"Indignant?"

"Arrogant even. Or entitled. Like I'm not supposed to have this problem. Like I don't deserve it. With Dr. Jacoby, and even Amy last night, my ego gets in the

way, and I think—I don't know what I think. I guess I think someone's gonna…"
I shrugged, "I don't know, dis me? Tell me I don't understand or that I'm not doing it right. That I'm wrong. I'm not good enough. Take your pick. Or maybe it's some version of all of that victimization at once."

"What does this have to do with your revelation about being a storyteller?"

"Right." I sighed. "Yeah. I'm still figuring that out. It was so clear this morning."

"Hmm." She looked sideways. "It got away from you."

"Yeah." I nodded.

"Slipped away."

"Sure."

"You lost it."

"Yes." I nodded. "I lost it after barely having it! Story of my life!" I threw my hands into the air.

"Ah. Is that the story?"

"I guess it is."

"That's your story?"

I thought for a moment. Romances. Career. Even my own dad. "Yeah, that's my story, alright."

"Is it anyone else's story?"

"What do you mean? Who? Like anybody? I guess. Probably."

"What's your favorite movie? First answer."

"Ahh…*Gladiator*."

"Second favorite."

"Okay. *Eternal Sunshine of the Spotless Mind*."

"Third, no thinking."

"Um." I laughed. "*Big Fish*."

"How are these similar to Van Morrison, Nirvana, and, is it Barenaked Ladies?"

I nodded, thinking. "Bittersweet. Nostalgic. Longing for acceptance. Regretful?" I searched some deep archive. "Maybe just angry." I shrugged. "Hopeful?" I nodded. "Yeah, I think they are all hopeful." I nodded. "Why are you making that face?"

"Pandora and her box. Let's put a pin in that shall we? For now, use another word?"

"Another word?"

"Yes. Another word for hope."

"Faith?"

"Faith. Television shows?"

"Television shows?"

"TV programs you've liked over the years."

"Oh. *The Simpsons. Family Guy.*" I smirked. "Then, *Breaking Bad,* the first few seasons. *The Wire.* Omar Little, best character ever. *Wilfred.* Well, I didn't really watch *Wilfred.* My Ex liked it.

"Is that the one about a man dressed like a dog."

I nodded, rolling my eyes.

"Similar themes?"

"Um…justice for the underdog. But I'm not really an underdog. Am I?"

"Are you?"

"No. But I feel like that." There was that victim thing again.

"Is that your story?"

"The one where I *feel* like I'm missing something? Or the one where I'm missing something?" I sighed, running my hand through my hair. "The one where I feel like a victim or the one where I am one?"

"It's a bit of a chicken and an egg, isn't it? Do notice though, that the boy you once were and the man you are today, both followed their nature, clumsily at times, but still with some faith that things would work out. You stayed in the game so to speak. Hero in your own story. Perhaps that's the more accurate story?"

"I never thought of it that way," I said, grinning and then shrugged. "Yeah. Maybe. Like a Cinderella story or rags to riches?"

"Victim to victor." She paused. "Everyone is the victim of something at one time or another. But such cause does not ensure a lasting effect."

"Right. Campbell talked about that. The hero's story. Causing an effect."

"Ready?"

Energetically, I reached for Pythia's hand and though we were an unfathomable number of miles apart, my excitement was instant. "We drop our arms to our sides and relinquish our history of losing our shirts in favor of the lapis rings," she orated, and the words initiated the familiar gravitational sensations. This time fully surrendering to the centrifugal force and the energy of the electric blue lights, I marveled at the rainbow lights before the hot jolt of red with its earthy aroma became the familiar clearing. That day, we landed at the edge of a golden patch of barley glowing in the afternoon sun.

Under a cerulean sky Pythia lifted her chin to the pastoral blue while bucolic white clouds, the likes of a Constable painting, drifted above us. "Oh, glory I am awakened!" She opened her arms. "Ah, the scent. Like the top of an infant's head or a horse, don't you think?" she headed into the heart of the field bathed in golden light.

"A horse? You mean like the sweet smell of hay? Okay, yeah."

"We are at the edge of truth here," she called back, high-stepping through the tall grasses. I followed, lacking her grace and feeling clumsy. "The beginnings of simple goodness," she yelled from the field's far edge and twirled in circles like a child, letting the tall grasses brush her palms. "Barley," she said, when I'd finally caught up. "It's symbolic of an awakening."

"What's this?" I pointed to a basket atop a folded blanket.

"Romance, I suppose." She took in another deep breath. "The scent is heaven." Then Pythia waved with great enthusiasm to a woman wearing a bonnet headed right for us from the woods' edge. "Jane!" Pythia shouted. The energetic woman waved in return, cutting a path without haste. The fabric of her high-waisted pale blue dress trailed behind, mowing down the grasses.

Pythia cupped her hands around her mouth, "We've found your picnic," she yelled. Then turning to me, clearly excited, she handed me the blanket. "Help me, please. She's coming!"

While down on all fours hurried and spreading the corners, Jane's pointed-toe slippers appeared. I lifted my gaze to a tall, slender woman, mature but with a rosy complexion that suggested she liked the outdoors. Her expressive eyes, wide-set and green, dominated her face and were only softened by the hints of girlish, curly brown hair spilling from her bonnet.

Pythia took Jane's hands. "It is so good to be in your company." Then, looking down to me, Pythia said, "Jane Austen, please meet our postulant of love."

I stood, taking Jane's hand. Her nose and chin were strong, making her overall appearance intimidating. "It's nice to meet you," I said. She blushed, then lowered her head and I blushed, too.

"Please," Pythia motioned to the spread and basket, "shall we picnic?"

"Oh, let's do!" Jane shifted to seat herself.

Pythia emptied the basket and passed around white china plates and linen napkins. Jane filled our stemmed glasses with sparkling cider and we helped ourselves to the generous spread. "Do tell of your thoughts on developing a story." Pythia encouraged Jane while licking sweet brown jelly from her fingertips.

Jane nodded, and then, sounding apologetic, said, "Although one might prefer to enjoy the pleasant party rather than to commandeer it with tutelage. But that is our purpose, I suppose." She finished a bite of bread over which she'd thickly slathered not only butter and figs, but a thick slice of chicken. She, too, licked her fingers and lips clean of the sweet and savory tastes before dabbing with her napkin. "Observation, improvisation, and participation." Jane lifted her brow looking my way. "This is the cornerstone of a good story." She picked a red grape from its stem, and before popping it into her mouth, she added, "Although, I must admit to you, I wanted to *create* stories. I didn't want to be a storyteller. I think we are the same that way." She hesitated chewing, then looked off. "Perhaps, though, I've been less successful than you."

My brow furrowed. I studied her.

"Oh, yes," she said, directly to me, "There is a difference between creating stories and telling them," she said without inviting discussion and took another bite of her open-faced sandwich. Then lifting her glass she stopped short of drinking. "On reflection, I can see I've invested far too much time convincing myself otherwise." She returned the glass to her lips and hesitated before turning to me again. "But I do hope the course of my life didn't stop me from telling others that love is valuable and worthy. That it is not measurable in money or acquisitions, but evident in the life one leads." She brushed her lap. "Well then, I do digress." She finally took a drink.

"A story," she said, sitting straight and speaking like an expert. "Your story about love, isn't just an idea. It must accomplish something. That is the challenge. The expression of the idea requires a clear purpose that guides action."

I shot Pythia a side glance and she motioned for me to jump in. "I know what you're saying, but before meeting Pythia," I gestured to Pythia, "I thought a story just happened."

"That is a common misunderstanding. Creating a story is work. The hardest part might be remaining equanimous. Without equanimity the story is not easily shared. It is in the collaboration that a story comes to life."

"By equanimous you mean," I paused thinking, "composed?"

"Yes, having emotional stability, self-collected. Particularly in times of high stress. One can't collaborate in a dysregulated state."

Pythia leaned my way and in a low voice, added, "The deep understanding that all of life is ephemeral, even in crisis."

Jane eyed me. "Something wrong?"

"Oh, nothing." I shrugged, minimizing, holding my breath. "I'm just remembering something with my girlfriend." I took a breath. "I have a girlfriend. And I wanna create a love story that is strong and self-possessed. But...I think I think too much."

She nodded. "I see what you mean. You think that you think you think too much."

"It's a lot of thinking," Pythia added.

"I know." I frowned. "And I don't usually think with a clear purpose that defines action. Instead, I jump to conclusions. I'm no good at equanimity and I didn't even know collaboration was a thing with love interests," I said, getting worked up, but then paused. "Except with Amy."

Jane popped another grape into her mouth. "I learned quite by accident that a story can become tiresome at about the time when it should become interesting. Perhaps you're there now." She reached for another grape, pulling it from its woody vine. "But if not," she paused to consume the sweet fruit, "your story could become lazy. Giving up and taking the easy old way that goes nowhere." She swallowed and patted her thin lips with a linen cloth. "The middle is the time to wake up, smell the barley, and prepare for harvest." She picked through the nut bowl. "A picnic always pays well. It's never time lost, only deferred for later." I watched while she ate only the cashews.

Sounding kind, Pythia spoke, "Love requires space to be nourished so that it can grow and later provide shelter. Think a bit less of your failings, agape mou. Consider instead where you're headed."

I nodded. "Equanimity. Victim to victor."

"Yes." Jane helped herself to another grape, and Pythia scooted the bowl in her direction. "I am afraid I have quite an appetite, and it may not be very lady-like. My apologies," she said, unbothered. "Pythia is correct. It isn't what we say or think that defines us, is it? But what we do. Nevertheless young man, and all the same, great stories are to be told in style. Truthful and not dressed up to resemble something they're not. There is no place for self-absorbed, tedious and prolonged ramblings."

I bit my lip knitting my brows.

You do have a tendency to rattle on as you wander the internal workings of your mind, dude.

I cleared my throat.

She shook her head and spoke with great certainty. "Verbosity in a story is only a distraction, it hinders intimacy. The more you explain, the less it is understood."

"Yep. Got it." I was curt but only in an effort to contain my compulsion for justification.

"Humor is necessary. Is it not?" Pythia asked. "It seems it eases the burden of sorrow. At certain junctures in a story, wit and amusement, even merriment, can provide perspective."

"Agreed, agreed. It lightens the load so that the heart can heal and trust that there is promise in the story. But know the difference between your story and its plot. Do you grasp my meaning?"

I looked at Pythia, and she nodded. "Um, well, like the things that happen, going out to dinner, buying a house together, or having children even, these things are not love or even evidence of love. They are the things that can reveal love."

"Yes," Jane said agreeing with an approving look, "like the patience of a parent, the investment in commitment, nourishing the body and the soul." She leaned back and, resting on her elbows, reclined on the blanket with her legs outstretched. She turned toward Pythia. "I am afraid it is hopeless. I am simply not minding my best manners. Do forgive my penchant for comfort, but I am settling easily into this one's own underestimated heroic qualities." She nodded in my direction.

"He is a remarkable character." Pythia eyed me while taking a slice of pear. "Alive and vibrant with contradictions. He is determined to thrive. And is committed to the dialectic of love."

"I can hear you both, you know." I blushed, playing along.

"Forgive me, won't you? It is only that there is no charm equal to tenderness of heart." Jane smiled, and reaching in my direction, she touched my arm. "Know that the best characters always have heart. It is their purpose and is contained in their story." Her ankles kept time with an invisible pendulum, her feet swinging back and forth. "Even when they haven't discovered it themselves, they still speak and act in congruence with their purpose; consciously or unconsciously. It moves the story forward. Anything else compromises, or worse, halts the story."

Was she suggesting my over-sensitivity aided my purpose? Could it even weave strength through my love story?

"You can be tender of heart and equanimous," Pythia added, seeming to read my mind. Then looking reassuring, she said, "Such balance can lead to a greater purpose in life and in love. It provides integrity."

"Balance," I said, trying on the word. It was true that my emotional outbursts with Amy had fueled a deeper understanding of myself and us. Despite the conflict, they had directed a new course of action.

"Balance." She repeated.

"See that cloud?" Jane said pointing. "The one that looks like a buggy. Chapters are like carriages; they are useful in that they allow you to travel and arrive. Each one is like a place on a map, perhaps seeming unlike each other, but all finally taking you somewhere specific."

"Oh, Earth is a lovely place from which to witness the heavens." Pythia rested back on her elbows. "Oh, I do see it now! Although it is losing one of its wheels."

"It looks more like a horse now," I said, joining them, leaning back on my elbows. We watched as the clouds passed. Then, breaking the silence, I asked, "But was the cloud a buggy and then a horse because of the association by language? Or was it always anything we wanted it to be?"

Pythia turned toward me. "Neurolinguistic programming: cause and effect? Or the infinite possibilities available via Higgs: causing an effect?"

"Was it ever even a cloud?" Jane challenged.

"Right?" I sat up. "Things don't have to be limited by your personal knowledge. They can be whatever you want them to be. You know, like letting one thing turn into another. Not jumping to conclusions. Not just accepting things as one singular thing." I leaned in. "Maybe there's always something waiting to become something else. I can't quite explain it, but maybe a love story can be created out of anything once you pay it enough attention. You know, give it time, like Pythia was saying."

"Miracles are possible," Pythia said.

"And reasonable," Jane added. "They are everyday occurrences, made more from that which goes unnoticed and less from the mystical. They are often accumulated from a series of quiet, unexceptional events. Take the caterpillar, for example. Did you know that if you sliced her open, you'd find her wings already folded neatly inside? And still, she faithfully eats everything in sight, hangs herself upside down under a leaf, and molts into a glistening chrysalis. Inside that cocoon, she reduces herself to a primordial goo before transforming herself into something worthy of the wings she always had within. This miracle happens as regularly as the seasons." Then Jane spoke directly to me. "Take my words to heart. Create a deep interest in an everyday story, and you will inspire the desire for manifestation. Not just for yourself, but for many others. The conscious collaboration of characters will exalt greatness."

"Without miracles, there is no faith in oneself, no faith in humanity," Pythia said like it was a fact.

Jane looked to the horizon. "Our hero must pay homage to the ordinary. Without this practice, the character is unsound. Erroneous in understanding! Deceptive even in observation of the day-to-day." She spoke with her hands. "Unable to recognize the daily marvels and mysteries and therefore simply can't inspire trust or faith." Worked up, Jane shook her head, hesitated, then turned to me. "I loved once," she confessed, searching my face, "and would have married for love had I not been declined for lack of money and social position. Later, I was asked to marry, but due to lack of love, it was *I* who declined." Looking forlorn, she faded off. Then catching herself, she enlivened with a shrug, shaking something off.

"Young man," she sounded quite serious, "your story may wander, but aid it in its arrival. It is fine to flow and meander, to bubble up or rush rapidly, to take unexpected twists and drops, but always turn up somewhere." She imparted with great passion, "Like love, a story is not a high art form. It is accessible and easily felt. Incongruences, ridiculous matters, and romantic sentiments prophesize its salient themes. Unexpected sage advice can provide divine intervention. Our teachers are many and can take unexpected forms. Take a break to consider the revelation before savoring it. And lastly, fight the need for resolution. That's something I never quite worked out." She admitted the last part in a whisper.

Still leaning on bent elbows, Jane looked to her feet, watching them keep time to something I couldn't hear. She chuckled. "Friendship is certainly the finest balm for the pangs of disappointed love." She reached for Pythia's hand. "I am grateful." She cupped Pythia's hand in hers before releasing Pythia and turning toward me. With a soft demeanor, she said, "I hope that we too can be friends."

"Of course," I said and with that Jane took both my hands and gave them a sturdy squeeze.

Letting me go, Jane said, "After all, none of us want to be in calm waters all our lives, and if adventure does not befall one, one must seek it out, I say!"

Pythia raised her glass. "To the story of love!"

Jane grabbed the bottle of sparkling pink elixir and poured our glasses full. "To love."

"To love." And we each hurried to catch the bubbly that was spilling over.

"Well, the sun is setting, my dearests," Jane said, with some apology.

"Indeed." Pythia stood to embrace her friend, and I hurried to my feet, wishing the sun would hang around longer. But at least the field glowed in the rosy glow of the fading light.

Jane slid on her white gloves and extended her hand. "It has been my pleasure."

I cupped her hand in mine, and then, emboldened, I dropped to one knee and kissed her hand. She blushed. "The pleasure has been all mine," I said, hoping she'd remember me more as a Colonel Brandon than a dashing John Willoughby.

23

I landed in my bed with a familiar whoosh that sounded like I'd dropped from the sky, but felt more as if I materialized. Cat appeared in the doorway, silhouetted by the moonlight. She mewed before sashaying across the floor with her tail held high, then jumped up onto the bed. Petting her, I caught a glimpse of myself reflected in my darkened bedroom window. I observed my reflection, observed his gentle manner, and noted the ease in his face and body. Outside of my mother, my relationship with Cat was the longest in my life. I kissed her head and scratched her ears. When she'd had enough, she kneaded the pillow beside me and curled up on it. "Comfy old girl?" I tugged her tail. She purred, and I flipped on my bedside lamp. Seeing it was still early enough to call, I picked up my phone.

"Hey, Mom." I heard the hiss of an egg frying and then the sound of a plate being pulled from a cupboard. "Sounds like you're having a late dinner."

"Hey, you." She sounded bright. "I know. Time gets away from me in these lighter, longer days. So, calling your old mom twice in a matter of a few weeks, huh? What's up? Everything okay?"

"I called to talk to you about something, Mom." The sounds of cooking diminished, and I heard her pull out a chair.

"What's wrong?"

"Everything's okay. Nothing's wrong. I just want to talk about ... dad." I rubbed my forehead and hoped I was doing the right thing. I didn't want to hurt her.

"What do you want to know?"

"Well, that's a good question." I scratched my head. "I don't really know, other than I've realized that I don't really know much about what happened. And I don't know why but we both seem uncomfortable talking about it," I said, lifting my brow in a soft arch hoping to sound kind. Waiting, I twisted the bedspread listening for her response. "Mom?" I said, my brow creasing in alarm. "Are you there? Are you crying? Oh, Mom, why are you crying? Mom? I'm coming over."

"I loved your dad very much." Her words were an odd greeting as she let me into the condo where I'd grown up. She motioned to the sofa and I sat while she poured me a cup of tea from a pot cozied on the living room table. The sharp, bright scent of peppermint wafted from the cup. "Take off your coat," she said, standing over me in a pink robe and fuzzy slippers, seeming composed, but her red, puffy face betrayed her. I pulled off my gloves with a bit of trouble and unzipped my jacket, feeling short of breath. Methodically, she hung my jacket on the back of a kitchen chair.

An untouched plate of two fried eggs and a slice of whole wheat toast loaded with jam sat cold on the kitchen table. Returning to the living room, she poured herself a cup of tea. The cup rattled in the saucer as she held it with a trembling hand. "I guess I'm a little nervous," she admitted, stooped and seeming bewildered, looking frail. The skin on her hands loose, transparent, revealing the blue veins beneath. Tendons obvious, knuckles enlarged. Her brown eyes searched my face from behind her stylish glasses. Then she turned away pushing her curly gray hair behind her ears, shuffling her slippered feet as she sat on the sofa.

"It's okay. I'm nervous, too." I stood, taking the cup from her, and returned it to the coffee table. "Sit down, Mom."

"Gabe," she said, still standing, making my name sound like a question. "I loved your dad so much. I don't think I'll ever love like that again." Her words carried no meaning for me. I had no context for them, and for a split second, I thought of my stepfather. "Gabe?" She panicked, her mouth agape as she panted.

"I'm here. I'm listening." I ran my hand through my hair. "But let's sit down." I lowered myself, but she still stood.

"I don't know where to begin." Tears ran down her face.

"Mom. Please. Sit down."

"We were inseparable, your dad and I," she started, then looking more at ease, she finally sat. "Madly in love, I guess you'd say." She made a slight smile. "Living together in a bedroom he'd rented in this little house in the canyon with four or five people. The two of us sleeping in his single bed." She paused, remembering. "It was the late seventies," she added as if that explained something. "Everybody was talking about free love and how people shouldn't own each other. We were going to just show up for one another. You know, just be there. No contracts." She hesitated. "I believed in it. The goodness of making a commitment out of love and not obligation. But when I found out about you, well, it turned out that I really wasn't that cool. I was pretty terrified of having a baby without marriage." She smirked. "I was ashamed of my lacking conviction. Embarrassed even that I was pregnant. I struggled to tell your dad, but your dad," her eyes twinkled, "he saw how my body was changing, and he was elated. Beside himself with excitement! And when I said I didn't think I could do it without a husband, he said, 'Well, let's get hitched then!'" She laughed, then shook her head. Her gray curls bounced, and I grinned before she burst into tears.

"Oh, mom." I gasped and reached for her hand.

"He was such a good man, Gabe." She nodded, squeezing my hand, fighting her tears.

Locking my jaw, I turned from her. Not meaning to, I took my hand with me. She rubbed my shoulder. Pulling myself together, I looked at her. "What happened after that?"

"I had to tell my parents." She sighed. "I was scared to death. They'd already disapproved. Your grandfather referred to your dad as, 'the pie in the sky potter,'" she spat, imitating my grandfather's cocky posture. Deriding him, she mocked in his voice. "'What kind of a man makes a living selling coffee mugs?' But once you were born, he said little, though still made his feelings well known. And my mother whispered, 'What kind of a life is this for a family?'" My mom's eyes narrowed. Then she frowned and threw the palms of her hands up and said, shrugging. "By then we lived in a two-bedroom apartment. We had a queen bed. You had a crib. It didn't matter." She scoffed, her face all pinched up.

I flinched, remembering my judgmental grandparents. The ways they managed their expectations: the cold shoulder, looks of disapproval, and the-all-too-often, "Is this the best you can do?"

"I'm sorry, Gabe," my mom said, touching my knee, "I'm so sorry." She groaned and closed her eyes, and when they re-opened, she grit her teeth.

"They wore me down, Gabe. I'm not proud of it, but it's true. I started to doubt your dad. I began to believe I couldn't trust him. Which made no sense. It was completely irrational." She looked as if she was still trying to figure it out. "I was young and scared, but I don't think I even knew I was scared. I just thought I was wrong, and they were right about your dad. That he wasn't the man I thought he was." She studied my face as if the answer were there. "The whole thing doesn't make any sense." She shook her head. "If they loved me, why would they create so much doubt for me? I lost trust in myself, your dad, and the dream of us. It was awful! I was desperate!" she said leaving her mouth open while the rest of her face contorted with disbelief.

"Mom." I tried to meet her frantic eyes. "Mom," I said, but she wouldn't look at me. "Mom!" I touched her shoulder.

She recoiled, "Don't touch me!" she snapped, then catching herself she frowned and shut her eyes for a moment before bottling something up. Then opening them, her gaze fell as her fingers worried at the edges of the belt on her robe. "I'm sorry," she said looking at me, then fixed her robe and smoothed her hair. Feigning composure, she reached for the teapot, then spotting our still full cups, she stopped short. "Oh! What am I doing?" Disgusted, she snatched her cup, the tea swirled and spilled over the rim. Her pink robe absorbed the brown stain. I quickly reached for mine and looked at her sideways as we pretended to be interested in the over-brewed tea, but her irritation prevailed. "Well, our tea's gone cold," she lamented, "What difference does it make? It was too strong anyway."

"It's okay. It's not bad." I set the cup on the table. "I'm okay, mom."

"Of course you are, but everything's ruined." We sat silent, and then she surprised me by standing. "I'll make more tea," she declared.

"Mom." I tugged at her hand. She flinched.

"I'm fine!" She pulled away. Her face fell, and with her jaw trembling again her mouth hung open. She looked more than hurt. She looked damaged. "Oh, what have I done, Gabe?"

"It's okay." I held her with my eyes. She exhaled loudly, waited a beat before nodding, and sat beside me. "Everything's okay, Mom," I said and this time she let me rub her back. Then without warning, she turned directly toward me.

"But is it?" she asked, her eyebrows hunkered down, making her look cross. She shoved her unruly gray hair behind her ears. "Because it wasn't fine, Gabe.

I had to pick between the love I had for your dad and some loyalty I believed I owed my parents. That's no choice." She rubbed her forehead and then got in my face. I drew back from her hot breath and the smell of sweat mingling with her usual earthy scent, but she didn't seem to notice. "I wasn't strong enough. I couldn't handle the pressure. I caved, deciding to see things their way. To turn your dad into something he wasn't—a failure! Arghhh!" She ran her hands into her hair, grabbing fists full. I edged away, but she wasn't paying any attention to me. She ranted, the cadence of her words determined, the volume climbing. There was no stopping her. "After you were born, I was always negotiating the difference between my parents and your dad. Trying to fix something that wasn't wrong in the first place. I was out of my mind. Afraid I'd lose him. But not because he was pulling away. It was because I was pushing him, despite the fact that all I ever wanted was to pull him in. It was insane!" She turned to me. Her eyes were wide and feral. "It. Made. No. Sense." She pounded a fist in the palm of her hand.

I drew back from her. "Mom," I tried to speak, but she wasn't listening and babbled on.

"My God, Gabe. Can you ever forgive me? It was the biggest mistake I ever made." She blubbered, her sentences became garbled. "I didn't know, I was young. Phone calls and letters. They badgered me!" She stood to pace, her hands flying, her body engaged in imitating her parents again. "'You're making a big mistake,'" she spat a mime of her own mother before switching to her father, saying, "'You'll regret this for the rest of your life.' Oh, I regretted it, alright. And for the rest of my life," she fired the words, "but not the way they thought I would." Worked up, her chest heaved. "Gabe." She lurched and hurried toward the sofa, her robe falling open, nearly tripping. She sat closer than she had before warming me with the heat of her heart working overtime. "I loved your dad." She took my hands. "He. Took. Very. Good. Care. Of. Us." She shook my hands with each word.

"Mom," I said meeting her eyes.

"No, no." Her eyebrows arched. "No, Gabe. It's true."

"I know, Mom. I believe you. I do."

"You believe me?" Her face softened.

I nodded. "Of course. Yes, I believe you. I do."

"We would've been really happy together," she said, reminiscent, gazing off before her eyes drifted to the floor and she settled. Everything about her lightened as she imagined another possibility for us. She smiled, observing some far-off, brilliant star-studded night that offered a new perspective. But when she turned back to me, she muttered, "If only I could have broken the spell." Looking bereft, as if she were watching her own words, promising clouds that drifted out her mouth and floated away into nothingness. Her only hope gone. "It was all my fault." Her words were barely audible. "I did something real and awful. Something unforgivable."

"Mom!" My voice was sharp, worried she'd drifted into la-la land. Frightened, I grabbed her. She stiffened and fought my hug. "Please, Mom," I begged her to be normal. To be my mom and not a grieving, guilt-ridden woman. Petrified of what she might say next, I sobbed into her neck, "Please. Don't."

With my words, she loosened her defense; her body melted and then heaved. She wailed, "It's too late, Gabe. It's already done." We held each other tight, rocking to our own wretched funereal sounds, a dark, old, lullaby. Our deep shared grief soothed something in both of us, and when the haunting subsided, she pulled away. "We loved each other. You have to believe that," she demanded. "Do you?"

I nodded, blurry-eyed and snotty-nosed.

"Now you have to know. I have to tell you."

I nodded.

"Okay," she said, nodding with me.

"We loved each other," she repeated, gauging the strength of the touchstone. Then stronger, she continued, her voice now measured. "After you were born, we fought about money. I'm ashamed of myself. There was no real concern. Your dad was an adjunct professor in the fine arts department. He had a few wholesale accounts for his pottery. The choices we were making weren't so untraditional. But I couldn't reconcile that I wasn't living my mother's life of a Midwestern wife of a lawyer and mother." She lowered her head, picked at a loose string from her terry robe, and tugged it. The thread seemed endless and finally caught, puckering the fabric. She yanked, and it broke, leaving a run in the nappy cotton. "Eventually, we fought so much we lost trust in each other. And that's when I did the terrible thing." Her words were chilling, but her tone was dissonant.

"I was so wrong. So childish. Ultimately dangerous." She sounded robotic but still owned the adjectives. "I pretended to have an interest in your dad's best friend. An artist who'd left studio work for a corporate job. Naturally, we fought. Your dad was hurt. Crushed. Blindsided, of course. And the whole thing blew up in my face. It spiraled out of control. I hadn't wanted any of that."

Something seemed to occur to her. "But you know?" she said, still speaking in a low disturbing monotone. "Maybe I did. Maybe deep down, I had wanted him to leave. Not because I didn't love him. But because I just couldn't take it anymore. In the end," she looked away from me, "maybe it made things easier if my parents were right. If I trusted them, instead of him. Or myself." Returning her gaze to me, she met my eyes unflinchingly and confessed, "I hurt him so badly. I will *never* forgive myself for what I did."

I was relieved when her face screwed up again, and she hid her head in her hands. At least she seemed alive when she slobbered and spit. "He was furious and walked out." She gasped. "I hurt him, and he didn't come back!" she bawled. I lowered my head into my hands; the weight of holding back my own agony was unbearable. I turned away from her, but she went on. I wrapped my hands around myself and rocked. Cradling myself like I was a baby, I was utterly incapacitated. I writhed until I became so disabled I crawled to the floor where I'd lain covering my face, trying to keep the awful sounds to myself. She went on and on. The room pulsed and throbbed, keeping time with the hastened beat of my heart. When I couldn't listen anymore, I covered my ears.

Still, I heard her. "I called his friends, the university and then finally the police. Everyone knew of our unhappiness, and after the police investigated, they said your dad likely deserted me, us. I didn't believe it. I just didn't. But pretty soon, it was a month, then two, then three. What could I think? I began to believe that he had left us."

"Stop!" I brought my knees up to my chest. I groaned and then heaved so deeply I thought I would die.

"Oh, Gabe!" Awakened, she hurried and joined me on the rug, cocooned me until we became an entangled, sloppy human mess of saline fluids. Time passed. Our sounds diminished. I wiped my nose with the back of my hand, and she let me go. More like herself, she shared soothing words and stroked my hair. Slowly, we rose and returned to the furniture. She blew her nose enough times the coffee table, littered with all the balled-up tissues, came to resemble an art installation illustrating the mathematical computation on the distance and angles between points of repose.

"Did he leave us?" I asked, feeling drained but wanting to know, and still hoping she'd say no.

She drew in a deep breath. She blew her nose again, this time tossing the dirty tissue into a cup of stale tea. I watched while it sank, realizing her resignation. She was quiet, so still that it alarmed me. Had she really come to the end?

"Mom?" I asked, not wanting it to be true.

She searched my face. "You look so much like him." She chuckled. "You *are* so much like him." She exhaled and then traveled back inside herself, disappearing through a portal, and into another reality, where she was estranged from me. A swimmer diving deep down to recover a lifeless string of words; sentences that would tie her to the past and anchor her to the sad story. At that moment, I recognized she was doing this for me.

"So, we packed up," she said, "and I took you to the flatlands. Moved in with your grandparents. Tried to be normal, whatever that means. A few years later, the state police called. Not far from where we'd all lived back then, they'd found your dad's motorcycle. And not far from there, they found the remains of his body."

In horror, I gasped and my hand shot to my mouth. My entire being took in the truth. I expressed myself again with deep, sustained moans, godawful sounds, but the story was the only thing in front of my mom, and so she continued. "It was speculated that he'd had an accident that night, the night we fought. He must have taken the curve too fast or even been blown off by high winds. Either way, he'd gone over the mountain. That call," she flinched, "was my wake-up call, my second chance. Your dad hadn't left us. He'd never left us."

She took a deep breath then. Her tone changed, and when she next spoke, she was my mom again. "I didn't tell you. That was wrong, and I'm sorry. At first, I couldn't trust myself to do it. How do you tell a child such a story? The longer I waited, the harder it was to tell. But I know in keeping it secret, I kept other things secret too, like his love. I can see now that I built a wall around myself that even you couldn't get entirely through. I am sorry, Gabe. Please forgive me?"

24

I didn't sleep well and woke grief-stricken, staring at the dirty, stained ceiling. Devastated, I couldn't even distract myself with the idea of Pythia. I simply didn't care. Nor did I pay any mind to Cat, fast asleep on the pillow beside me. That morning I never noticed the absence of her persistent morning head-butting to be fed. I only had eyes for the yellowed blemish that all too often overshadowed me. Finally, tired of even that, I exhaled and swung my feet to the floor, only to stall again and lingered at the side of the bed, waiting until some internal cue prompted me again to rise.

In the kitchen, I stood at the sink, clasping the coffee mug. Feeling the hot weight of it in my hands, I stared out the window. The smooth, thick glaze burned against my palms, but even Amy felt far away. Fuzzy and out of focus, as if she'd never existed. Outside, someone honked their car horn. Startled I narrowed my brow before returning my attention to the coffee, but the cup had gone cold.

Emptyhanded, I levitated up the stairs. Hovering at my desk, I smoothed the spine of my journal. Then soothing the urgent black scratches and sharp slashes with a finger, I wondered when I'd embossed the paper with such pain. Last night? My mind floated out the window. I chewed on my lip. Then, BANG! I startled. My lip throbbed with the beat of my heart. BOOM, BOOM, BOOM. I tongued the raw spot.

A bird hovered and tittered, threatening to crash, dizzy from slamming into the window. Then, it righted itself, lifted, and flew off.

Get your shoes, Mendes. You need a run.

Once out of the neighborhood, on the move up the dirt path into the snow-covered mountains, I fought a steady blast of frigid glacial air. Broken frost-covered branches littered the ground but sparkled when they caught the sunlight.

Struggling to breathe the sharp air, I decided to skirt the summit by way of Realization Point, where the grove of pines would provide shelter from the wind. Deep snow banked either side of the slippery trail, sure-footed I dodged the icy patches.

"Madly in love," my mom had said. I thought of Amy. Are we like my parents? My shoe slid on the slick snow. Losing my footing, I nearly took a dive, remembering how my mom had yearned for a do-over. One where she'd remained committed to my dad and the life they'd dreamed of despite her parents.

Thinking of Dr. Jacoby and her lesson in epigenetics, I wonder what it must have been like for me, a little zygote, a secret, hidden, maybe even denied by my mother? She hadn't any idea my cells would record her experience, but still, they had. It could explain my desire for and fear of intimacy. How much love and recognition could a zygote miss?

I huffed, hoofing it up the mountain, thinking about my mom's uncertainty and the torment it'd caused her. My arms swung, propelling me against gravity while my legs did the same, shortening the distance up the mountain. As a developing fetus, I was likely fed a low-grade diet of melancholy and fear with an erratic dose of humiliation. While I wanted to believe I'd felt my parents' honest love for each other, the odds were good that I'd lived in my mother's hope. The hope that she could someday freely love my dad without conditions. Nearly numb, my feet pounded the frozen trail. I wondered, had I absorbed my mom's hope against her desperate longing and deep disappointment and recorded that as love?

Approaching Realization Point, I slowed my pace. Ahead of me, a lone coyote slunk across the iced land, its thick gray fur indicating health. It could see I stopped. Panting, I paced in a circle, then bent over with hands on my knees to catch my breath. "We're not my parents," I whispered to Amy as much as myself. My Ex crept in. "We were never madly in love." I denounced her.

That's right, Mendes. You were too worried about what people thought to trust yourself enough to trust her.

A dreadful, hot shame rushed my heart. Determined to rattle it loose, I threw my head back and belted out frustration. The coyote turned around, and I watched the creature watch me.

Dude, you do have a habit of pushing people away, all the while wishing you felt closer to them.

The coyote trotted off, disappearing into the woods.

If Pythia was right and my parents were my first gods, in what kind of king-dom had I lived? One in which they loved me but resented each other? As a tod-dler, had I felt a duty to protect each from the other, all the while acquiescing to their power as deities? Were they untrustworthy gods? They weren't Santa Claus gods, rewarding me only for my good behavior. Or gods of fire and brimstone, damning me for my mistakes. They may have been gods distracted by their own troubles. Gods less likely to notice me through the fog of their bitter battles. Gods who unintentionally taught me more about helplessness than they'd ever intended.

Recalling my mom's story I frowned. Is this my destiny? My wet face stung in the stiff, March mountain air. Considering my own behavior and beliefs around love, my chin quivered fighting the ache in my chest. And then, without any prov-ocation, I peacefully realized this isn't what my mom had wanted either. She never wanted to pass me this generational baton, the one where love is untrustworthy and a struggle. Thus the secrecy, our unspoken agreement. At last, I understood why she'd never told me and why I'd never dared to push her. It had been all too much for us both back then.

Beneath the nearby pine boughs heavy with the weight of snow, naked un-burdened trees tucked into the white of the mountains revealed themselves in patches of purple bark.

"I really do want something different from my parents' story," I spoke into the winter silence. With hands-on-hips, seeing beyond the wilderness, the front range came into focus. Without thinking, I picked up my legs, high-stepping to warm up before jogging again toward the majestic peaks. My breath puffed white clouds against the stiff wind that burned my face. I tugged my hat down over my ears and headed west toward the Continental Divide. Picking up my pace, I wished I was already home calling Amy. I could hear her voice. The way she gave me her full attention. How she never held back.

"I'm ready for love," I spoke under my breath, trying it on. "Despite all the stories," I hollered, raising my arms to the distant blue peaks dusted in snow. I slowed to a stop and looked to the heavens. "Okay," I said to myself. Then a louder declaration: "I am now ready to freely love Amy." I imagined myself telling Amy and how we'd melt into each other's arms.

"Do you hear me?" I boldly bellowed, and my voice echoed, "Do you hear me? Do you hear me? Do you hear me?"

The snow-covered mountains looked back at me like ancient etchings. Their fine details were only revealed in the contrast of color. I yelled, this time calling him out by name, "Are you listening, old Gabe Mendes?"

"Old Gabe Mendes? Old Gabe Mendes? Old Gabe Mendes?" the echo echoed.

Beaming, I grinned from ear to ear. I cupped my hands around my mouth and shouted, "Today's Gabe Mendes." I waited.

"Today's Gabe Mendes. Today's Gabe Mendes. Today's Gabe Mendes."

"Is already living in love."

"Living in love, living in love, living in love."

25

Pythia sat next to me on my old brown sofa perched at the sagging cushion's edge, attentive and silent except for the occasional jangle of her bracelets. Listening to everything I said, from my mom's confession to the run at Realization Point, she made a kind face when I finished and reached to touch my hand. Wafts of her unique resinous and earthy scent drifted my way. "I'm glad you trusted yourself and me enough to know you only need ask," she said, and I thought of Higgs.

The morning light spilled through the picture window casting her in a warm glow. She brightened my dull room, making me wish the place was nicer for her. Then remembering Amy's crystal in the kitchen window I looked over my shoulder. Soon the rising sun would illuminate the glass heart. Knowing it would then sparkle for Pythia, I leaned toward her. "I trust you," I said, nodding, then shrugged and shook my head. "I don't know about trusting myself, but something about seeing you ... well, I just really wanted to talk this out in-person."

"Intimacy, yes?"

I scratched my head. "Yeah, maybe. So much has happened over the last few days. Epigenetics, equanimity, Dr. Jacoby—that's a whole other story." I shot her a look. "And last night with my mom. So, trust? Intimacy?" I paused, considering how these things might fit together. "I don't know. All I know right now is that my love story is complicated, and it's not just about My Ex." I leaned in. "Pythia, if I don't figure this out, I'll just go on doing the same thing. I don't want that. I am *really* ready to create something new with Amy."

She leaned over and tapped my knee. "The good news," she said, "is you are already figuring out this sticky wicket. Hmm? No doubt it's complicated! The foundation of your story was laid long before you ever stepped foot on planet earth. It's in the stars, so to speak." She gestured out the window where the Sun, a massive, fiery star spun, climbing into the sky to feed the Earth its lifeforce. "The laws of nature and motion have had a hand in it, too. Not to mention your own life experiences," she continued. "All of this and more have nurtured that old love story. But we shan't let that stop us, shall we?"

Cat lumbered across the room, eager to rub against Pythia's legs and it occurred to me I hadn't seen Cat since breakfast. "Well, there she is," Pythia said, turning her attention to Cat. "I wondered where you were." She petted Cat, who now danced circles in Pythia's lap, purring at Pythia's attention.

"Cat." I tugged her tail. "Where've you been?" But she remained insistent with her affection for only Pythia, rubbing her head along Pythia's chin. "She's always so happy to see you."

"And I, her. We're old friends, aren't we, Cat?" Cat meowed, and Pythia laughed. "You see?" she said to me and scratched Cat's neck, then behind her ears. Finally, satisfied, Cat climbed off Pythia's lap and curled up beside her. "Now," Pythia said, "Mother?"

I closed my eyes. "Well," I said, then as I opened them, this came out on the wind of a long sigh. "I was raised by a heartsick god who couldn't forgive herself. Who came to think of love as elusive and easily lost," I shook my head, "but also wanted to think otherwise. Now that's a god who couldn't trust her own instincts because she agreed to believe someone else's. That's some trick."

"Quite a dilemma."

"Right?" I gave her a boy-don't-I-know-it look. "Like me, she wanted intimacy but then was afraid it was too much, and then pushed and pulled my dad. That's not very intimate at all. It makes people feel like they can't trust you, and if they can't trust you, they can't feel safe."

"What is intimacy?"

"You're asking me?" I pulled back.

"Well, you've got a little computer right there." She nodded to my phone on the coffee table. "Look it up."

"Now?"

"If you're suspecting you've inherited a fear of intimacy, you might want to be clear on just what it is you are afraid of." She handed me my phone. "Well, go ahead now. I-N-T—"

"I can spell," I said, already typing. "Intimacy: a noun meaning: 1. Characterized by close personal acquaintance or familiarity; 2. Relating to or indicative of one's deepest nature; 3. Essential; innermost; 4. Marked by informality and privacy; 5. Very personal; private; 6. Of or involved in a sexual relationship." I stared at the screen. "Relating to or indicative of one's deepest nature and marked by informality and privacy." I paused, shook my head, then frowned before tossing my phone to the coffee table.

"Healthy intimacy requires trust."

"Healthy? How's that supposed to relieve my anxiety? What did that say?" I snatched my phone. "Here it is: essential; innermost; very personal; private. Honest, right? That's what that means. That's some risky business, right there." I shook my phone. "If I'm honest, Pythia, my greatest intimate experiences are of guilt and shame, and I venture to say it is the same for my mom. The apple doesn't fall far from the tree. That's it, right? A destiny of guilt and shame for pushing and pulling. For being a liar, really. Never being honest about who I really am or what I really want. Not on purpose but because—"

"Because—"

"Because." I eyed her.

"Go on."

"I can't!" I stood. "Because I don't know!" I stepped away.

"Sure you do."

I rolled my eyes. "Because I didn't know what I wanted." I barked back at her.

"And why didn't you know?"

"Because I'm pathetic and don't know how to relate any other way." I dared her.

"Why?"

"I don't know," I said like I didn't care.

"Yes, you do." She was firm but kind.

"Because it's in my genes!" I plopped next to her. The broken-down sofa creaked at the force of my weight. I sighed, then shot up and spun around. "Really, though? Is it as easy as that?" I loomed over her, the thin crown on her head glinted. It was set with little sparkly stones.

"What makes you say that's easy?"

I threw my hands up, flopped back into the miserable piece of furniture, and blew my cheeks out. "Why can't it be easier?"

She shrugged.

"I want it to be." I bargained.

"Maybe it can."

I turned to her. "But there's so much in my genes. There's so much in my family history that I don't know."

"And probably never will. That adds to the complexity of healthy intimacy. A greater understanding of what you can know may help."

I pointed a finger, accusing my phone of expectation. "Like letting others see my weaknesses with confidence that I'll be accepted."

"And sheltered. But not just for your liabilities, for your strengths, too."

"Whatever." I shuttered.

"Equanimity, agape mou."

"Equanimity." I stood to pace.

"Agape mou," she said, sitting alone on the sofa, her posture erect, hands in her lap fidgeting with a ring. "Intimacy is a deep biological need to belong. This isn't going away. Baby steps."

I bit my thumbnail, still pacing.

"Intimacy is something you build over time. Remember how it was when you first met Amy?"

I stopped and hurried to sit beside Pythia. "I'm not as afraid. Not as distrusting as I was." Focusing first on Pythia's blue eyes, I noticed the slight sag at her jowls, the crow's feet at her eyes. I thought for a moment. "Or as my mom was." I paused. "Pythia, I've never seen her so lost. She was desperate last night."

"Such sadness can be frightening."

"What if Amy hadn't engaged in ludus at the grocery store? Would I have ever seen her or her interest in me? She was in plain sight! But when I saw her, I only saw her as threatening." I remembered how she seemed to be popping up all over the place. "Back then, I thought she was too much to handle." I grinned, thinking of her boldness, but then scowled. "Instead of seeing her and the sea of possibility, I only saw one familiar outcome: overwhelm followed by helplessness." I paused. "Why, though? I mean, I'm smart. I've achieved things." My eyes darted. My brows crawled in critical judgment, and then, dumbfounded, my jaw dropped. "Is this my mom's story? But what about my dad's story? I don't know what history his semen brought me, but I can feel his love in my cells. His history, our history, the knowledge that his love is real. That's what I was missing!" I grabbed Pythia's hands. "Don't you see? Something really was missing! The admission, the permission to see and feel that his love was always there." Amy's crystal flashed. Rainbows dazzled the room. "It was in plain sight all along. I could feel it; his love, her love, their love. But in some unspoken agreement, I've been protecting her from the truth she was hiding from me. The two of us protecting each other. From what? Love?" I stood and stalled at the sofa before stepping away. "That's so messed up." I scratched my head. "And for how long? Before I was even born?"

"Humans are comprised of complicated systems for self-preservation," Pythia said still on the sofa, lifting her chin to meet my gaze.

"Yeah." I nodded, walking the floor, the dirty old green-gray sculpted carpet. "And my self-preservation strategies would only be as sophisticated as my programming. How could I know anything else?" I shrugged, shaking my head.

"Programmed by the old stories, you would unconsciously replay them. In doing so, you would reinforce their truth, but only as you understood that truth."

Van Morrison, Dude.

"Right," I whispered, while Van's hypnotic music drifted through my mind, his honest voice lulling me into a melodic stream of consciousness. "Could you find me? Would you kiss-a my eyes to lay me down in silence easy to be born again. To be born again."

I eyed Pythia. "Until I met you, I was only reacting to what I thought love was. And in some weird way, making myself gallant. Heroic."

"How so?" she asked from one end of the sofa while Cat blissfully slept at the other, soaking up the sun that now filled the room.

I hurried over. "Through sacrifice," I said, sitting beside Pythia.

"What did you sacrifice?"

"My own love story; my free will to create my own love story. I sacrificed the chance at a brand-new story, and unconsciously went on recycling the same old one."

"How old?"

"Right?" I scratched my beard. "Old. Real old. Romeo and Juliet old. Maybe ancient."

"Take a moment. Close your eyes."

I obeyed.

"Make yourself comfortable."

I leaned back into the forgiving sofa. Warm sunlight lit the insides of my eyelids. The corners of my mouth lifted with the flood of brilliant orange-red light. My shoulders dropped and scooched deeper into the cushions.

"Now. Imagine your parents sitting behind you." She waited while my parents took their seats in my mind and I turned to greet them, my mom sharply dressed and grinning, my dad soft and fuzzy. The edges and details of him missing but I knew he, too, smiled, "And your grandparents seated behind each of your parents." I frowned, wishing she'd suggested something different, at the same time worrying how I'd conjure my dad's folks. Then my face relaxed. There they were, blurry, but all the same I could feel them behind me. "That's right. You don't even know your father's parents, yet you can see them behind your father. Behind you. You don't even know them, but they have your back." I agreed. "And behind your grandparents are their parents. And..." instantly, the crown of my own family tree populated behind me. A sea of people sharing my DNA. "Do you feel them, agape mou?"

"I do!" I grinned, my spine lifting so much I thought I might stand. "I can feel their strength. It's—it's for me, Pythia!"

"Now. In your mind, turn around. Face them. Ask, how many know your helplessness, your struggle with self-love, your anxiety over love? Ask, how many might help you by sharing their wisdom."

When I did as Pythia had instructed, many stood, peppering the vast crowd that was my family. People I did not know or know anything about. A man with a gaunt face and a top hat several rows behind my father removed his hat and placed it over his chest. Then nodded at me before helping the woman beside to her feet. She waved and blew me a kiss. "A lot!"

"Now. How many of them want you to feel confident in the experience of self-love and love for others?

"Holy snickerdoodle!" My eyes popped open. "All of them. They all stood up. Is it really possible they have my back?"

"That's a useful perspective, yes? Now, my applicant of love, you know our work." She made a sympathetic smile. "Please, do tell the other side of this beautiful realization, the unraveling before the reconstruction."

"You mean?"

"What have you been deconstructing over these last few days to rebuild your foundation? What have you been letting go of to move forward unencumbered? What have you been processing for digestion to harvest wisdom?"

"Umm. I don't even know if I know what you mean but what comes to mind is how defensive I was with Dr. Jacoby, even Amy."

"See, you do know. Sometimes you don't even have to think about it. So, no one gets angry or defensive without feeling afraid."

"I was afraid of being made a fool. But then, with Jane, I was hopeful. What? Why are you making that face?"

"Nothing." She shook the expression from her face.

"It was something."

"You are right."

"What?"

Her lips parted. But then a look crossed her face, and she made a little gasp and shut her mouth.

"What? You have to tell me now."

"You are right. And I don't want to undermine your intuition. And I want to tell you. And I will. But can you finish first?"

I eyed her sideways.

"I'm afraid my reaction has made what I do have to share seem far more important than what you have to share. For that, I am sorry. Please?" She gestured, inviting me to continue.

"Okay," I said but studied her. She met my eyes. Her crown shown in the sunlight.

"Please," she asked and cocked her head. Her wavy-red locks followed while her green dress shifted, and yet, she was my mother's age.

"Sooo." I deliberated taking her in, and then, without a thought, said, "I'm embarrassed to say that I was pretty suspicious and guarded with Dr. Jacoby. And like I'd said, a bit with Amy, too." I scowled, hoping Amy'd forgiven me. "But then, with you and Jane, I felt like maybe I could be vulnerable."

She nodded.

"And then I wanted to know what I'd always wanted to know but had been too afraid to ask. I wanted to know what happened to my dad. I was afraid of what my mom might say," I shook my head, "but I had to know. I didn't want to hurt her, but I knew it would. Not the way it did, not that badly." I shrugged. "I don't know, maybe unconsciously I did know. Maybe that's why I never really pushed hard. But over the years, I resented that I couldn't ask. That I had to protect her when really, I wanted her to protect me. To be strong, not helpless." Feeling guilty, I looked away. I shook my head again. "I had no idea, Pythia," I said, "no idea at all how much shame she carried. And while she didn't mean to, my mom let her fear and shame keep me at an arm's length from not only her love but the love of my dad." I took my head in my hands. I went for my curls but let them go, turning to Pythia instead. "She couldn't change what happened. But if I could have talked with her about him? If she could have shared with me the kind of man he was? What kind of a man might I be today? Instead, the ways his love could have inspired me was just a big, fat, gaping hole in my heart. And he was a hard brick wall neither my mom nor I could ever get over."

"How did that influence your beliefs about love?"

"Oh, it made me believe that love hurts, that it devastates. That it's a burden. Honestly, it terrified me. I believed I couldn't live happily in love, and I couldn't live happily without it." I looked out the window. A squirrel maneuvered into the bird feeder like a performer in a defying circus act. Soon the sun in the cloudless sky would blaze, but for now its golden fingers joined the birdsongs instigating a coming flurry of morning activity.

"What you've described *was* the foundation you built your life's love story upon. Tell me that story. Help me see a picture in my head."

I searched her face, but really it was my own internal workings I explored. I surveyed some resistance. A hesitation to shift from the profound information I'd just shared to the more academic analysis she'd requested. I noticed a pull toward that warm wrap of self-pity but instead looked for the truth. "I couldn't trust my mom." Then the words amounted to something greater than language. I could feel them. "She couldn't trust herself. So, she couldn't teach me trust, and of course, I'd be afraid of intimacy. It's so clear now. The story I'm deconstructing is about a boy whose dad goes missing. And the boy's profound loss becomes a shroud of heartache that seduces the pained boy into believing that love is harrowing and haunting. And the hopeless boy becomes a helpless man." I winced remembering that time in college, the surreal red restaurant. Me, a grown man crawling into my mom's lap. That plush den of thick foam. Everything, soft and red. Or me, tiptoeing around My Ex—a good boy keeping secrets.

"Agape mou?"

"Oh, right. Yeah," I said, bringing my mind back to the soft green folds of Pythia's gown and the scratchy brown sofa. "That is," I said, smiling, "until he finds the courage to lift the veil of secrecy and at last sees love clearly."

"A beautiful story. But sad, yes?"

"Mostly, but hopeful too." I frowned. "I mean, I hope so."

"Oh, Pandora!" Pythia closed her eyes and pursed her lips. "Well, here it is," she said as if something had finally come to its reckoning. "Hopeful is for the hopeless. Wasn't it Nietzsche who said something like, 'Hope is the worst of evils, for it prolongs the torment of man'? Hope is the craving for a mere and fleeting hint of a future place when you aren't satisfied with the place where you currently reside." Then throwing up her hands with her bracelets making a racket, she asked, "Are you hopeless?"

"No," I said more loudly than intended. Catching myself, I modulated my tone. "I am not hopeless." We stared in a stand-off. Then she arched a brow, and I shifted my weight drawing back. The sofa squeaked, then boinged, and the vibration of the spring sprung jabbed me in the butt.

"Then what are you doing with hope? You have trust." She crossed her arms.

Red-faced, I frowned and swiped a hand across my damp forehead. "Well, isn't hope a good thing? I mean, isn't it good to be hopeful?"

"I don't know. Is it?" She grabbed the key on her necklace and slid it back and forth. "Hope does die last, I suppose. I don't know what Zeus had in mind for that. Did he lock hope in a jar to save it *for* or *from* humanity? It's never been clear, but hope eventually seems to make people angry."

"I do feel some resentment at the idea of being hopeful about love."

"That makes sense."

"It does?"

"Hope springs eternal." She nodded while Cat passed me and climbed into Pythia's lap. "In other words," Pythia continued petting Cat, "it is human nature to find a reason for optimism. Hope is the desire for a particular outcome. In order to desire something, you must trust in your ability to attain it. But hope is not a permanent state of being; instead, it facilitates desire. Once desire is in place, hope properly diminishes and refers to desire for manifestation." She paused. "You see," she said, shifting on the sofa, and springs sprung. My eyes widened but she carried on despite the offensive coil. "With desire in its proper place, you no longer hope for love; you are free to act to create it. Why? Because you can trust in the process. You believe in it against all the odds. If all you had was your hope for love, it would eventually make you angry. You have every right to manifest it. Make sense? Ready to write the next chapter?"

"Wait. What?" I laughed. "You are a taskmaster, Pythia. But yes, I am ready like I've never been ready before."

"Well, then. You'd better get busy!"

Cat sat at the big window watching Pythia stroll down the sidewalk. The little girls from across the street called out to Pythia. I shot back from the glass, Pythia waved and I scanned the street, but when no one else took notice of the high priestess I grabbed my phone to text Amy.

Hey, I miss you. Can I take you out to celebrate?

The familiar speech bubble hovered as Amy typed.

Celebrate that you miss me???

I laughed, texting the laughing till crying emoji, and felt heated at the thought of missing her.

No, that I'm buying a new sofa.

26

Grinning from ear to ear, fantasizing about shopping for home furnishings with Amy, I shuffled through the mail, heading up the stairs. "The Institute of Intimacy. Huh?" Curious, I slid my finger beneath the flap while I slipped into the desk chair, opening the red envelope. Cat mewed from the floor. "Well, hello, old girl." She meowed again. "What lazybones? You wanna be picked up?" I asked, already bending over. She pranced on the desk until I stroked the length of her body and tugged her tail. Happy, she rolled over and flicked her tail in my direction.

The envelope contained not the usual junk mail, but a letter, and a small, neatly wrapped, pink parcel. Thinking of Amy and her attention to detail, I went for the little bundle tied with a teeny-tiny red bow. I considered the dexterity required for such delicate wrapping while the soft sounds of crisp tissue gave way, revealing an inscribed key fob nestled inside. *There are no regrets in healthy intimacy; if there are, it isn't healthy intimacy!* I fingered the words punched into the metal and palmed the weight of the well-made freebee. The letter, while printed on fine stationery, was an over-the-top marketing piece, boasting with bolded type and exclamation points. But ultimately, it struck a nerve. Intimacy requires vulnerability, and vulnerably requires self-trust.

Uncomfortable, I cleared my throat. Thoughts sat on my chest. The late black nights after breaking-up with My Ex. How I'd sit in the La-Z-Boy stirring the pot of regret. Ranting to no one about betrayal, dishonesty, and broken trusts. Stewing about time wasted while guzzled beers fueled my arrogance. There'd been stupid calls, mostly initiated by yours truly.

Muttering, I grabbed the cube and rotated the puzzle, grumbling. A fact surfaced. I'd often expected something in relationships that I wasn't willing to give.

I twisted a few squares seeing a clear move toward resolving a whole face of the puzzle. Studying the now neat squares, seeing the simple pattern, there was nothing left to decipher. I set the game down and, without hesitation, reached for my phone.

"Hello? Oh! Hold on a minute," My Ex said, her voice as familiar as the game. "Yeah, this is not a good time. I'm not home or maybe I'm screening calls. Either way, you know what to do."

"Hey," I said, leaving a message after the beep. "I know it's been a while, and you can call me back if you want, but the onus of this, this thing I want to say to you, is on me, and I don't want you to wait another minute to hear it. So I'm leaving you this message." I stopped and searched for the right words, "I wasn't honest with you about who I was or what I wanted from you. I didn't mean to be dishonest. I guess I didn't really even know I was doing it, and that's not an excuse. I am not calling to make excuses. I am calling because I'm sorry. I'm sorry for all the ways I hurt you, for the ways I was shut off and guarded. And what I really want you to know is that I expected things from you that I, myself, never delivered to you, or even to myself. I didn't trust myself to be alive as me, and so I didn't trust you to be alive as you, either. So, I'm sorry, and I hope you can forgive me. I hope you're happy. Call me if you want, but I'll understand if you don't. And, I am really sorry, okay?" I sat holding the phone, hoping that perhaps, finally, I was honest and intimate with her. "Okay, take care."

I sat listening to the muffled outside sounds. Then on some internal cue, I opened the window and let the sweet spring scents into the room. Cat stretched into a downward dog, then crossed to cackle at a bird out the window. Spotting the stack of mail I'd tossed aside on the desk, I shuffled through it. "Hey!" I waved a mailer. "Ask, and you shall receive, Cat! Look at this. It's a furniture sale!"

27

Outside the showroom, rain was pouring. Inside, I couldn't help paying attention to Amy as she raced ahead of me in her tight jeans, weaving in and out of the staged rooms. "Oh, check out this one," she called back to me, headed to a blood-red, curved sectional. By the time I caught up, Amy was already sitting with her legs curled up beneath her, her arms outstretched across the sofa's tufted back. "It's velvet," she whispered, running her hand over the luxurious covered cushion.

"It reminds me of Trane's," I said, noticing how the designer had paired the furniture with rich exotic woods and a Persian rug.

"Trains?" She made a face, and I was relieved she didn't ask more. "Eighty-five hundred," she mouthed and grabbed one of the faux filled champagne glasses from the coffee table which looked real, right down to the bubbles. "Sit," she murmured, tapping the seat. Before I could, she exchanged the drink for the Lucite framed marketing piece. Playing with the turquoise earring, Amy rotated the stud between her thumb and first finger as she spoke in a seductive tone, "Proudly handmade in America by skilled craftsmen since the nineteen-seventies." She interrupted herself and, dropping the affect, made an apologetic face. "Sorry, no women build their furniture." Then resumed the pompous air. "Sure to become your legacy, our rebelliously yet poetic designs pack a bold punch of modern glamour and cheeky nobility that never goes unnoticed." She returned the frame to the table. "Sexy," she said, and played her brows, "A family heirloom harkening the good old insurgence of the nineteen-seventies." She slid her tongue over her upper lip with great exaggeration. Fake candles flickered all around us.

Overwhelmed, I wished I was clever.

"Oh, I see." She cocked her head, and with her tongue at her cheek, said, "This is one of those moments where I say tomayto, and you say tomahto."

I scratched my beard but couldn't come up with a thing to say, so I pointed a remote at the fake stone fireplace across from me. With a hiss, a blaze sizzled and cracked, the lights above us dimmed. Amy's deep blue nose stud glinted in the candlelight.

"Let's Get It On," the effortless soulful sound of Marvin Gaye set a mood.

"Is that…?" I pointed to the airwaves.

"Creepy!" she said with a nod and sprung off the couch. "Let's get out of here!" She grabbed my hand. We dashed up a set of stairs into a fake rooftop garden and took refuge on a pair of modern barstools.

"Nacho?" I offered, edging a mammoth plate of plastic chips across the thick glass hightop.

"Thank you." She accepted the glossy food before raising a pilsner. "To a new sofa. May it be what you've always dreamed."

I lifted my glass. "I don't know if I've ever dreamed of a sofa."

"Not a problem." She looked very sure of herself. "I have."

We toasted from the heights of our urban terrace and that's when Amy noticed the postcard on the floor.

Retrieving the giant card, she flashed it at me climbing onto the tall stool. "What's the matter? "Hey, let's do this," she said wide-eyed. "Why do you look like that?" Concerned, Amy ditched the card, tossing it face up right under my nose. "Hey." She lowered her voice. "Are you okay?"

Lightning flashed. Boom! Thunder cracked, and I jumped in my seat.

"Wow! Listen to that." A deluge of rain pounded the roof. "Gabe?"

I massaged my chest. "Nothing, it's just," I pointed to the ceiling, "unexpected," I said, catching my breath. "I'm fine." I frowned and snuck a glance at the oversized card referencing Jane Austin and featuring her and a couple picnicking in a golden field. The woman was a dead-ringer for Pythia. "Wow, yeah. Rain," I said, flipping the card over with one hand while pointing out into the opulent world of furniture with the other. "We should look over there," I said, breaking out in a sweat.

She turned and followed the trajectory of my finger. "The bathrooms?"

I ran my hand through my hair. "Is it warm in here?"

"Gabe, what's up? Your entire demeanor changed when I showed you this." She snatched the card. "Picture this, a love story, words by Jane Austen," she read aloud. "I don't get it. What spooked you?" She turned the card in my direction and pointed. "Do you know these people?"

I'd previously considered telling Amy about Pythia and my quest for love, but it seemed impossible to explain. Amy would think I was crackers for sure. Honestly, I wasn't sure myself if it was all for real. Sometimes I worried I was making it up.

"Hello?" She waved. "Hey! Look at me." She'd raised her voice. "Gabe?"

My heart raced. "I have something to tell you, and it's not easy to say." She drew back and narrowed her eyes. I waved my hands. "No, no, no. No! It's nothing like that. I mean, it's nothing bad. I don't know *her*." I gestured to the card. Then breathless and dizzy, I jabbered. "I mean, how could I? She's a stranger to me." I swiped at sweat beading on my brow. "It's complicated. That's all. It's hard to explain."

"Why would you know her?" She paused and studied my face. "You do know her." She looked horrified. "Oh, my God! Are you married?" Then, she pointed to Pythia's look-alike on the card. "Who is this woman?"

"No, no." I laughed before realizing laughter wasn't appropriate and gathered my composure. "No," I said, as flatly as I could, "I don't know *that* woman."

"But a woman that looks like this woman, and you thought—"

"No. No. Listen, there's no other woman." Pythia passed through my mind. "I mean no *other* woman." Amy looked away, snubbing me. "Really," I pleaded, taking her hands. She recoiled. "No. Come on, please. Listen to me." I waited, worried. "Look at me, please. I know Jane Austen. That's all."

She looked at me sideways. "A lot of people know Jane Austen."

"Well, yes, but I met her."

"You met Jane Austen? *The* Jane Austen. Is that what you expect me to believe? That is absolutely ridiculous. Is this your way of getting out of telling me about some woman who looks like this?" She shoved her finger hard at the picture and poked it for emphasis.

"It's hard to explain."

"It's not that hard. Either you are in a relationship with another woman, or you're not."

"I'm not." I could feel the look on my face betray me. "Not like you think."

"Oh, my God. I can't believe this."

"Let me explain." I reached for her hands again, but she turned her back to me. "Please, I want to explain. I want you to understand." I goosenecked, trying to make eye contact. "Oh, you are so upset. I'm doing this all wrong." I looked hard, trying to gauge her reaction, but she wouldn't face me. "I knew this wasn't a good idea!" I rolled my eyes and then mumbled, "I don't know what I was thinking." I threw my hands in the air. "Why did you think this was a good idea?" I shouted to the ceiling.

She spun around. "Lower your voice." Then alarmed, she asked, "Who are you even talking to?" Frightened, she stammered, "Are you—are you talking to someone? Do you think, I mean, is someone talking to you?" Then fully alarmed, she demanded, "Do you hear voices?"

"No! No, no, no, no, no." I shook my head violently. "I can explain," I argued before noticing nearby shoppers gawking our way and lowered my voice. "I just need to gather my thoughts. Will you excuse me?" Then, rising so quickly that I had to right the stool to keep it from toppling over, I tried to look normal and made my way to the bathroom.

I stood in front of the low-lit mirror. "Holy mother of God. What have I done?" I bent over the vanity and laid my face on the cold black granite. My sweat-stained shirt clung to me. I closed my eyes. A toilet flushed, and then the hard-clipping sound of a woman's heels on the tiled floor echoed.

"Remember, opportunity lies at the center of adversity," she said with a thick German accent. With my head cooling on the stone, I peeked. "What a fancy-schmancy place this is." A grandmotherly looking woman washed her hands. I closed my eyes, hoping she'd leave, but when I opened them again, her face was only inches from mine.

"Ahh!" I shouted. She grinned. Her eyes twinkled behind a set of oval-rimmed glasses perched high on her broad nose. Wearing a loud pink suit, the short, yellowed-haired woman resembled a kewpie doll. I'm losing my mind, I thought, and of all times in my life! Why now?

"You see, you're not losing your mind," Dr. Ruth Westheimer began, "but a person who never makes a mistake never tries anything new. Are you a turtle who never leaves its shell? No, of course not. You must stick your neck out!" She dried her hands with a towel from a gold tray. "You're not crazy. Insanity is doing the same thing again and again and expecting something different. Now straighten up!" I lifted myself up. "Get your feet on the ground. You look like you're dangling from a thread." She pointed to my reflection in the mirror. "Let them carry your spine. You see what I am saying?" She threw her shoulders back to show me. "Go on now. I'll wait." Half-heartedly I seated my shoulders and lifted my chin. "Okay," she said and raised a finger to make her point. "First, stay grounded in love. Not what happens to you, but what you can make happen. Okay?" She nodded once, sharply snapping her chin, commanding my agreement.

"Okay." I sighed.

She patted my arm before turning toward the door. With her back to me, she hesitated at the ornate brass handle. Then turned my direction. "You know, hotshot, that's The Thang—recognizing the difference between miracles and psychotic episodes." She smiled and added, "Oh! I hope you don't mind. They're cleaning the lady's room." And with that, she raised both eyebrows and her finger again. "Joie de vivre!" she said, and the door slowly closed behind her.

Oddly, I felt relaxed and it somehow seemed rational that if I had departed from my senses, the world's most famous sex therapist would've appeared in the men's room to assure me of my sanity. "Okay." I searched my eyes in the mirror, trying to catch a glimpse of stability. Then, pacified I splashed my face with cold water and headed out the door. Outside the men's room I surveyed the fake rooftop. "Oh, thank God!" I said, spotting Amy still seated in the high-top chair and raced in her direction.

"Amy," I said out of breath, sliding into the chair, "I'm sorry I scared you." Her eyes fell to her lap, revealing her damp lashes. She sniffled. "Amy, look at me," I pleaded.

"I trusted you. I really, really liked you, and you—I don't know what you did. But I know you're lying." Her eyes filled with tears.

I leaned across the bar-height table. "I am really, really sorry because I really, really like you, too."

She broke down. "So, you *are* cheating on me."

"No! Let me explain." I pulled out my phone.

"There are pictures?"

"Amy, I am gonna show you a website."

"Oh, Gabe! I just wanna go home." She stood.

"Okay, no. Please. Sit down. Look, it's just the search engine listing." I held my phone up for her to see. "Please?" I slid the phone her way.

Still standing, she took the phone, read the entry, then returned it to the table. "Gabe, I'm gonna leave now."

I picked up the phone. "But Pythia's the other woman in my life." I pointed to what I'd first seen that New Year's Eve. "She's my teacher, Amy. She's helping me learn about love."

Amy stood weighing something. "Learn about love? What do you mean? Like what is it? Or how to find it?"

"Yeah." I nodded, and my whole being softened. The whole furniture store seemed to disappear. All I saw was Amy. Her short black hair, her nicely shaped head, her thick lashes. Even with her blotchy red face she beautiful. "I want love in my life. Love is the single thing we all want most, but it turns out it's the thing we least understand. How can we have love if we don't even know what it is?" I took a step toward her. "Amy, I wanna love myself." I tapped my chest. "So I can love you in a way that is healthy for us both."

She looked to the floor. "I want to believe you, Gabe." Then looked at me. "But you are not making it easy. You expect me to believe in the Oracle of Delphi?" She spat the words and then scoffed, searching her phone for the site. "That Pythia," she snapped, "who by the way, Gabe, is a Greek goddess. You want me to believe a goddess is teaching you about love? Really?" She frowned while her thumbs flew at the phone, typing and then retyping.

"She's a high priestess. That's different than a goddess. I was confused about that at first, too."

"Oh, my God, Gabe!" She glared at me like I was crazy. "This just gets worse when I want it to get better. You really expect me to believe you? You're a well-educated man, and you want me to believe you find some cheesy site a reliable source for your greater understanding of love?" She ranted, then typed and re-typed again. Then scowled. "Wait," she said, "What's the site? I'm not finding the link in the search."

"Here."

She looked at my phone. "Yeah, that's what I entered about a hundred times, and nothing's coming up." She took my phone and studied the search results. "Is this some trick? Why can't I find it on my phone?"

"Let me see." I stood next to her. Together we tried various ways but ultimately failed to reproduce the search results or the website on her phone. "That's so weird," I said, and then something occurred to me, "Maybe it's because I was hopeless." Amy looked like that might be possible. "But here it is." Encouraged, I showed her my phone again. "Do you think if I was going to make up a story, this would be the story?"

"I don't know." She sighed. We stood face to face. Then she slid into her chair. "Okay, tell me everything from the beginning."

"Well," I began and told her how lost I'd felt that New Year's Eve, the ludicrous link, the far-out umbilicus, my friendship with Pythia, and all the characters I'd met. She listened, and when I finished, I took her hand and held it between my two. "But the greatest thing to come of it all is the love I am feeling, not only for you but for myself, too. I'm a changed man, Amy. I owe that to you."

"I thought Pythia was your teacher."

"But without you, the story of love is only a mere idea."

"Oh, Gabe." She softened. "This is crazy." She shook her head before hiding her face in her hands. "It's all too much. You can't be…" but then she paused as if afraid and looked away. Turning back, she shook her head. "Gabe, you can't be unstable," she said tearing up, "I'm in love with you."

"Oh." I rushed to her side of the table and hugged her. "Oh, don't cry." Her shoulders lurched, and she heaved. "I'm so sorry I didn't tell you sooner, but I didn't know how." We huddled until she pulled away to blow her nose.

"I don't know what to think. This is all very, very, very strange." She laughed a little and then a little more, and I laughed, too, and wiped away her tears.

"I know it is not funny, but is it okay? I mean, are we laughing because we're okay?" I wanted to cross my fingers.

She shrugged. "I don't know, maybe I've lost my mind, or maybe it's expanding. I'm certainly beginning to realize there's more to the world than I ever knew with the multiverse and all its parallel universes." She made a little shrug. "I guess maybe you were in one of those parallel universes with this, Pythia."

"She's really a good person, Amy. You'd like her. There is nothing to worry about there."

She nodded. "Maybe your helplessness was a superposition."

"I said hopeless, but I've been pretty helpless in my life, too. Maybe they were or are superpositions but not that night. That night my superposition was determined. Something different happened that night. Space, time, matter, even energy opened up through that search."

She sized me up. "I want to believe you." She tilted her head, then crossed her arms over her chest.

"So, come on, let's step out of *this* preposterous superposition."

She chuckled but eyed me hard, her hand going for the stud earring.

"What'd ya say? A sofa and dinner? Come on. Trust me."

She looked away, then back at me. "Gabe, what if you're whackadoo?" She studied me.

"Maybe I'm just crazy for you." I tried to sway her.

"I mean, what if you're…unbalanced?" She stared at me, twisting the crystal stud, her ear blooming red.

"Come on," I said, motioning with my head and hand, "Walk this way." I rose and walked with an exaggerated limp.

"Very funny." She grabbed my hand.

"Let's find a sofa," I said, doing my best to sound sane. I kissed her forehead, and we descended from the chic faux rooftop. Out of the corner of my eye, I could see her sizing me up once more.

She sniffled. "What do you think of that one?" she asked, making an effort.

"The white one?" But she was way ahead of me, already plunked down.

"Oh, it's very comfortable. Feathers, I bet." She stood and turned over the cushion, rummaging for a tag.

"Wow, it is comfortable," I said after sitting, and then put my feet up on the modern coffee table and spread my arms across the sofa's back.

"Yeah?" she asked, her eyes still glassy but never-the-less hypnotizing.

"Yeah." I smiled overcome by her. "Hey, Amy," I started, but she was fixed on something across the room.

"Gabe," she whispered, scooting close to me. "Look over there." Her eyes darted, indicating something of interest. "Is that…?"

But before I could say a thing, Dr. Ruth was extending her hand to Amy. "I would like to introduce myself. I am Doctor Ruth Westheimer. I was talking to this good-looking, hotshot here," she teased, motioning to me, "and he said you wouldn't know who I was, but I was hoping you might recognize me by my accent." My mouth fell open. What audacity! Amy stood and accepted Dr. Ruth's hand. Speechless, I sat feeling every eye in the furniture store on us.

"He underestimates me." Amy gave me a glance. "Of course, I know of you. It's my pleasure to formally meet. Won't you sit down?" Amy said, and then realizing we weren't at home, stammered, "I mean—"

Not missing a beat, Dr. Ruth sat, and quite close to us.

She grabbed our hands, squeezing them in hers. "When you have a lot to talk about, one place is as good as another." She patted our hands. "Okay?"

Confused, I nodded, hoping agreement was the fastest approach to rid ourselves of the unpredictable doctor.

"I'm not sure I know what you mean," Amy said.

"Okay," Dr. Ruth said, giving a quick karate chop to one hand with the other. "First order of business, call me Ruth. Second, as a trained Israeli army sniper, I know how to give instructions. Third, we've all survived something, and that obliges us to help others survive—to be teachers. Now, new ideas are always a touchy topic, but they keep us agile. See?" She tapped her temple. "The greatest six inches are between the ears. Not in this hot shot's pants," she said, unabashed as I blushed.

A composed salesperson stood waiting for Ruth to finish before asking, "May I just interrupt to say it is a pleasure to have you in our store," and he made a little bow to Ruth. Then with a confident demeanor, he asked. "What can I help you all find today?"

Before Amy or I could say a thing, Ruth spoke. "What's your name?"

"Gerald."

"Gerald, these two here are ready for love. It calls for a toast." She grinned, slapping her lap and looking quite nuts.

"Ah," the associate's mouth fell open. "Ummm." He raised his eyebrows, trying to figure out what to say. "Well," he began, sounding diplomatic.

"I'll take this sofa," I piped up, standing and taking my credit card from my wallet.

"Do you have any Dixie cups?" Ruth asked.

What appeared to be a manager made her way swiftly from across the store.

Excusing herself through the growing crowd of shoppers gathering around us, darting through the furniture with two other staff at her heels. "Dr. Westheimer," she said, emerging, extending her hand, "I am Shanice, the manager here, and it surely is a pleasure to have you in our store today. What can we help you with?" It was clear whether we liked it or not, we were about to receive exceptional customer service.

"Thank you, Shanice." Ruth acknowledged the manager, and then to the staff asked, "And you are?"

"Amir."

"Anya."

"Amir and Anya!" Ruth repeated their names and nodded to each respectfully before turning back to Shanice. "Shanice, do you have some paper cups? The cute little ones?"

"Paper cups," Shanice said to Anya, who then hurried off.

"Because I have a bottle of champagne," Ruth said, pulling one from her black patent leather purse. Dr. Ruth motioned for Shanice to come close and whispered in her ear.

"Oh," I shook my head and then looking apologetic toward the store employees, "I don't think—"

Someone whizzed by me and handed Ruth a sleeve of Styrofoam cups. "I'm sorry, this is all I could find."

"Perfect!" She paused, making eye contact with the accommodating staffer. "What is your name?"

"Roger."

"This is perfect, Roger!" She touched his shoulder, then turning to a random shopper, she asked, "What's your name?"

"Maria."

"Maria, will you do us the honors?" She passed Maria the bottle.

I looked at Amy, and she looked at me and smiled. POP! Startled at the burst of bubbles, I jumped, but Amy stood and looking enthralled, she accepted a cup of bubbly passed her way. I copied her composure and followed her lead. "A toast to new love," the outspoken doctor raised her glass. A sea of disposable foam cups rose above our heads. "May sex always be respectful companionship, a mitzvah. And," she paused, eyeing a few from the swarm, "may it make for better lovers."

"Here, here," many called out, and we each drank the droplets spilled into our cups from the split bottle.

I snuck a sideways glance at Amy. Feeling the thrill of it all, I set the foam cup aside and pulled her to me. She leaned her warm, soft body into mine and rested her head on my shoulder. I wished we were alone.

In the background, someone called out, "Dr. Ruth, would you say that sex has become a commodity?"

"And with a 5th Avenue marketing campaign claiming that it's free," Dr. Ruth answered. The crowd roared, but my thoughts were only of Amy. "But," I heard Ruth interrupt and I didn't need to look to know she'd raised a finger, "it can come at a very high price. Especially if you make it transactional."

"Amy," I whispered.

"What do you mean by transactional?" someone asked.

"Let's go," I suggested in a hushed tone.

"Now?" Amy looked incredulous. "We can't go now." She indicated to television crews pouring through the doors, dripping wet from the storm.

"She means sex in exchange for something like dinner," someone said, and the crowd chuckled. "No, seriously. Or loneliness, or even shelter."

"This brilliant young woman is right." Dr. Ruth worked the crowd. "Mark my words, when sex is exploited, it will fall into two experiences. Not enough and too much."

"But those aren't the concerns of sex," Amy piped up, surprising me, already fully engaging with the group. "The bio-mechanical activity of coitus *is* the nature of sex. Copulation, screwing, a roll in the hay, hanky panky—"

"I think we get the point, Amy," I said, under my breath, eyeing those who might be within earshot.

"Yes, well, but I'm making a point," she said, out-loud and directly to me. "Those things," she said, in deference to me, "have no concern for emotional, mental, or spiritual well-being. Their single focus is the insertion of the excited penis into the aroused vagina until both have orgasmed. Or in the case of homosexuality or queer preferences—"

"Amy," I interjected, red as a beet. People laughed while some joined in a debate.

"You're so cute when you're embarrassed," Amy mouthed to me.

"Please," Ruth spoke over the crowd. "Sit everybody. Sit. Amir?" she called, and the salesman raced over. "Please. Can we get an assortment of hot dogs from Colonel Mustard's? Some vegetarian. Some kosher." Amir nodded and hurried away.

"Sex is not everything." She looked serious and karate-chopped her palm again. Then lowering her voice, she added, "Don't say I said so, but you can't get fed anywhere like you can in this town. Not even in New York City." Then full of enthusiasm, she said, "Because it takes chutzpah to talk about orgasms, we must eat! And!" she paused, "you can say you heard that from a little old lady." She nodded sharply and beamed while the crowd roared with laughter. "Okay, see? It is fun to laugh. It feels good. Sex is like good conversation. It's fun when the intention is for pleasure between partners. Then!" she lifted a finger, "it provides more than just intense release of sexual excitation." She licked her lips, accepting a bottle of water from Shanice, who was passing them out.

Accepting a bottle myself, I enjoyed the wet, cold weight of it in my hand. I had something I wanted to say. I cranked the cap and took a long gulp, then another slug, but still my heart raced. The crowd chattered with an intimidating rhythm. Wondering how to jump in, I eyed the cameras, and that's when I noticed the crew from Colonel Mustard's making their way in with large aluminum trays. I closed my eyes and sighed. Things were moving too fast. I cleared my throat fighting the urge to give up, and when I opened my eyes, Amy and Dr. Ruth were looking my way.

"Go ahead, hotshot." Ruth encouraged me in her own serious way. "Listen up, everybody. This is Gabe. He is a professor of love. He has something to say."

"Umm," I stammered, dizzy until Amy put her hand on my knee. "Um. Okay. I've done a lot of research on the topic of love." I looked at Dr. Ruth.

"Yes." She nodded. "He is a prophet of love. Searching for the meaning and healthy application of the world's most sought experience. Please continue."

I exhaled. I scratched my head, remembering the timeline. "I want to say that we are confused about sex because this idea of shared pleasure, to share in the experience of healthy sex, is exactly what the Christian church sought to control centuries ago." I looked around to gauge people's reactions, but found they were just listening. "A long time ago, way before any of us can remember or know anyone who could, the church preached that sex was practiced as gratitude for god's sacrifices. And that sex glorified god, but only through a divine union in him that gifted a godly offspring in his image. For these reasons, most of us were taught that shared pleasure in sex is selfish and immoral. Handed down centuries ago, these moral mandates hijacked the joy of sex and further complicated our understanding of love. I know that's been true for me." I finished a little breathless, hoping I'd made sense. I soothed my anxiety by grabbing the chili dog Amy'd set in front of me.

"Well said." Amy clapped. I felt warm but didn't blush and took a bite, listening to the low rumblings through the crowd that eventually erupted in some clapping and voices of agreement.

"It's good, huh?" Amy watched for my reaction.

"Delicious. How's yours?"

"Super." She smiled, and I understood the word transcended the dog.

I prepared for another bite, still shaking off awkwardness when someone spoke.

"But wouldn't you agree that the 20th century took us from sex shame to shameless sex? It only took a few decades to pitch a 5th avenue marketing campaign against St. Augustine's philosophy, I assume that's what you're referring to, and turn sex into a money-making industry."

I nodded with the hot dog in midair.

Someone else chimed in, "But sex for any other reason than God's glorification is lustful." There were low voices of agreement. "And contrary to the will of God," someone shouted. Television cameras moved in closer. I thought about the centuries spent arguing the purpose of sex and its relationship to love.

Then, from somewhere inside what I hoped was not a mob in the making, came a voice. People turned and parted to reveal an elderly woman in a wheelchair. "I am Mavis," she declared, revealing a southern drawl as she eyed Ruth. "Like so many other important things, sex has been a pawn in the historical play for power over the people. We've barely ever had a balanced idea of sex thanks to privileged people telling us what it means." Heads turned, and all eyes were on Ruth.

Without looking, I tried to get a feel for Ruth's posture. Amy cleared her throat and shot me a look. "Dr. Ruth," she began, sounding diplomatic. "What was it like to be at the forefront of such change?"

"Well, it wasn't always easy. And," Ruth paused with great intention, then smiled, "it is true that not everyone saw things as I did. It might surprise you that

I have been accused of having an ego." She laughed, and people laughed with her. "But I am a celebrity," she said and let the fact sink in. "Someone even called me a sex titan." Another pause before she grinned and shifted to her playful demeanor. "I was in *Playboy*," her eyebrows arched, "not naked, of course!" She hesitated, then looked like she'd fondly recalled something. "You know, Fred would tell you, 'Don't listen to her about sex!' He'd say, 'She's all talk.'" Ruth softened as she spoke of her late husband. Then sounding apologetic, she began. "I didn't set out to be famous, but I am. I have that privilege. And that's why every day I remind everybody that good sex is healthy and wonderful. You see, in sex, we must teach each other love and respect. Good sex is Heavenly sex with a capital 'H.' It is not learned on the school bus; it's not derived through the maturation of genitalia and the release of hormones. No, no, no!" She frowned, shaking a finger. "In good sex, you take responsibility for your ability to create life. Whether you create it or not makes no difference. Okay? You see? In sex, teach each other to make love. Fail so you can succeed. And take your time. Okay?"

People nodded, and voices agreed.

Dr. Ruth clasped her hands. "Now! You've endured enough from an old lady like me. I must go now. That is, now that I have proven *this* hot shot wrong." She nodded at me. "See," she bent to me and pretended to whisper, "I told you that people would know who I was." Then, turning to leave, she stopped mid-step. "Oh!" she called back, "Joie de vivre!" and left.

Afterward, Amy and I strolled almost giddy on the pedestrian mall, chattering and laughing as we recounted the evening. The rain had stopped, and the air was fresh. It was late, but some buskers still played guitars under the warm yellow streetlights. Occasionally, I stuck my hand in my pocket to find the crisp folded edges of the large pink receipt and marvel at how good a sofa could feel.

"How in the world does he do that?" Amy pointed to a muscular man suspended upside down from an elaborate harness playing a piano.

Taking the opportunity to get close, I leaned in and pointed. "See how that pulley—"

"Yeah, but I mean, he must be really strong. What would it take to do that?"

"A lot of confidence and trust," I whispered into her ear.

"Right." She grinned. "Speaking of which, what's that song he's playing?" She goaded, weaved her arm through mine, and leaned into me.

"Hm?" I pretended to think.

"You don't know?"

"Well, it's not that I don't know."

"Oh. So you know, but you won't say. Don't you trust me?"

"Oh, no! I trust that you just wanna hear me say it."

"Would that be wrong?" Her tongue poked the inside of her cheek, daring me.

"Well, right or wrong, I believe that impressive fellow suspended upside down by not only ropes and pullies, but by the brute strength of his core is playing a song called, 'When a Man Loves a Woman.'"

"Is that so?" She lifted a brow, challenging me.

"It is."

"I don't know if it is?" She flirted. "Can you sing it?" She was smug.

"Ah, I think the lyrics go something like this," I cleared my throat, lowered my head to hers, and sang just above a whisper. "When a man loves a woman, can't keep his mind on nothin' else. He'd trade the world for the good thing he's found."

She caressed the side of my face then slid her hand along the back of my neck. We kissed while walking until the passion was so great that we staggered to a bench where we made out like kids until she pulled away. "We gotta stop."

"Agreed."

"Would you like to come over?"

I nodded, already imagining the future, feeling it my body.

"Yes?" She looked directly at me.

"Yes." I returned her gaze.

"I think we owe the piano man a sizeable tip."

"Not a problem," I said, pulling a twenty from my pocket and dropping it into his hat as we hurried off the mall.

28

A my lived in a complex north of town in a tiny but new apartment. The kind with granite countertops and wooden floors.

"Kitchen." She announced, indicating with both hands like a traffic cop toward a breakfast bar and two stools. Then motioning ahead. "Living room." She stepped left. "Bathroom." Then looking straight at me, she raised her brow and indicated to the room beside the bath. "Bedroom," and she let the word linger before adding, "of a woman, serenaded earlier by a handsome man. Very romantic." She emphasized the last two words before sounding casual. "Can I take your coat?" Helping me take it off, she took it to the bedroom, calling back, "Would you like something to drink? I have water."

"I love water." I shoved my hands into my pants pockets past the receipt and began poking around the place. Her modest furnishings felt like her. Multicolored handknitted throws dressed up a worn but contemporary sofa, and an old pine trunk functioned as a coffee table. I paged through an art book atop the table before spotting the modern floor light, its long neck craning high and wide overseeing a comfortable-looking chair. The light illuminated pale-green walls that hosted art posters, one featured a realistically painted light bulb that reflected an entire scene apart from the one in which the bulb existed. Trading my interest in the book for another hyper-realistic print, this one of orange slices dropped and sinking into a glass of water, I crossed the room and squinted to see the artist's signature. "The perspective on this Jason de Graaf is fantastic. It looks so real," I said, calling out to Amy while I noted the place was filled with books—some in cases and others stacked like cairns against the wall, often topped with a hand-thrown pot or jug. All kinds of titles peppered the spines both new and well-loved.

"I know, right. I love the water splashing from the glass and puddling on that shiny surface. Everything's reflecting something else," she said, returning without my coat and went to the fridge. "See," she said, pouring two glasses of water from a Brita pitcher. "I like water, too. We're so alike."

"Here's to discovering more things we both like." We toasted, and then I relieved her of her glass, setting it beside mine. I lifted her chin, and she met my gaze. I kissed her, strategically holding back desire and then gently consuming her soft lips.

"Oh," she moaned. The sound escaped as if she were falling deep inside herself, taking me along.

I kissed her again, pressing against the cushion of her breasts. "Where's my coat?"

"In the bedroom." She was breathless. "Going somewhere?"

"The bedroom."

"Let me show you the way." And she took me by the hand.

29

In the morning, I awoke relaxed, even happy, as I lay on my side between the sheets, soft from the heat of our bodies. Dust particles danced in the sunlight that spilled through Amy's bedroom window. Under the warmth of her fluffy white comforter, I remembered the way the full moon had cast us in a cool blue light as I explored the soft round shapes of Amy. How Amy and I harmonized our low sounds with the ease of fitting into each other. Somewhere behind me, Amy now lay. I listened for her sleep-breathing, and when I heard none, I reached behind myself and carefully felt for her.

"Looking for something?"

"Not anymore." I rolled over to see her in an oversized T-shirt and reading glasses. Her legs were bent at the knees with a book in her lap. "You're reading?" I asked lifting the book to see its spine: *Esoteric Healing: A Treatise on the Seven Rays.*

"Be careful, hotshot."

"Oh, I'm always careful. You should know that by now." I pointed to the book. "Author, Alice Bailey, huh? Any relation to George Bailey?" I asked climbing out of bed to head to the toilet.

"Nope," she quipped, confident as usual despite her bedhead.

"Are you sure? Do you know who George Bailey is?" I called back while relieving myself.

"Yes, I'm sure. And, yes, I know George Bailey and how he comes to a deeper understanding of love through the trials of life and in the end takes shelter in the basic goodness of himself and his community, which restores his faith in humanity and helps him realign his life with greater purpose."

"Wow," I said loud enough for her to hear as I washed my hands. Catching a whiff of Amy's familiar scent, I sniffed the soap.

"High school English teacher, remember?" she shouted from the bedroom.

"Right," I said, returning the bar to the dish and for a split second I imagined her in the tub shaving her long shapely legs. Catching myself in the mirror, I hesitated but before I knew it, I'd hurried through the vanity drawer and found a new bar: goat milk and honey with tea tree essential oils. I shoved the bar back in its rightful place and closed the drawer quietly.

"Right. So, who's Alice?" I asked, heading back into the bedroom and climbing into bed, taking in her sweet honey scent, the medical tea tree aroma only faint.

She gave me a sideways look. Then closed the book and retrieved a leather-bound journal from her bedside table. Clearing her throat, she opened the diary and read aloud. "Alice Bailey, 1880 to 1949, author of twenty-four books about the seven rays." She paused and looked at me over the top of her glasses before proceeding. "Rays are subtle creative forces of energy that live inside our body and connect our physical, emotional, mental, and spiritual bodies to the world. They are how we communicate and connect with all other energies."

"Ah," I said, "And after just one night, you're already trying to understand me and my ray."

She eyed me, resembling a teacher more than I liked, before continuing. "Each ray relates to certain body parts. The second ray relates to reproductive organs and especially helps us enjoy creativity in hobbies, work, relationships, and sex." She raised a brow.

"Well, sure." I fidgeted, wondering where this was going. Hoping to keep it light, I gave humor another go. "I mean after last night with me and my ray you probably—or it probably—"

She looked at me with great skepticism and reached for her earrings on the bedside table. "Go on. I'm listening to your creative ray as it attempts to make you witty," she said sliding in the turquoise studs, the Navajo silver work catching the bright morning light.

"Well, I would go on, but after last night's performance, the competency of my second ray is anything but funny."

"Yes. Well, I am happy to have provided the inspirational vessel for such an occurrence."

I waited a beat, hoping for my own inspiration, when an indiscernible thought shot through my head. Something about creativity and the second ray didn't feel funny. With my hands up, I surrendered. "I can't keep up with you. I'm callin' uncle."

"Of course, you can't." She crawled over and touched my lips with her fingertips. "You need say no more." She kissed me, and I was glad again.

"I think I'm feeling those rays now." *Score!* Finally, a comeback.

"Magnetic energy?" She playfully bedeviled. "Tingling body parts waking to their only real purpose?" She bewitched me between baby smooches so that I forgot my morning breath. "Is the second ray turning you on to our deepest partnership?" she whispered, sounding very sensual and smelling of sweet sweat, the soapy scent gone.

"Yeah." My hand followed the curves of her body.

"Yeah?" She drew out the question in a way that made it feel already answered. "You know the rays have fields, Gabe. All round your body. Like spinning hula hoops." She drew in a breath. "Gabe? I think I feel you in my field."

"Me too." I fumbled at her T-shirt and panties.

"Yeah? Are you feelin' physically and emotionally free? Spiritually liberated?"

"Um-hum." She tasted salty-sweet.

"Let go of yourself." Her words, barely audible, were like some incantation. At that moment, my eyeballs rolled, fluttering back into my head. A wave rushed through me, sweeping me deeper into myself. Down, down, down, I drifted. Her soft, hidden, wet places smelled like earth after long and heavy rain. She was right. No fear. No boundaries. Only bountiful joy.

Afterward, Amy buttered a piece of toast while we sat at the breakfast bar. I waited for her to finish with the knife. Passing it to me, she reached for the peach preserves, waited for me to return the knife, and then spread a generous helping. She bit into the toast, returning to reading aloud from her notes.

"All seven rays reside within and have fields that extend out from the body." With her hand, Amy showed me their placement by drawing invisible circles on her body and motioning in circles around her body.

"Got it," I said, licking butter from my fingers, wondering if sex would always come with a lesson.

"Good, because it's about to get real."

"Oh, it wasn't real before? Wasn't that…?" but instead of finishing with words, I smirked, pointing toward the bedroom.

"Funny."

"I'm hot."

"Cocky is more like it."

"Confident. I kinda like it. Being funny, I mean."

"I know."

"Do you think this qualifies for intellectual intimacy?"

"I'm not sure I'd call it intellectual."

"Hey! I was clever."

"You were flirting."

"Was I?" Ludus, I thought.

"And just so you know, you and I don't want for intellectual intimacy."

"No?"

"No."

She waited. "May I?"

"Please. Proceed." I reached for another piece of toast, my pride at flirting fading to a rising teacher-resentment. Did Amy want for something else?

"Okay, where was I?" she asked herself while her finger wandered across the paper. "Hold on." She climbed off the barstool and dashed to a second-hand desk to grab paper and a broken-handle mug full of markers. Sliding back into her chair, she drew a picture. "Look." She scooped egg onto her toast and took a bite, pushing the paper at me.

I studied the diagram.

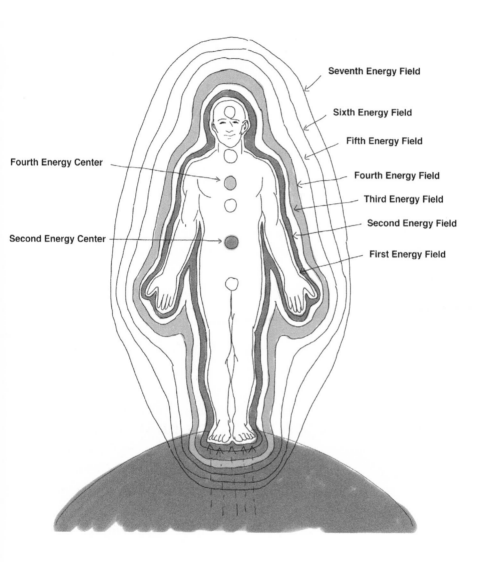

"Subatomic energy from the Earth's core fuels the seven and their fields. Energy, not matter. Quantum, not Newtonian." She looked at me, and satisfied I was keeping up with her, she took a bite. "But here's what I really wanted to share. The second ray is how we connect emotionally. It's all about personal power and making moves in life. She tapped the man's belly. "It's responsible for desire. The yearning to be alive. To create the life you want." She looked at me with expectation. "See? Sex requires a creative mind."

Did she think I wasn't creative? Wait, how creative did she want me to be?

She hopped off her chair to stand beside me and pointed again at the picture I was beginning to begrudge. "When your second ray is open, you feel dynamic. Stimulated. Full of ideas. You have the confidence to make significant changes in your life. That takes creativity." She nodded like we agreed.

But to what? That I lack creativity? Confidence? Red-blooded virility! Feeling a sucker punch coming, I bided my time pretending greater interest in the drawing. Was Amy looking for Eros?

"What?" She drew back.

"Well," I began, fearing the weight of a conversation about my sexual prowess, "I was hoping sexual intimacy would be more than just sex."

"Yes. Me, too," Amy said like we were on the same page. "Our own unique sensual expression. Of course, consensual, and shared for pleasure and joy." Reaching for her plate, she scooped the last of her eggs onto toast. "Otherwise," she said before pausing to gobble the last bite right in my ear, "it's only a mechanical means to an end."

I stood. "Well, yeah." I rubbed the back of my neck. "We talked about this with Dr. Ruth. I mean, why are you bringing this up now? Are you trying to tell me something?"

"Gabe?" She seemed surprised. "Are you angry with me?"

"No." I blew her off. "No, I just—" but then I decided it better to shut my mouth and reached to clear our plates instead. "Do I rinse first?" I asked, trying to sound cheerful as I headed toward to the sink, but my head sweltered.

"No, just put them in." I could feel her watching while I turned loading two plates into the empty dishwasher into a big deal. "Are you okay?"

With my back to her, I massaged my pained heart. "Yeah, I'm fine," I lied, feeling hot.

"I'll wash the flatware." She rose from her chair. "The dishwasher never gets it clean." She plugged the sink and ran the water.

I wiped my brow and hung over the open dishwasher far longer than necessary. Hiding, really.

Dude, get a grip!

I heard the sound of dish detergent squeezed from the bottle. Then her hand swishing about. I imagined bubbles. "You know what?" She sounded perturbed. "I'll just wash the plates, too. Do you mind passing them?"

Pulling them out of the dishwasher, I handed them over, doing my best to re-engage, working hard to resist my preoccupation with self-absorption.

Don't make it into something, dude? Just be normal. Just do the dishes.

She scrubbed the plates, circling the sponge far too long and with far too much vigor. "I don't know the last time I washed the dishes beside a hotshot like you," she said, the line sounded forced despite her hip-bumping me in the little galley kitchen. "There's a towel in that drawer there. Would you mind?"

Fighting confusion and bruised feelings about the whole second ray bit, I took out a thin cotton towel. "How do you keep these so white?" I asked forgetting myself for a second. "Mine are thick and, I don't know, fuzzy. They're way dingy."

She made a face like she'd been caught. "I buy new ones. And only linen. It's an indulgence."

"That's indulgent," I said, sounding more judgmental than playful, and relished it more than I liked.

"I know. I hope you can overlook my weakness for clean, white dish towels."

"I noticed your bath towels were quite white as well." My demeanor was dry, almost resentful.

"I like white." She sounded apologetic. I could feel her looking at me. "But enough about my fine taste and extravagant lifestyle." She tried to banter but then sighed. I wanted to say something but couldn't muster a sound. "Gabe? I think I offended you. I'm sorry."

"Nah." Resigned to disappointment, I couldn't look at her and played it down with one of those faces. "I'm fine," I said, and then Pythia's voice floated into my head.

"Agape mou," I heard her say as if she were with me. "Emotional intimacy *is* sharing protected personal information. Such vulnerability strengthens trust in oneself and others. It can diminish fear and aloneness. Practiced, it will create a safe space for working through difficulties."

"Gabe, I don't know what I said but—"

"Amy, it's not you. I just don't want…" but then I had to pause. I closed my eyes before I continued, "too often, sex has been a tool and not anything akin to love. I want a love life where sex is complementary and not the creative focus."

"Oh, me too, Gabe. Let me explain."

"Amy, I don't want you to backpedal. We have to be honest with each other."

"I am honest. I don't need to backpedal. Please, Gabe? I know we want the same thing."

I frowned.

Dude! Emotional intimacy connects. It deepens the ordinary and opens possibilities for the extraordinary. Come on. Cut the defense. Trust a little.

Yeah, well, Mendes. You were never much for rollercoasters.

You're strapped in, dude. It's just the dishes with Amy.

What if risk could come with reward? Wasn't this the point of my work with Pythia? Hadn't Dr. Ruth said as much? And Trane. And Higgs.

"Amy. I feel foolish. I overreacted. Maybe my second ray got too creative. You know, not in a good way."

"No, it was me. I pushed you too hard." She lowered her eyes, and I narrowed mine.

"What do you mean?"

She hesitated. "Well, being too creative in the wrong way, that's what I was, well, trying to illuminate." She lifted her gaze.

What'd I tell you, Mendes? Epigenetics, not to mention your real-life experiences. Love's not your game.

"Oh, I see. So you think my ray's—"

"No, not your ray, but—" She grabbed her notebook and began paging, rambling under her breath, speed-reading. "Okay. So, here it is. The second ray helps us feel alive through our emotions. Freeing us from our limited thinking so we can feel desire inside our bodies. Desire precedes all creation. It is impossible to manifest anything without desire. However, if one is not conscious of one's true desire, the outcome may not be healthy and will not promote the evolution of humanity's highest good."

I scratched my beard and shook my head, scoffing. "Is that supposed to make me feel good?"

She set the book aside. "It's complicated, Gabe. This is not about you feeling good." Then seeing my expression, she quickly added, "Come on, you know what I mean. This is hard to explain. Let me try it in my own words." She thought for a moment. Then licked her lips. "Okay. Our sexual identity is essential to us as humans."

I nodded but glared.

She eyeballed me. "I feel on the spot," she said as she rolled her shoulders and stretched her neck. "I can't do this with you staring at me like that. Can we just be normal for a minute? Dry the dishes and talk?"

"So, you insult my ray, and now you want me to clean?" I tried to joke but sounded hostile. I sighed, and with a towel in hand, I nodded to the few dishes in the drying rack.

"You're making me nervous," she said, pulling the sink plug and draining the water.

"I didn't know you got nervous." I hip-bumped her.

"Everybody gets nervous." She rinsed the suds from the basin.

We were quiet for a moment, then Amy spoke, this time sounding easy, almost casual, more like a peer. "So, the rays can get jammed up. You know, like from cultural or familial expectations. And then they don't work as well, and we can't get their full benefit." She paused and I turned toward her, drying the frying pan.

"I'm listening, I said.

"So," she began again, "with the second ray, it can really mess with a person's ability to feel safe and free to be intimate. And I don't just mean sex. People can disconnect from their emotions and even their bodies when the second ray is compromised." She waited for my reaction, but I kept my head down, drying a fork. "Then, there's no flow, and grasping begins." I felt her sideways glance. "That's when controlling and addictive behaviors, fear of abandonment, a loss of personal power, even career ambivalence can happen," she said and straight up looked at me.

Ruminating I ran the cloth back and forth over a fork, its chewed-up tines evidence of time caught in the garbage disposal.

"Are you always that thorough," she pointed to the fork, "or are you just trying to impress me?" I could tell she was nervous.

"What? Oh." I set the fork aside. It lay alone on the fancy quartz counter. "No, I guess I was lost in thought," I said taking in the brand-new white counter with its sparkly flecks, looking so clean and modern. "See?" I said, sounding agitated and tossed the white towel atop the remaining dishes waiting in the drying rack. "This is what I was afraid of, having a broken ray, and that's not a euphemism," I began to rant as I grabbed a spoon from rack. "And I'm not trying to be funny, but you should know mine is messed up. No passion or creativity. Controlling relationships. Stuck in a job. No career! No guts! I might as well be dead for the amount of life I live. That's me to a 'T'! Okay?" I looked straight at her, feeling a lifetime of self-pity, and dared her to deny it.

"Oh, hey!" she said, looking right at me and when I looked away but she craned her neck to get up in my face. "Gabe?" she asked.

I shrugged and took a risk, but still clung to the spoon. "I should say, that was all true before I met you." I didn't move. I stayed frozen right beside her. Her hip was just a bump away. I was at a crossroads. A tug of war between my strong desire to trust in Amy and a love life with her, or my downhearted fear of betrayal and rejection from her.

"Gabe, look at me," she said, "Please?" and I remembered asking her the same just a day ago, so I looked at her and she looked right back at me. I searched her face; she tilted her head. Something flashed, and a plethora of options appeared right there in front of me.

"What if my second ray is wrecked?" I asked taking a different path and re-trieved the towel. The cells of the grid shifted and populated with all the varieties of my busted ray. "I mean, does the book talk about treatment?" and in an instant, they shifted again, everything brightened.

"Gabe, nothing's broken. The rays are organic and dynamic. They're chang-ing all the time, but..." as she paused, she licked her lips, and I could see she was figuring out how to make me feel okay. "If something happens that is scary enough, or often enough, the rays can become..." this time she seemed to search in general for the right words and not so much for my sake. I looked away, giving her room to do so. "I guess they can get stuck."

She craned her neck again, trying to get a look at me. "But they can heal. Not to worry. Okay?" She brought her hand slowly to my back and I'd actually felt the heat of it before she touched me. "Are you worried? Look at me. Everything's okay. Let me tell you about the fourth ray. It'll make you feel better. It's in the heart center." By the sound of her voice, I knew she thought she had me by the hand, helping me down off the ledge. But boy was she wrong!

"Amy," I said, giving the spoon and the towel a toss into the sink. The mangled fork laid on the counter, ugly and alone, while the brilliant quartz flecks flashed in the morning sun. "I might not be clear on the second ray, but I already know my heart is broken."

"Listen," she said, looking at me, but I couldn't face her. "Things aren't always what they seem to be. You're resilient, Gabe. That's the foundation of health. It fortifies a person's ability to problem-solve." Amy grabbed my hands. Hers were warm and wrinkled from the hot soapy water. Somewhere the electric blue cells shifted. Inside my body, my own cells accommodated the adjustment. Something reorganized inside my head.

Amy's real, dude. She's really real.

I drew in a breath, on the exhale my muscles relaxed and I let go of the old broken idea about my worth.

"Gabe? Hear me out. Okay?" Her voice drifted into my awareness as space and time opened into the infinite sea of possibility. "Gabe?" She squeezed my hands.

"Yeah. Okay." I squeezed back.

"Thank you." Sounding relieved, she inhaled. "The fourth ray is a bridge between our earthly and the spiritual experiences in life. Without this bridge, our physical life's struggle is meaningless, and the value of the spiritual body is of no practical use. This bridge, the heart center," letting go of one of my hands, she lay hers at my chest, "cleanses the emotional experiences of the second ray, making it possible to feel intimately and spiritually connected to everyone and everything." She retook my hands. "Look at me," she demanded, and while I wasn't looking away, I also wasn't exactly looking at her, that is until she insisted.

"Once a person lets this happen," she said, her eyes making meaningful contact with mine, "they realize they belong, they see their purpose, they feel the power of their own love, and they love like they've never loved before. That's what I've wanted to say." She paused. "Well, that and this." She rolled her eyes. "Sorry to ramble, but in a nutshell, sex can become lovemaking by simply participating consciously in the energetic experience of life. By being fully alive. Not numbed. Not altered. Not deluded."

"So? I have to bridge between the second and the fourth?"

"Well, I'm just learning too, but yeah, something like that. We can figure it out together."

I searched her face. "You would do that with me?"

"I thought we were already doing it?" Her voice was soft. "I already started. Are you telling me you haven't because I think you have." I blinked a few times before my brow creased. "Close your eyes." I obliged. When her plump lips blessed my eyelids, I surrendered and the word "tender" came to my mind. She slid her hand to the center of my chest. "Heart center," she whispered, her breath heavy at my ear, the edges of her teeth tugging gently at my lobe. "Next stop, second ray. Very hot."

I disappeared, fell into the space between us. Floating. Drifting nice and deeply down until my eyes popped wide open.

"Amy!" I pulled away. "I gotta tell you about my job."

30

Later, Amy sat cross-legged on her sofa meeting my intensity. "Okay. I'm all ears," she said. I fidgeted in the quicksand trap of the over-stuffed chair across from the sofa wishing I'd never mentioned my job. "Go ahead," she encouraged me while yanking one of the afghans from the back of the sofa and wrapping herself in the super chunky yarn.

"Well," I began, still trying to assimilate all that had happened in the last 24 hours while gauging Amy's sincere interest in me and all my problems. She met my hesitation with uncompromising attention, looking completely earnest except for the bed head. I ran my tongue over my unbrushed teeth before admitting to myself that despite our physical intimacy, Amy's frankness still frightened me. "Okay, well, my mother's a nurse. My grandmother was a teacher, and my grandfather and stepfather were/are both lawyers. I thought I wanted to be a lawyer, too," I said, trying to shrug loose from my propensity for self-judgment. Allowing my shoulders to drop, I shifted in the floral-patterned chair, my hand appreciating the smooth cotton finish.

"I didn't know you wanted to be a lawyer."

"Yeah. Well, I mean, I don't know if I ever really thought, I want to be a lawyer, but I did want to help people. And at some point, I realized being a lawyer wasn't the way to help, not how I wanted to help anyway. Looking back, I had a sense of that even before law school, and I am not proud of this." She continued to listen directly facing me, her legs still crossed, her back erect, her eyes tracking my story. I drew a breath and continued, "I was blown away by my acceptance to Northwestern. I romanticized the Midwest. You know, true grit and all. Like it would be the place for an aspiring young Atticus Finch." I snorted at my naivety while stealing a glance at Amy to see if the risk I was taking was worth it. "I think it was just an indication that I really didn't know what I was *really* doing," I continued after registering that Amy was 100% engaged in my story. "In my defense, I was this kid from the mountains, from the west." I felt small, making such a confession.

"Well, *really*, Northwestern is really nothing to sneeze at."

"Okay, but..." I said, scowling, at the same time finding a flaw in the smooth cotton fabric with its pretty flowers. I had her attention, but she was missing the point. I wanted to be honest about everything, lay the deal I'd been dealt down on the table. Reveal my personal protected information leaving nothing hidden between us. "What I'm saying," I began and picked at the nub, "is less about my successes. It's more that I didn't know much about the world. I don't want to harp on it, but I was this kid from Colorado."

"You were *really* a cowboy?" She teased, grinning from across from me. Still cross-legged and now leaning so far forward that she braced herself with a hand on the coffee table full of books. I thought about abandoning the conversation, but the chair had laid claim to me. It was too late. I'd never get out now.

"Look, I didn't know about the workings of big-city politics." I raised my voice struggling in the chair. "Or big business and the law. Like I said, I pictured myself as this small-town Atticus Finch." Embarrassed, I blushed and hoped she'd seen how vulnerable I'd made myself.

"*To Kill a Mockingbird*. Fabulous story and world-class character, Atticus Finch. You *really* could have done worse."

"Okay, I *really* want you to stop saying *really*. It's *really* annoying, and this *really* isn't easy for me. I am trying to share something really personal. Private. Something I want to be upfront about. I've never done that before. Not even with myself. But if you're not interested in this level of conversation, just say." Breathless, I wished I could take back the last part, having said it only out of self-protection.

Not too equanimous, Mendes.

Dude, seriously? She's not gonna break-up with you because you were honest. Use the bridge. Be a little big-hearted to yourself.

Amy closed her eyes before she covered her face with her hands. "Argh!" she growled and then slowly toppled over sideways until she laid still on her side.

Confused and a little scared, I waited. Then leaning in, I asked, "Amy?"

She slid her hands to reveal only her eyes.

Perplexed, I cocked my head orienting to her perspective. "Are you okay?"

"I'm an idiot." She covered her face again and growled. "I'm embarrassed." She sat upright on the sofa. "Ugh!" she said, looking like something tasted terrible. "I don't know why I do that. I know you're telling me something really significant. I can feel how personal it is, and what do I do?" She threw her hands up. "The thing I just did. Instead of taking you up on this really personal moment, I act like a third-grader." She covered her face again. Then revealing herself, she said, "Sometimes I do that. I'm sorry."

"It's okay. I do it, too," I said, feeling a foot on the bridge. "Amy?" I leaned toward her in spite of the overly soft chair and with the strangest sense of confidence. "Like you said, we're both learning. We're gonna make mistakes, fail even." I maneuvered, edging to the outer limits of the cushion. Pushing not only against some unseen physical boundary but moreover opposing my usual fear-based emotional programming, I finally stood. Gangly and awkward at first, I covered the short distance to sit next to her.

"Healthy emotional intimacy connects us at that second ray, but love's more than that. If we're gonna trust each other, we gotta trust ourselves. We gotta have faith it'll be okay no matter what happens when we make ourselves vulnerable." I held her with my eyes and brushed her messy hair from her face. I kissed her. Then meeting her eyes again, I said, "Intimacy is the gateway to love. I guess that heart thing is the bridge over." She searched my face. I shrugged. "How can we practice intimacy without exploring the habits that prevent it? Maybe exploring the behavior and the limiting beliefs that drive it *is* a part of emotional intimacy."

She wiggled, shaking off the crocheted throw. "Because our limiting beliefs are Newtonian. Cause and effect. If I'm vulnerable, I'll get hurt." Fully engaged, she carried on in her Amy way. "But you and I are dancing with Higgs." She pointed between us and the well-worn sofa cushions absorbed her excitement. "We can't expand beyond the center of ourselves without journeying the distance from our own self-preoccupation to witnessing each other. There's wisdom in the journey. It provides a sense of security. Holy moly, hotshot. Discovering intimacy is as beneficial as the actual acquisition of it."

Then something internal caught her attention. Her expression fell. She reached for me. "Oh, my God, Gabe. I really did push you. I was disconnecting when you wanted greater connection." We shared an honest look, a transparent exchange that revealed our vulnerability and then weighed the trust between us. "I am so sorry," she said, "Please, tell me about wanting to be a lawyer."

"Well," I chuckled, "Law is far more political than I'd understood. I became miserable thinking my dream was dying and believing I wasn't good enough for what I thought I'd wanted. Basically, I lost my confidence, and it nearly killed me. I felt I had no choice but to move back to the foothills and settle for the job as a paralegal." I shrugged. "Yeah, so I've been bored and disappointed ever since, professionally, that is."

"It takes a lot of courage to step away from an expectation you had of yourself. One that other people shared, too. That's not easy."

"It's still not easy. But I know I'll figure it out."

"Of course, you will! I have no doubt. Raining frogs is a game-changer."

I tucked my chin and drew back. "Raining frogs?"

"You know, letting go and forgiving; self-acceptance is self-love."

"Huh," I said, making myself comfortable on the sofa, watching her.

"Also, it's sexy to think about you in Chicago, a big lawyer with all those gangsters." She giggled.

"Exactly!" I sat forward. "That's what I thought," I said, returning to a more relaxed pose.

"You know, we could have passed each other on the street back then. Or maybe we were at the same Cub's game. Did you ever have a cheeseburger at Billy Goat's?"

"How do you know Billy Goat's?" I grinned.

"My dad was from Chicago." She nodded, but then winced and went pale.

"Your dad?" I asked, confused as well as beginning to sense the need for concern.

"Yeah." She eyed me, then dropped her gaze. "So, my dad," she began and picked at the piping on the sofa cushion, "had an accident." She lifted her eyes to gauge my reaction.

"An accident?"

"And he died." She looked directly at me, her face slack.

"Oh, Amy. I'm so sorry." I inched forward.

"The *accident*," she said, articulated the word like it was her enemy, stopping me in my tracks, "well, let's just say, was not by accident. I took it hard, didn't make it easy for my mom." She picked at the afghan. "So a few years later, she shipped me off to my dad's folks in Chicago." She rolled her eyes. "Daddy's little girl." She looked at me with heavy eyes. "I've wanted to tell you, but I didn't know how."

I touched her knee wishing I could figure out how to come closer. All too familiar with the failure of words, I found her hand.

"After college, I went back for the summer. That's when we might have passed each other." She made a weak smile. "They're dead now, too. But they would have liked you, Gabe."

We sat, both of us seeing the scene, passing each other on the street or sharing a bench in Lincoln Park. Feeling the grief reverberating in the room both of us well knowing the haunting of such an echo.

"I don't know if I've ever really, *ever* told anybody about my dad," she said, reaching to fiddle with one of the studs in her lobe but instead took the earrings out. Setting them on the table, she pointed to the jewelry, "Turquoise means friendship. Did you know that?" she asked.

I barely shook my head and instead held her gaze.

"There was no note," she shrugged and sighed shaking her head, "but we all knew," she said, then tried to smile, but only looking sad, she looked away.

31

Returning home around lunch time wearing yesterday's dress shirt and black jeans, I was more jazzed about Amy than I imagined possible. Not for her sadness, but for how we'd come through some stuff that morning. Grabbing the morning mail before unlocking the door, I called out, "Cat, I'm home!" Shuffling through the letters, I headed to the kitchen. "Cat!" I called out again, filling her bowl, and then made a pot of coffee.

Carrying my favorite mug made by the loving hands of my favorite gal, now brimming with hot coffee, I headed upstairs, careful not to spill. I took a sizeable gulp seated at my desk before pulling out my journal. I ran my hand over the geometric design, remembering Amy's hand-tooled leather journal. Even though mine was only paper, I appreciated the colorful composition. I flipped to the back cover. *Passage—the Divine Rite to The Corridor.* I slurped from the cup, better appreciating Rusty Caldron's musings. *Organized expressions of the creative forces revealing life as vibrational rays in geometric forms.* I wondered what Rusty knew about the second ray. "How's that for things coming together, Cat?" I began paging through the notebook before realizing I hadn't yet seen Cat. "Cat?" I called, then listened. I imagined her stretching before jumping from the bed. I cocked my head to hear the familiar sounds of her footsteps traveling down the hall to see me at my desk. "Cat?" Her name died into the stillness. Concerned, I rose, making my way from room to room, checking in all the usual places, but the old girl was nowhere in sight.

Finally, on all fours beside the bed, I craned my head sideway. "Oh, Cat," I said, short of breath. She barely lifted her head, drooling, her eyes sunken. I army-crawled under. Once out, I could see the situation was grave. I grabbed the neatly folded Spider-Man tee from beneath the pillow and wrapped it around her unbelievably frail body. How did this happen? Her eyes now dull sunken, her beautiful coat matted. I kneeled beside her, feeling like a clumsy giant, afraid to touch her again but wanting nothing more than to make her better. When had she gotten so thin?

"This is a good-looking cat." The vet, about my age, donned blue scrubs, her brown hair pulled into a ponytail, her freckled face sans makeup. "She's got perfect markings: white chest and socks; no Hitler mustache. Those are always funny, aren't they?" She turned in my direction, but obviously seeing I was in no shape for small talk, she unwound her scope from around her neck and listened to Cat's heart and lungs. She palpated her abdomen and then checked her ears and teeth. "Beautiful tuxedo. What is she, about sixteen, seventeen?"

"Probably older." I stood next to the table with one hand on Cat's haunches, hoping to comfort her. Feeling Amy's presence just a few feet behind me, I turned to her. "I should know how old she is." Amy placed her hand at my back and I turned to the vet and said, "It seems like she's been with me forever." A flash of heat shot through my chest, my stomach turned, and my knees weakened. I needed to sit, but I didn't want to leave Cat's side.

"She's badly dehydrated," the doctor said, finishing her exam. "It could be the beginnings of kidney failure…." She went on, but I didn't hear a word. Instead, "no," looped loudly in my head. No, no, no, no, no. Amy put her hand on my shoulder, and I tuned back in. "So," the vet said, her voice on a frequency I could hear again, "Does that sound like a good plan?"

I looked at her wide-eyed. "I'm sorry. What did you say?"

"Let's get her started on some fluids. Okay?"

"Alright." I gently stroked Cat who reached toward me and rested her paw on my hand. I leaned over and kissed her.

"I think it's good news," Amy said, making her way to the other side of the exam table once the vet had gone. "It could be an acute kidney episode due to simple dehydration, or it could be symptomatic of something else. She suggested bloodwork, or you can wait and see how she does once she's hydrated."

"Thank you." I nodded but still wasn't really hearing anything other than the one question I had in my head. "Do you think she'll be okay? She's not gonna die, right?" I knew I sounded like a child.

"Well, yes, she is going to die, but I don't think it will be today or tomorrow. Let's make it our business to help her feel better. Okay?"

I bit my lip.

She walked around to my side of the table and put a finger to my lips. "Stop."

"What do you say, Cat?" I asked, soothing my lip while bending down to meet the face of my most treasured friend. "Sound good?"

An hour later, the clinic sent us home with one well-hydrated Cat, a bag of fluids, needles, written instructions on how to deliver fluids twice a day, and our next appointment time. Amy got busy setting things up while I made Cat comfortable upstairs. By the time I came down, the kitchen had taken on the look of a medical setting. A clamped fluid-bag dangled, suspended from one arm of the chandelier that hung over the table, that was now covered in a large bath towel with packaged needles neatly arranged at the end. Amy had taped the cheat sheet to a cabinet. The paper illustrated how to insert a sharp needle through a pinch of skin tented at the back of Cat's neck. Someone had highlighted, *move swiftly and efficiently through the tough skin.*

"It's a lot to remember with all the worry. I really don't mind staying to help, especially the first time." Amy offered again as we stood at the door.

"Thanks, but I'll remember," I said, feeling queasy thinking about pushing something sharp into my best friend. "You should lunch with your friend. We'll be fine."

"I'll come every day if you like. You're not alone. Okay?"

"Okay."

"See you later?" She locked in on me, showing unwavering support.

"Yeah. Okay. Thanks," I said, not meeting her eyes and closing the door. Then I spied on her from the small diamond-shaped window. Amy walked with her head down. Once in the car she looked at herself in the mirror before backing out, and I wondered why. In my mind, I imagined our roles reversed. Me leaving her after such happenings. What would I see in the rearview glass? What would I be looking for?

Still on vibrate from the vet visit, my phone buzzed in my pocket. *No Caller ID.* But no sooner had I terminated the call than the phone hummed again.

Persistent marketer! Annoyed, I made a show of declining the call. But without haste, the phone whizzed again.

"Stop calling! Whatever you're selling, I'm not interested." I could barely hear over the static.

"Oh!" the caller said, followed by a stream of incoherent barrage, and then, "Cat." Thinking it might be the vet, I pulled the phone from my ear, hit speaker, and raised the volume.

"Hello!" I shouted over the top of the garbled rambling. "Call back! Our connection is bad!" The caller carried on, so I brought the phone close and listened hard.

"Agape mou?"

"Pythia! Can you hear me?" I listened hard. "Pythia? WE HAVE A VERY BAD CONNECTION. Please, Pythia! CALL. BACK." I listened, but there was nothing to hear. All that was left was white noise. "PYTHIA! ARE YOU THERE?" I hollered while thinking I should just hang up. But I couldn't. I couldn't just let the connection go.

"Can you hear me now?"

"Yes, yes! I can hear you."

"Oh, agape mou. I've just learned about Cat."

"Oh, Pythia." I pinched the bridge of my nose and squeezed my eyes shut. "How is she?"

"Weak." My chin quivered. "But she's a real trooper, Pythia. You know Cat. She's, um, she's gonna be fine." I squeezed my eyes shut again and took a breath. "Ah. I, uh, I gotta give her these fluids." I pointed to the hanging bag even though Pythia was on the phone and couldn't see me. "Amy took us." I pointed to the door, then ran my hand through my hair and paced. "Amy was great. I don't know how I could have done it without her. Things are good with Amy. Really good." My voice cracked. I swiped at tears. "So," I said, sitting down, saying nothing more, only running my hand over the bath towel, hoping to anchor myself to something real.

"Gabe." The sound of my name sounded like a prayer. "How are *you*?"

"I'm a mess, Pythia," I said, breaking down. "Why would this happen? Why now? When I'm falling in love with Amy? Why would something bad happen when I trusted things to be good?"

"Oh, agape mou. Love does not require sacrifice, and it certainly doesn't punish."

"But Cat was fine, and then I went home with Amy, and we—" I caught my breath. "I should've never spent the night at Amy's." I felt wobbly all over again. "This is bad. So bad. And right after a really good thing. Why would Cat get sick when I'm falling in love? It doesn't make sense. I know that some people might think it's silly that a man loves a cat. But Cat has been as true to me as anyone or anything, and I love her. I'm not embarrassed to say it. So, the thought of her," I choked down the unspoken words. My heart plunged into my stomach, but setting my jaw against it, I changed the subject. "But Amy's been great." I paused, trying to catch my breath. "Everything that's happened seems to have brought us closer, and we're starting to trust each other." My hand went deep into my curls. Was I making this up? Or was it real? "And that's weird, too. That bad stuff should make us more intimate. I don't know," I said, mouth-smacking an awful metallic taste, "nothing makes any sense."

"Are you quite alright?"

Crowded by her concern; our bad connection overwhelmed me. It was too much. Almost hallucinating, I worried her head would bust through the phone and push itself up into my face. Ginormous with misgivings. "Woah," I said, "I'm a little dizzy." Things spun.

"Close your eyes. Take a nice breath through your nose."

I did as she said, then gasped as the sensations slowed. "Thank God." I opened my eyes. The room was leveling off. Pythia no longer loomed over me like an awful caricature and then she was back inside the phone where she belonged. Where I could handle her.

"A lot has happened. You're grappling with the profound sorrow of grief. At the same time, you are integrating trust and intimacy. No wonder you're dizzy."

"I also told Amy about you."

"You did." I heard her smile. "You've certainly made yourself vulnerable to the hard work of self-trust and trust in others. No doubt you are ahead of schedule rounding the corner into the land of self-forgiveness."

"You'd have been proud. I told Amy how I'd thought becoming a lawyer would make me a shining knight on a white horse." I rolled my eyes and snorted, happy to think about something ridiculous. "The grandeur of it still makes me laugh. Nobody saves anybody, really. What a fool I'd been." I laughed, but then sighed and my eyelids fluttered. "I've told her everything now."

"You are tired. And if by pride you mean I am in awe of you, you are correct. I'm struggling myself just thinking of what you're processing. I wonder to myself, should I help Gabe see his realization that 'nobody saves anybody' has him eyeball to eyeball, wrestling with old fears around risk and reward?"

Her words were a lullaby about a man named Gabe.

"And then I shudder to think of the courage my friend Gabe gathers while he battles an old limiting belief. One that threatens to shadow not only great love already in his life but love that's blooming."

"I just don't want to let anybody down, Pythia." I slurred my words. My eyelids flickered and then closed. Letting go, I began drifting off beyond any hope of concentration. Then, barely uttering my deepest wish, I laid my head on Cat's soft towel, "I just wanna be loved," I mumbled and slipped into sleep.

32

The next time I saw Amy, she stood on the art museum's steps waving the postcard. As if I'd ever miss noticing her with her long legs and boyish figure or the way her short hair accentuated the grace of her neck and the shape of her head. She was unique and bold as one of O'Keeffe's brilliant poppies; the sun illuminating her like a Vermeer.

I kissed her, and she wholeheartedly kissed me back before we mounted the steps.

"Remember last time?" she asked, gesturing to the cement we climbed.

"I think we took them two at a time."

"I thought we flew."

I turned on the step and spied the tree where we'd taken shelter and remembered her struggle to breathe. Amy stopped and turned a few steps ahead of me. "It certainly looks harmless now," she said while we surveyed the park, green and glistening after a cool spring rain. "Well, at least there's nothing scary about this." She read from the card, "Picture This: A Love Story—Words by, your good friend," she looked to me, "Jane Austen."

Inside the gallery, once a railroad warehouse, most walls were stark white, but some revealed the old handmade red bricks. Big, tall rectangular windows cased in golden oak moldings soared to the high ceilings. Light flooded the room. The energy of the place was disciplined yet richly intimate.

I took a moment to consider the men who'd once worked in the same space, rolling handcarts full of boxes, stacking them deep and tall day after day after day. What would they think of the walls, now stenciled with Jane's words and filled with staged shots. Pictures depicting the same couple at the same location having nearly the same picnic with nearly the same props year after year after year.

Snapping a wad of gum, Amy reached for my hand. I leaned, searching beneath her sugary bubble gum breath, wanting a waft of her clean soapy scent. Unearthing it, I kissed her neck while she read aloud the exhibition text printed on the wall, "A stake in love spares no risks of abandonment and makes no room for pride. Only vulnerability births intimacy—the genesis of love, the balm of the aggrieved. Introspection and self-examination usher the morally discerned into a life well lived in love."

"The balm of the aggrieved?" I asked, studying the crisp paragraph of jet-colored words. I frowned thinking it'd always seemed to me that vulnerability had equaled grief, then wondered what was meant by the morally discerned.

"Speaking of the morally discerned," Amy whispered, making me think she'd read my mind, "I like this one." Together, we snooped, voyeurs drawn in by the intimacy. Peering deeper into a snapshot of life, Amy pointed. "The way she's turned, it's almost like she has her back to him, holding the knife like it's a secret."

"The distance between them is greater than in the previous pictures."

"But last year," Amy said, pointing, "she was leaning into him. Look, he had his arm wrapped around her. I wonder what happened." She moved on.

Following her, I gestured to the walls covered in the staged shots. "I don't know. But I guess they worked it out." Their hundreds of eyes meet mine, and while the pics had been made public, they were still private. What had the couple wanted of us in making themselves so familiar? Had they hoped we could see something they couldn't. Or couldn't admit?

"Yeah." Amy sounded pensive. Standing behind her, I wrapped my arms around her. She leaned into me, and I kissed the top of her head. "Do you think you'd ever do anything that'd make me want to kill you?" she asked, then with her gum blew a bubble in my face before walking away.

"Probably. I know I've wanted to kill myself before."

She spun around. "Don't say that! Seriously. I was kidding about what I said. And you're kidding too, right?"

"Of course," I said right away. "I'm sorry. What I meant was what everybody thinks about, well, being eradicated in some way." I looked to the pictures but again thought of the men who'd worked here, some traipsing, some rushing across these very floors a hundred years ago. How often does anyone want out of their commitments? Was it merely moral discernment that kept us obliged?

"Okay, agreed, but…." She took my hand and led me to the black leather bench in the middle of the gallery. Before sitting, she took a wrapper from her pocket, deposited her pink gum into the paper, looked around, then tossed it into a not-so-near-by can.

"Wow. Impressive," I said, returning my gaze from her slam-dunk.

She brushed off her hands, then sat and taking my hand, said, "Can we agree to be there for each other at such woeful times? I'm sorry I said that. I want you to know, I want to hear everything you have to say. Crazy, or desperate, or haunting, or—"

"Loving?"

"Yes, loving, too. Like that." She pointed to an early photo where the man carried the woman in his arms, and she wrapped hers around his neck. They both looked directly into the camera. "Love is not a state to enter with a heart half-full of doubt," Amy read the stenciled quote above the picture.

"That woman looks like the cat that ate the canary." I grinned, witnessing the trust the photographed couple had in themselves and each other.

"She does. And he looks like he caught a big fish. They look happy, don't they? I wonder how old they are. What do you think, twenty?"

"Barely," I said, imagining the pictured pair's spontaneity.

We made our way through the photographs. Their vulnerabilities. Their secrets. Things they'd traded for convenience. The woman, indeed nine months pregnant. The man, middle-aged, extended a casted leg resting atop a pillow. There was a duplicate of the one where he was carrying her over the threshold, but this time they were in their fifties, still appearing confident and satisfied. Sometimes the spread of food gave insight into their habits or trends of the time. Buttermilk fried chicken wrapped in wax paper, with sides of pickles and potato salad in glass refrigerator dishes, all spread out on a floral tablecloth. A kite in the grass. Years later, a transistor radio sat on a red checked cloth with plastic utensils rolled in paper napkins and a lime Jell-O ring that had been flipped from its Tupperware mold. A Frisbee in the grass. Then, a bucket of chicken with dinner sides in Styrofoam containers and cans of Coke. An easel in the grass with the beginnings of a painting capturing the creek-side willow. In others, the basket was closed, its contents kept secret.

Fifty years of moral discernment, dude.

I nodded to myself and, under my breath, said, "There is no righteous moral-ity in love." Equanimity, I thought.

Amy stood ahead of me several pictures down and only three from the end. "Oh!" I heard her gasp.

"Amy?"

She turned in my direction with one hand over her heart, the other covering her mouth. I rushed to her. Her eyes were desperate for mine as she pointed to the old man in the picture, forlorn and staring past the camera, sitting in the tall grass, alone, without a blanket or a basket.

"Oh," I sighed.

Did he regret making himself vulnerable to her, to us? Or was it true that in the face of abandonment, his vulnerability had gifted him intimacy that now sheltered him in grief? Was that the way of the healing heart?

33

Pythia appeared as always. First like a mirage, her reflection rippling as if on water instead of the laptop, and finally in high definition so that it seemed I could almost reach into the computer and touch her.

"Hey!" I waved tossing the Rubik's cube aside and pulling my chair closer to the desk.

"Hey, yourself." Pythia smiled. "I've good news. I've finally connected with Francis of Assisi. He's on Cat's case. She's in good hands."

"St. Francis?"

"Yes, the patron of all sentient and non-sentient beings. We've been working together since he put his indulged and high-spirited ways behind him." Then she whispered, "He was a devotee of troubadours and then had a sort of come-to-Jesus moment." She further lowered her voice. "Zeus is very touchy on the subject of Jesus. He may have instigated that whole business about the name Jesus meaning 'Hail Zeus.'" She made a face as if something smelled foul. "But like you, Francis was awakened to love, that greatness that lies within. So, how's our Cat?"

"Ah, well, she's right here." I nodded at Cat, curled up in her favorite spot on the desk. "Aren't you, Cat?" I asked, tugging Cat's tail, but she slept too deeply to notice. "She's so, so," I murmured, frowning, waggling my hand. "On the mend," I added loudly, not wanting to speak of Cat as if she weren't right there. "She'll be herself in no time. Isn't that right, old girl?"

"And you?"

"Okay. I'm okay. I just …." I paused to observe the rise and fall of Cat's breath, its rhythm a song to distract me from telling the truth. I came closer to the computer's camera. "I don't want to let her down." My voice was low. "She's always there for me, and I wanna do right by her. You know?" I weighed how honest to really be, wondering what I was supposed to say.

"I know you will." Pythia sounded so sure and wanting to join in the glass half-full, I exaggerated the arch of my brows.

"You know, Pythia," I said, loud enough and in an attempt for Cat's attention. "Cat used to fetch."

Impressed, Pythia's brows arched too.

"I know, right? Way back in high school when I'd crumple a homework paper, I'd give it a toss over my shoulder. Next thing I knew, Cat would be sitting on my desk with the paper in her mouth." I grinned. "It got so that whenever I sat at my desk, I'd have to throw a wadded paper ball just to keep her from pestering me. Eventually, we made a game of it. I'd throw it down the hall and she'd race off to bring it back. Right old girl?" I asked, while the smile spread farther across my face, but Cat only slept. "You know," I continued my sales pitch, "when she was a kitten, she used to sleep in the crook of my neck," but Cat didn't stir. I frowned. Then noticing the cube somehow clutched in my hands, I shoved it aside again. "Anyways, I don't know what made me think of all that. It just popped into my mind."

"Cat medicine." Pythia made a little smile.

I returned her sympathetic gesture but then blinked rapidly before turning away.

"Eyeball to eyeball with grief, agape mou, your vulnerability will be soothed through the intimacy you've shared," Pythia said, and when I returned my gaze to her, she met me with the kindest eyes. "It's how you'll forgive yourself, hmm? Cat has been your prophesier of love," she said, but I was mute and only stared. Concern crossed her face and she crossed her arms to hold her elbows. Her bracelets jangled; the soft green gown shifted. Then letting out a little sigh, she dropped her arms to her sides and cocked her head.

I blew out my cheeks. "Yeah, she has." I nodded rubbing my neck, wishing for some other topic.

"Far more than just storge." She pulled at a thin lock of hair and twirled it around her finger.

"Yep." I nodded, thinking months back to that chart. "Yep. There's ludus. Anyway, when Cat's feeling well, we are very playful and affectionate. I'd say

our love is unconditional." I wanted Cat to hear, to understand what I was telling Pythia was meant for her too. "I think she'd say that, too. So that's agape." I
looked sideways at Cat, really wishing she'd rally. "Philia, there's definitely comradery between us. We've been through some stuff for sure." I paused, wishing
for a half-hearted flick of her tail at least, but all I got was the steady rise and fall
of her breath. "And pragma, the test of time, each of us accepting the other as we
are." I nodded, realizing that it wasn't so easy to accept Cat as sick, but soldiered
on as if that would make it bearable. "Even philautia. Cat's love has helped me
see myself lovingly as I've loved her, and it's helped me believe I am loveable as
she's loved me." I cringed, my vulnerability becoming sentimental. "My mood's
all over the place. One minute a pushy salesman peddling that-a-boys to Cat and
the next a pathetic fool, and it makes no difference anyway," I said beginning to
sound sloppy, tossing a hand toward Cat, still fast asleep. I lowered my voice.
"But even if it doesn't matter," I said chewing my thumbnail, "I still believe everything, all of it."

"You need say no more. I know you love Cat and she you. Partners in crime, yes?"

"Yeah, partners in crime." I pulled my thumb away and fingered the rough
edges of the nail, but agreeing with Pythia only ramped me up again. "Hey, that
reminds me of this art I saw with Amy. The message was kinda like life's a picnic.
You know what I mean, ants and rain, too much sun and sometimes just enough
shade from a tree. You know you don't picnic alone!" I laughed. "What I mean
is that love is messy, and you gotta make yourself vulnerable to the picnic." I
rambled.

Dude, you're yelling.

"The good, the bad," I rattled on. "You know surviving it all fortifies self-love,
and like the Greeks said, self-love amplifies all the other loves. It's just one big
circle of love that spills into a bigger one—love and grief are never-ending, always
pushing life forward."

"Yee-ess," Pythia said and nodded as if in slow motion. "Theee ele-phan-nnt
innn theee roo-oom."

"Well, six out of seven kinds of love, that's pretty decent." I babbled pretending things were fine. "Of course, no Eros. Yeah, that'd be weird with Cat." I dabbed
at beads of sweat forming on my brow, fighting the awareness that no matter how

hard I tried to stop thinking about Cat, she was really all I thought about. "But I am madly in love with her!"

Dude, stop!

"Are you quite alright?" Pythia asked, sounding normal again.

"Yes, yes. It's the heat in here. I think it's broken. Well, look at the time." I pointed to the clock. "We should get working." But I couldn't budge from the eddy of grief. Wretched and sinking down under, I made a valiant attempt to save myself and clawed my way to the nearest lifesaver I could find, "So," I began, "speaking of eros, does it *have* to be dangerous?" I feigned intellectual curiosity, raising my brow, but really it was to keep sweat from my eyes.

"Agape mou, are you ill?"

"No, no. Not at all, not at all. Please, please," I blinked against the sweat.

She studied me hard.

"I'm fine. Really. Let's just talk about eros." I swiped my sleeve quickly across my face.

"Eros?" She sounded suspicious, eyeing me.

"Yes, yes, I'm very interested."

"Well," she began but paused, and I nodded like my life depended on it.

"Please, please," I said.

"Eros," she said, "rightly refers to all passion. In healthy expression, the divine desire of any passion can draw out a deep desire for collaboration. Sexual passion is just one kind of passion."

"Is that so. Well, good, good." I smiled like the idiot I'd become, suddenly having no idea of what she'd said.

"Why do you ask?"

"Why? Yes, well, of course, it's because Amy and I, we had sex," I blurted out.

Dude! Really? Some respect.

This isn't a locker room, Mendes.

"Sex?" Pythia asked, sounding like she didn't believe me.

"Yeah. I don't know what I'm talking about." I scratched my head and pulling back from her and the second elephant, now in the room, I apologized. "I'm sorry. I'm not myself."

From the frying pan to the fire, Mendes.

Dude! Where's the moral discernment? This isn't just your protected personal information.

Not to mention, Mendes. You just opened a giant can of some get-real emotional intimacy.

"Pythia, I don't want—I can't—I don't know—" And then, suddenly, I saw a way out of being honest. Narrowing my eyes, I turned the tables. "I mean, you know about sex, right?"

Dude!

Well. But did Pythia? Did she really know about sex? After all, she was a high priestess and had sent the good doctor. Maybe she wasn't at all intimate with the subject.

Really, dude? Is this what you want?

Ah, yes, Mendes, a nice turn of events, indeed. The arrogant coward, prodigal son, returned and fully kicked back in the La-Z-Boy to savor the warm, smooth sensation of two-fingers of doubt and skepticism with a splash of gas-lighting.

Somewhere something low grumbled vibrating my chair. A low frequency rolled through followed by a sharp, loud crack that clapped, roared, and rumbled. Feeling the thunder, I startled upright out of my seat when the jolt of lightning shot through the room.

Now standing, it was clear to see the sky was blue. There was not a cloud to be found. "What was that?!" I asked and then bending over, I scrutinized the seemingly frozen screen. Pythia stood perfectly still, somber faced. "Pythia?" Frantic, I pounded the reset key. "Please, no," I begged. "Let her just have glitched," I said, hunched over, my face to the screen. "Pythia!" I yelled, sure she'd been hit, killed, and at any moment would collapse to the ground, dead.

Pythia blinked, and Cat startled, looking herself like the awakened dead. "Oh, thank God," I whispered lowering myself to sit and stroked Cat all the while monitoring the rise and fall of Pythia's breath. I waited, but Pythia only stared past me, and for long enough that I turned and looked over my shoulder.

"Pythia! Over here!" I waved.

"I *am* the high priestess appointed by Zeus," she barked flashing anger, "filled with the spirit of Apollo, oracle and son of Zeus."

"Oh, my God. She's been struck! Her brain is hurt," I muttered wide-eyed, bringing my hand to my mouth. "Oh, Pythia," I whispered.

"Celibate as a deity, it is true," Pythia snapped, then paused to eye me, "but not virgin as a human. It is the womb of a woman that provides grace for human-kind. The vessel that energetically connects the mortal to the divine, allowing divine inspiration to guide mortal insight and govern the will."

See? Moral discernment, dude.

Yeah, Mendes. Nobody likes a spineless—

"Okay, okay," I said, cutting myself off. "Pythia, Oh my gosh. I'm sorry—"

"For your information," she interrupted me, sounding uncharacteristically curt, "moral character is of the utmost importance as a high priestess. To infer sex, rites of passage, and sacrifices for purification are unfamiliar to me is to doubt my capacity."

Told ya, Mendes. Nobody gets out alive.

I scowled, pushing the black ram out of my mind and rushed in. "I'm sorry. Please forgive me." And then, for some reason I couldn't help myself. "But you did seem perplexed when I'd said that Amy and I'd, you know, had sex."

Dude, put down the shovel!

"*I* seemed perplexed that *you* had sex?" She paused just long enough with her brow arched. Then in her Pythia way, she dismissed it with a wave. "Not at all. But after everything, I thought you might refer to it differently."

"Good point," I said, making sure to maintain eye contact. "I guess I'd said it that way because, I don't know, we're always rationalizing, sanitizing things down here on planet Earth."

"But not you," she said, then waited. "Certainly, you're not afraid of intimacy." It was a bold move.

"Ahh. Well. No. I mean, yeah. In fact, I think that's exactly my struggle. I'm not. I mean, I was. Well, I am, but I'm—"

"Confused?"

"For sure! I don't know the rules. Like, how do you talk about sex? Or, how much is too much about Cat? Plus, I don't want to kiss and tell."

"Moral discernment."

"Right? I mean, love is really complicated. Seven kinds of love, four kinds of intimacy, the effects of cultural and personal history. Neurolinguistic program-ming, not to mention epigenetics, and causing an effect instead of cause and ef-fect. And now, morality! There's a pretty good chance I don't figure this out."

"I think what you mean is that love is complex, comprising interwoven and interconnected parts."

I tossed my hands in the air. "Whatever!" I snorted rolling my eyes. "So, if that's not complicated, then what's wrong with me?" I got right up in the camera. "Because as I understand it, love hinges on intimacy, which depends on vulnerability. Well, I got the vulnerable part of the equation covered, but I can't say that's made me very competent at intimacy or love. I'm uncomfortable just talking about intimacy." I sank back into the chair, running both hands through my hair. "Oh, my God! I'm so uncomfortable even talking about being uncomfortable!" I shoved my face into the camera again. "What if I'm incapable of true intimacy? Did you ever think of that? Be honest. I can take it."

"Agape mou. Slow down."

"Pythia! I'm finally in love. But I could blow it! Right? If I can't get this intimacy thing down. Wait, maybe that's always been the problem? Is it possible that I've never been intimate? That I've never loved anyone before?"

"While it's true—"

"Oh, my God! Oh, my God! I knew it. I'm chicken left on the bone. A sofa on the curb." I rocked in my chair like an imbecile.

"Gabe!" Her sharp tone cut through my madness. I pulled my head out of my hands and looked up wide-eyed. Pythia stood with her hands on her hips leaning into the camera. Her brows hunkered over her eyes. "That's right," she said, "slow down. You've much in your life right now. Some things you've desired and some you've feared. Everything is as it is. Breathe through the nose. That's right. Now, agape mou. It is true that if you are loving unconsciously, meaning without intention or attention, you can only love as well as you've been loved. But—"

"But what?"

"But, in that ignorant state—"

"Ignorant?"

"Well, yes," she paused, "without this new consciousness, you have been operating in ignorance."

"You're saying I'm ignorant in matters of love."

"You have been." She pulled her lips into a tight straight line.

"Seems harsh." I massaged my brow. "Pythia," I said, "I don't think I can be made happy in this conversation." I rolled my eyes and grabbed the stupid puzzle off the desk.

"Yes, you can." She was the voice of reason. "I certainly don't mean for you to feel uncomfortable or for the content of the information to be insulting. It is all just what it is. If you don't know what love is, how do you expect to recognize it, create it, and participate in it?" She paused, tilting her head.

"I suppose." I twisted the thing scrambling the colors.

"But even in ignorance, there's grace."

I lifted my gaze. She was generous, but I shook my head, embarrassed and worried I'd never leave my old smoke-and-mirrors ways behind.

"So, I do believe you've loved." Her voice was soothing. "And now, you are learning that love isn't something you can *honestly* do a little bit. It isn't something you stick a toe in to test it out. It isn't even something you do the best you can do. It is something you *do*. Either you love, or you don't."

"So, I've loved?" Please, please, please, say yes, I thought feeling the hard plastic edges of the cube.

"What does it matter?"

Sick to my stomach I let the puzzle remain in my lap. "This is too much. It's not what I want to hear. None of it." I looked at Cat, who'd fallen fast asleep again, and returned the Rubik's cube to the desk.

"I know," she said and said nothing more until she added, "All that matters now is that you *do* love. You now know that intimacy precedes love. That it's a slippery umbilicus, not meant for backing out of. Intimacy shoots you right into the spotlight and at center stage, exactly where you *can* create love. Do you see?" She played with her necklace while her eyebrows cast concern in my direction.

"I suppose." I rubbed the back of my neck and then reached for the cube. Stretching across the desk I placed it left of me, farther back and out of reach. "But I'm not a centerstage guy," I began now sitting square in the chair facing her head on, "and I want this so badly now." I brought my face close to the camera. "I wanna believe I can have it. I want my cake, and I want to eat it, too. Who wants cake you can't eat?" I nodded to Cat, unable to further articulate the fear that good things come with hefty price tags. "It's not like before. It's different now. I know things. I feel things that inspire desire in my cells, in my bones, in my heart.

Please don't let me mess this up. Please." I pleaded with my eyes. "I still don't *really* know what I'm doing, and that scares me."

"You are doing it just as it is done." She waited, then said, "It can be helpful to see that. Sometimes it's important to take inventory of what you've done and what you've learned. So, tell me, what have you learned about intimacy?"

Taking a breath, I looked aside to think. "Well, intimacy does emerge from vulnerability," I said, meeting her eyes. "And if you want to love someone, you have to make yourself vulnerable enough to learn who that person is. And if you want someone to love you, you have to be vulnerable enough to let them know who you are. So, if someone thinks you are a certain kind of person and you're not, or they expect you to be a certain kind of person, then that's a problem." I stretched my neck from side to side before continuing. "First, because they expect you to be different than how you see yourself or who you're practicing to become, but more importantly," I cracked my knuckles, "because the relationship is developing without an honest willingness to share who you are and/or to learn who the other is." I crossed my arms on the desk and leaned in. "And that's dishonest," I said noticing that insight felt plain, ordinary, normal even.

My muscles softened as a picture spilled into my mind and splashed through my body. That first date with Amy. The playful banter, moments of mutual admiration, the fabulous kiss before sharing our intellectual interests, and then the snowbow. "Intimacy is like a prism," I said, relaxing into the chair. "It changes the nature of the space between people. And when it's healthy, it refracts the white light, reflecting it into seven newly organized arcs of choice. A rainbow of color." I paused to take in my own words. "Like the seven kinds of love. You can choose one, or you can go for the gusto. Intimacy is not love, but it is the vehicle for experiencing love. Pythia?"

"Yes."

"I wanna give this another go."

She nodded.

"As mentioned, Amy and I, well, you know." I fumbled, wondering what Amy would want me to say, and then I knew, "We made love," I said and then, something stirred inside my chest. "Pythia," I said, trying to be very still. "I feel something. I think it's my heart." And there it was again—a quivering fledgling. Cat opened an eye. "Something's unfolding." Cat stood and stretched.

"Opening?"

"Yeah," I said like we were telling secrets. I giggled; there was no other word for it. Tickled at some effervescence. There it was again. Whatever it was, flashed and twinkled. "Yeah! It's opening now. Pythia, I'm in The Thang! I'm in love!"

"Splendid!" Pythia clapped. We both laughed, and Cat sat up, then yawned until her eyes crossed. I scratched her ears until she lifted her head, inviting me to do the same under her chin. Tall and pretty, she purred.

"Oh, this is beyond the Sun and the Moon!" Pythia crossed her hands over her heart. Cat headed across the keyboard, striking keys as she went. Leaving behind the word VULNERABILITY in all caps. "Yes. Indeed. Thank you, Cat." Pythia said.

Cat jumped from the desk, a bit wobbly but all the same very independent, and left the room. "Pythia, are you and Cat—" I gestured to the keyboard.

"Research the 'V' word. Lunch at your place, noonish?" She waved and the screen began to fade. "Oh!" I heard her say and then coming back into focus, she said, "see if you can compose a mathematical equation for love. You know, something like $E = MC^2$? Toodles!"

"Wait, what?" But she'd already vanished.

Gazing out at the rainy day from my desk, sipping peppermint tea, I lingered, enjoying the refreshing, bright taste before doing as Pythia had asked. The pond ran full, and I wondered how big the fish had grown over the winter. Cat cleaned her face with her paws, then circled and laid down in her usual spot. Taking the last warm gulp, I set Amy's mug aside, cracked my knuckles and typed v-u-l-n-e-r-a-b-i-l-i-t-y into the search bar. The definition was as I'd thought: *1. capable of being hurt; 2. open to temptation, persuasion; 3. liable or exposed;* but with one exception. It didn't include any reference to weakness.

I reached for my journal and pondered Rusty's reverie.

From the incalculably minute to the stellar, this metaphysical gestalt pervades the natural order of things. Exalted and unbounded shapes that tirelessly encircle the circles that make life, reminding us of our sacred beginning in oneness.

No matter the distance of space or time, was everything always dying to be reborn? Circling and cycling and recycling itself. Was this some natural mechanism for evolution? Could it be an unspoken agreement of love?

The book was rich with my writings. Patterns of letters informing patterns of thoughts that were penned, inscribing the paper with patterns of emotion. Some thoughtless and automatic but still leading to a consciousness. I looked to Cat breathing in life and breathing it out. The occasional flicker of a whisker, the rapid eye movement of her deep sleep. I'd always known it was likely I'd outlive her, and I'd loved her anyway. Could I bring such awareness and practice to my relationship with Amy? Could I decide and commit to love despite how it made me vulnerable to the rich, warm red world of intimacy?

Pen to paper I drafted. *We want love, but in fear of being hurt, we vacillate between the desire to connect deeply and the terror of rejection. Ironically, the tense marriage of desire and fear can produce vulnerability, the necessary component for the most profound experience of love. Terrifying, it requires that we lay down our defenses and stand honest, exposed for who we are.*

I ran my hand across the words as if they were brailled. Desire to love Amy and to receive her love swelled. "I want this," I told myself and prayed for it. Then, proactive, I answered the unspoken, ancient, and looming 'what if?' "I'll be okay," I said and then wrote. *Believing that we can be competent in the face of fear perpetuates inner integrity that emphasizes confidence and allows us to trust in ourselves. When we trust ourselves, we can better endure all of life's complications; we can trust our ability to discern the dependability of people and situations despite the uncertainty. Vulnerability means we trust in our own resilience despite the risk. We can live alive in love despite death.*

"Okay, Dr. Einstein. How about this?" I said, scratching the formula into my journal. *Confidence precedes trust. Trust precedes vulnerability. Vulnerability precedes intimacy. Intimacy precedes love. Therefore, trust multiplied by confidence divided into intimacy multiplied by vulnerability equals love.* $TC / I \times V = L$

34

"Dr. Ruth?" Having expected Pythia, I drew back from my front door. Through the downpour, I looked past the short, colorful woman standing in my doorway, but Pythia was nowhere. Across the street wearing pink raincoats and hats, Bubbles and Mushkin stomped in the puddled sidewalk. An abandoned umbrella lay open on the ground.

"Please, call me Ruth. May I?" Ruth asked squinting up at me, her glasses wet from the storm. "May I?" she asked again, but was already closing her sopping umbrella, stashing it on the front stoop, and stepping inside.

"Certainly. Yes, of course. It's nice to see you again." I scanned past Ruth, searching again for Pythia while strategically overlooking the kids who were now waving at me. But besides the girls, all I saw was rain pouring onto the empty streets and sidewalks. I cocked my head and lifted my brow. "How can I help you?" I asked asking closing the door and looking down at her.

Ruth hung her bright slicker on the coat rack by the door and wiped her feet before heading straight to the sofa. "Please," she patted the beautiful cushion as if it were her new sofa and I was the guest. "Have a seat," she narrowed her eyes, "I have something important to tell you," she said, waiting in a blazing bold blue suit with her black patent leather bag perched on her lap. Making my way across the room, I glanced out the picture window. The steady spring rain puddled on the gray and dreary sidewalks. Still there was no one but the kids in sight. "You needn't look for her. She's not coming."

I sat, but at the edge. Then misjudging the new sofa's depth as I turned to face Ruth my knees bumped the old Gothic style coffee table. Massive, the solid wood piece didn't budge. "Who's not coming?" I asked, trying to ignore the sting while realizing I was sitting uncomfortably close to her despite the sofa's comfort.

"Pythia." She nodded sharply.

"Pythia?" I asked, my gaze ping ponging from her to the window and back again.

"Now, listen," she began with I've-seen-it-all eyes. "She won't be here today, hopefully, tomorrow. But, we never know with these things. Especially at her age. She's no spring chicken. Please. Don't worry yourself so, you'll get wrinkles making those faces." She touched my knee. Her short fingernails painted bright glitter pink, her little hand hot on my leg. "Now, look, she told me, 'Tell him I will be fine.' So, she's fine. Okay?"

"I don't understand," I said shaking my head and shifting to scoot from under her hand to slide farther back and away from her.

"Where are you going?" she demanded waving at me, "I don't bite."

Ignoring the comment I leaned toward her, and asked, "Did something happen? What do you mean she'll be fine? What happened to Pythia?"

"Oh! I didn't say? Well, she fell snowboarding and maybe broke a leg. Can we turn on the lamp? It's dark in here."

"Broke her leg!" I shot up whacking my shin on the coffee table. "That's no little thing," I said, hobbling out from behind the table. "Where is she? Can I see her?" I asked bent over rubbing leg, my face screwed up in pain. "Wait," I righted myself to stand, "I just saw her. When did she go snowboarding?" I asked realizing I didn't even know where Pythia lived, or how she existed, let alone that she snowboarded. "I'm confused." I ran a hand through my hair. "Snowboarding? We've never talked about snowboarding. Am I going to see her again?" I paced on the old green carpet while Ruth sat tall on the sofa with her hands folded in her lap. Now on, the old lamp cast the room in a depressing thick yellow light. Nothing about her seemed so bright. Even the suit took a dingy green hue. "Wait," I halted, "are you her replacement?" I asked, sticking my neck out and leaving my mouth hang open. "I mean, she's the high priestess, and we're discovering the true meaning of love and how to secure it." Then catching sight of Ruth's stone face, I rushed over. "Oh, oh. No. I'm sorry. I didn't—I mean, I like you, and I'm sure we'd work fine together." I sat closer to her than before. "I'm sorry." I touched her arm. "Please, forgive me."

"It is quite alright. You're worried." Then she leaned in to whisper, "But you're right, she's no business snowboarding. But," she shrugged, "what business is it of mine?" She pulled a paper from her handbag. "Here are our instructions," she reported. "Review vulnerability and how it relates to intimacy and sex. Discuss the difference between intimacy and sex. Consider the mathematical equation for love. Introduce the concept of morality."

Sex! How much more could there be to discuss? I thought but instead said, "You know, a broken leg takes a long time to mend. I can't imagine any of this. Pythia skiing. It seems, well, ridiculous, really." I stood and made a wide berth around the table to stand at the window. "I'm sure it's true," I said with my back to her watching the rain. Then turned and said over my shoulder, "I guess. I mean, why would you lie? Of course, you wouldn't. I believe you. But it was only a few hours ago that Pythia and I spoke, and now you're telling me she went skiing in that time." I turned fully around to face her.

"Snowboarding," she said meeting my eyes.

"Alright, snowboarding!" I shrugged and paced again. "That's not the point. I'm trying to piece this together. I guess I don't know much about Pythia, and still, she's really important to me. We've been intellectually, emotionally, and experientially intimate. That's not nothing. It's a big deal. I've been vulnerable with her. I've trusted her. I guess I love her like a dear friend, and yet, I have no idea where she lives or what she does when she isn't with me. Do you think that means I haven't really been intimate with her? That I don't really love her?"

"She mentioned that the intimacy thing had your goat."

"I'm sorry?

"Pythia said that intimacy had you in a fix from the get-go, you know, twisted your melon, stirred up a hornet's nest. Figuring out intimacy has you flummoxed."

"Well, it's the key to love, you know? And, sometimes, I'm still afraid I'll—"

"Listen to me, okay! Sometimes, trust is all we have," Ruth said, and I nodded, but my tongue worried at the sharp edges of the crown on my tooth. "Now, let's get started," she said, then pointed to the sofa which looked so perfect despite the clunky table, the worn carpet, and the heavy drapes at the window. Smart casual, that's what Amy had said. "Sit," she frowned, "You're headed to the top of the mountain tomorrow, and I want you ready. Okay?" She smiled, but I barely noticed.

"Did she break her tibia or fibula? I hope it wasn't the femur."

"I don't know, and that's the truth. Look at me, please. Can you trust me?"

She eyed me hard. "Good! It's time to get busy. Oh! This must be Cat." Ruth patted her lap, and Cat leaped in response; while she wobbled she managed to balance so Ruth could scratch behind her ears and under her chin.

"You have a way with her. She doesn't purr for everyone."

"Well, the World's Authority on Sex ought to know how to make a pussy purr, don't you think?" She laughed. "Oh, that's right. You're a blusher. There's nothing to be shy about. You're among friends. Cat's and my lips are sealed about purring pussies." Then she pretended to turn a key and lock her lips. "Alright. So! We all have a lot of habits that we believe identify us as individuals. Like, I strut around talking about sex, so I believe I'm easy to talk to. And you?"

"Oh." I pointed to myself. "My turn? Oh um, I don't walk around talking about sex, so, I believe I'm polite."

"So, you can see that's confusing. Just because you and I believe something about ourselves doesn't make it true." Cat climbed off Ruth's lap and curled up between us.

"Cause and effect."

"Ha! You got it, hotshot. And when that happens, we've reduced ourselves to some specific thing and then tend to look at ourselves and other people, too, as those things, as objects. As if these define who we are. The beloved becomes something to possess. Nothing more than an object of desire. This is dangerous." Her expression signaled a warning, and eros flashed through my mind. "But!" she said, "there's a remedy."

"Intimacy," I said, remembering it led to alliance and cooperation. Not the illusion of control. Not madness.

"Ha, Ha! Intimacy! The very thing that breaks down the constructs of who we believe we are, who we project to be, or even who we think other people are. Intimacy is surrendering, letting go of that grasp." She clawed at the air and grabbed a fistful. "That clinging to an independent identity in favor of interdependence." She illustrated by weaving the fingers of her two hands together.

"And that surrender is vulnerability." I recalled the other day with Amy. "I just realized my anxiety has blinded me from seeing vulnerability as anything but a death sentence, but, really, it's a portal." I said, noticing the rain had stopped though the sky remained cloud covered.

"A portal. Yes! And portals are a risk at first because they take you to a place you've never been. Vulnerability is no different. And," she paused, "as a risk, it seems like an invitation for harm, having us believe that intimacy will reveal our weakness."

"So, either we'll refuse it," I said, recalling the morning and how much I'd fought myself and Pythia. "Or, it's what happened with My Ex. We pretended we'd entered the portal of vulnerability as if we'd revealed the truth of ourselves, but we'd really both just held back. Not intentionally, but as a safety measure. I think we were afraid vulnerability would weaken our negotiating position, and so, inadvertently, we jockeyed for a position of power. It's messed up. Because it actually raised the stakes and made intimacy a game of chicken." The arrogant coward inside me came to mind.

"And?"

I flinched. "If My Ex and I had stayed at it, I don't know. I think it would've killed me."

"Or worse than death." Ruth looked serious. Cat stirred. Yawning, she rose then stretched before jumping to the back of the sofa where a heat vent kept the spot toasty warm. "A lifetime of manipulation and distortion. Playing mind games that perpetuate dishonesty around vulnerability, intimacy, sex, and love."

Off in the far-off distance, I knew somewhere those old, jazzed amphetamine sounds played while a curl of smoke was plenty willing to lure me down the hall of shattered mirrors of the arrogant coward's mind. "Yeah." I averted my gaze, knowing full-well I'd been the player and the receiver of those games. "When that happens, the body knows. It can feel dishonesty." I met her eyes.

"The chest tightens; the stomach becomes upset; the mind races."

"Yeah, but you tell yourself it's okay. That this is intimacy. You lie, telling yourself this is what intimacy feels like. That's what I did. Honestly, it's what I sometimes still do. I did it as recently as this morning with Pythia. I'm not proud of it, but I denied my own feelings and instead believed a lie about myself."

"Which lie?"

"That I was polite by not bothering anyone with my feelings." I smirked, feeling foolish. "That I don't know how to be intimate. That it's too much. That I'm crossing a boundary or someone's expecting more than I can deliver. The strange thing is, none of *that* makes me feel any safer," I said, and the room brightened, fresh clean light spilled from parted clouds that revealed a beautiful blue sky.

"That's right! Because intimacy-fiction requires you to deny your own intuition. The thing you always know deep down."

"That everything will be alright," I said, reaching to turn off the dull lamp with its sickly light.

"And, without access to that belief, it's curtains! Trust me. When we're afraid of being authentic, vulnerable, and intimate, our energy will attract others who are fearful, confused, even dishonest."

"Perpetuating a pattern of disappointment in love." I felt the plain truth of it.

"And what about good sex?" Her German accent made the question sound like an intellectual inquiry.

"Good sex?" I suspected I blushed but forged forward.

"Yes, we have a list." She waved the paper, a crisp white flag.

"Oh, right," I said, conceding to what I hoped was the last of such discussions. "It's more than the mechanics of reproduction." She waited. "Or pleasure." I definitely blushed, both cheeks burned hot as I tried to look unbothered.

"The orgasm! Okay? But what's an orgasm if it's not the joie de vivre? Good sex, Heavenly sex is more important than pleasure. More beneficial." She waited for my nod, then raised her finger. "Sex! Is important. It is our life force. But! Believe in something greater than the climax, which is very good, of course. Don't misunderstand." She shrugged. "It's not everything. Good sex, Heavenly sex, lovemaking is everything. Okay?"

"Okay," I said, noticing her suit was brilliantly blue again in the after-storm light.

"Okay!" she said and cackled, the sparkle in her eye undeniable. "Now, shared with pure joy, lovemaking is a physical way to be vulnerable, express trust, and experience intimacy on an emotional, mental, spiritual, *and* physical level."

"It's what you were talking about earlier. The thing about the object of desire, right? Transforming self-regarding to regard for the other." I faced her, our knees lightly touching while Cat slept between us.

"Yes! Making a mutual consciousness."

"A mutual consciousness? Moral discernment?"

She nodded. "With a goal of unbounded unity."

"Not a transaction for the acquisition of the object of desire." I nodded. "I get it. It's a decision. Deliberate."

"Exx-Actly! Yes! And a human doesn't stumble into this experience. Like love, lovemaking must be created." She grinned, and the sun broke through the clouds. Her soft yellow hair glowed. She was magical to be around. "And remember! Responsibility is practiced with birth control, not to control birth, but to take responsibility for your ability to create life."

"I understand." I smiled, thinking the reminder silly for a man my age. "But why is there so much confusion around healthy sex?"

"Good question! Will you carry my purse?" She opened her bag and pulled out sneakers and sunglasses before passing it to me. "By the way, the sofa looks fabulous! Nice choice!" Seated on the sofa she slid on the sneakers. "Now the rain has stopped, and the view from the bench at the foot of the Flatirons is beautiful. And! That's as far as an old lady like me can hike." She handed me her dress shoes. "Put them in the bag. Okay? Let's go." She put on the glasses while I wriggled the shoes past an unusually large magnifying glass and into her purse. "Oh, I have to say goodbye to Cat." She took off the glasses and leaned to speak with secrecy to Cat. I turned away in politeness, and after what seemed like paragraphs of whisper-speech, she said, "Okay. There! Now, we can go." She stood.

"We?"

"Of course! You don't think I'm going to hike alone, do you? Besides, we have to finish the list. But in the sun. Okay?" She slid on the glasses again, slipped her arm in mine, and then just as quickly slipped out, grabbing my journal. "Here," she said, handing it to me. "Put it in the bag."

The afternoon sun felt good on my back as I pulled the door shut and locked it, juggling her shiny black bag. By the time I finished, she was well down the sidewalk. I jogged to catch up, taking in the sweet and loamy scents of the wet April earth. I knew there was a rainbow somewhere.

"You've heard of St. Augustine of Hippo?" she asked when I was at her side.

"Yeah, that's a messed-up story."

"Go on."

"Well, his dad was all for him having sex, but when his mom found out, she went ballistic. He basically spent the rest of his life rationalizing his urges for sex and searching for salvation from the evils of it." She gestured with an impatient hand for me to continue. "So, he preached that because Adam and Eve had seen each other's, you know, stuff." Turning red, I scanned for a neighbor within earshot, once satisfied that the coast was clear I continued, but lowered my volume, "they'd infected humans with the sin of lust. Which was evident in involuntary arousal and all its evils. He believed denying our desire in favor of imbuing our hearts with God's love was our only redemption."

"Exactly!" she exclaimed as we'd turned out of my neighborhood and onto the sidewalk of the busy road heading to the Flatirons. "Adam fell from the grace of God because he chose an orgasmic life with Eve. Today, if you are Christian, only Jesus, born of the Virgin Mary, can free you from your sin. This theology influenced the Western world. Make sense?"

"So, if it feels good, it's bad and best kept secret," I asked, my breath labored more from the thoughts of prostitution, sexual abuse, and rape coming to mind than the increasing altitude.

"So," she continued, pumping her arms and walking at a nice clip, "the church pairs the necessity of sex with procreation, but leaves everybody on their own to manage their natural sexual desires, and sex becomes a dirty secret or a power play."

I frowned. "There's nothing healthy or intimate about that."

"Fetch the instructions from Pythia." She pointed to the bag and we stopped on the sidewalk while cars flew by on the main fairway. "Let's see how we've done." I fumbled with the shiny clasp before the bag popped open releasing a puff of spicy perfume, then dug around the shoes, trying not to notice a roll of condoms. "Don't mind the prophylactics," she said, now excavating with me. I made a face pretending I hadn't noticed, even though she wasn't paying me any mind, now pulling out a wooden ruler and then an apple. "Okay," she said wrestling out the paper and a pen. On the sidewalk, she read, "Vulnerability? Check. Intimacy and sex? Check. The difference between intimacy and ...." She squinted at the paper. "What does this say?" She passed me the sheet, and I expected the task of deciphering Pythia's chicken scratch, but instead, the stationary was marked with several exclamation points, many large and declarative capital letters, and monogrammed with a big "R."

"Sex," I said, under my breath, scanning for bystanders as the sun disappeared behind clouds.

She turned her ear in my direction and leaned in. "What do you know about intimacy and sex?"

"Um. Intimacy..." I said, lowering my head, hoping no one was anywhere near us.

"And sex?" she asked, stepping closer. Hunched over with her head hanging, she turned an ear to listen hard.

This wasn't going to be comfortable. I waited until someone passed, then launched, speaking low and fast like a secret agent. "Sex is a natural and biological drive that's designed to be a pleasurable urge, and intimacy requires a willingness to be vulnerable; sex doesn't." Finished, I scanned my surroundings.

Dude, seriously. What's the big deal?

What *was* the big deal? I asked myself.

"And?"

"Um." My mind wandered to the greater scope of our dialogue, and I pictured vulnerability as a magnificent shoot. A pulsing, funneling black hole. A mysterious midnight swirl of indigo and purple, that once within, the experience of passage cocooned and imbued us in a rainbow of deep self-trust. So, utterly and completely unexpected that on exit, we are cleansed of doubt and fortified to inspire the creation of love. "You can't have Heavenly sex or love without intimacy, and vulnerability is the only bus headed to that show."

That, Mendes, is the big deal.

"Excellent! Now, what is this?" She leaned, showing me the paper.

"Oh, that's referring to my mathematical equation for love. It's in your bag."

"Go ahead." She motioned to the bag. "But don't wake the Lindberg baby, okay?"

We laughed as I rooted for my journal to show her the math. Leafing to the last page, a cloud cover drifted from the sun and light illuminated the text.

"Confidence precedes trust. Trust precedes vulnerability. Vulnerability precedes intimacy. Intimacy precedes love. Trust multiplied by confidence divided into intimacy multiplied by vulnerability equals love. TC / I × V = L. That's some pretty fancy-schmancy math." She eyed me. "What does it mean?"

"Well, it means that before you can love, I mean truly love—you know, like the seven kinds all bundled up in one."

"Yes. Yes." She waved me on, looking seriously interested and impatient.

"Before you can love yourself or anyone else, you must have the confidence that you'll be okay—no matter what happens. That's the only way you can be vulnerable. To really trust, you gotta show your soft underbelly and take the risk of being hurt. Trust is a risk. It's faith in yourself and the belief that everything works out."

"Go on, go on!" She waved again, this time grinning.

"Once you trust yourself, you can trust the other person. This whole process *is* love. Love is creating this special place of trust where evolution happens. Inside the circle of trust, everyone agrees to support change. Whatever it is and however it's figured to be done. Love lets you believe in evolution, in change. That's love."

Cars honked, and people shouted, "Dr. Ruth! I love you!" and Ruth grinned, waving. Then for the benefit of an excited-looking woman making a beeline right for us with her hand already extended. Ruth elbowed me, "See! I told you, people know who I am!"

"Dr. Ruth Westheimer!" The woman shook Ruth's hand. "I want to thank you for talking about sex."

"Heavenly sex is good sex! I was just telling this hotshot, big-time lawyer exactly that. But he says nobody knows who I am."

"I never said that," I said to Ruth and laughed. "I never did," I said to the fan but the woman's attention was with Ruth.

Ruth shrugged frowning, then tossed her hands and broke into that signature smile. "What's an old lady to do? But! This here hot shot's destined to change the way the world thinks about love." She grabbed her bag from me and dug around until she passed the woman a business card. "There'll be a book."

"A book?" I asked.

"Look at this hotshot, will you?" She saddled up next to the woman and pointed to me. "Big-time lawyer. He's always got something up his sleeve." I shook my head and went to speak, but she filled in the space. "Mark my words. This guy's writing a book. Look for it. You don't wanna miss it."

"What did you give her?" I asked above the shouts and honks while the woman walked away.

"Your card, of course." She passed me her purse, and we resumed, huffing up the mountain incline. "How do you expect people to find you, hotshot? It's not every day somebody sacrifices the black ram."

The black ram! I dropped back and blew out my cheeks.

How bad can it be, dude? Maybe it's like running of the bulls.

People die running the bulls, Mendes.

Yeah, people die.

People do die, dude. That's life.

"What a view!" she shouted down to me, already sitting on the bench swinging her legs, seeming perfectly content, and entirely out of place—the way something very interesting always does.

She's perfectly harmless. And Pythia adores you, dude. You got this black ram.

"Come on!" she motioned for me to join her while fellow hikers gawked, some whispering, others pointing. By the time I sat down beside her she was still catching her breath.

The wind blew the wet spring grasses flat. Delicate flowers with their furry green leaves bloomed in pink clusters nestled around the rocks. Farther into the field, the tall goldenbanner showed off its tubular yellow blossoms. The ancient blue flax colored the path edges with a broad stroke of lavender. The wildflowers were as reliable as the spring rain.

But much had changed since I was a kid. The streets were now congested with cars, buildings had popped up everywhere, and the population had grown by over twelve thousand people. I gazed down on my house, over the university with its sandstone walls and red-tile roofs, and past my little town tightly packed against the foothills. "It's pretty awesome, alright. Despite everything, I can always count on this. It never lets me down." I gestured to the horizon, where the flat land met the blue sky. "I know this view well. In all seasons and nearly any time of day. I grew up sitting pretty much in this very spot." I surveyed the landscape. "Nursing bruised feelings, contemplating life, drinking beer with friends."

Clutching her purse and sitting that close to Ruth, I could feel the heat of her body. She smelled of roses, the way all grandmothers should. She leaned in. Her sleeve brushed against my arm. "The view from the mountain only improves the higher you go. That's morality," she whispered like we were in church. "It's one thing to climb the mountain, navigating all the life its sides sustain, and then another to sit at its peak, transcending all the life it nurtures."

"And!" she said, in her unique singsong way. Being with her was like an amusement ride, intimidating at first but eventually an inspiration for self-confidence. "Joie de vivre!" She smiled. "And!" She raised a finger, "Remember! Responsibility! Not to control birth, but to take responsibility for your ability to create life." She nodded, plucked her bag from my lap, spun on her heels, and headed down the mountain. Heads turned. People called out. I shook my head and watched the real hotshot in action.

35

Surveying the valley after climbing an hour farther up the mountain, the bench Ruth and I'd occupied, along with the hikers, all looked like props from a train garden.

"Hey, Amy," I said into the phone, seated on the rocky mountain top, catching my breath.

"Hey. What's up."

"I just wanted you to know I can see you."

"What do you mean, you can see me."

"I can see your place. I can see you. I can even see you rubber-necking out the window searching for me."

"Rubber-necking!" I heard her open her door and head down the stairs to the outside. "Where are you?" I imagined her shielding her eyes to the sun while she scoured the area for me. "I don't see you."

"I'm at the first Flatiron."

"Oh, you can't see me from there!"

"Oh, no? I bet you've found a shady spot and are picking grass blades."

"How do you know that?"

"Because I can see you."

She laughed. "No, you can't."

"In my mind, I can."

"Oh." She sounded intrigued. "Well, I can see you, too." I knew she'd closed her eyes.

"What'd you see?"

"You. Sitting on a rock with your phone to your ear grinning like it's nobody's business."

"So, you can see me."

"Yeah. I can see you." I knew she, too, was now smiling like it was nobody's business.

Standing over me at the summit huffing, Amy asked, "Why not?"

"I'm just tired of talking about sex. Come sit with me." I waved her over.

"Won't Pythia quiz you tomorrow?" She was finding her footing on the rough terrain sporting colorful yoga pants, an athletic top, and hiking sneakers. "It would be good to review with me." She dangled the suggestion, lifting her brow like she knew something about test-taking.

"There are no tests. It doesn't work like that. Pythia uses the Socratic method." Amy lowered herself, her hip against mine. Her skin was damp with sweat, but she still smelled of that astringent camphorous scent. "You made good time."

"Don't change the subject." She took another swig from her canteen. "Come on," she whined. "I want to hear what Dr. Ruth said. Please?" She straightened her back and folded her hands in her lap. "I'm all ears."

"Well, that makes me nervous." Caving in, I flipped through three-quarters of my journal, looking for my most recent entry. I could feel her eyes on me. A breeze blew the pages and likely tousled her short hair.

"I like how all those inked pages are wavy. How they expand the book, making it greater than its spine." She reached, brushing past me to touch the page.

"Me too." I closed the book and gripped it with both hands to show it meant something more than ink on paper to me.

"Nice try." She plucked the book from me and took in the front cover before she flipped it over. I wondered what she thought of Rusty. Then, cocking her head, she turned to me and narrowed her pale blue eyes. I enjoyed the way her mind and body worked together, even if it was at my expense. "Hey, I just realized something. Why were you meeting with Dr. Ruth anyway? I thought this was a Pythia day."

But our attention was highjacked by the sound of feet on the loose rock and the nasal twang of a singer whose voice failed to maintain the proper pitch. "I keep a close watch on this heart of mine. I keep my eyes wide open all the time. I keep the ends out for the tie that binds. Because you're mine, I walk the line." The singer scrambled into sight wearing skin-tight jeans and turquoise cowgirl boots.

"Whew!" she said, taking out her earbuds, standing with hands-on-hips to take in the view. Her red T-shirt read, *Clippity, Do-Da* in a fancy gold script. "Welp, *hair* I am!" she said turning toward us, then pointed to her shirt, "See? I'm a hairdresser. I work at Shear Genius. You mighta heard of it." She cast her gaze back to the view. "Good golly, this sure is pretty." She widened her eyes and let her meticulously painted mouth fall open. Then, clumsily making her way to sit right smack next to me, she asked, "You mind?"

Flabbergasted, Amy gave me a look from behind the young woman's back.

"Sure," I mumbled, but she'd already squeezed up next to me.

"Oh, glory be. I thought I'd never catch up to you." Practically nose to nose, she stared right at me.

"To me?" I pointed and while inching backward on the rock, I shot Amy a sideways glance.

"Oh, sorry. Am I all up in your space?" But she didn't budge. "I'm so used to talking to people in the mirror. You know, their reflections? That I forget about personal space. Most people don't realize that a good hairdresser has to get real intimate with her clients. I betcha never thought about that. Anywho, I guess you'd say it's an occupational hazard." She nodded, and her golden curls bounced while her head bobbed. "So, you were the one with Dr. Ruth, right? Gabe, right?"

"Do you have word from Pythia?" I asked, lurching toward her now with intense interest, but she craned her neck around me to speak to Amy.

"I sure hope I didn't follow the wrong fellow up here." She snort-laughed. "This is a right far piece from East Jesus if you know what I mean." Then she turned back to me and looked as if she was thinking about something, and said, "No, Gabe. I'm sure I don't know anyone named Pythia. I'm real sorry." She wrinkled her nose. "But I met Dr. Ruth, and she asked me to chase you up this mountain and go over a few things with you." She wrestled with the back pocket of her jeans, trying to make room for her hand, wiggling about. Then nearly toppling over, she finally extracted a paper.

"Can I see?"

"Ohhh! Sugar!" She snatched the paper back from me after allowing me to take it. "Sorry," she said to me and made a face, and then turned to Amy. "I wasn't supposed to do that. Dr. Ruth was pretty insistent that I was to initiate the talking points." She pointed to the paper. Then lowered her voice and spoke only to Amy. "On account of he's real shy about s-e-x."

"I can spell," I said.

"Oh, Gabe, I get it. Talking about sex with a stranger is like hair in a biscuit. It's just not right." She scrunched up her nose.

Amy tried not to laugh. "I think that's a fair assessment."

"About me or the biscuit?" I asked.

"Both," Amy said, and then to the singing hairdresser, "Your timing's perfect. Gabe was just about to tell me the details of his conversation with Dr. Ruth." Amy played me.

"Oh, you're so sweet," she said to Amy, and when she turned my way, Amy stuck her tongue out at me. "Isn't she sweet?" the hiker asked me, not having a clue about Amy's third-grade behavior. "And you're shy." Her false lashes blinked. "There's not too many shy men around anymore. By the way, you've got super great hair." She touched my curls, and then to Amy, she said, "He really does." She smiled at us for too long. Then sighed. "Okay. I guess we better get going with this test."

Amy made a told-you-so face at me.

"It's not a test," I said.

"Oh, don't be nervous. I'm sure you'll do real well. Okay, now it says here," she said, but then paused. "Ready?" She sounded sweet.

"Sure."

"Okay." She smiled at me. "Here we go." She cleared her throat. "If sex is a physiological function meant to procure the evolution of the species. What two self-interest activities are naturally and automatically prompted for self-preservation?"

"We already covered this," I said, beginning to feel warm and fearful I was outnumbered. "Maybe not in those words, but Ruth and I've already discussed this. Can I just see?" But the singing hairdresser yanked the paper from my reach.

"Sorry, but Dr. Ruth's a super bossy lady. She was way firm about me asking and you answering. Oh, my gosh, Gabe!" She fanned me with her hand. "Look," she said, enlisting Amy, "he's turning beet red."

"He'll be okay. But you know, we didn't catch your name. I'm Amy."

"Nice to meet you, Amy. I'm Lacy, but everybody calls me Moe."

"Well, Moe, you seem like a very understanding person. And you probably don't know that Gabe has already had several discussions with Dr. Ruth. I don't think she'd mind if you gave Gabe the list to read himself."

"I'm afraid she would, Amy." Moe frowned.

"Stimulation and arousal. Okay?" I did my best to sound like those were my final words on the subject and hoped I'd stonewalled any further discussion. "What's so funny?" I snapped at Amy with her smirk.

"Nothing. I just enjoyed the way Moe's drawn you out. That's all. Sorry." Amy said, faking defense.

"Well, Gabe's correct, Amy. But, Gabe?" she said, getting my attention, "just because 'nature' is calling," she used air quotes, "doesn't mean it's your right to have sex. A conversation about sex has to include a conversation about privilege, Gabe."

"Okaaay. But that wasn't the question, and I know you don't know me, but I would never think it was my right. I'm not that kind of person," I said, refusing to think about the slippery slope of manipulation that Ruth and I had discussed earlier.

"I don't know what kind of person you are," she said, clearly reserving judgment. "You seem nice, but as long as we're talking about sex, I think we should discuss both sides of the argument."

"But I'm not arguing."

"He's not arguing," Amy said. "But I'm glad you brought it up. I agree." Then, looking at me, she said, "It should be a part of any conversation about sex."

"Right? I know. Thank you, Amy." Then to me, Moe said, "Gabe, you see, desire incites creativity, and that's self-serving. When sex is celebrated exclusively as a pure expression of bodily desire and not for the advancement of the species, it becomes isolated from its true nature and is then imposed with a false nature that values only desire instead of procreation."

"That makes me wonder about friends with benefits." Amy sounded far too interested for my taste. "If creation requires desire, then it must be unadulterated to be wholesome, meaning healthy."

"I know! Balanced, right? Exactly, Amy!" Then to me, Moe scolded as if I'd disagreed. "You know she's right, Gabe." Her tone was cool, but before I could say a thing, she went on. "This arrangement, Gabe," I began to think she'd thought I'd personally invented friends with benefits, "known as 'friends with benefits,'" and she used air quotes, "is a rationalized agreement for the exchange of arousal and stimulation. There's no intimacy in friends with benefits, Gabe. Somebody eventually gets hurt or at least feels used."

"I agree with you and would add that without moral discernment, objectification is inevitable." I'd hoped to win her over.

"That's correct, Gabe." She was sarcastic and clearly not impressed. Maybe even disgusted. "Without its natural context, manipulation can arise, and persons acquiescing to transactional sex can become only objects of desire."

I opened my mouth, but she cut me off.

"You're interrupting Gabe," she said with scorn. "Conflating sex for one's singular pleasure does lead to objectification and power dynamics. Now I hope you can see how sexual abuse and assault are rampant." She spat her words.

"Okay." I put my hands up and scooted back from her. "Look. I don't know what happened here—"

But before I could mend things, she snapped, "Really, Gabe?"

"Why do you keep saying, 'Gabe,' like, I repulse you?"

"It's your name, isn't it?"

I sighed and ran a hand through my hair. "Yeah, it's my name," I said resigning to defeat. "Somehow, you think something about me that just isn't true. I don't know what gave you that idea, but you're attacking me in this discussion. A discussion I didn't want to have and one *you* pushed on me. Soowa, I think, things should just simmer down here." I gestured with my hands.

"Oh, you do, do you?" She scoffed and turned her back, the heat of disdain rising off her. I looked to Amy, who shrugged, making a face that conveyed my suspicions were correct; Moe hated me. Sighing, I weighed the options. I could throw my hands up in the air, or I could try to persuade her she was wrong about me, which already wasn't working.

"You can trust him, Moe. He does think about these things. He wants to understand." Amy touched Moe's shoulder.

"Moe," I said with caution, "maybe you're mad at me because I'm a man, and your experiences with men have led you to believe that all men disregard women. But, however I've upset you, I am genuinely sorry."

"Good lord. I don't know what I thought when I agreed to do this." Her curls flew about as she shook her head. "Gabe, I've been tougher than a two-dollar steak. And you'd think finishin' up my dissertation on attachment, and the rituals of sex without moral discernment oughta make me level-headed about sex!"

"Attachment and the rituals of sex without moral discernment?"

"Gabe," Moe said, sounding tired, "please, don't make me lose my religion again. Your teachers are everywhere. Even on top of the mountain resembling a cowgirl."

Amy cleared her throat. "Why is sex so complicated?" she asked, shepherding us clear of emotion.

Moe sighed. "Thanks, Amy. Yes, let's keep both oars in the water, or I'm liable to argue with myself on this topic. Well, sex is pretty biological," she said, sounding better regulated. "It was never meant to be intellectualized or rationalized. It's not even meant to attract or even indicate love! But lordy be, do people want it to. I know I did."

"I did too," I confessed. "But sex can't be casual when it's really a life-creating activity." Feeling the flat-out truth of it, I leaned in. "Healthy sex, or what Ruth calls Heavenly sex, or what Amy calls lovemaking, that involves a conscious agreement in expectations," I said, realizing sex was a Thang.

"Gabe?" Moe eyed me, and I knew we were about to make up. "You right. It wasn't you." Then to Amy, she said, "It wasn't him." And to both of us, she said, "I've had some bad experiences, for sure!" She laughed, but we knew it wasn't funny. "And let's just be clear, I didn't just fall off the turnip truck. I've been a rockin' chair in a room of long-tailed cats plenty a time!" She closed her blue lids and pulled her red lips tight. I looked to the slippery scatter of rock that made getting to the top difficult and recognized the struggle of pride. "Glory be, how the past can sneak up on you," she said opening her eyes. "I think Faulkner said, 'The past is never dead. It's not even the past.' All that daddy and momma drama, well, it's running in our cells."

"Generational epigenetics," I said.

"Generational epigenetics," Moe repeated like we were all in a club. "All I wanna do is break the cycle. But those pheromones! Jesus, Mary, and Joseph! Those scent-bearing chemicals instantly attract us to others with not only similar IQ and compatible genes, which would be okay, right? But they attract us to partners with a history of likened evolutionary impulses. We're like Narcissus gazing into the pool, falling in love with himself over and over again."

"Nature's way of ensuring the propagation of a healthy species. The unhealthy breed and over time the lineage degrades while the healthy evolve." I commiserated.

"I sure do want to evolve," Moe said, with longing in her voice.

We all nodded.

"Hard as I try, it's no secret I've had a time with men." She carried on. "Squeaks out sideways. Like today, my love drama is always just one hop, skip, and jump away. I suppose that's why I've made it my life's work: that and cuttin' hair. My momma had it too, the triggers. And my daddy, well, let's just say, he wasn't a sack of kittens. No, sirree! Still thinks the sun comes up just to hear him crow." She smacked her glossed cherry lips.

"I'm sorry," I said, wondering what to say. Then, pretending I was Pythia, I asked. "Moe, if there was one thing you wanted me to know about sex, what would it be?"

"That's a good question, Gabe." She drew her tight-jeaned legs up to her chest and wrapped her arms around them. "Well, I guess what I'd want you to know in a nutshell is that sex is a powerful activity designed to result in the production of another human being. Because it's pleasurable, it can be easy to forget that it's designed to literally create life—a baby! So because it is a means to a significant end, some people get confused. They think its importance means their worth is measured by their sexual prowess, and when that happens, manipulation or full-on power plays are inevitable."

"So are you saying that healthy sex can be either a conscious biomechanical function for creating life or a physical expression for conscious and collaborative coupling? Anything else is reckless?" Amy asked.

"That's correct, Amy. Because it's a life-creating activity, sex cannot be casual. Healthy sex involves a conscious agreement in expectations." Moe nodded.

"Responsible creation of anything requires conscious desire. What did Higgs say?" I said and then thought to ask Moe, "Do you know Higgs?"

"Higgs Boson? Oh, my gosh Gabe!" She looked like I'd just given her the keys to my car, then swatted me. "You underestimate me. I am more than just a pretty face! And I'll just tell you what Higgs says, 'Know *what* you desire before you create. Once you know the "what," the "how" follows.'"

"Is it snowing?" Amy asked, standing to catch flakes.

"Oh, it surely is." Moe stood. "Well, this has been more than I can say grace over for sure." She gave us each a hug.

"Hey, Moe!" I called after her, now standing too. "I've been wondering, where's your cowgirl hat?"

She stopped and turned around with her hands on her hips. "He'd worry the horns of a billy goat, wouldn't he?" she asked Amy. Then to me, she said, "Glory be, Gabe! Everybody knows you don't wear a cowgirl hat hiking," and she disappeared down the mountain.

That night, I listened to Amy sleep-breathing. Warmth radiated from her body. Cat slept curled up, tucked into Amy's arms. My best girls were fast asleep in a swath of soft moonlight. I lay thinking until the words in my head required a pen, then pulled my journal from the bedside table and sat up in bed.

Spiritually, we may be drawn to sex as an intentional activity that reflects our connectedness within the physical multiverse. Consciously, we may recognize sex as a life-giving force that, like the sun, illuminates light and therefore reveals shadow. Like a Vermeer painting, sex can be evidence that every object absorbs and reflects the color of its adjacent object, that nothing is ever seen honestly in only its singular nature.

Sex may be the closest we can come to immortality; casting our own light for the absorption of another form and creating a deep convergence of souls. Such a meeting may relinquish us from our attachment to permanence and provide us with the ability to trust in the perfection of our own mortality, allowing us to love ourselves and others freely. Sex's highest purpose may be to reconcile separateness. By partnering with another, sex can connect the emotional, mental, and spiritual human desires with the body's physical mechanics.

Satisfied, I closed the journal, then my eyes. Darkness received me. I let go and fell into sleep, where I dreamed of Amy. She was bright, almost sparkly, taller even as she came to me, bringing me the tiniest kitten. The size of a minnow, and pink for lack of fur, its eyes were unopened. Cupping the delicate thing in the palm of her hand, she showed me. "See how fast her heart beats?" she asked. Astonished, mesmerized even, by the little thing with its bones and blood, I did see. Yes, I thought. Yes!

But by morning the dream was a mere ghosted memory.

36

S tanding over my laptop at the kitchen counter, I refreshed the page. Nothing. "Oh, Pythia. Where are you?" I muttered, refreshing it again, but it remained the same. I stared at the blank screen. I waited. With no idea of her whereabouts, I sat blind to the myriad of possibilities that had always existed. She could be lost in the Bermuda triangle with Amelia Earhart or in jail. For all I knew, she could be caught in some phone loop with her insurance company. My fingers fired on the keyboard, striking the question mark. *Where are you???* It was fair, but I tapped the delete key. *I hope you are okay. I missed you yesterday and this morning. Hope to see you soon.* I read the message in my head once, then out loud before adding, *Sincerely and always yours, Agape mou.* I sat. I waited. Then finally turned away and headed downstairs.

From the kitchen window, I witnessed the spring snow erasing all evidence of the world I knew. It took its time absorbing the history, the marks of humanity. From my perspective everything seemed to have stopped, space contracted and dilated time. Or was space expanding? Time accelerating? Without a point of reference, it was hard to know. I twirled the crystal prism. It won't cast any rainbows today, I thought, feeling its smooth planes of glass.

"Hey," Amy said, stomping her feet as she came through the back door. "It's like a ghost town out there." Her greeting floated in on her breath, alive in the cold fresh air she'd brought with her. "Well, this isn't what I expected." She pulled off snow-caked mittens. "Nobody's been out. The cars are buried." She warmed her hands standing next to me in the kitchen. "It's ridiculous. Did you expect this?"

"Well, April snow's always the heaviest." I offered her a cup of coffee. "School's closed."

"I figured." She grinned, her hand-knitted hat, cockeyed on her head.

The hot mugs warmed our hands while the drafty window whispered a steady stream of cold, crisp air. We stood side by side, sipping coffee, staring out the window, mesmerized by the big wet flakes falling. The tree branches strained under the snow's beauty, the tips of the red tulips now devoured.

"The mountains are about to leave us," Amy said as a distant mist absorbed them, and they disappeared as if they'd never existed. We peered through the kitchen window, the scene unfolding, the world surrendering in silence to the nature of things.

"Well," she sighed, "that's that." She gestured to the storm. "You're stuck with me. For a while, anyway."

"And you with me."

"In that case, let me see if you're still as good looking this morning as you were last night." She took my face in her hands. "Oh, yeah, and still a hotshot, too." She locked in on me. I met her gaze head-on. Our eyes danced for a bit.

"Your hat's crooked," I said, daring her.

"That's how I wear it." She steadily eyed me, and I smiled, betting my life her tongue poked at her cheek.

"Come on." I nodded to the living room.

"I win," she said, following.

"What?" I said, making myself comfortable on the sofa.

Straddling me, she grinned and pinched my cheek. "You looked away first. You were clever about it. I'll give you that, but I still won."

I smiled at her ease. "Maybe I'm more clever than you give me credit. After all, here we are eyeball to eyeball again." I fixed her hat and kissed her.

"Maybe." She didn't concede but climbed off. "Any word on Pythia?" she asked, loving on Cat who'd staked claim to her beloved warm spot on the back of the sofa.

"Crickets," I said and kicked back, propping a throw pillow at my head and placing my feet in Amy's lap.

"What happened anyway?"

"To Pythia? I didn't tell you?" I craned my neck. "She went snowboarding yesterday. And she broke her leg!"

Amy's mouth hung open.

"I know!" I said.

"Oh, my God! Wait," Amy replied, "why are you smiling? You're pulling my leg!" She swatted me.

I faked protecting myself against her. "No. It's just fun to see you, flabbergasted. Not much shakes you."

"Except an old lady gone missing from a picture at the art museum. Or gunfire on the creek path." She rolled her eyes. "So?"

"That's it." I shrugged. "That's all I know. I just checked again. No Pythia."

"You're worried?" She situated my feet in her lap and then studied me hard.

"Not worried. Well maybe. Pythia's my friend."

She cocked her head, making a sympathetic face. "Sorry, she's MIA."

"Well, it's not your fault, but we were in the middle of this quest for love. What if," I began and then caught myself.

"What?"

"I don't know. I gotta be patient. I just don't want to lose any time. I mean, of course, I'm worried about Pythia. It's not just about losing momentum on this love thing." I fussed with the pillow behind my head. "It's hard to imagine. Inconceivable, really, that she was here one minute and gone the next. Maybe forever. I don't know. I suppose it kicks up my 'abandonment issues.'" I used air quotes.

"Is that what you and Pythia talk about?"

"No, but I've seen *Oprah* clips on YouTube." I joked.

"What do you mean you're in the middle of finding love?"

"Well, what is this April? So, we've got two more months to figure this out."

"I don't get it, Gabe." She slid out from under my feet and curled up at the far end of the sofa. "I thought you wanted to understand what love is or learn more about it or something like that. And—well, it would seem to me—I mean," but instead of saying, she worried at a dangly earring with her eyes fixed on me.

I scratched my beard. "Well, it was like a six-month program, and what if the whole thing's canceled?"

"So?" She looked hard at me.

I sat up. "What's up with you? You know how much I've put into this."

She was silent. Then pulled her legs and a pillow up into her chest and wrapped her arms around both.

"Are you mad?"

She picked at the pillow. "I'm not mad." She didn't look at me but shook her head, scowling. "God, Gabe." She slapped the pillow. "Do I have to spell it out?"

"Are you jealous because there is nothing—" I leaned toward her from the opposite end of the sofa.

"I'm not jealous!" She tussled with the pillow before shoving it to the floor.

"What then?" I wanted to get closer to her, but she seemed furious.

"Okay, that's how you want to do this? All your work on love and intimacy, and sex, and this is how you treat me. What am I? An experiment?"

"Amy." I went to her side. "What are you talking about? I love you."

"Do you? Because you just made a fool out of me begging to hear it. I don't get it. If I'm really your love, then what's the big loss if the thing's canceled."

"Oh, Amy. I'm sorry." I sighed. "It never occurred to me that you'd think—"

"Exactly, Gabe. That's what communication's for. To understand what another person thinks. To take the risk to ask *and* to tell. That is, if you really want intimacy."

"Of course I do." I paused. "Look at me. Yes, the point was to find love, and yes, I have found it with you. I'm sorry if I'm not very good at it yet." I took her hands, but she looked past me. "Amy, I wanna be good at this, but love is far more complicated—"

"What's so complicated about it? I love you. You love me. And we build a life around that love. I don't think it's that complicated. It's just a commitment. Do you ever notice how you always want to make things complicated?"

"Amy," I said, wanting to make things right, "maybe it's not complicated, but it's complex. Things are interwoven and interconnected in a way I've never noticed before. Maybe all my life I've confused that with complicated, messy."

"Life is messy, Gabe. That's not a bad thing."

"I agree, but I don't know how to be in the middle of messes like you do. I'm just learning that it's okay to be messy. What did Zorba the Greek say?"

"The full catastrophe of living."

"See how smart you are? What? I mean that." Our eyes locked. "Amy, I wanna see this thing with Pythia through to the end because it feels like I'm not done yet. I feel like there's a big breakthrough coming, and I don't even know what that means."

"You missed that *Oprah* show?"

"See? Smart, and funny. You're so fearless. Like this thing we're doing now.

If that had been me wondering if you loved me, I'd have really struggled to even admit to myself that something felt off. Let alone to confront the fear."

"Well, I struggle, too."

"You struggled figuring out how to talk it out. I've mostly struggled figuring out how not to figure it out. I've had a tendency to give up. But I don't want to do that anymore. I want to show up for you, and for me, and for us."

She sat, eyes scrutinizing me weighing my words. "So," she began, "just to be clear. You're not still looking for love?"

"Nope. Love is all seriously good now that you're here."

"Yeah?"

"Yes, it is," I said, with the greatest deliberation I could muster.

"You're sure?"

"I am sure."

"Then let's find Pythia."

37

"**A**re you for real?" Amy stood in the bathroom, holding the lampshade with two hands while I filled the tub with hot water.

"I already told you. I don't know how to do this," I said, feeling Amy hovering right over the top of me in the tiny room. "I only know how we did it the first time, and I don't know if that's how all first-timers do it. I don't know if I have..." my voice echoed off the old blue tile while I struggled for the right word. "I don't know if I'm strong enough to take you. I don't even know if I have the power to take myself without Pythia. I don't even know if this is going to work. And if this is absurd to you, I can tell you I feel ridiculous."

"Okay, okay, okay. Sorry," she said, with her hands up. "Should I light the incense?"

"Not yet. There are some things you should know." I turned off the faucet.

"Why?" she asked fixing a stare, dropping the lampshade, letting it dangle from her hand at her side.

"We don't have to do this."

"No, please, I want to," she whined. "We have to find Pythia." I thought she might stomp a foot, but then she hesitated. "Are there rules about bringing someone else along? Pythia knows about me, right? She won't be mad, will she?"

"No, of course not. I mean, I don't think she will. She's not like that, but Zeus is a little unpredictable."

"Zeus?" She sat on the tub ledge.

"Well, of course. Zeus runs this whole thing." I ran my hand through my hair. "I have no idea what I am talking about. I don't want to disappoint you, but I don't know how this works. At all!"

"Okay, okay. Let's just see what happens. Let's just make it fun." She threw her arms around my neck and leaned her forehead against mine. Then in a low voice, she added, "But we're not going to blow up like the Challenger space shuttle, right?"

I exhaled, making a show of it. "I don't know! This is crazy. Where is she?" I motioned to the computer. "And what the heck?" I pointed out the window. "How long is it going to snow? Look! It's like the world we knew never existed?" My voice was extra loud, then under my breath I added, "I'm sorry. Nothing makes any sense anymore." I sat on the toilet lid with my head in my hands.

"Are you tired of me?"

"I am not tired of you." I stood in the cramped space. "I just don't want to disappoint you. I have never done this before. None of it. I've never been in love like I am with you, and I certainly have never time-traveled without the high priestess, let alone taken my girlfriend."

"You know, it's kinda serendipitous."

"What? You think Pythia planned this?"

"I don't know." She shrugged flirting. "I don't know her. Never met her. Never been introduced."

I rolled my eyes. "Okay. I gotta change out the water in the tub; it's too cold now," I said, already draining it. "Here." I set the shade on her head. "You gotta steady it." I steadied it for her. She looked nervous, letting me fix the ridiculous thing on her beautiful head. "I'll wear one, too. So you don't feel silly." I kissed her nose before donning a shade myself.

"Oh, yeah. That definitely helps."

I made a goofy face, and she laughed. "Alright! Once we go," I said, steadying my shade, "it'll feel like something is pulling us down hard and fast. Then there'll be the sensation of passing through hoops."

"Hoops?"

"Like a tunnel. I keep my eyes closed, but even with your eyes closed, you'll see bright colors. Sometimes they're so intense I have to peek just to see if my eyes are really closed."

"Are they?"

"Yeah. It's cool. I don't think you have to close your eyes." I thought about it for a minute. "Wait, maybe you do. I think you do. I think that helps you travel. You squeeze them like this." I contracted all the muscles in my face, and when I opened my eyes, she looked like she'd witnessed something painful. "It doesn't hurt." I shook my head. "You'll see." I nodded. "So, you'll close your eyes, hold my hands, and I'll say some words. I hope I can remember them." I stopped to think. "I'll do my best. And if it works, we'll drop down, circle through, and land. Oh! Be prepared to bend your knees right after you smell fresh dirt."

"What?"

"The last thing you'll notice is a scent, like fresh earth. Or no, like clay. You'll recognize it for sure. It smells just like clay."

"Okay, so we stand next to the tub?"

"No." I shook my head. "No, we have to climb up and straddle the tub with the steaming water and burning incense."

"You're making this up!"

"We don't have to do this." I looked at her sideways with a brow arched.

"You're serious?"

"I am as serious as a Baptist preacher on Sunday. Hey, don't make that face at me."

"I don't think we need to be that serious."

"Okay, let's just be normal-serious. Do you want to do this or not? All of these questions erode my confidence."

"Okay, okay!" She climbed onto the ledge of the tub, and wearing the shade, she did her best to balance.

"Make room for me," I said, and once she'd inched herself backward, I steadied myself before her, taking her hands. "Let us go down the viaduct of vertigo dreams and slip into the slipstream. Come as we are like a fish to the dish and a Chinese chicken. Memoria, memoria, memoria."

"Ahh!" she cried.

"Here we go!" I screamed, feeling the familiar pull and the tube of sparking blue light. "Hold on!" I shouted above the roaring blast. And then, we floated down, descending through the rainbow rings. When the last red ring deepened to the color of blood, the earthy clay scent enveloped us.

"Bend your knees," I told her, and we landed with a soft thud.

38

"Holy moly, that's a big moon. Geez!" Amy said, looking to the heavens and staggering backward into a tall hedge. "Woah!" she cried, falling into the bushes, their dense foliage catching her. The small, dark-green leaves shone in the light of the full moon.

"You okay?" I rushed to help her out of the meticulously groomed boxwood and steadied her, holding her elbow.

"Yeah." She dusted herself off. "But it's weird here, right? I feels like something is about to happen. You know like a storm is about to brew. I don't know, or like anything could happen. Something's strange."

I scratched my head, looking around. "Yeah, I see what you mean." I walked about, trying to feel something the way you want to hear something. "I don't know if it always feels like this."

Amy walked about. "It's as if the space wants us to make something happen. Feel it?" Her hands surveilled the area. "How does this work? What's next?"

"I don't know. It's different every time." I poked around in the hedge. Finding an opening, I reached for Amy's hand and we wove our way deep into the labyrinth until we arrived at a crude sign, windblown but still staked into the earth.

In the space created by love, we are one and in union of all that is, was, and will be, yet we are still ourselves and seemingly separate, unique, and mortal beings. What is the formula that opens this space?

"Oh, this is my formula. Um, trust multiplied by confidence divided into intimacy multiplied by vulnerability equals love. Ah, so TC / I x V = L."

"Woah." Amy steadied herself as a violent wind blew. The tall bushes and outlying trees roared, resisting the blast. "Look!" she shouted, pointing to a rabbit, and the strong current died down. "Come on!" Amy grabbed me as she hurried after the rabbit who'd darted off into the labyrinth. We followed the rabbit, racing around corner after corner until, at a crossroad, she dodged into the bushes. This placard read: *Love is a set of points satisfying a specific geometric truth. Round-shaped and moving in circles that oscillate ecstatically, without subjugation. What must you acquire to see this mechanism?*

"Trust," I said. The wind picked up again. The boxwoods quivered; their strict bows bent. Our leader sprang with big feet and agile legs, and we serpentined behind until the next signpost.

What simultaneously embraces the individuation of one's nature and the unification of all nature, begetting a single soul charged to expand into the concentric vibration of solidarity?

Amy looked at me. "The circle embraces the parts *and* the sum of the whole. So, love embraces me and the me-you," I said.

"That's vulnerability, right?"

"Maybe." My brow narrowed. "There is a willing deconstruction of me to create the me-you, but it's a risk. So, maybe, vulnerability precedes intimacy?" I asked. A darkness, previously unnoticed, lifted, and we looked to the heavens. A cloud drifted past the moon. Everything had become still in the moonlight. We looked at each other and then to the ground. Our friend grazed nearby on clover. I scratched my head.

"You're right," Amy said. "When we trust in the process of me and me-you, vulnerability naturally happens and leads to intimacy." A stiff breeze blew, and off our guide went. "Come on!"

"But that's what I said!" I called from behind. "How come we didn't get the go-ahead when I said it?"

"Because you didn't say it, you asked," she shouted back. We traveled deep into the labyrinth, turning far more corners than before. "Do you see the rabbit? I've lost her," Amy yelled back to me.

"Oh, my God!" I said, inhaling a sour odor: the humid smell of a rancid, festering wound. Feeling like I'd vomit, I covered my nose and mouth. And that's when the grotesque creature appeared. Stealthy and fast, it ran on hooved feet straight for Amy, its eyes were glowing red holes. Its face was framed by an impressive but matted and dirty golden mane. Its brown fur was patchy, and its skin scarred, presumably from years of battling. "Amy!!!" I cupped my hands around my mouth, gagging at the putrid smell. "Watch out!"

The monster carried two sharp spears, one in each hand, both perfectly positioned to pitch in our direction. Its hands were human-like with fingers and thumbs, only long claws replaced nails. The thing lowered its head and snorted as it advanced, preparing to ram us with its great horns or impale us upon the deadly arrows or both. Fire shot from its enormous leathery black snout. At first, the savage's tail trailed behind like another demon, but then the tail snaked its way forward as the beast charged. In close range of Amy, the tail sprung on its own as if to strike her.

"Holy frack!" I grabbed her arm, dragging her back in the direction we'd come. We ran screaming bloody murder until we'd lost the thing. Finally stopping, I bent over to catch my breath. Amy gasped for air and pulled her inhaler from her pocket. "You okay?" I put my hand at her back.

She nodded. "Do you think we're safe?"

"I don't think it followed us past the first turn."

"He stank so badly. Do you think we gave the wrong answer?"

"I don't know." Finally, able to stand upright, I drew in a deep breath. "Maybe we took a wrong turn when we lost the rabbit."

"We're in the right place, right? This is where you usually meet Pythia?"

"I think so. Each time the setting is different, but it's always within the same clearing. But it's never been dangerous."

"What? What're you thinking?"

"Nothing. I'm not thinking anything. Well, I just thought that it's not necessarily true. Even the first time with the Greeks, I was scared. I mean, I thought I was going to die when I left for the Higgs field. And even Higgs made me deathly sick when I met him. It looked so much like me that it freaked me out big time." I stood to scan the area.

"What?" She shot up, following my eyeballs scouring the place. "You're freaking me out. Is it coming again?" She looked over her shoulder.

"What if that monster is just some fear projection?"

"Oh." She sat down in the grass, and I joined her. "Of course." We both let out sighs of relief and leaned against the green wall. Then she lay her head on my shoulder. "What do we do now about our projection of fear?"

"Find our confidence. And we need to rest to do that, so let's just sit for a minute and get clear about what we are really doing here."

"Okay. Well, we came to see Pythia. I guess I was looking for adventure, and we both were a little, shall we say 'wigged-out' about the trip. I guess we didn't begin very grounded."

"Look!" I pointed to the rabbit.

"Don't scare her." Amy hushed, and together we rose in slow-motion.

The rabbit hopped ahead, keeping a few yards between us, before stopping to graze. We followed like that until she took off leading us, but this time never racing out of sight.

"Confidence leads, trust follows," I said, jogging alongside Amy.

"And that supports the willingness for vulnerability and in turn allows for intimacy. I'm keeping up, hotshot." She elbowed me.

Then, there was a familiar voice. "Love, influenced by mutual relatedness, folds the desires of one into another and the other into the one, transcending humankind from the craving for permanence to the joy of infinity." Pythia hobbled out from around the corner of the upcoming bend.

"My God! Pythia!" I opened my arms. "I didn't know if I was ever going to see you again." I hugged her and her crutches. "So, it's true. You broke your leg snowboarding?" I gestured to the place her leg would be visible if not for her chiffon gown.

"Oh, nothing's broken, just badly sprained." Flushed, and looking vulnerable for the first time, she twisted her biggest ring, one with a thick engraved band and a large milky-white moon-like stone. "But enough about my foolishness." She touched my elbow and extended her hand to Amy. "This must be Amy. May I?" she asked, opening her arms.

"Of course." Amy welcomed Pythia's embrace.

"Please." Pythia motioned ahead. "Let's sit at the center of things."

"I'm glad you know your way around," Amy said, "We just had quite a scare with a minotaur."

"Oh, for goodness' sake! That was a chimera. Harmless really, all bark and no bite these days." Then she whispered while working her crutches, "Deplorable hygiene. Lost most of his teeth, and the others had to be removed. You know, streptococcus sanguis, the bacteria in periodontal disease; it can play a huge role in heart disease. He's terribly old. We've only a few of them left. Phasing them out and all." She said the last part like she was sharing a secret. "We are moving away from those fear-based practices now. Very old fashioned."

"You are pretty good on those." I referenced her crutches.

"I'm not too bad. Thankfully, the talus wasn't fractured. The bone that joins with the shin and forms the ankle joint." With her wrist, she demonstrated the flexibility the joint offered. "I needed new boots." She blushed again and swiped at a strand of hair that had fallen into her face. "It's my own fault."

"So, you snowboard?"

"I do, but I hadn't in some time."

"I'm so confused. We'd met that morning, and I'd expected to see you at lunch. So, you went snowboarding right after we talked?"

"I did." She didn't elaborate.

"I know it's none of my business, but why? I mean, I was so worried about you, and then you didn't write or call."

"I was taking a lesson." Her words were clipped, and she averted her eyes.

"A lesson? I know I don't have any right to ask, but I care about you. I was worried." I frowned. Amy was quiet with her hands clasped and her gaze on her own feet. "Right, Amy?"

"He was pretty anxious. He thinks the world of you." Amy made it sound loving.

"Oh, of course, you were!" Pythia hugged me, still smelling like pine needles and gingerbread. "You are so right, my darling friend. But I wanted it to be a surprise for you. You know, we're headed to the mountains this session, you and I, and I thought it would be fun to snowboard in. I know you rather enjoy the sport, and I normally have good balance and am quite confident. Maybe a tad too much faith in myself this time," she said, showing us the tad with her thumb and first finger. "But honestly, it was the boots. Too loose, not enough support." She shook her head, and her crown gleamed glints of gold. "I fell and twisted my ankle. The pain was incredible, but it was Apollo who wouldn't hear of anything short of a full medical. And he was right to do so; I have responsibilities. But the pain meds made me loopy and unprofessional at best." She blushed again. "So, I lost that whole first day of our meeting, and then, if that wasn't enough of an interruption to our work, the umbilicus has been out. Well, in and out, which is really worse than completely out because I kept thinking at any time it would be back on."

"You're kidding me? The umbilicus goes out? Like the Internet?"

"What's Apollo have to do with anything? I thought you said Pythia reported to Zeus." Amy looked confused.

"No, no." Pythia shook her head. "I would have never lasted as high priestess if I had to work directly with Zeus. It is enough to see him socially or at strategic meetings. No, I report to Apollo. Son of Zeus, but he doesn't favor him in the least. He's wise, you know, an oracular god."

"The umbilicus goes out?" I leaned in, cutting in front of Amy.

Pythia caught my eye.

"Oh, oh. I'm sorry." I stepped from between the two women. Then seeing Amy, I reached for her elbow. "Are you okay?"

"I'm not feeling too well." She licked her lips, looking pale. "This is a lot. Can we sit?"

"Yes, of course," both Pythia and I said, leading Amy around the hedge into a beautiful topiary garden with fountains and flowers. Lightning bugs twinkled like fairy lights. "Sit here." Pythia accompanied Amy onto a white wooden gazebo where a cushioned wicker love seat offered respite, then fetched Amy a glass of water. The crystal cut pitcher cast rainbows on the pond under the full moon's light. Jasmine, sweet and exotic, like pipe tobacco swelled in the breeze, intoxicating. The scent seemed to be coming from a large bush smothered in star-shaped flowers with deep tubular throats. Their heavy heads weighed-down the green boughs as they swayed in the soft breeze.

"Is someone singing?" Amy looked around, and above the sound of falling water, I heard a familiar melody and then made out the words.

"Love is real, real is love. Love is feeling, feeling love. Love is wanting to be loved."

Two shadowed figures, one at a piano and the other with a guitar, appeared from across the garden. Their voices were well-known. Amy and I craned our necks, straining to better see in the dark, but instead we only heard music.

"Love is touch, touch is love. Love is reaching, reaching love. Love is asking to be loved. Love is you. You and me. Love is knowing we can be. Love is free, free is love. Love is living, living love. Love is needing to be loved."

"Is that," but Amy paused as she craned her neck again trying to see, "John Lennon?" As the piano faded and a guitar strummed the well-known riff, Amy sprung up. "Is that George Harrison?"

Sure enough, wearing a loose-fitting white cotton shirt and jeans, George stepped into the bright beam of moonlight as if he were on stage strumming and singing,

"My sweet Lord. Mm, my Lord. Mm, my Lord. I really want to see you. Really want to be with you. Really want to see you, Lord. But it takes so long, my Lord."

Leaving the piano wearing a lightweight denim jacket and black turtleneck, John joined in with the hallelujahs tapping his foot, and by the third verse, we sang the Hare Krishnas from the gazebo. Amy and I clapped to the beat while Pythia slapped her good leg. Her bangles took the place of a tambourine.

When finished, the duo joined us. George extended his hand. "Nice to meet you both. We've been looking forward to this meeting," he said, flashing a mouth full of teeth, and sat beside Pythia across from Amy and me.

John raised his eyebrows above his signature glasses in two fast successions, as if to say "Hello" and lowered himself comfortably in the remaining chair. He messed with the trumpet flowers taking in their sweet scent before settling in. "Hey ho," he said, in his lyrical Liverpool accent. "Ditto on what George said." Then turning to Pythia, he said, "Better be careful, eh?" and gestured to her crutches. "Everybody loves you when you're six feet under, you know. Is this what kept you yesterday? Are you alright, then?"

"Thank you, John. I am." Pythia spoke in a way that ended any further discussion on the matter.

"Oh, I see." He looked around at each of us. "Well, I suppose, I don't believe in yesterday anyway."

George smiled, and the two leaned toward each other and sang, "Yesterday, all our troubles seemed so far away."

"Well, everything is as important as everything else, isn't it now?" John drummed his fingers on the arms of the chair.

"I don't know if I agree with that."

"Of course you don't, George."

"Much of life is unimportant. If you don't know where you're going, any road'll take you there, won't it? It's being here." George pointed to the ground. "Now, *that's* important. Time's very misleading. We can learn from the past, but it's behind us. We can hope for the future, but it's ahead of us. All there ever is— is now." He looked at us, and then looked off, a contemplative but melancholy prophet.

"He's thinking," John pretended to whisper. "He's thinkin' I might be right."

"You might be, John," George said. "With every mistake, we must surely be learning."

John arched his eyebrows my way and grinned.

Amy shifted in her chair. "Can I ask a question?"

"Of course," Pythia said.

"Well, the two of you," Amy began, pointing to John and George, "certainly influenced the way many people in the western world came to think about their responsibility for living a loving life."

"Pardon me," George said, "but as a reminder, they rather liked us quite a bit in Asia and India, too."

"I stand corrected. Your influence did reach all the way around the world. In fact, it has been suggested that it was your overwhelming success that drove you to seek greater internal satisfaction."

"That's right." In the soft light, George's chiseled features softened. "I wanted more than fame or money. I wanted to know happiness, love. Peace of mind, I guess. And I realized if I really did want that, I'd have to figure it out."

"So, what ethics—" Amy stammered, "what moral obligations led, or drove you? Either of you?" but she turned to John.

"Amy, is it?" John asked. "Yes, well, you don't really need anybody to tell you who you are. You are who you are, and you do know it, you know?" He shifted to the edge of his chair. "And knowin' who you are *is* your moral obligation. Then doin' something with who you are, well, that's your ethical obligation, isn't it? So, for me?" He relaxed back into the chair and crossed his legs. "Well, a dream you dream alone is only a dream, but a dream you dream together is reality. We've all got this gift of love. It's like a plant here in this beautiful garden. You can't just expect it to get on by itself, can you? You've got to water it. Really look after it. Nurture it. And I'll tell you this, George is right. Love is not just somethin' you wish for. It's somethin' you make, somethin' you do, somethin' you are. It's somethin' you give away."

"Well, thank you, John."

"Certainly, George. I wanna give peace a chance." John grinned and did the eyebrow.

"Love will show you life, Amy," George said. "How it flows within and without you. In love, we welcome all of life. In fear, we pull back. When you've seen beyond your own life and death—well, then you can find peace in knowing that love is always there." George's deep-set pensive eyes searched beyond us for answers before they returned to study us. "This is it, really." He motioned to the garden. "It's not what you get; it's what you give. It starts within." He thumped his heart. "Then it spreads and blooms. Basically, that's your obligation."

"Do you know about the Higgs boson?" I asked.

"Ah, Higgs. Creatin' opportunity just for the asking, eh? But I thought you two were lookin' for the source of moral obligation," John said, pointing to Amy and me.

"He's right, you know. Moral responsibility is that of a person, not Higgs or even God, for that matter."

"It's like George said before." John leaned to poke my chest. "It's right there."

"That's exactly what I'm sayin'. Love, morals, God, it all begins within," George said. "The only way to make it real on the outside is to make it real on the inside first. If we can't love ourselves, we can't fully open to our ability to love others or fulfill our obligation to create. Evolution, and all hopes for a better world, rest in the fearless and open-hearted vision of people who embrace life."

"We all have to live with that, eh? Like George said, we're all haunted by the existential vacuum of our inner emptiness, as it were. No person or tradition can or should fill that. Only each person can fill that void for themselves by discovering *for what* and *to what* they understand themselves responsible." He finished with a straight face and then arching his brows, he said, "So, Amy, now you know what we believe—"

"So, what do you believe?" George flashed that boyish grin.

"And what're you gonna do about it?" Then looking my way, he added, "And you, too. Go on now. Don't be shy. We've all been monkeys in the zoo, haven't we, eh?"

"Okay. Yeah." I organized my thoughts. "Well, I believe in the value of love and its power to improve, not improve, but—"

"Maybe, in its power to *transform* humanity?" Amy offered.

"That's right." I nodded at Amy. "Love allows us to live in our own potential, not in someone else's idea of our potential."

"To learn how to be you in time," John said.

"Right? If you don't know who you are, it's pretty hard to love yourself. And loving yourself is a big deal. Loving yourself allows you to figure out how to love others and then inspire others to do the same. Love changes the world," I said.

"You both are really on to something here." George narrowed his eyes. "I struggled all my life," he confessed, "tryin' to balance the sacred and the profane. But I do believe my devotion to the path of spiritual awakening made me more than just the lead guitarist for *that* band." He nodded sideways to John. "By travelin' the scope of creativity, and the depths of introspection, I learned I hated promotin' myself. That I was never really much for competition. And that I worried what everyone else thought. You see, I was afraid for people to see me, and I was even more afraid to see myself. But I went out on a limb anyway. And you two," he said, pointing to Amy and me, "have shown me that everyone's out on a limb. The trick's to open your eyes, isn't it? To see the risk and balance anyway." His eyes narrowed again. "And I say if that's the moral obligation? So be it."

"Or do you mean, let it be, George?" John quipped.

They stood, gave us the peace sign, and turned, vanishing into the night edges of the garden.

"I had a really nice day with you," Amy said, gathering her things in my living room. "I don't know what I expected but I never imagined that. It was magical."

"I'm glad we did it," I said standing over her, waiting to hand her a pair of socks while she shoved a stack of ungraded papers into her backpack.

"You know, I just want to say, when John Lennon was alive, he admitted to some abusive stuff. He had a lot of shortcomings when it came to being a partner and a father. But people are a product of their environment, right? They're not just all good or all bad. It's tricky to not throw the baby out with the bathwater."

"I was thinking the same thing. These people I've met on this journey have had their blind spots. Places in their lives where they've failed to progress. But that doesn't mean their contributions won't go toward the evolution of the species. I guess bringing equanimity to their stories is the key to extracting the wisdom from the good and the ugly."

"Balance, right? It's necessary to literally and figuratively move forward." She smiled. "At the same time, you can't be balanced until you've learned from your mistakes, and you can't learn from mistakes without the freedom to make them."

"And you can't evolve if the only outcome of your mistakes is judgment."

"Forgiveness."

"Yeah. Forgiving your own shortcomings. That's critical, isn't it? I mean, how can you change if you don't make the space to forgive yourself."

Headlights shone through the window. Amy parted the curtains. "Looks like my ride." We kissed goodnight. Then she shifted her backpack and opened the front door a crack, letting in crisp, dry air. "See ya, hotshot." She waved and headed out.

Outside, she opened the car door. The interior light illuminated an elderly man. They exchanged what looked like pleasantries as she climbed into the back-seat. I watched until the car was well down the snow-packed road.

39

Weeks had passed since Amy and I'd traveled the portal. The late spring breeze now boldly crossed the threshold of opened windows, blowing in summer promises, predicting a coming season of abundance. Already birds nested in branches, well-hidden like secrets in the fully green tree canopies. That's when my workdays became nothing more than hours spent away from Amy.

Cat clumsily jumped onto the bed. Nearly not making it, she tottered across the mess of sheets, determined to make her way toward us as we lingered in bed following the most recent impromptu after-work rendezvous. With the sun still high in the sky in the late afternoon, the open window let in the sounds of children and squirrels. The calibrachoa Amy and I'd recently planted in the window boxes bent and waved like they were sending kisses while Cat situated herself between us.

"That stain sort of looks like a rabbit," Amy said, cocking her head. "See?" She pointed to the ceiling. She lifted herself up onto her elbows and squinted. "I think there's a crack there too."

"Yeah, I know," I said, but feeling the fullness of my life, I reached toward my bedside table. "Hey, can I show you something?" I asked.

"Oh. I thought it was going to be something fun." She frowned at the folded paper.

"Listen to you. Get your mind out of the gutter for a minute, will you?"

"I keep telling you, there's nothing dirty about my mind," Amy said, turning on her side, supporting herself on a bent elbow. "Where'd that come from?"

"Pythia always sends me back with a note. Well, not always." I sat thinking. "Sometimes, she does. Anyway, that's not the point."

"Okay, what's the point? Because that was weeks ago." She collected Cat's fur from the pillow.

"Well, yeah. But I just got it out again since we're meeting this week, and well, the point," I said, waiting for Amy's attention, "is I want to keep you in the loop. You know, cause we're in this together." Looking smug, she snuggled up, interested in the note.

"Dearest Philosopher of Love," I paused to explain how Pythia always calls me something clever like that, "Next we meet, we shall explore attachment, the belief system, and morality. Though, you, my agape mou, need do nothing but enjoy the love for life you've been creating. Your advancement is beyond the moon and all of our expectations."

"That's her handwriting?" She sat up.

"Yours Truly, P."

I nodded. "Yep." I ran my hand over the precious note.

Amy laughed. "It's not what I expected. I mean, she's a high priestess and all. I don't mean to be judgmental—"

"But you are." I folded the note.

"Can I see it?"

"You saw it." I was already stashing it in the drawer. "I thought you might be interested in what the note implies."

"That you're a teacher's pet, and you had no homework." She made it sound juvenile. "So?" She slid onto her side and lightly ran her fingers up my arm and onto my chest. "No more conversations about how sex plays a huge role in our human understanding of love."

"Nope." I rolled onto my side to face her. "It's been talked to death."

"Really? Because biologically, procreation is our primary function as human beings, we have to perpetuate the species."

"But love is our primary pursuit, our soul's purpose."

"So, don't you think the marriage of the two is important?" She batted her eyes. "But not to worry, hotshot. You can count on me for more than just thinking about it." She grabbed my thigh through the sheets and squeezed until I squirmed laughing.

"Hey!" I cried out, wriggling free of her hold. Then, gathering my composure, I said, "Look what you've done. Cat's upset."

Cat stood wearily, poised to jump from the ruckus. "Sorry, Cat," Amy said, throwing back the sheets and crawling to the floor to kneel beside the bed.

"Forgive me, Cat," she said, in her Cat voice, face to face with Cat. Cat rubbed noses with Amy. Amy scratched her ears, then gathered her up in her arms and placed her neatly beside me. Cat watched Amy.

"Oh, so you'll love on Amy, but not me, huh?"

"She ate everything at lunch again today. Didn't you, Cat? And then we laid down right here, didn't we, Cat. And she purred really loudly before she fell asleep."

"Thanks for all your help."

"No problem. Cat's my friend, too." Amy balanced, sliding one leg at a time into her slacks. "Oh, that reminds me," she said, zipping her pants. "I forgot to tell you that Cat and I bought a bed."

"A bed?"

"That's right. For Cat. Right, Cat? She deserves something soft and pretty." Amy kissed Cat. "It should show up today. Well, I gotta go." She looked around the room. "I guess that's it."

"I don't rate a kiss?"

With a big grin, she came at me and laid such a sloppy fat kiss on me that I had to laugh and wiggled to get out from underneath her. I swiped the back of my hand across my slobbered-up face, and she straddled me. "Don't wipe my kiss away, hotshot."

"Or what?"

"Or." She kissed my forehead. "I." Then the tip of my nose. "Won't." She pecked my lips. "Give you sweet kisses!"

"Oh, yeah?" I pulled her close, and we kissed. She rolled over, and I followed. Sliding my hands beneath her bulky sweater, I discovered her silky naked body all over again.

40

"**G**ood morning, old girl," I whispered in the wee Sunday morning hours, already showered but exhausted. Blurry-eyed, I cleaned the crusty glaze of thick morning mucus from Cat's eyes. Once on the floor, she wobbled a few steps before giving up and waited for me to scoop her up. I swaddled her close to my chest. Feeling her heartbeat, I tried to ignore the knobby round ends of her bones as they poked back at me mercilessly, reminding me of something that was always there at the edge of my mind.

Balanced on crutches, Pythia appeared on the screen. "Good morning!"

"Hey. Glad to see that you and the umbilicus are up and running without any hitches." I tried to match her zest despite my arms crossed in front of me. Cat lay fast asleep beside me on her new pink heated bed. As promised, it had arrived and was addressed to *Cat, the world's most precious cat.* "Still with crutches, huh?" I grinned, then frowned at my strange satisfaction in her lameness.

"Oh, yes. What a lesson in humility." Her self-disgust surprised me. "It seems I've overdone it. And so," she threw her hands up, keeping her elbows close to her sides, hobbling for balance, "as you can see, I've yet to ambulate with much poise." Then lowering her voice, she said, "And if that wasn't humble pie enough, at our last roundtable, I even found myself obliged to the kindness of Zeus."

"I didn't know Zeus could be kind." Out of character, I was eager to trash-talk.

"I didn't either. But he can." Animated, but in a low voice, she dished the dirt. "He offered me the use of Pegasus. His immortal winged horse? The one that sprang from the blood of Medusa and was tamed by Bellerophon? Do you know the story? No? Well, it's not important, other than to say Pegasus is really the muse of all muses, inspiring high-spirited imagination and that kind of thing."

Challenged to remain interested, my gaze drifted to the babbling brook that always bubbled behind her. Remembering our first meeting, I recalled how it had been winter. A cardinal had flown from the same branch that now launched a robin. I looked more closely. A breeze blew a distant stand of cattails.

"Oh! And you'll appreciate this." She carried on. "It was the fecundity of Pegasus's clever genius that spurred Bellerophon to slay the chimera. Of course, not that daft old one you saw."

"How's that old chimera—" I began asking while the robin flew again en route from the tree to the water.

"Oh, it was grand!" She was all dreamy and clearly not paying one iota to me while I pored over the cattails bending to the wind again.

I sat back and let my thoughts poke around the edges of betrayal and deceit. Practicing equanimity, I rested my thumb against the sharp edge of a tooth. But I couldn't help remembering the outlandish advertisement all those months ago.

Then pulling on the chain around her neck, Pythia said, "I'm a little jazzed just thinking of riding that grand stallion. It was fantastic!"

My heart picked up a tribal beat. Something smelled fishy. Short of breath, I madly recounted my meetings with Pythia, our interactions.

Dude, she's real.

I thought how she'd taught me new ways to think, new ways to believe in myself and in the world. She'd changed my life.

I don't know, Mendes. Pegasus? Medusa? Bellerophon? Really?

Sticking my neck out, furrowing my brow, I scrutinized the scene behind her.

"Oh! You've already spied my surprise." She'd mistaken my keen study to be about her and leaned in to reveal a charm dangling beside the key and pendant she faithfully wore. "Zeus gifted it to me." She beamed, showing off the golden oak leaf, shoving it into the camera, and then clasped her hand tightly around it.

"Nice." I made myself lean in and tried to sound enthusiastic. "Did you expect this?" I asked, watching the bird again in flight and the cattails swaying in the wind.

"Gads, no! The oak leaf is Zeus's own symbol of strength, endurance, and noble presence. It is quite an honor he's bestowed upon me. And you know what else?"

"Huh?"

"He made it sunny every day. Said he didn't want me to endure any rainstorms through my recovery. He was good to me. You know what he said when he gave me this leaf?" She was sliding it on the chain again.

"Pythia?" I squinted, biting my lip, focused on the goings-on behind her, the running stream, the water rushing around a large stone.

"Well," she babbled, clueless, "you know that humans were originally created with four arms, four legs, and a head with two faces?"

I scratched my beard, frowning. "Pythia?" I pointed behind her.

"Well, trust me, they were. And it scared the bejeebers out of Zeus, so he sliced them right down the center and told them to busy themselves finding their better halves. Well, that was just awful, all that mindless searching for love. You can imagine. And that's when I got the idea and told Zeus about the project. Oh, he wasn't happy about it in the least!" She made bug eyes shaking her head. "He said I'd never succeed. He said humans were too consumed with themselves, that they'd never look beyond their own reflections for the experience of love. But when he handed me this?" She slid it back and forth like a prize she wanted everyone to see. Then she straightened her spine, held her chin high, and channeled the great God. "He said, 'For you have persevered and saved humankind from the poverty of thoughtless searching and, instead, have enthralled their craving and aroused their curiosity for an Elysian life.'" Finally, finished jabbering, she appeared very self-satisfied. "So, my dearest, what do you believe about love? Any of the following resonate?" She pointed to the air but there was nothing to see.

Then seeing my confusion, she flapped her hands. "Oh, for goodness' sake!" She rolled her eyes and bent over, juggling the braces. I heard her shuffling through something. "So sorry," she said, coming back into view. "One moment." She lifted a finger before ducking down again, only to pop up and say, "I'll be right back. Hold on. Yes?"

"No. Wait. Pythia?" But she'd already limped off.

"I am so sorry," she said, stepping back into the picture out of breath. "It is completely my fault. I forgot to reserve the portal." She fussed with a loose strand of hair, and her bracelets rattled as she tried to tuck the stubborn lock back in with the rest. "I've couriered the information. I'm sure it'll only be a moment." She looked cross-eyed at the hair that was determined to hang in her face.

"Hey, Pythia?" I sounded casual. "Is that a set behind you?"

"No." She looked behind her, then at me again, and the disobedient strand of hair strayed into her face again. "No," she repeated. "You mean the babbling brook and all?" she said, adjusting her thin gold crown.

"Yes," I barked surveilling the robin and pointed. "And the birds, and the trees."

"No." She shook her head and took a hairband from her wrist. She shoved the crutches into her pits, put the band into her mouth, and bent over, gathering her hair into a ponytail.

I cleared my throat. "Pythia?"

Still upside down, she twisted the tail of her russet-colored hair about itself, then stood to pile it atop her head, securing it with a couple of chopsticks she seemed to pull out of nowhere. "Much better." She smiled.

"Pythia." I frowned, pointing. "I can see it's not real. The bird's looping." I motioned with my hand.

"Did you not hear me? It's a green screen."

"When?"

"Just now."

"You mean when you were bent over with your hair? No. I didn't hear any-thing. It's a loop then?"

"Yes, exactly." She looked over her shoulder and shrugged. "Nothing here but me." She cocked her head.

As much as I tried not to, I knew I'd eyed her with great suspicion.

"Agape mou." Her tone was of someone standing their ground. "It's meant as a soothing and comforting backdrop. That's all." Then seeing my skepticism, she changed her tone. "I would never trick you."

Unsure of what to think, I lowered my gaze. I shook my head. Then looking sideways, I noticed Cat was gone. I scanned the surroundings.

"I don't know what to say. This has never come up before."

I stood for a better view and scanned the room for Cat.

"Honestly, few people make it as far as you have." She called out. "Gabe? Do you hear me? Gabe?" Her voice grew louder. "I *will* take this under advisement." She shouted as I ran down the hall and to the bedroom.

Nope. I popped my head into the bathroom. No Cat. Frantic, I eyed the stairs. Thank God! She wasn't lying in a heap at the bottom. I took the steps two at a time and raced through the kitchen. I looked under the table. I surveyed the living room. In giant strides, I headed back up.

"Oh, my God!" I said, on seeing Cat.

"I don't know what more I can say. You've quite romanticized me, you know." Pythia's voice now faint but sounding like her feelings were bruised. "I suppose that was the 'marketing' intent of it all, but that doesn't mean I'm not real. I care deeply, Gabe. Gabe? Please come back."

"Pythia," I said breathless, sliding into the chair with Cat purring in my arms.

"Oh!" she sighed, shaking her head. "I thought I'd lost you. You must believe me when I say that I can't bear the thought of letting you down. I am real, Gabe. I'm not a god. I have bad hair days and fall off snowboards. I'm prone to gossiping, and I can be self-absorbed. Some of my mistakes are more egregious than others." She twisted a ring with ferocity. Her poor finger was red and swelling. "Your point is a good one. This," she said, gesturing behind her, "certainly could erode trust. I see that now."

"Pythia, Cat went missing and—"

"Oh, no!" she said alarmed. "Oh," she said, piecing things together. "Oh, Cat, there you are. Well, it's certainly nice to see you up." To my surprise, Cat leaped from my arms and rubbed the side of her face against the screen before slowly lowering her old bones to the soft heated bed. Then, Cat pulled her tail in around her and closed her eyes to sleep.

"Wow, she's not moved this much in weeks." Wide-eyed, I studied Cat. "She did look like her old self, didn't she?"

"She did." I wondered what to think.

"Sometimes, it's hard to know what to think."

"Yeah." I eyed Pythia. Then feeling bold, I said, "Maybe, in the future, after you meet with someone a few times, you might fade out the set and let the reality of you become what's real. Because you are the real deal. All those things you just talked about. Those are the ways you're real, and that's what's helped me learn to love myself."

"Awe." She cocked her head, grabbed the charm, and slid it again. "I am sorry about the whole set thingy." She looked behind her.

"I'm just tired." And for the first time, I considered just how true that might be. "Life's good, but I gotta admit, it's been action-packed since the Beatles. It's been non-stop since your accident. Everything's moving at such a clip, but I still gotta show up to work. And there's Cat. Her fluids and three feedings a day now. Thank God for Amy. I don't know what I would do without her. But there's Amy, too. And then my mom! I didn't even tell you. She's talking about Nursing Without Borders." I brought both hands into my hair and massaged my head before doing the same to my face. "I'm beat." I sighed. "This is what I wanted, though. Right? I've been aching to feel alive and in love. But there's a pace to it. You know? I mean, it feels like I'm always trading one thing for another." My hands went to my hair again. "I don't know what I mean. I guess the whole Beatles thing got me thinking."

"Tell me."

"Well, I wanna be awakened. I really do." I sank back into the support of the chair. "But honestly? I'm scared. Those guys?" I sat up and leaned into the camera. "They had the world at their fingertips, and yet they struggled to understand life and love." I looked to Cat, her breath circling in and out. I thought about the Rubik's cube. Even scrambled, it was neatly contained. I sighed. "I guess there's this romantic sense of how things are supposed to be, and then there's the reality of what a person can do given human nature. But there's a finer point."

"Yes."

"Well, there's this big picture of love or how to live life, but we don't regularly consider that. Instead, everything's divided into just two choices: the good and the bad, the right and the wrong, and really those choices are no choice. I mean, the vast majority of people don't intentionally pick the bad or the wrong, and even those who do often rationalize it as good or right. And now that I say that, I wonder, how do you ever know for sure what's right and what's wrong?" I picked up the puzzle and palmed it. "Circumstances, and even time or perspective, influence that." I returned the puzzle to the desk and leaned into the camera. "The whole thing about the woman who steals the loaf of bread to feed her starving children, is she right or is she bad? You know what I mean? The higher we climb the mountain, the more we see, and what happens when we see things differently? Do you see what I'm getting at?" My hands went to my head. "I don't know what I'm talking about."

"Keep talking."

"Well, if I'm gonna live a conscious life, whatever that really means, it's entirely on me to decide how to live, how to love. And I'll wanna take responsibility for those actions, right or wrong, because they'll lead me to a greater truth about myself, about life, about love. That's pretty intimidating, you know?" I said, more to myself than to her. "The idea of living life with the intention for deeper discovery as opposed to living the way I've been told I am supposed to. That's pretty heavy stuff."

She shifted on the crutches. "Consciousness."

"Yeah, but I don't know if I can let go of judgment and live in equanimity.

That's consciousness, right? Those are some big shoes." The black ram popped to mind. "I'm up against something, Pythia. Like either, I slay this dragon, or it fries me to a crisp." I paused. "The world is full of cowards." I paused again, weighing the black ram. "What if I'm one of them?" I said in a hushed voice and looked sideways at Cat.

She hobbled closer to the screen. "Love and bravery come *in* the face of fear. You're hardly a coward." Then she asked, "How's Cat?"

I faced Pythia down, challenging her.

"You're worried." She noted.

"Of course, I'm worried. Where's the good news in that question?"

"You're angry."

"Not at you, but yeah. If this mindset applies to everything, does that mean I have to trade the love of Cat for the love of, I don't know, the love of Amy, of life? Those guys?" I pointed and then wondered where I was even pointing. "The Beatles? They gave up one dream for another. I thought you were showing me that love isn't a sacrifice. But grief makes it feel like it is. It's confusing. What *am* I supposed I do with the realization of loss?"

"Much of life is in its potentiality and not in a single thing. Respectfully, I ask you, agape mou, where is the potential in such profound loss?"

"Oh, Pythia." The question felt like a sucker punch. "Don't ask me that because there's nothing in the world worthy of trading Cat's life. I'm exhausted just trying not to think that's exactly what's being asked of me. What kind of choice is the exchange of one thing you love for another?"

"I know." She held me with her eyes. "And this matter is awfully close to your heart for debate today. Let's stay with the Beatles. Yes? But first, let me say that this matter is not a transaction, nor is it a case of cause and effect. The opportunity is not in the loss itself but in the grief."

I looked away. "I'm not ready for that."

"I understand."

Feeling angry, I wrestled with resentment toward Pythia. Part of me wanted to punish her for asking so many questions, and another part wanted to fall apart in front of her. To make matters more uncomfortable, I could feel her eyes on me, and there was nowhere to hide. "How about those Beatles?" I said, with a dead stare, daring her.

She waited a beat and then cleared her throat. "Very well, then," she said, arching her brow and fussing with her hair she became unsteady on the crutches. "Why do you think they traded their public lives of fame and glory?" she asked, hopping to gain balance.

"Ahh." I tried to shift my agitation. "Maybe, for greater understanding and deeper glory. No, not glory, but deeper self-appreciation." I thought for a moment. "I guess for a richer life experience?" I closed my eyes. "I don't know."

What'd I tell you, Mendes? This is a bunch of claptrap bunk. When you gonna wake up and see it all ends in sacrifice.

"Pythia." I shook my head, feeling a tantrum coming on. "I can't do this. I'm not that strong."

She made a loving smile. "You are strong. And courageous. And you're already doing what it takes." Then she added, "But it matters less what I think."

"Am I, though?" I was desperate to believe her.

"I think so. But only you really know." She paused, letting me appreciate my own agency. "You're a bit lost right now. Tired, yes? When that happens, it can be hard to remember what you believe, and without appreciating that, it'll be nearly impossible to create the life you want."

"What do you mean?"

"Well, in what sort of intelligence do you believe? How do you think the world is organized? By a god that punishes or one that rewards? A god that tells you how it is? Or one that asks you to participate in some greater plan of co-creation? It doesn't matter to me what you believe, but it does to you." She pointed to me and waited. "Agape mou?" She cocked her head.

"Ahh. I guess I'd say, I believe in an intelligence," I sighed and shrugged, rolling my eyes, "that supports my participation in a pattern that creates a life lived in love." I glared at her.

"And what happens when sad, or worse things happen? How do you sustain yourself? What nourishes your ability to believe in your belief?"

"That it all works out. That I'll be okay." I cast my eyes downward, feigning interest in my fingernails, particularly the thumb.

"And what's required to believe that?"

"Trust." I sighed. "Okay." I gave up a small smile that she returned.

"Life's always headed to the place of balance where things can grow and flourish. This perspective is always easier when you've gotten some rest, and sometimes rest comes in the form of letting yourself be. Letting yourself feel. Hm? Now, before we head to Mauna Kea let's talk about Lawrence Kohlberg."

"Mauna Kea?"

"Yes. The sacred Hawaiian mountain."

"Oh. Because of the snowboarding thing, I thought we were going to Mt. Everest or the Alps."

"Not today." She drew her lips into a tight line. "And I am afraid the chances of visiting Mt. Everest are nearly gone. Too many people. I hadn't considered the Alps, though." She thought for a moment with a finger at her chin. A glint of light flashed from one of her many rings. "While beautiful, the Alps are too small for this trip. Sacred is a criterion. I had thought to take you to Mount Olympus, but after that snowboarding business, I was inspired by an even grander idea. Now, I don't want to spoil it. You'll see soon enough."

"I'm tired. Can we talk tomorrow?"

"Hmm." She studied me. "How about we take a break now, and resume at three post meridiem today. And yes, let's pick up tomorrow with Dr. Kohlberg. We do have our schedule," she said, by way of reminding me of our overarching agreement.

41

"For heaven's sake, why? Agape mou?" She argued at about five minutes past three. "Do you remember that without consciousness, you *were* merely a product of your thoughts? And those mindless thoughts became your beliefs. And that jibber-jabber reinforced your next thoughts and those turned into your words that befit your actions, and your actions settled into your habits, forming your values, and your values determined your destiny! Do you?" She gasped after wielding her words like a pointy stick.

"Not exactly," I said, feeling defiant despite her exasperation.

"Did the courier arrive?"

"No."

She closed her eyes and bit her lip, then slowed her breath.

"Agape mou, you have forty-thousand to seventy-thousand thoughts a day." She began back in teaching mode. "That's a lot of thoughts. Some are helpful, some downright hurtful, some important, some absurd, and some are brilliant. Some you will deem with paramount importance, inscribing them with intrinsic value. These thoughts will become your beliefs. Why?" she asked, creating a space that required my attention, but I only stared back. "Maybe your family or culture shares such thoughts. Or because of a personal experience. Or maybe they were inspired by genius. But some, Mr. Mendes," she said, grabbing my attention, "are birthed out of defense."

"Okay! Message received."

"Believing in a sacrificial god is not gallant."

"I never said it was."

"It's not healthy physically, emotionally, mentally, or spiritually."

"So, I'm not healthy. What's new?"

She rolled her eyes. "Agape mou, everything in the multiverse hinges on everything else."

"Like the turning of the seasons with their changing landscape."

"Your sarcasm is unbecoming. If you blindly believe that you're weak, you will not feel fully alive and therefore resign yourself to a lacking life." She waited with her brow furrowed and her lips pursed. If it hadn't been for the crutches, she would have held her hands at her hips. "Everything turns against or with something, revealing something else. Birthing, you see?"

I twisted my neck, trying to crack a kink. Mindlessly, my hand found Cat's tail. "I think you think I am braver than I am. I think everybody thinks that. I told you about my mom, right. That I," I poked a finger at my chest, "inspired her to leave the country. For a year! Maybe forever. And why? I'll tell you why, because she feels useless. She's a nurse, for God's sake. It's reckless! Her leaving me is reckless. I mean—wait—that's not—or—I'm confused. You confused me!"

She held my gaze but said nothing.

"You believe, I believe she's reckless? Is that why she's always trying to be helpful. Like it would undo the things she's done, making her useful. Are you saying she believes she's reckless and can't be trusted, and for that reason, I can't trust myself? Seems a bit of a stretch, don't you think?"

"It can be confusing for a child to know the difference between his beliefs and those of his first gods. But it may be more important what *you* believe about yourself?" I didn't deserve her soft tone and found the tip of Cat's tail. With it between my thumb and forefinger, I felt for the bony tip beneath her thinning fur.

"How many things do I believe that I don't even know I believe? What's the math on that, Pythia? Because I bet it's a black hole. A never-ending, hungry, sucking, devouring hole."

"Blackholes birth alternate realities."

I stared her down.

"Respectfully, I ask you again. What does this make you believe about yourself?"

"That the world is a cruel place."

"Stay with my question. What does this make you believe about yourself?"

"How am I supposed to be alive and well and happy in love if things are always changing? That's reckless!" I knew I whined and hated myself for it. "There are no good choices."

"Consciousness is the only choice. The rest is rote."

"I don't know how to live and die every single day."

"Yes, you do."

"No, I don't" I gave her a look that declared it was my final answer.

"Yes, you do."

"No." I shook my head with exaggeration. I found the length of Cat's tail and again ran my hand down it a few times before her muscles trembled, and her whiskers flickered. On reflex, an eyeball opened and closed. My eyes stung while I let go and carefully situated her long beautiful tail neatly around her haunches, then forced myself to leave her be.

I looked up, intending to surrender but instead was snagged up by my own vile contempt again. Fierce, and with scorn, I made a face that dared Pythia to say a thing.

"You cannot pass through the door if you refuse to cross the threshold." She matched my intensity.

"I don't even know what you're talking about anymore."

"The hero's journey? There are two doors. You've passed through the first; you know you have. You're well aware that there is no return from the knowledge of Higgs. If you choose not to proceed through the second door, you will be stuck here. Perhaps not infinitely, that is up to you. But you will stall the story. There's no moving forward if your beliefs remain rooted in cause and effect, in the finite reality of any one thing, including life or death."

I rolled my eyes, but my heart wasn't in it, and my stomach lurched in fear. My body already knew the truth. I couldn't think my way out. "Fine! I am stuck. My history, my epigenetics, maybe it is my beliefs. Hell, maybe it's the stars! Whatever it is, it hijacks me." Off in the distance, far away, I could barely make out that dissonant sound of Ornette Coleman's blasting saxophone. "You ever heard of the butterfly effect, Pythia?"

"Cause and effect, agape mou." She shook her head. "I wonder if your belief about weakness may be linked to your mother's belief about recklessness. It's hard to feel your strength when you worry you might be dangerous."

I said nothing, trying to harden myself to Pythia and her tricks. The inevitable staggering had already begun. The long hallway of busted-up, looking-glass walls was narrowing in. My hands went to my head. My fingers crawled into my hair.

"Perhaps you're finishing up her storyline. Maybe that's what holds you back from the second door."

"This isn't Narnia, Pythia. You're not Aslan." I looked right at her and shoved away from the desk.

"Perhaps, as you help tie up her loose ends, it does create an opening for you both to believe and create anything you've ever wanted to create. As I recall, you indicated yours was love. Yes? And you do have love. But you can't see that. You can't feel that if you aren't willing to live alive."

"I don't want to fight with you."

"You were warned in the beginning, Gabe. This journey is life-changing."

A low, sweet warble sounded. Cat lifted her head. "Coo-coo. Coo-coo." A pale gray bird with purple and green metallic-flecked feathers stood amidst the freshly planted flowers in the window box.

Driven by instinct, Cat's saucer eyes locked in on her mark. Alert, she righted herself and "Ack, ack, ack," chattered at the bird.

The pigeon's red eyes, ringed with yellow, blinked as if she were taking pictures. "Pythia, is the courier a pigeon?" I stood, relieved for the distraction, already opening the window to take the scroll of paper from the leather pouch on the bird's back.

"I do believe we've exhausted this lesson. I'm feeling unwell, agape mou. Please, just post to the website, and we'll meet in the ante meridies. Yes?"

Website?

But by the time I returned to the screen, she'd already signed off.

42

The next morning Cat stood on shaky legs before laying down slowly. "I know, old girl. It's early," I said, hungover with grief, struggling with the dead weight of what a big fricking mess everything seemed.

Not everything, dude.

I rolled my eyes, catching my reflection in the big picture window, a black mirror in the early morning hours. How strange to believe my reflection was the only witness to Cat and I illuminated in the yellow kitchen-light for anyone to see.

I smoothed Cat's fur as her skin crawled with the rush of fluids, and when she'd taken in the seventy-five milliliters, I removed the needle and dotted the site with a cotton ball before tugging her tail and giving her a kiss. But she made no effort to move. "Hungry?" I set her to the floor and watched her eat. Eyeing her slow efforts and wrestling the usual worry, I waited, and when she wobbled toward the steps, I carried her upstairs where we waited for Pythia.

"Good morning!" Pythia shifted right into teacher mode. I sighed, fighting the old pull of drifting to the bottom of abandonment and drowning in self-loathing. "In the middle of the last century, Lawrence Kohlberg concluded that moral reasoning is a perspective and not a natural occurrence. It cannot be instructed and only evolves through social interactions that provide cognitive conflicts at certain stages of human development. Therefore, ethical conduct develops in six stages. Each building skills of competency for the resolution of moral dilemmas and resulting in a higher stage of moral development." She teetered on her crutches and did her best to appear composed while steadying herself. I resented her balance. Everything seemed effortless for her. "In this case, greater conflict is good news." She paused and smiled.

I snorted. "Sure," I said, slinging the word like a weapon and with half of a mean smile. Cat twitched in her sleep, and I petted her, keeping my hand light, beginning to admit I owed Pythia an apology.

"So, I ask you, is love a moral dilemma?"

I searched Pythia's face and then looked away.

Come on, Dude.

"Gabe. You have to be alive. You can't play dead. Breathe."

I exhaled and groaned. "But yesterday, I thought—" I shook my head, "I felt. You don't, I mean, I feel all alone."

"What do you believe love is?"

"I don't know."

"You have a mathematical formula. Yes?"

I didn't want to answer.

"TC / I × V = L." She paused. "Trust multiplied by confidence divided into intimacy multiplied by vulnerability equals love. Yes?"

I shrugged.

"But you don't believe it. You believe something else."

"Love is sacrifice. It hurts." My eyelids were heavy. My face muscles lacked any integrity. "And when you believe it will make you whole, love becomes a moral dilemma."

"Trust multiplied by confidence divided into intimacy multiplied by vulnerability equals love, could be a moral dilemma?"

"Pythia." I moaned and shook my head. "We both know that if the only goal in trusting is for the acquisition of a specific self-serving outcome that assures your safety, well, that's not love, is it? The whole point of trust is relinquishing control, letting go of a certain outcome, and allowing yourself to be vulnerable to the outcome. And even if that change is not what you wanted or expected, you gotta trust in the process of evolution, that's love." I argued. She was silent, and that's when I realized she'd tricked me.

"No, agape mou. Despite tricking yourself into believing something else, you've now spoken your truth. What if you let yourself see what is actually before you and then decide what you want to think and do about it. Letting yourself believe in your own competence, trusting that you do belong living in a loving life." She did her best to look patient, but the crutches challenged her ease, and she flinched adjusting them. "Can we please move forward?"

"Pythia, I'm sorry about yesterday."

She waved a hand and said, "You owe me no apology. It is hard work to face the pain and move forward, trusting in love." She wobbled, and her lack of usual grace somehow helped me navigate the strange distance I'd come to believe existed between us but clearly didn't.

Just then, a very ordinary fellow appeared on screen, hurrying toward Pythia. Other than wearing a headset, he was the kind of man nobody would ever remember. She fumbled with her crutches before shuffling through index cards he'd passed her. Frowning with her mouth twitching, she spoke presumably to the man who'd exited. "Thank you," she said, sounding curt, "but this is far too much for today. We can post it to the website."

He mumbled something from out of sight but all I could make out was a garbled, "Wha, wha, wahht."

Pythia shook her head, "No. Please inform Zeus that this level of detail is unnecessary. Post it to the website."

"What, wat, whahh?"

"Yes, please."

"Wat, wat."

"Thank you." Then looking flustered, she rolled her eyes before leaning in to whisper. "Zeus! Just as soon as I let my guard down with that god, he's all up in my business again. Really?" She held up the stack of cards. "If anyone wants for more info, you can direct them to the website."

I scratched my beard. Website?

But before I could ask, she came close enough that all I saw were her lips, thin and a natural red color framing her straight teeth. "Control Freak." She mouthed and backed up, arching a brow. "Six Stages. Shall we? Alrighty then. The first stage," she said, sounding official again but was interrupted.

"Wha, wha, whahh?" the invisible man droned.

"I'm sorry," she said and looked at someone I couldn't see. She hesitated, then looked to the cards, and sorting through them, she shook her head, held them up to me, and whispered, "I promise, you needn't know all of this." She waggled the cards, and the fellow appeared. "We'll use that game show set," she said, to him, handing him the cards.

"Wat, wat, wat, wat, whahh?"

"No, not, *The Price Is Right*." She frowned and shifted her weight. "The other one." She looked hopeful that he knew what she'd meant.

"Whahh?"

"No, no." A wayward lock of hair fell across her face. She pushed it behind her ear. "Agape mou, I am so sorry. This was meant to be a nice surprise. Something fun, yes? But there seems to be, shall we say, confusion. Do you know the name of that game show, the one where they say, 'Survey says?'" she asked, doing a perfect imitation. Cat twitched. Her eyes flickered.

"*Family Feud*?"

"*Family Feud!* Yes." She turned to the man. "*Family Feud*."

"Wha, whahh?"

"Yes. Please!" She widened her eyes, and he scurried off.

Then without notice, and as if someone flipped a switch, the familiar bucolic scene vanished, and Pythia suddenly stood on the set of *Family Feud*, complete with the colorful board and flashing lights. The man dashed back into view handing Pythia a new stack of cards.

Referring to the first card, Pythia read, "In the first stage of Obedience and Punishment Orientation, a person believes their own agency is outside of themselves and therefore makes moral decisions by way of avoiding punishment." She sounded just like the game show host. "In your life, when have you done this?"

"When?" I was still taking in the set, the blinking lightbulbs outlining the board, the contestant's desk complete with a buzzer.

"The clocking is ticking."

"Um." I giggled and leaned in, my heart beat fast.

"Picture it in your mind."

In my mind, I saw myself as that clean-cut contestant hitting a buzzer. Ding, ding, ding! "Me as a young boy. My grandfather refers to the untouched pork-chop on my plate, saying something like, 'You don't want my finger in your eye!' My mom looks worried, and when the old man looks away, I slide the chop into one of the cargo pockets of my pants."

"Survey says," she called out, and with a 'Ding!' a tile on the board flipped revealing, *Porkchop*, followed by canned applause.

Having fun, I imagined myself as that game show winner. A young man who knew his curly mop was charming. He let himself move at the podium in a way that interested women. In my mind, I saw him bend forward to speak directly into the microphone, "I'd like to dedicate this answer to my girlfriend, Amy," he said, with a boyish grin, "who never makes me feel like I have to hide things." The camera would zoom in on his pearly whites. There'd be a devilish twinkle in the champ's eye as he'd take the microphone. "Not in my pants anyway," he'd say, and the audience would roar. Their admiration was amplified in their hearty handclapping.

"Gabe!" Pythia shouted sharply, and I was awakened to her face so close to the screen that it was mostly a single eye. Then she hobbled back and fussed, adjusting the crutches at her armpits before touching her hair and straightening her dress.

"It's perfectly fine," she assured me. "Change of plans, though." She forced a smile from the set of *The Newlywed Game*.

"Is that?" I pointed.

"Hey, hotshot." Amy waved.

"Son of a monkey, Pythia! Is that My Ex?"

"Holograms." Pythia hurried in to say. "They're only holograms." Looking too friendly, Amy waved. Unsure and feeling foolish, I made a little wave. Thankfully, My Ex seemed disinterested and painted her nails while a young woman in the next booth had her nose deep in a book.

"They'll keep you focused on the topic of morality as it relates to love. Porkchop was an excellent example of stage one. Very Newtonian. If I do this, that happens. Hide the chop; the problem's solved! Your answer referenced personal history, possibly epigenetic info. You know, like secrets or deception as a family coping mechanism, and it did refer to intimacy. But no romantic challenge. See what I'm saying?"

Still keeping an eye on My Ex, I thought about this idea of secrets and deceptions, and that's when one of the women, a girl really, caught my eye. Squinting, I asked, "Is that Brittany Duncan from high school?" Brittany gave me an embarrassed smile, and I blushed. Amy giggled, but the Amy I knew didn't giggle.

"Alright, ladies." Pythia turned to the contestants. "Describe a time when Gabe participated in the second stage of morality known as Self-Interest Orientation. This will be when he navigated a romantic situation using the guideline of, 'How can this benefit me?' This would be a time when his moral actions were guided by personal advantage. Here again, Gabe behaved as if his own agency was outside of himself."

"Brittany?"

"Pythia, I'd have to say—" and she flashed a card that read, *Gabe's big mess!* and smiled for the camera.

"Oh, no!" I hid my face.

"Back then, Gabe and I were neighbors, and we used to hang out and watch the *Simpsons* in my basement. Pretty soon, things got romantic. We started fooling around, and he unzipped his fly." Brittany paused, and a canned audience gasped. "And I said, 'No.'" Brittany lingered, allowing the audience to boo. "And he said, 'I love you.' But before anything happened, he, you know, made a big mess." On cue, the audience roared, and Brittany laughed too. "I'd say, he said he loved me because his moral compass was set at self-interest orientation, because after that he never came over again." She looked sad, and the audience uttered a collective, "Ah."

"Brittany, I'm sorry. I'm so embarrassed. I was so humiliated. That's why I didn't. I mean, I wasn't. Well, maybe I was trying. Anyway, I'm sorry. I don't do that anymore." But she just blinked. I looked to Pythia and then Amy. "I'm not like that," I said, but Amy only giggled, and then the audience giggled, too.

"Perhaps you've advanced from objectification and making interpersonal relationships transactional. Hm? Such self-awareness could indicate you've evolved. That's something to feel good about. Yes?" Pythia shot me a feel-good smile before flipping to the next card while some of the audience whistled, and others called out, "Way to go, Gabe!"

"Well, these certainly aren't my finest moments," I whispered to Pythia, hoping not to engage the audience.

"No one here thinks you normally operate today at stage one or two." Her speech was clipped, and she gestured to someone off stage. "Cut the audience, please," she said, then turned back to me. "But you could, and some people still do operate at those early stages of morality. Today, it's essential to understand your moral intelligence so you can partner with someone who behaves from a similar ethical standard."

She returned to the women seated in the bank of cheesy, white lattice-covered booths, and said, "Ladies," with a Bob Eubanks-esque smile and charm. There was nothing about any of this I liked. "Third stage. Interpersonal Accord and Conformity Orientation. That's a mouthful that describes a time when Gabe collaborated exclusively with a like-minded group to harness greater agency. This will be when he decided on a matter along the lines of living up to some outside group's prescribed values and expectations. Seeing their regard as personally beneficial to him by deeming him a worthy human."

"Amy?"

Amy held up a card that read, *Gabe's the bomb!!!* She flirt-smiled and giggled, looking absolutely ridiculous. "Pythia, why is Amy acting like that?"

Pythia looked concerned. "I don't know. The algorithm's set to defer to her trauma response. Something does seem wrong."

"If I understand correctly," Amy said, beaming with pride, "this would be a time when Gabe believed his core importance was dependent on his relationship with a group and that group's values. Gabe's never projected *anything* like that into *our* relationship." She boasted.

"Count yourself lucky, Amy," My Ex said, revealing a card that read, *Gabe's a dick.* "Back when I was with Gabe, it was the league of lawyers, and they ranked royal! That high horse included teachers, bosses, grandparents, his stepfather, even his mother," she said to Amy, then turned and looked right at me. "He's a momma's boy," she sneered.

"Hold on," I shouted, shooting up, my chair rolling out behind me. Cat startled. But My Ex was on a roll.

"He drank the Kool-Aid. Granted them all sovereignty, and I fell into his good graces the way a bad habit makes someone likable. I was his currency." She spat the words. "Slumming with me, he found a whole new way of objectifying and transacting, and he tied it up in a delusional white-knight bow. That is until he fell off his horse." She snorted. "And boy, did he fall hard. That's when I conveniently became just some effed up girl dragging him down to the other side of the tracks."

"Oh, my God! I called and said I was sorry." Then to Pythia, I said, "I called her." I turned to My Ex. "And what about you?" I asked. "You belonged to some club that valued marginalizing people's dignity!" But she only blinked. "Pythia, that's not—she's making me sound like a monster. My God!" I turned to My Ex, "Is that what you think? That I used you to feel better about myself?" But she only blinked. I picked up the computer, wishing I could climb through and set everybody straight, while at the same time, sick to my stomach, I knew what she'd implied wasn't entirely a lie. I'd made some real mistakes.

"He did the same thing to me at a bar. Led me on with all this talk about being a musician when he really lived with his mom. Totally messed up. When I called him on it, he tried to make me feel ugly," she said, wearing a crop top, flipping her straight blond hair over her shoulder.

"Who are you?" I squinted at the woman. "Pythia? Who is that?"

"The young woman from the bar on the hill," Pythia said, looking apologetic before flagging the off-stage man.

"That one time at that bar on the hill? The one who gave me the finger? Oh, my God, Pythia! What the—" and for a split second I remembered the woman's heavy perfumed scent.

But Pythia was already hollering something about an algorithm and then outright yelled, "Right away!" Breathless, with beads of sweat on her forehead, she said to me, "I do apologize," trying to sound as if the situation wasn't a complete circus. From off stage, I could hear the man firing some order.

"A few kinks in the programming. That's all." Pythia minimized. "Not to worry."

"Pythia, in case you haven't noticed, I'm in the hot seat here. Some of the nuts are out of the nut jar!"

"Do take what they say with a grain of salt. Hmm?" She wrinkled her nose, still playing it down. "Holograms. Yes?"

"Yeah, but they hate me. Except for Amy, and she's a complete nitwit. I can hardly stand to look at her. Look at her!" I pointed, and Amy waved wiggling in her seat, then cocked her head and when her eyes met mine my stomach sank. "Amy?" I whispered with a real distaste in my mouth.

The young woman with her nose in a book looked up. "We can only speculate how much of Gabe's moral dilemma around love is nature and how much was nurture. But a little self-awareness goes a long way in evolving to a higher moral code. Self-awareness is critical to the consciousness required to change any pattern of thinking, despite epigenetics or personal or cultural history."

"Is that the psych major from college?" I asked, but Pythia was distracted. "We never even dated!"

"Gabe?" The Prettiest Girl In The Sixth Grade, sniveled. "I thought all those looks at our lockers meant you liked me, but you never even tried to ask me to the sixth-grade dance. And after the dance, you couldn't be bothered to even say hello. What did you expect me to do when Theo Winner asked?"

"Ladies, please!" Pythia yelled, and her crown slid crooked on her head. She wobbled, and the unsteady crutches shifted, revealing dark stains of sweat at the armpits of her green chiffon dress. Then, furiously waving to someone off-stage again, she lost her balance. The crutches crashed to the floor, and she toppled over.

Without being cued, a Moe look-alike held up a card: *Gabe's a sexist.* "The fourth stage, Authority, and Social Order Maintaining Orientation is when Gabe made a moral decision by granting paramount importance to civic laws and social conventions. On top of the mountain, Gabe defended his male privilege for sex as a moral right. He refused any responsibility for rape culture relinquishing his own agency to the good-old-boys justice system."

"No, I did not!" I grabbed the computer and screamed into it. "I did exactly the opposite of that! My God, I quit my job over exactly that kind of thing. Pythia!" I shouted for her, "do something!" But Pythia was sprawled out on the floor like a beetle on its back in no position to even hear me.

Someone I didn't recognize held up a card as tears streamed down her face. It read: *Gabe made me feel used.* I sank into the chair and closed my eyes. My heart raced. It was that girl. Eva, or was it, Ava? I sighed, rubbing my forehead while the off-stage, headset-wearing fellow raced to help Pythia.

Utterly clueless to the chaos surrounding her, the Amy look-alike spoke, "Recently, Gabe and I agreed on an informal rule to hold each other accountable to sincere and forthright discussion that bridges, not breeches, trust and builds, not impedes, intimacy. This informal rule is a guide that allows us each to find our way toward a deeper shared truth, moreover than holding each other to the letter of the rule. Therefore, Gabe and I are morally suited to each other."

Another man carrying a chair hurried toward Pythia and the two men helped her into the seat. Both buzzed about her trying to fix her hair and adjust her dress but Pythia flapped her hands and they scurried off.

"I think Amy is referring to stage five," The Psyche Major piped up. "She's really describing the evolution from stage four to five. If we only use the rule as a measure of judgment, it won't ever help us find trust or intimacy. It seems to me that while each of these stages becomes more complex, graduation from one to the next only results in greater contemplation about the meaning of justice and the realization that there is no intimacy in the service of justice.

"I agree," the Moe look-alike said. "People don't live or love in ideals. But if there is a moral obligation in love, can Gabe love if his moral judgments are fixed?"

"Ladies, ladies!" Pythia shouted from the chair but then stuck both her first fingers into her mouth and produced a loud, sharp whistle. Each hologram pixelated and wavered, jeopardizing its image before restoring itself to its recognizable form. Finally, when they all sat blankly staring and blinking, Pythia asked, "When have you witnessed flexibility in Gabe's judgmental tendencies in favor of a moral obligation to love."

"Cat," they said in unison.

"Stage five, Social Contract Orientation, as was discussed by Amy and The Psyche Major, as well as all of you when you acknowledged its relevance in Gabe and Cat's love. These were times, are times, when Gabe took deep consideration for his or another's determination with a willingness to find common ground for health and welfare despite any of the previous stage considerations. In these situations, Gabe's moral conclusion was drawn completely from his own agency, and he did not relinquish it to another."

My Ex was back to her nails, and The Psyche Major was deep in her book. Amy waved and giggled. They'd each returned to their resting place.

"Ethical Principles Orientation." Pythia sounded weary. "Very few people evolve to stage six because these courageous individuals determine their actions based on their ethical principles rather than laws. They have a profound commitment to secure moral equilibrium. Even if it means disobedience on their part, they commit to taking action utilizing their full agency regardless of the consequences."

The Prettiest Girl In The Sixth Grade waved, while the others were motionless.

"Thank you all for your participation," Pythia said. The holograms shimmered. Pythia nodded to someone off stage, and the images began breaking up. Fully dissolved, the set sat empty except for Pythia, and the room went green before the familiar scene returned. The robin and the babbling brook.

"I am terribly sorry." Pythia looked a complete wreck with her crown in her hand. "I can only say, that is not what I'd intended. I take full responsibility for the utter," she hesitated, "shall we say, comedy of errors. Can you forgive me?" she asked with a hang dog expression, but almost like it didn't matter either way.

Definitely still shaken, but seeing Pythia as such a mess, I took the lead. "I know without a doubt that this was not your idea of a … meaningful experience." Imitating her, I paused, letting her take in my words like they were medicine. "It wasn't all bad."

"It was pretty bad."

"Well, sometimes things aren't what they seem to be. Huh?"

"Agape mou," she said, in disagreement.

"I have to say, I think it was helpful. I mean, sure, it was intense. But, intimacy? Love? Moral discernment? None of them is any singular thing, and you wrapped them all up here together in a way that revealed they are interconnected. The Prettiest Girl and Brittany Duncan are interconnected to loving Cat, who is interconnected to Eva or Ava, My Ex, the girl at the bar. Even Moe and The Psyche Major." I scratched my beard. "And they're all interconnected to me loving Amy. I don't get to be where I am today without the real Amy, and all of them. And you're in there too. It's The Thang. And in The Thang, there's no liberation in love when morality is based on cause and effect. Love is only nourished in a conscious collaboration that causes an effect. Right?"

"Well, yes, that is correct."

"And that's what you wanted me to understand yesterday. That when I transmute my grief, I will see it as more than only loss. I will be able to find the opportunity. Some greater meaning that I can apply for a broader application. The health and welfare of Cat is her journey, and mine is inside of hers." Something caught in my throat and I swallowed hard shaking my head. "I'm not ready to apply that, Pythia. But today, you brought me face to face with a lot of grief. If I'm going to understand the moral obligations necessary for creating love, you were right to show me my part in the grief. I can't create a space that allows for change if I'm clinging to the past, especially with judgment." She looked pale. "Are you alright?"

"I've been better."

"Pythia, life's messy," I said, trying to make my voice sound the way my hand might feel at her shoulder.

With her head lowered, she nodded, and I made out the sounds of sniffles. "You're very right." She lifted her head. Looking exhausted, she attempted to fix her hair.

I made a little laugh. "I'm afraid it's hopeless, Pythia." I pointed to her sloppy, sweaty hair.

"You think?" She looked me in the eye. "How about now?" She dropped the crown atop her disheveled hairdo, and we both laughed. "Some high priestess, I am. Oh! Agape mou? What was I thinking?" Her eyes pleaded as she tugged her ring on and off. She shook and hung her head.

"I think you were thinking, how can I show Gabe that most people are raised to value morality as a means of keeping out of trouble, finding validation, ensuring protection, or providing the *right* kind friends or experiences. Even though deep down most of us want it to provide more meaning than that. I think you wanted me to see how the stage of morality correlates with the experience of love. And how even that can be transcended with the creation of a space that allows people to change—to heal, to evolve."

She listened, looking at me hard.

"I have a question for you, Pythia."

"Please. Yes." She perked up, sitting tall, all eager to find a way back to her engaging self.

"How often did the village that raised you applaud your defense of social injustice, or support your decision to take a stand against inequity?"

"Oh, well." She chuckled. "You know Zeus. It's his way or the highway. I do my best, but that *is* his privilege," she said like it was a truth. "At the same time, it's that very privilege that blinds him to injustice and inequity. He can't even see that his beliefs are outdated. It's fair to say, mortality is a sticky wicket with a god like him." She laughed and shrugged.

"He's not much for morality that challenges the status quo, huh?"

"No. Zeus's not a fan of cultural evolution." She waved a hand.

I nodded, glad for our easy rapport. "I guess if you don't evolve past stage four, your ability to develop a complex understanding of love will be limited."

"Pretty much." She sighed and then reached to slide the charm on the chain. "Do you know he refuses to even recognize the seven types of love? He's Greek, for God's sake," she said in a low voice.

"Somebody's got to be the squeaky wheel. A whistleblower, even."

She grinned. "Well, we do our best, don't we?" She fidgeted with the necklace.

"I don't know about me. But you sure know how to shake things up and blow out the cobwebs. You've got me thinking in a way that makes me believe in an experience of love I never even knew existed. You've changed my life."

"Well," she said, making a little shrug and looking shy. "I, um, I," but then she just laughed. "Well, we do our best, don't we?" and straightened her dress.

43

As always, there she was at the crack of dawn. I stood from my desk and reached through time and space for her hand. Joining her, I recited the invocation with her as easy as a prayer I'd known all my life. The powerful downward surge pulled me, and I completely surrendered. This time, feeling as if I was dissolving into billions of tiny particles. Whooshing through space with greater intensity than ever before until the fertile, humus scent clung damp and heavy in my nostrils. Then, the soft thud. The kindness of earth at my feet. "Whoa!" I opened my eyes, balancing on the edge of rocky terrain, and looked out from atop the mountain.

At the peak, I stood surrounded by a blue wall of sky. Below it merged with the sea, and the setting sun lit the horizon in fiery orange while a rippling cirrocumulus drifted in. Clouds rolled in, covering the world in a dense white blanket.

"Look." A soft British voice floated in from behind me. A tall, slender woman bundled in a heavy parka emerged from the mist. I recognized her immediately, her voice and gait a dead give-away. She pointed west to the blazing red orb as it sank into the thick white fog. "It's enchanting to see you. I don't think we could have asked for a finer night," she said, as she greeted Pythia with a hug and a kiss to each cheek. She cast her eyes downward and handed us each a jacket. Then helped Pythia, who hobbled about, leaning on me while sliding her arm into the coat. In-person, Diana was as endearing as she'd ever been portrayed on American television. Something about her drew me in and I wanted to like her, but I acquiesced to her celebrity, minding a boundary I thought appropriate.

"It was a fine idea, Diana. I only wish I'd thought of it. I might have saved myself the grief of this snowboarding business!" Pythia nodded to her foot.

"Well, yes. But it couldn't have happened to a nicer priestess." Lady Diana flashed me an intoxicating smile as she helped Pythia. Then lifting her seductive blue eyes, she extended her hand. "Hello, I'm Diana. It's nice to meet you." Batting her thick eyelashes, she grasped my hand between two bulky wool mittens. Then laughing, she said, "I'm sorry. I'm afraid it's a bit of a clumsy introduction all bundled up like this." She turned, and still managing to sound soft, she called out to two men approaching. "Martin, do you have the extras?"

The taller of the two pointed to the shorter. "Bapu has them." The short man waved the mittens.

"Cold, isn't it?" She sounded friendly and looked fresh with a ruddy nose and cheeks, but her beauty transcended her physical features, and I worried about what I could possibly say.

"It is." I tried making two words sound engaging but not needy.

Rubbing Pythia's thickly coated back, Diana leaned her head on Pythia's shoulder. "It's certainly nice to be with you again. I've missed you." No matter the volume, her tone was always hushed.

"And I, you." Pythia struggled to figure out how to hold the princess's hand while managing the crutches.

"We're coming, Pythia!" Bapu jogged with open arms, Martin at his heels.

Diana watched while the three hugged. She stood lanky with her arms crossed, holding her sides swaying like she was rocking a baby.

"Have you known Pythia long?" I asked, trying to grab a quick sideways glance, hoping I sounded nice and normal. Maybe interesting.

"Yes, I have." She looked to the snow-covered ground. "It seemed to me I was a lamb gone to slaughter back when the eyes of the world were upon me. I wasn't used to that, you know. I was only a girl and a virgin at that." I felt her glance my way and imagined her doe eyes, honest now and not playful. "My immaturity was tremendous on so many levels. Later, after I'd departed the physical world, Pythia explained to me that I'd been idolized because I transgressed all the traditional rules, the ideas of morality, really. And those transgressions became virtuous to so many who were waiting for the repudiation of the old order." She hesitated, and I worried I'd missed some cue. Finally taking a chance, I looked right at her. She searched my face as if she needed assurance.

"You'd stumbled into a powerful position," I said, surprising myself.

"Quite by accident, it seemed." She looked relieved, as if we were sharing secrets and then confessed. "But in the beginning, I was so shattered by the dissolution of my fairytale that I felt abandoned; forced, even, into a cocoon of myself where my only choice was to reduce down to nothing but a maudlin, viscous mess. I wasn't easy for anyone, myself included. And I certainly wasn't clever about my transformation. I was troubled, very lost indeed." She paused and knowing she was pained, I mustered the courage to witness the sadness in her eyes.

"I'm sorry," I said, finding the greatest sincerity. Hoping Diana would feel I did, in fact, understand.

"Thank you." She paused, and I took in her gratitude. "But it was my good fortune, really. It forced me to find that inner determination to survive." Her eyes fell, and she stomped her boots. Then from beneath her long lashes she lifted her gaze. "It's cold if you stay in one place. I finally figured that out! Don't ask me how." She laughed. "I was a slow learner. But, eventually, I re-created my own mythology by helping others, and then I embraced it like it was my own destiny. I believe every one of us must practice caring for others. It's how we can care for ourselves, and that is our ethical responsibility. Everyone needs to be valued, don't you agree?"

"You must be cold? Please." The small, bald man, who I fully recognized as Gandhi, interrupted, offering me gloves, his moon face full of laughter. His eyes sparkled with kindness from behind his round spectacles while his nose took center stage above a bushy mustache. His ears stuck out like handles for his head, and I wanted deep in my bones to be his friend.

"I am Mahatma Gandhi," he said, "but those who know me call me Bapu. It is my pleasure to meet you." He bowed his head, then turned to the handsome man beside him. "This is my friend, Martin Luther King Junior. He was the leader of the American Civil Rights Movement." Gandhi then leaned in and whispered. "He's reserved but friendly."

Martin removed his mitten, and vigorously shook my hand.

"Yes, of course. I know you all. I mean, I know of you." I could feel myself blushing.

"We know what you mean." Gandhi smiled in a way that had me feeling at home, and in the dimming light, I couldn't help but want to believe he already liked me.

"When Pythia said we were headed to the highest mountain in the world, well, I never imagined. I'm certainly, I mean I hope—"

"Tell him a joke." Gandhi nudged Martin. "He's nervous."

Clearly excited, Martin grinned, and I couldn't help but feel I'd known these people all my life. "What did Gandhi say when the British tried to push him out?"

"Oh, Martin," Pythia said, and then to me, "He could have been a comedian for all his joke telling."

"He is funny looking," Gandhi said. "But, Martin, please, do tell us what it is I said."

"What you said when the Brits tried to push you out?" Martin asked, setting up the joke again.

"Yes, Martin. What did Gandhi say when the British tried to push him out?" Pythia asked.

"Nah," Martin said, waving his hand, "ma stay."

Pythia groaned. "Martin, did you make that up?"

"It's very clever, Martin. But I don't remember the British having much luck getting rid of me."

"Alright, I have one." Pythia jumped in. "Let me see, now."

"While she's preparing," Gandhi said, "what did the Buddhist say to the hot dog vendor?"

"Make me one with everything!" Martin clapped and belted out with laughter.

"How does he do it?" Gandhi turned to Diana and included me. "He knows every joke."

"Alright, I have it," Pythia said.

"Please. Let's all come close." Gandhi motioned. "Pythia has a joke."

Diana took my hand. "Come on." Then she whispered, "Pythia's terrible at telling jokes, and Martin tells terrible jokes."

"A Baptist preacher was struggling in the water when a boat came and offered help," Pythia began, but I only half listened. Not on purpose, but I wanted to feel who I was while in their company. "The preacher said, 'Thank you, but God will save me.' Another boat came by, but again the preacher refused. Then, nearly drowning, the preacher denied yet a third boat, saying the same. Later in Heaven, the man asked God, 'Why didn't you save me?' and God replied—"

"'Fool, I sent you three boats!'" Martin burst, stealing the punchline he clapped his hands and roared with laughter.

"You're impossible, Martin," Pythia said.

"He is," Gandhi agreed.

"Everyone!" Diana called out over the din. "It'll be dark soon. Who's ready for a toasted marshmallow? Martin?" She lifted her eyebrows, asking me.

"Sure," I said, feeling like maybe I could be like them.

"Bapu, you will have one, won't you?" she asked, opening bags and packages.

"Of course."

"You don't need to ask me twice, Diana." Pythia hobbled, and we all found seats in a big circle around a campfire perfect for toasting.

Martin handed me a stick with Gandhi seated beside. Then, speaking only to me and in a low, deep voice, Martin began his story. "I was fifteen," he said as we both sat holding sticks we'd later load with a marshmallow and hold over the flames. "A middle-class son of a prominent black family from Atlanta headed to spend my summer working the tobacco fields in Yankee territory." I could tell this was a story he never tired of telling as he eyed me like we were old friends. Then he shook his head, and poking the hot coals with his stick, he confessed, "Changed my life. Back then? North of DC?" He frowned, closed his eyes, and sealed his lips. "Nope, past DC, there was practically no discrimination as far it looked to me then." He fixed an extra-large marshmallow onto the end of the long stick. "This look big to you?" he asked, showing me the confection. Unsure if he was setting me up for a joke, I nodded my agreement; it did look extraordinary in size.

Diane leaned over me to explain, "It's a giant roaster, Martin," she said.

"Oh, did you hear that? It's a giant roaster." He smirked, passing me the bag. "Well," he said, gazing into the fire. "In the north, it seemed like we could go anyplace, sit anywhere. Back then, in comparison to the south, the white people were down-right friendly. There were even racially integrated church services. But once I was back home, I couldn't enjoy such freedoms again." He turned down the corners of his mouth while he browned one side of the marshmallow, and then the other. "After that, I felt an inescapable urge to serve society, to be a constant and unwavering promoter of human dignity, and without this guy," he nodded at Gandhi, "I wouldn't have known how to stand up and change things." He drew his stick out of the fire and called down to Pythia, "Where would I find the chocolate and crackers?"

"Over there." Seated across the fire Pythia pointed to large boulder. "Would you make me one? Mine's about toasted."

"Excuse me," Martin said, standing. "Would you like me to make you a smore, too?"

"Oh, I like mine on the charcoaled side. I'll be a little longer here," I said, being honest.

"Me too," Gandhi said, sitting beside the empty seat that was Martin's. "Nothing beats the crispy carbon with the caramelized sugary inside. I like burnt toast too. With slabs of butter."

"Me, too," I said, surprised at these some things I had in common with such an extraordinary person. "Can I ask you something?"

"By all means, after all, I am all ears." He grinned, showing off the size of an ear with his free hand.

I chuckled. "Did you ever imagine you'd leave such a mark on the world?" I hoped the question didn't bore him.

"Not at first. You see, I was terrified of speaking in public. They say humans have two fears: of falling and of being heard. Well, I was certainly afraid of being heard, but I suppose I got over that. Love is brave, and I loved India and her people. That love transformed my fear into a gift. You see, it made me an excellent listener. It taught me patience. And because I was hesitant to speak, I learned to say more with fewer words. Sometimes the very things that hold us back are the vehicles for our greatest success. In time, I knew that the only way to change the world was to embody that change. And I hoped that I would inspire others to do the same."

I blew out the licks of fire from my flaming marshmallow. The thing was encrusted in charred black sugar.

"You've roasted it perfectly. I only hope I can do it as well." Gandhi grappled with the stick, turning it this way and that, trying to secure the burning confection from falling. "But glory lies in the attempt to reach one's goal, not in reaching it." His voice climbed as he rose from his seat, dancing to better maneuver the stick and its contents. We all laughed at his performance. "If I believe I can do it," he said, playing to the crowd, swinging his hips and the stick, "I shall surely acquire the capacity to do it!" He lifted the stick and placed a hand beneath the gooey mess. Martin ran to his aid with a pair of crackers and a square of chocolate. Using the crackers like mitts, he slid the mallow off the stick and presented the treat to his friend. Gandhi grinned, licking chocolate from the corners of his mouth. "No matter your opponent, always conquer with love. Or chocolate!" He declared, his mustache all sticky.

"Is there a difference?" Diana licked her sticky fingers. "Look." She pointed to the navy sky, dazzling without the interference of ambient light. It seemed we hovered in blackness, surrounded by millions of brilliant bright diamonds, sparkling in the infinite night. Diana rested her chin in the heels of her hands with her elbows on her knees. "I always knew that life was outside the walls imposed upon us and those we impose upon ourselves. It's beyond truth and beauty. Do you suppose that's where humility lies? In such generosity as this?" She referenced the dreamy, celestial sky.

"Amen," Martin said, and for a while, we were quiet.

"Did you know that Mauna Kea is the most sacred of the Hawaiian volcanoes because of its height? It's taller than Mount Everest." Gandhi broke the silence. "If you measure it from its oceanic base, it's thirty-three thousand one hundred feet. Everest is just over twenty-nine thousand feet."

"The summit of Mauna Kea is where the Sky and Earth separated to form the Great Expanse of Space and the Heavenly Realms," Pythia said, trying to stand, precariously leaning on a crutch and struggling for balance. On one side of her, Gandhi shifted, trying to anticipate Pythia's need as Diana did the same from the other side. "It is the zenith of the Native Hawaiian people's ancestral ties to creation. An umbilicus of sorts. The core of their existence. This summit itself is a temple created to bring the heavens to humanity. The laws of man do not dictate its sanctity." She teetered against the crutch. "The laws of the heavens do."

"Pythia?" I stood up. "Can I help you?"

"Thank you. That would be a relief. I'm so terribly uncomfortable." She leaned on me, handing me her crutches. "I can't decide if I want to sit or stand."

"It's okay," I said. We were eye to eye.

She nodded. "I suppose." She lowered herself to the chair.

"Here," Martin said, sliding a nearby a rock beneath her bum foot.

"Thank you, Martin," Pythia said. "Ah, yes. Much better. Thank you, everyone. Now, where was I? Oh, yes." She wiggled to sit tall. "This is where the life-giving waters originate, where the very first breath can be seized, where we can be born again, only this time, fully alive and without fear. Tonight, we honor that for ourselves and for each other. That we may proclaim the summit's sanctity and commit to carry and share its great purpose with all of humankind. Our duty cannot be abridged."

"Over a thousand years ago," Gandhi said, nodding to the sky, "Polynesians followed these same stars and journeyed to Hawaii. Today the stars are at the heart of great controversy."

"Who has the right to stake claim to the stars and this mountain top?" Martin orated. "Morality cannot be legislated, but behavior can be regulated. Judicial decrees may not change the heart, but they can restrain the heartless."

"What are we talking about?" I asked.

"Astronomers want to build an observation center with a monstrous telescope, believing that will answer the most intriguing question of all," Gandhi said.

"Ah, the age-old dilemma, infinitely battled out between science and spirituality: are we alone?" I asked and everyone nodded. "Well, from this perspective," I looked to the stars, "we are not alone and never have been."

"But wouldn't an observatory with a thirty-meter telescope a hundred times more powerful than current instruments prove that?" Martin deviled.

Gandhi pointed through the darkness to a shadowy place. "Perhaps, but the footprint of this proposed observatory will sit in the Ring of Shrines, the sacred peak, the burial ground of the highest-ranking native ancestors and home to divine deities—the meeting place of Earth Mother and Sky Father, the progenitors of the native people. It may be a testament to human curiosity, but from what moral lens does this scope see the world?"

The steady trade winds blew in from across the Pacific. Somewhere in the dark, the wooden and stone altars of the Hawaiian natives bowed to the mountain, standing in stark contrast to the tall white observatory and telescopes that already loomed over the landscape.

After some time, Gandhi spoke again. "I must say, I understand not wanting anyone to walk through my house with dirty feet."

"Life is full of differing opinions, and there is plenty of competition for the right to maintain one's own beliefs," Diana said.

"Adversity," Gandhi added.

Feeling bold, I asked, "So, tell me, how did you all let go of the oppression? How did you forgive those who disrespected your cause or, worse, set out to annihilate it? Because I get stuck in the persecution, the injustice of things. And then I can't move forward. How did you recognize the inhumanity and make a difference despite it?"

Diana spoke first. "The world is plagued by the disease of people feeling unloved. I saved myself from my own bitterness and resentment by offering others what I needed—love—and thereby gave it to myself. I didn't do it gracefully, but in time I learned to be happy with myself, to love myself, and then forgiveness was easier. I think forgiveness requires loving oneself first."

"That's correct." Gandhi cast a serious eye. "I would add that forgiveness is an attribute of the strong. And, it is easier to discover that strength when you are acting in the service of others. But it must be said that service rendered without joy helps no one. There is no forgiveness in martyrdom." He spoke with great conviction.

"Darkness cannot drive out darkness." Martin's voice boomed. "Only light can do that. Those who passively accept darkness are perpetuating it just as those who have inflicted it. There is some good in the worst of us and some evil in the best. We must forgive such humanness, first in ourselves, and then in others. Without that, there is no humanity. And what is a cause without humanity?"

"Please?" Diana took my hand, inviting me to stand. Martin and Gandhi rose and helped Pythia balance on her crutches.

"Wait, what?" I feared the worst. The time had come for the black ram.

Diana placed a lei of pink flowers over my head. "Carry out acts of kindness from your heart, not your head." She reached for my hands. "May you be free from your expectation, but safe knowing that you may have inspired someone to do the same." She squeezed my hands, then kissed me on both cheeks, dropped her gaze to the ground, and fell back with the others.

Martin leaped forward, grinning, and beamed. "As God is my witness, there is no starless midnight of depravity that a single act of humanity cannot unarm and inspire the act of love." He shook my hand hard and laughed heartily while I laughed with him. "Love is the only force capable of evolution."

"The lei." Pythia reminded him.

"Oh, yes." He looked at the string of white flowers with yellow centers already in his hand. "Well, let me see now—ah, yes!" He lifted the aromatic necklace over my head and did his best to look solemn. But his nose twitched while he fought a grin, losing the battle he beamed as he broke into riddle. "How do you make holy water?"

"Oh, Martin!" Pythia rolled her eyes. The others groaned.

"You can't trust him." Gandhi made a show of disgust. "Even if he is a Nobel Peace Prize winner."

"Boil the hell out of it!" Martin snorted, then guffawed.

"Oh, that's terrible. That's the worst he's told yet," Gandhi said, stepping up with a violet lei in hand. It was odd looking down at him as he looked up to me. But Gandhi didn't notice and instead clasped my shoulders, met my eyes, and then seized me in a bear-hug that I returned. When he finally pulled back, his eyes were wet and alive, meeting mine, also filled with emotion. He shook my hand with vigor and sincerity. "It has been my greatest pleasure to meet you." He raised the lei, a bit worse for the wear of our embrace. I bent to receive it. "My comrade," he paused for emphasis, "where there is love, there is life." And he beat his heart.

44

When I landed, Cat was fast asleep on her pillow. With great care, I lay my head, resting it as close to hers as possible. She was breathing but didn't stir. "Cat," I whispered, then beckoned quietly, sounding like an enchanting siren from afar, I sang out to her, "Caaat." I stroked the nape of her neck, my fingers barely touching her warm body. I wanted to tug her tail and tell her about Diana, Bapu, and Martin. About being in the clouds and burnt marshmallows. But I rolled over feeling all alone and listened to the sounds of the house. Cat's whiskers flickered. Her eyeballs rolled behind her lids, revealing her deep brain state. "I love you," I whispered. She stirred but didn't wake. I lingered for another moment, then rolled over.

Home now. See you tomorrow after work? I texted Amy after struggling to text her at all. Bothered by my indifference, I pasted a heart emoji, turned off the light, and that's when the phone rang.

"Wow!" she said as soon as I picked up.

"Yeah. It was pretty action packed." I turned on the lamp. "I'm pretty beat."

"I bet. I've been feeling kinda blah, myself. Aah!" I knew she'd stuck out her tongue. "Know what I mean?"

I chuckled. "I do," I said, wishing I wasn't still bugged about Amy's look-alike hologram. Eyeing Cat, I adjusted the pillow at my head. Still uncomfortable, I shifted the phone from one ear to the other before engaging the speaker and laying the phone on my chest. Then trying to shift the weight of wondering—was Amy for real, or was she only pretending to be—I breathed in deeply before exhaling slowly.

"What's wrong?"

"Nothing. Everything." How could I ask if she could *really* be there for me?

Not some cheerleader or some strong, perfect version of herself. I wanted her to be real.

"Cat? I know. I'm so sorry."

"Amy?" I retrieved the phone to scroll, searching for a photo. The three of us looking right at the camera. Me holding Cat, grinning. My arm around Amy.

"Yeah?"

"Nothing." I closed the photo. There were no clues, but somewhere there was a parallel universe where the mystery had already been solved.

45

Days later, I hit the snooze button before realizing the alarm was more about hydrating Cat than getting to work. I rolled over and spied Cat sprawled out on her side with her mouth hanging open enough for it to look worrisome. The days of her sleeping sweetly curled up next to me on the pillow were gone. I watched, a ghoul looming over the dying, until, unlike a goblin I was satisfied she was breathing.

"Hey, Cat," I said. She stirred, then looked bewildered to see me. Her eyes were sunken; she'd become a bag of bones. "Hey, sleepy-head, ready for a big drink?" I scooped her up and carried her frail body downstairs to the table where we did our thing. Afterward, she rubbed against my legs, begging for breakfast, and when she'd finished, she headed up the stairs on her own, resting every few steps. "Well, look at you!" Encouraged by her independence, I followed her upstairs. She mewed at the desk, and I lift her onto the plush bed. Squinting at me, the equivalent of a cat smile; she purred, soaking up the morning sun.

I showered. Then dressed and knotting my tie, I crossed the house in wide strides to kiss Cat goodbye, promising Amy would come to feed her lunch, and headed out. Biking down the big hill approaching the traffic light, I applied the back brakes, signaled turning into the parking garage, pedaled hard up the nine floors, flashed my badge at the sensor, and entered the exclusive Dumas, McPhail & Cox's lot. I locked my bike alongside many others and traveled the enclosed glass bridge to an elevator that opened onto the black terrazzo-tiled floor. Its flecks of quartz flashing refracted light. Fanny was on the phone. I grinned, waving. "Good morning," I mouthed. She winked and waved back.

Down the long, carpeted hall and past my own office, I stuck my head in at Josh's.

"Hey, Gabe!" Josh waved me in. "Take a load off. You know Matisse? Tech support. Always a good man to know." Matisse stood like a tower despite Josh's office, a bigger, plusher version of mine, and shook my hand with might. His man-bun withstood the force.

"Gabe Mendes. Paralegal." I slid into one of the very, very comfortable chairs in Josh's office.

"How's Cat?" Josh leaned in from behind his desk.

"About the same." I nodded and shrugged, wishing he hadn't asked. Josh made a face of condolence.

"You got kids?" Matisse asked.

"No, his cat's sick," Josh explained.

"Yeah," I shook my head. "It's just Cat and me."

"Hey, don't underestimate your relationship with your cat, man. Stuff's for real. A relationship's a relationship. My lady got a bun in the oven. Just telling Josh here how my old lady's learning that a kid's central nervous system starts gettin' programmed the minute they pop out. You hear what I'm saying?"

"Yeah, well. That's intense." I nodded.

"You gotta touch and love on 'em a lot. That produces hormones and neurotransmitters and some kinda pathways that get their brain wired for life. Life bro! Could be a death sentence if you screw it up." He eyeballed Josh and raised a brow to me. "Something called attachment. Look it up, bro. It's critical to healthy interpersonal relationships. Kid could be all messed up. Afraid of the world. Always be searchin' for security, needin' assurance he's competent and safe in the world. I sure as hell don't want that for my boy." He cackled. "You two are lawyers. Should be some kind of law about it. You know what I'm sayin'? I'm just sayin', attachment issues are for real. Love makes the world go round, but looky here," he leaned in, "attachment's a biological drive, bro. It isn't somethin' you decide. It accounts for all social bonds across a bro's entire lifetime: lovers, friends, relatives, or creatures." He pointed to me. "You and your cat, bro. Am I right? It oughta be a law that kids get some healthy attachment. Whole species countin' on it. I'm just sayin'."

"Well, I have a girlfriend, too." I felt compelled to say.

"Okay, okay." Matisse nodded. "So, you know, just like everybody here knows, we've all confused attachment for love. I bet old Josh here's had a hard time or two letting go of someone, even when he knew they weren't right for him. Other times, it was easier letting go. Now I bet old Josh here assumed the latter was less significant. But maybe he was more attached to the idea of a certain relationship but not really to the relationship itself. See where I'm going with this? Maybe the ones he let go of with less complication were the healthier relationships. Maybe you're like old Josh here. I know I was."

"Can you believe this guy?" Josh put his feet up on the desk. "How do you know all this? You're a computer programmer!"

Matisse's eyes widened. Bug-eyed, he stared Josh down. "Well, I guess you've underestimated the pearls of wisdom dropping from my ruby red lips. I wonder what other gems you've neglected to behold. And," he changed his demeanor, "I *am* a programmer." He cackled again. "This is just programming, bro." He looked at me. "You ever notice how some folks hook-up as a way of pairing. They're mistakin' sex for a committed relationship when really, it's just their biological drive. I'm tellin' y'all. That's infantile stuff. You gotta bring awareness to the idea of attachment, or you'll end up grabbing partner after partner, valuing their acceptance of you over your own self-acceptance. Think about it." He tapped his head. "Use the old six inches between your ears, boys. Don't go being big, old king babies."

No one said a thing.

"Listen up." He leaned forward. "Interrupt those patterns of transgenerational epigenetics by forming healthy attachments."

"What?" Josh looked confused.

"Bro," Matisse said, wincing. "Everybody got an *Oprah* episode. Some got *Jerry Springer* show variety." He made a face. "Welp!" He slapped the arms of the chair just as his phone rang.

The lulling voice of Elvis Presley cradlesonged a confession from Matisse's phone, "Wise men say, only fools rush in. But I can't help falling in love with you."

"Ah! That's okay, baby, you call me anytime you like," he said, answering the phone and giving us a wave as he exited.

I threw my backpack and helmet onto the side chair in my office, hung my jacket, and slid in behind my desk. Still thinking about Matisse, I leaned back, letting the ergonomic chair recline as I opened the manila folder someone had left for me.

"PETA. v. A. Peman." I stared at the photo from the file. "What?" I leafed through the file. "A gorilla?" I looked hard at the grinning ape. "This can't be for real."

"Hey," I said, poking my head in my boss's office, holding up the file, "do you have a minute?"

"Wild, isn't it?" She invited me in. "I'd hoped it would be fun for you."

"So, it's for real?" I purposefully showed my exasperation.

"Yeah, it's for real." She frowned, looking irritated. "Remember? It's our job to protect the intellectual property of creative minds. You know, so they can make a living. Not to mention, afford our services. This is no different than Haagen-Dazs owning the right to invent Scandinavian-sounding words. Or Amazon owning the one-click checkout." She finished with her eyebrows in high judgment of me.

"Okay, yeah. But seriously, an ape protecting his intellectual property? Come on."

"The question of who owns the rights to a selfie taken by an ape is not ours to judge but to argue." She shrugged and then made a show of checking her watch.

"But for what gain? What are we protecting?" I demanded. "I am beginning to lose sight of the purpose. I mean, can anybody really ever own anything? Shouldn't ownership mean some responsibility to others and not only exclusive rights for self-promotion?" My face contorted with disgust as I looked down on her, preaching. "This is just," I stuttered, then threw my hands up and blurted out, "privileged objectification for the purpose of attachment!" She looked at me, both confused and concerned.

She groaned. "Sit down." She pointed to a chair. "Close the door first." I shoved the door just enough the weight of it pushed it the rest of the way, the sound of it shutting, satisfying. "What's going on here?"

I took a breath and sank deeper into the chair. I shook my head, then sat up, slid to the edge of the chair, and placed my hands on her desk. "I don't know if I can do this." I looked right at her. "I try. But I just don't get it. I don't care about the blue ink on the Klondike wrapper. I went into law to change people's lives. I know. I know." I raised my hands. "I was naive, innocent, really. I thought defending people's rights meant I'd wanted what they wanted. But it was foolish to think the measurement of goodness was finite and determined somewhere in those books." I gestured to her cases of leather-bound volumes. "I thought the law was the holy grail." I blushed but didn't turn away.

"You could make a damn good lawyer." She leaned forward. "You are smart, detail-oriented, yet you see the big picture. You've got passion and humility that's attractive, but…." She looked down at her desk blotter where her fingers found a loose paper clip to play with it. Then she lifted the silver lid from a glass jar and dropped it in with all the others. It disappeared. She shook her head and frowned, then shrugged. "For some reason, you don't want to be a damn good lawyer. And that reason, while I don't understand it, means there's something else out there for you. And it's time. You owe it to yourself to go find it."

We sat sizing each other up for a minute. "Are you firing me?"

"No."

"But you're telling me to look for another job?"

"No." Her face remained open and patient. "You just told me that you fell in love with an idea about law, but not law. So essentially, you just broke up with me."

"Yeah." I leaned back into the chair. "I guess you're right. So how do we do this?"

"Break up?" she asked, holding back a smile. "Well, let me start by saying that I want you to be happy. Go with your strengths. You've got a good education, and you know how to use it. Have you considered publishing?"

"Publishing?"

"A lot of big professional publishing houses have legal staff. You understand how to protect and enforce copyright. That's a significant value to a full spectrum of potential employers. I think you'd find you have a lot in common with the people drawn to publishing. They're often well-read and interested in the humanities." Then distracted, like she'd remembered something that had nothing to do with me, she said, "Do some research. Keep me posted, and in the meantime, research the rights of our chimp. Okay?" She made that double-clacking sound and pointed her hand as if it were a gun.

"I think it's a gorilla. Or maybe an orangutan."

"Well, whatever, get on it." She shuffled through papers on her desk. "I gotta get ready for a meeting," she said, grabbing her phone.

"Thank you," I said, rising, but she didn't respond. Her back was already to me as she dug through a large leather bag on the credenza behind her desk.

46

"What's this?" Amy asked, over the Saint Louis Cardinals and the Chicago Cubs swinging it out on the television. "Are You Really in Love or Simply Attached to the Idea of Pairing?" She read from the article I'd left on the kitchen table. "I thought you didn't have any homework?"

"Oh, I just did some poking around the Internet," I said, not making eye contact, wishing I'd stashed it before she'd arrived.

"Yeah?" She grabbed the old throw off the sofa and, wrapping herself in it, she returned to the kitchen chair.

I pounded hamburger into two palm-sized patties and then ripped a paper towel from the roll and wiped my hands. "I think my lifetime of longing for love might've been more about attachment issues than actual desire." I snatched open a cupboard and grabbed the grill basket that Amy had given me.

"Really?" she asked, and I caught sight of her shutting the window. With the throw draped at her shoulders, she reminded me of a superhero, and that bugged me. I wielded a big knife, with my back to her, chopping a couple of sweet potatoes. "Careful," she said, coming up behind me.

I dropped the knife and shoved it aside. Snatching a couple of stalks of broccoli, I flipped the faucet on full throttle and rammed the veggies into the strong cold stream. Water splashed everywhere. I felt her eyes on me, but she didn't say a thing. Then, with my heart thumping for no reason I understood, I tried to sound casual. "Have you ever heard that a person can perpetuate the infantile state of wanting to be cared for, like through other relationships when they're older?" Towel drying the broccoli, and a bit breathless, I added, "And when that happens, a person will abandon their free will, and therefore deprive themselves of opportunities to create new loving experiences." I paused, and when she didn't reply, I continued. "And so," I shrugged, lifting my brow like it was an off the cuff comment, "they'll become more dependent in the infantile state and less able to evolve."

"Well, that's gloomy."

"Yeah, it is." I went at the broccoli with the same knife. "But I think it's how I've lived my life. I've got some romantic sentiment about sacrificing my needs for the person I love."

"Well, don't do that for me."

"I don't want to." I tossed the chunks of sweet potato and spears of broccoli in olive oil and sea salt with enough vigor that some flew to the floor.

"And you learned all this today?" She got up to retrieve the lost veggies and tossed them in the trash. Then stood beside me and stole a salted stalk of broccoli.

"Yeah. Something got me thinking. Maybe it was this guy at work today. Or all those women in the stupid game show." I shrugged. "I think I've convinced myself in all those relationships that I was the one who'd sacrificed. But that's not really right. The greater truth was that I sacrificed being honest with them out of fear of rejection. It was really me who was dishonest. In some weird way, I think I'm screwed up because of this attachment thing. You know, my parents were preoccupied. My mom was ambivalent, and I don't have a clue about who my dad was, but I've always felt afraid I'd lose my mom. Maybe I didn't attach properly, and now I'm afraid to be dis-attached." I finally turned and looked at her. Something deep inside of me wanted *it* to be her fault. What *it* was, I had no clue.

"You seem really worked up." She put her hand to my back. "Do you think this is about Cat?"

"No!" I pulled away from her, and then in a more measured voice, I said, "I don't know why everyone thinks that."

"Okay, so it's not about Cat." Her voice was soft. "But I think probably every-body is afraid of being dis-attached."

"No." I let myself feel angry and backed away from her. "You're not listen-ing. At twenty-five years old, everybody's executive functioning matures. I'm well past twenty-five. I should have full access to my free will and my own agency to secure my fundamental needs, Amy. This is what I'm telling you. Not everybody's afraid, compulsive, obsessive, addictive even, around their need for security. It's only the people like me who are practicing the illusion of control as a means to secure their hierarchy of needs."

"Gabe." She came closer.

"There's little difference between security and control, Amy." She reached for my shoulder, and I wriggled out from under her hand. "We both know they're fear-based illusions dependent upon mistrust. This article talks about control." I picked up the article stepping away from her with it.

"Gabe—"

"No, Amy. Don't try and talk me out of this. Control is the belief that something can be contained within a set of determined conditions to secure a singular outcome. You have to admit that it doesn't make any sense. The very fact that life is fluid, dynamic, and organic is proof enough of no certainty of outcome." She opened her mouth, and I raised my hand. "So, do you believe buying strawberries is within your control?" I looked right at her. "Well, do you?"

"Gabe? I don't understand."

"It's a simple question, Amy."

She threw her hands up. "Sure. It's America, right? I can buy strawberries any day of the year."

"But what if you got to Food King, and they were all gone?"

She smiled. "I shop at Super King, sometimes Super Food, but never Food King. Too expensive."

"This is not a cute little joke, Amy. So, what if you arrive at Super King, and there's not a strawberry in the place? How could securing something as simple as a strawberry elude you?"

She feigned disbelief, shrugging.

"Well," I began, my voice wavering, "to control procuring strawberries, you'd have to control all the other customers who might buy them before you got yours. Or the stock person who's surfing their phone instead of stocking the berries. Or the trucker who delivers the produce; the pickers, the farm, the weather, the seeds! It goes on and on, Amy. Each of those variables has as many variables, and those variables have another whole set of variables. You'd have to contain *all* the variables! All of them, Amy! Put them all in pristine boxes so nothing could influence them."

"Gabe, slow down."

"But that's impossible! That's atrophy. And that kind of thinking denies evolution! Don't you see, Amy?"

"Gabe, you're all hopped up. How much caffeine have you had?" She looked around like there might be a clue.

"We all desire to be cared for as an infant so we'll survive, right? What do we fear? Death. As adults, we unconsciously think that if we don't control things, we'll die. But we are gonna die no matter what. Neither life nor death can be contained or reduced to favorable circumstances. It is impossible! To believe otherwise denies that the multiverse is in constant evolution. Love's the only antidote to fear, Amy. It's the only way to evolve!"

"I understand, Gabe."

"You're placating me. Don't think I can't see that. Do you really understand that to live as if there is permanence in an impermanent world is insane?"

"I do." She looked like she thought I was crazy. "Like we said the other night about forgiveness, remember? What you're saying now is along the same lines. We can only trust each other when we trust our own right to value our own freedom to be ourselves. No objectification. No ownership. No matter the obstacles: cultural, familial, tribal, epigenetics, attachment, even our own beliefs. We have to rise above them all in consciousness and choose trust. It is the only thing that saves us from going crazy with the knowledge that someday we will all disconnect. I know you know this, Gabe." Her soft voice made me want to pull my hair out.

"Let me see if I've got this straight, Amy. Without trust in the natural order, we're afraid of dying, cling to attachment, and deny our free will. So, congratulations, Amy. You just made this all about Cat. Right?" Spit flew from my big mouth, and Amy winced, wiping it from her face.

Wild, I couldn't stop myself. "You don't think I know how to live intentionally with the knowledge that we all die. You think I'm a baby?" I asked, making it sound like the stakes were very high, and it wasn't until then that I realized I had no idea what I was even talking about.

Seeing my vulnerability, she moved in. "Or is the question, how do we intentionally love knowing that we and our beloved will die?"

"Forget it," I said, resenting her, just wanting her to go. "I can see you just want to gloss over this and pretend like everything's peachy keen between us."

"And it's not?"

I looked away.

"Is this your way of telling me you're unhappy?" She snatched the article and tossed it across the counter. "You know, I am a little tired of the deep and profound window of consideration we have to peer through on a regular basis. I think you are a bit addicted to this whole thing."

"Maybe I am. And you know what I learned about that? That my single-minded fixation on security and my grasping at a sense of self-permanence has led to a longing for things to be as they once were."

"Instead of how they are now?"

I didn't answer.

"What're you saying, Gabe? And you know what, Gabe? Think about what you're going to say before you say it. Be sure of what you want to say to me before you ring that bell, Gabe."

"I don't even know what interests you. It feels like all you ever do is go along with whatever I'm doing. Like you're along for *my* ride."

"Okay." She narrowed her eyes to slits. "You're not making any sense. You know damn well what interests me. Intellectual discussion, artistic pursuits, and, and," she got up in my face, "having fun! Which I might say has been lacking!"

"See! You never said that before. You are a wonderful woman, Amy, but I don't know if you're right for me."

Ata boy, Mendes. You don't need her.

Oh! Dude!

Her eyes searched mine, reading me while I read her. I held her gaze, challenging her in my madness, fully aware I was so far out, I was in left field.

"Okay." Her tone was hushed. She took her eyes off me and shifted them to her feet. "Okay."

"Amy, I'm stuck in attachment. In a false sense of security. A baby cries, and the mother feeds him."

Dude, what the hell?

"How's that false?"

"Well," I hesitated, "there is no true security. Anything could happen at any time. It's magical baby-thinking. It's Newtonian. It makes sense for a baby whose life experience is limited to the fundamental purpose of healthy attachment. So, while it is false, it is critical in infancy. But I'm not a baby anymore. I don't want to sacrifice the truth of what I want or feel in a relationship anymore. I want a woman I can be honest with."

Ouch! Dude! Where are you going with this?

"Okay, well, that's on you." She bit back. "But do tell me, Gabe. How exactly have I kept you from being honest? I've done nothing but accept you after everything you've told me." Her arm flew out in a grand sweeping gesture. "Plenty of women would have thought you a raving lunatic. Maybe you are. You're certainly talking some bat-shit crazy right now."

"See!" This time I narrowed my eyes. "That's exactly what I mean. Like on *The Newlywed Game* when you just sat there, giggling and waving." I mocked her look-alike version.

"Oh, my God, Gabe! That wasn't even me. You know that, right? This is me!" she screamed, poking herself in the chest. "This is me. So, if you want to break up with me, then do it! Go ahead. But don't hold me accountable to some bizarre-o version of me from one of your psychotic road trips with Pythia." Right away, her face fell. She shook her head. "I'm sorry." She sighed. "That's not what I meant, the part about you and Pythia. I was angry. That's not what I think."

"Maybe it is."

"It's not. I don't know what this is all about. I'm guessing it's about Cat, and I can understand how that's poking at your attachment-slash-abandonment issues."

I shook my head and muttered, "I don't even know what I'm talking about anymore." I staggered to the counter, where I took my head into my hands. Then, giving in, I looked up at her, "I'm exhausted."

But she just couldn't shut up. She wouldn't leave me be alone.

"Gabe." She took a step toward me, and every muscle in my body hardened against her. She stopped dead in her tracks. "Okay." She put her hands up. "But do you remember when you told me that our parents are our first gods? Well, attachment is our first experience of love, Gabe. And if it doesn't instill trust, it creates fear that security will be lost, just like you said. It does seem like you're determined to find a way to control the current circumstances so you can feel secure right now. Which, as you said, control is a false belief."

I closed my eyes.

"You're just afraid right now, Gabe. It has you grasping for control."

I wanted to disappear. Crawl into a hole. I couldn't face her. She was right, but there was no way back. Obsessions, compulsions, and addictions! There they were! All behavioral manifestations of my infantile needs.

"I think you should go," I said, never looking up.

47

Long before dawn, with no reason to be up, I rolled over and sat at the edge of the bed, feeling the weight of my troubles. Still, I stood, only to be exhausted by the idea of moving my feet. In the bathroom mirror, I stood weary, witnessing myself washing a warm cloth over Cat's eyes and mouth, sponging her backside clean while the vet's recent words preyed on me. "She's not suffering. We all die. This is hard. Too much to bear. No one would blame you." Cat squinted, smiling with her eyes, enjoying gentle cloth on her face she purred. Still, over and over again the vet's unbelievable words echoed, "No one would blame you. No one would blame you. No one would blame you."

Deeply sad that my life had lost all purpose in the matter of a week, I snapped my eyes shut against the hot salty tears, and when I dared to open them, there it was. The once red cotton T-shirt had faded to pink; almost transparent from wear, it had already frayed at all its edges some time ago. It didn't take Einstein to see that Spidey had seen better days. The hole was nothing more than evidence of the garment's faithful service. On closer inspection, I could see where the worn threads had broken and could no longer weave a connection. In the mirror, denying the fate of my beloved shirt, I held my hand over the hole as if it were a wound.

"Mom?"

"What's wrong?"

"Everything. Absolutely everything."

"Cat?" Her voice trembled.

"Yeah, we're coming to the end. I can't do it. And Amy." My voice broke apart.

"And that course I'm taking...it's a scam. And I'm gonna get fired, and it's all because I'm way messed up."

"Is Cat okay?" She steered me.

"No!" I sobbed, circling the old La-Z-Boy in my office.

"Has her condition worsened?" She triaged.

"No."

"What happened with Amy?"

"We planted those little petunia flowers in the boxes a while ago." I pointed out the window. "And everything was good, and then it just seemed like she was too good, Mom." I pinched the bridge of my nose hard and, squeezing my eyes shut tight, I still held the phone to my ear. "Or I wasn't good enough. Or she wasn't. I don't even know."

"Oh, honey."

"I know." I swallowed another lump in my throat that was so big it physically hurt. I squeezed my eyes shut, fighting back the tears, and slumped down into the chair.

"Oh, I'm so sorry." She choked on her emotion. "Are you there?"

My chest heaved with my silent sobs. I set the phone down and doubled over. "Honey? Oh, my. What can I do?" She sounded too far away. I wiped the tears from my face and retrieved the phone. Plunking my way downstairs, I shuffled around the kitchen.

"Gabe?" she said panicked.

"I'm here." Flushed, I opened the kitchen window. The crystal spun and sparkled in the damp breeze, flashing a rainbow of colors in the dull kitchen. "I love her, Mom. This completely sucks. I feel like I'm gonna die."

"I know. I know."

I pulled out a kitchen chair, set the phone on the table, and turned on the speaker before sitting. "Ah." I caught my breath, then blew it out again. Then, everything was so still. The chair sank into the floor, but the kitchen drifted away. It was only a cardboard set. Unreal. Cold and empty. I felt for Cat's soft pink towel and saw how the place looked like a M.A.S.H. station. "I better go, Mom." I sounded robotic.

"Not just yet, sweetheart. Stay with me for a while. Talk to me."

I wanted nothing more than to lay my head on her lap and let her draw her fingers through my hair like I was a boy.

"Everything's falling apart," I said. Stacks of dirty dishes consumed the counter.

"I am so sorry, love. There's no easy here, is there?" I knew she was rubbing the back of her neck and likely had stood to pace.

"Nope."

"Can you call Amy?"

"What would I say?" I fidgeted with Cat's collar. Too big for her now, it lay on the table.

"I don't know, but it sounds like, I'm sorry, is probably in there somewhere." She likely adjusted her glasses.

"What? Sorry, I'm so pathetic and lost?" I fingered the worn leather.

"Apologize for what you did. Tell Amy why you behaved the way you did and commit to something different. But Gabe," I knew she was sitting herself down, "you can't love her until you make friends with yourself. You won't be able to let her forgive you if you don't forgive yourself for whatever it is you're holding yourself accountable for. Without forgiveness, there is no trust. And without trust, there's nothing."

I nodded.

"Call her. Don't hold it against her that she might be the best thing in your life." I heard her unwrapping a Werther's candy. "Do you hear me?"

"I do. I will." My shoulders eased; a sense of peace descended over me. We sat quietly. Across the street, the little neighbor girls carried paper baskets as they climbed into their car seats. "Remember when we made those baskets out of strips of construction paper and filled them with flowers?"

"Mayday baskets." I knew by the sound of her voice that she was smiling. "Gabe, everything turns on something, and when it does, it makes a new beginning. Life rebirths itself in the seasons and in every breath we take."

My neighbor adjust the rearview mirror, and then, with an animated face, she said something that caused Mushkin to laugh while Bubbles clapped and I realized I only knew the girls by their silly nicknames.

"So, what's this about your job?" my mother asked, and I walked from the window.

"I'm not getting fired, but my days are numbered there," I said, feeling a prick of fear. My mom had been so proud at one time to call me a lawyer. "And that's on me. It's what I want."

"What are you thinking?" I heard her sucking on the candy.

"Maybe teaching?" I bit my lip. Even though my grandmother had been a teacher, my grandfather, a lawyer himself, had made no bones about teachers: the whole "those who can't do, teach" thing.

"Oh, wouldn't that be something?" In my mind, she clasped her hands in front of her heart.

"Don't get too excited. I'm not committed to anything." Then frowning at the sound of my own words, I added, "Yet."

"I know, but do you think you would teach at the university?"

I laughed. "I don't know, Mom. One thing at a time."

"You know your dad taught there?"

"I know," I said, thinking about what I did know about my dad. "I've thought how funny, or odd—I don't know—how *something* it would be if I ended up teaching there, too. But I gotta figure out if I want to teach first. Mom?" I started to ask, risking a question that had been on my mind. "Do you think Dad always knew that's what he wanted to do? Do you think he ever questioned the importance of his career?"

"Your dad was a passionate man. He was clear that beauty was meaningful to a person's spirit, that beauty inspired a person's life, and, conversely, that a person's life could inspire greater beauty. He had a saying, what was it? Let me think. It was a quote." She paused. "Oh, yes. William Morris, 'Have nothing in your house that you do not know to be useful or believe to be beautiful.' Your dad wrote that in big letters on his studio wall."

"Amy would like that." I smiled before my stomach knotted, then winced.

"I bet she would."

"How did he know, though? How was he so sure?" I asked, glancing at the time, remembering my job.

"I don't know. I'd always admired your dad for that. That kind of thing was harder for me. I felt more beholden to my parents than I ever did to my own thoughts."

"Well, that can't be true, Mom. You did make it out to the mountains twice because you believed it was where you belonged. That's something. That's passion and commitment. And nursing?" I talked, heading upstairs, "And Nursing Without Borders?"

"Hmm. I suppose you might be right. I've never thought about it that way." She thought for a minute. "But I guess your dad just knew himself earlier in life than I knew myself. It's not a contest, of course. I suppose what's important is that eventually, I did feel inspired to follow my dreams."

"Maybe there's hope for me yet," I said, squeezing paste onto the toothbrush.

"Don't be silly. You don't need hope. You have the rest of your life before you. This all works out. I promise. And if it doesn't, well, it's just not happened yet. Stay with it," she said, sounding just like my mother always did.

Not long after getting home from work, and after I'd seen to Cat, I found myself in the kitchen. Methodical, and with purpose, I cleaned until all that was left was polishing the faucet. I snapped the new, bright white, cotton dishtowel open and rubbed down the chrome until I took satisfaction in making out my reflection. Then, appreciating the now tidy place, I pulled on my baseball jacket and headed out. The sun was sinking behind the mountains, and in the fading light things in my neighborhood were turning into shapes, just beginning to lose their details and all the ways they identify themselves.

In the distance, the mountains had already become a broad black jagged band between the earth and sky. That, too, would soon vanish. The playful sounds of children were diminishing into cries. Doors slammed. Bikes abandoned as balls lay littered in the yards. I zipped up against the dropping temperature and wished I'd worn a hat. It was predictable how fast things can change, and still, it somehow always seemed as if it happened by chance.

"Amy," I said, rehearsing, making the sound of her name carry the sentiment of contrition.

"Oh, Gabe!" She'd be breathless.

"Oh, thank God, Amy. I thought you'd never speak to me again." I smiled, walking at a good clip. Then nodding to myself, I tried again. "Amy." This time sounding serious and measured. "No," I shook my head. "Amy." I tried again, talking to myself, preparing, as I headed unannounced to Amy's with a grocery store bouquet of flowers in hand. My olfactory senses already anticipating her goat milk and honey with tea tree scent.

Finally, at Amy's complex, I cleared my throat and pushed the buzzer.

"Yes?" she asked, and I sighed with relief even though her voice was not embodied.

"Amy," I pleaded into the door intercom, making the sound of her name equivalent to, 'I'm sorry I was such a jackass,' and lifted the flowers as if she could see.

Silence.

"Amy?"

"Yes." This "yes" was less friendly than the first, which was the kind of "yes" saved for someone you didn't know.

I leaned against the cold brick building clutching the flowers.

"Can I come up?"

"What for?" she asked, and I imagined her rolling her eyes and shifting her weight from one hip to the other.

I shuffled my feet, glanced at the bouquet, then tightened my grip around the stems. "To say, I'm sorry. To say, I'm really sorry." I tilted my head and looked extra mournful, not as a trick but in hopes she could hear it in my words. Inside the paper cone some of the flowers were already wilting.

Crickets.

"Amy, please."

"You shut me out."

"I know. That was wrong."

"And you never called."

"I'm sorry. That was wrong, too."

"You disappeared."

"No." I shook my head and found myself showing her the flowers again. "I'm here."

"You disappeared, and you know it. And the worst part is that you tried to make it my fault."

"I'm really sorry." Someone shoved past me and into the building, evil-eyeing me like I was "that guy." "Can I come in?" I asked while the prudent man eyed me, pulling the door until it latched.

"You don't get to tell me to go away and then walk out of my life. I can't be with someone I can't count on. That's the minimum, Gabe, and you failed at the very least requirement."

"Amy, I am sorry. I'm just learning that I have some limiting beliefs."

"I don't wanna hear all that."

"I know, I know. I'm sorry. Please, though, I'm not making excuses. I just want you to know that I realize what I did and why it happened. So now when I say, I'm gonna do better, I know how. Can I come up?"

"No. Tell me the what, the why, and the how."

"Well, I learned a person can believe anything they want. What if I believed, um, I was a vampire? No, a pirate." I frowned, scratching my head. "Then acted like a vampire, I mean a pirate." Someone exiting the building gave me a strange look and made a wide berth around me. "Some people do think they're pirates, you know," I called out to the stranger's back. "Not me, though!"

"Why are you yelling?"

"I'm not. Sorry. What I mean is that people believe all sorts of things. Like, I'm learning I believed in judgment. You know, the polarity, duality of things. That either, things are good or bad. That the multi-universe is full of either opportunity or obstacles."

"Yes, Newton. Cause and effect. What's your point?"

"Well, my point is that I didn't know that I *really* believed in that. So, I didn't make a choice about what I wanted to think. That led me to believe some unfortunate things about love."

"Like what?"

"Well, Pythia sent over a long list."

"You told her?" She sounded hurt.

"No," I said right away. "Not about this. Pythia had sent the list a while ago by pigeon, but now it makes sense."

"A pigeon?" She sighed. "Like what beliefs, Gabe?"

"Like, love's a sacrifice. Or, it's not for me. Or, that it hurts." She groaned, and I hurried to say, "That's not what I *want* to believe! And now that I know I did, I'm gonna stop. I'm going to think differently, and then create different beliefs, like believing that loving myself *will* allow me to change. That's what I'm gonna organize my life around. That's how I'm going to change. And I was doing that, Amy, but I got tired, and it's not an excuse," I said right away. "But it's true. With Cat, and all of that, and Pythia not being the same since her accident, and my mom and her nursing thing. And then at work, well, that's a whole other story."

I shrugged. "They're not excuses, but now I know when I get worn out, I have a tendency to clam up and start thinking things that scare me, and then I pull away. That's why." I let the flowers dangle from my hand, hanging at my side. I licked my lips. "And, honestly, Amy, I still worry that I'm not enough. For you. Or for anybody."

"Gabe, you have to be enough for yourself."

"I know. I found out about transparent beliefs. They're like these clean windows I looked through every day, but they're so clean I never even noticed they were there. I couldn't see them. I never noticed how they distorted my view. I just thought that was the way the world looked. The way it was. I've lived in a world where I filtered my life experiences through the transparent belief of, 'I'm not enough.' That's screwed up, and I didn't even know about it."

"You can believe anything you want, but you gotta know what you believe, Gabe."

"I know that now. I know I've believed in thoughts that were counterproductive to the life I've wanted to create. I know that now."

"How can I trust that I know what you believe in if you don't even know? The depth of intimacy reflects the strength of any relationship. It's the gateway to love. It's what diminishes our experiences of aloneness and fear. But there's no intimacy without honesty. How can you love yourself if you don't even know what you believe? I get that it's a process. I'm not shaming you, but I can't be with you if you aren't honest with yourself."

"I know. I was blind to that. I couldn't see that my beliefs were driving the effect. I'm conscious of that now. Now I know what I believe. I even wrote a formula. That's the 'how.'"

"Hmm. A formula? I do like the window part. That the glass is at least one degree of distortion."

"Amy?"

"Yeah?"

"I know you don't want to see me tonight, but could we maybe get together another time. Just go for a walk or something? I could tell you about the formula."

A couple exited the building arm in arm. The woman spied my flowers and gave me a knowing smile while her partner mansplained something to her.

"That'd be nice. Gabe?"

"Yeah?"

"How's Cat? It must be hard for you to get home in the middle of the day."

"No, actually, it's been kinda nice. But she does miss you."

"I miss her, too. What're you gonna do about your next meeting with Pythia? Maybe if it's okay, I can help out then."

"Sure," I said, setting the flowers near the door wishing things had gone differently but leaving room for hope. After all, I was hopeless. How would I live, never again drawing in her freshly-cut wooden and honeyed scent?

By the time I made it home, night had enveloped all the evidence of people. All that was left were the glowing yellow porch lights. I threw my jacket to the new sofa and headed upstairs, thinking I'd surf the net for job opportunities. But once at the computer, I found myself on hospice sites.

We all join the big hum. Each of us seeds, sexual and creative by nature, expressing our unique vibration. Agreeing with some greater intelligence, we are planted in masses. Programmed to activate the forces of evolution, we secure the resources for our physical lives. Then, the push and pull of the turning tides that births us, separating us from the great hum. We grasp with our desire to hold on to the past and to secure the future. We are lured into the hope that we are not short-lived in this world, that we will bloom but not decline. And when we do wither into the soil, our unique decay composts and nourishes the earth; then we can accept that our bodies were never designed for permanence, perhaps only our souls.

Cat had come into my life from some greater intelligence, perhaps even with intention. I liked the thought of her going out that way too. Turning with some tide, returning to a place where she'd never needed a body, but not before—

My muscles clenched. Then deciding to think for myself, I braved the question: Not before what?

The waning moon shone only a silver sliver, its shape sharp and distinct; something was coming to an end.

48

After exiting the cyberspace of interdimensional travel, and with our feet on the ground in Cambodia, Vishnu, the supreme Hindu being, greeted Pythia and me. It was the first I'd seen Pythia without crutches since before the Beatles.

"This is a good thing. You've picked a place with few lily pads," Vishnu told me as we all three retired to a blanket at the water's edge. The sun would soon light the tall black peaks across the reflection pond, revealing the temple spires of Angkor Wat.

"This is my favorite spot." Pythia unpacked a picnic, stretching with ease.

"You see, the lotuses are alluring in the daylight, but at sunrise, they're like blemishes on a mirror, disturbing the picture the sun paints across the moat." Vishnu gestured at the water with one of his four blue arms.

"High on the hill is nice, too." Pythia drew up her legs, wrapped her arms around her knees. "But I rather like the way the sun-god rises from behind the temple and illuminates opulence and nobility first. Then reflects such beauty onto the still water before the pond casts back a reflection of Angkor Wat. It's like a nudge as if the day is saying, 'Reveal yourself two-fold in all your majesty. Be seen and accountable for grandeur.'" For the last part, she wiggled until her spine was straight and tall and assumed a bold voice. "Or something like that." She relaxed her shoulders and reached for a slice of a baguette stuffed with veggies. "This is spicy delicious." She held her sandwich for us to see. "Anyone? A num pang? Sweetened iced coffee?"

"Oh!" she said, remembering something, and she touched Vishnu. The god was reclined on two of his elbows while a third held an iced coffee, and the other cradled bread in his periwinkle palm. "Thank you again for arranging such lovely weather. Nothing compares to the sun rising in the open breadth of the clear blue sky."

"It was my pleasure." He smiled and setting everything aside, his arms worked together in a choreographed dance. Then rising off his elbows, he took our hands. "Let us dream the multiverse into reality." He closed his eyes and breathed in deeply. "Let the artistry begin." On cue, golden rays burst across the horizon, and the atmosphere took on a hot atomic light.

A circular, blood-orange god levitated from behind the temple, blazing crimson at its edges and radiating yellow and pink heat waves from its heart.

My mouth dropped and my eyes softened. I wished Amy could see this, too.

"It is most remarkable, is it not?" Vishnu asked while dawn revealed his topaz-blue skin and the odd complexity of his many limbs. His chest was bare except for the ruby necklace that dazzled in the morning light and a single curl of jet-black hair. Red cloth draped his shoulders, and a mala of white flowers hung from his neck. A gigantic collar of peacock feathers showcased the intricate crown on his head, and his hair was so black, it shone indigo in the sunlight. "Let us recognize the precious nature of the only day before us," Vishnu said, letting go of Pythia's and my hands. "Every day we return to the first age of creation, and the ancient world meets us gladly in servitude. It is the way, the nature of things." Two large hoops swung from his earlobes as he spoke.

The rising sun revealed an unkempt dirt path. Then filled the inner shrines, unveiling intricate carvings on the temple's walls just as a man wearing a white tunic tied with a rope headed our direction, his expression one of abundant joy despite a single black cloud that followed him.

"Oh my!" Pythia jumped up. "You made it!"

Vishnu turned toward the beaming dark-skinned man who hobbled along, using a long stick as a cane, but without haste. "Jesus of Nazareth!" Vishnu cried, and his bright red lips broke from their usual composed heart shape to reveal a hearty grin.

"Hey, dude." Jesus waved.

"I dare say, you are a sight for sore eyes!" Vishnu stood, and his luxurious, yellow-silk harem pants glistened as the two embraced. "What's happened here?" He pointed to the wooden staff.

Out of breath, Jesus rolled his eyes. "Oh, dude! Whew, that's a hike." Then, lifting his foot, he revealed a broken strap and angry blister. "I need new sandals." He pushed his long brown hair behind his ears. His brown eyes danced, and I couldn't keep from grinning, too.

Pythia grabbed my hand, pulling me to stand. "Jesus, this is Gabe. He's all I've said, and more," she said, raising her hand to make a generous sweep and the little black cloud drifted off.

Jesus extended a warm hand, but instead of shaking mine, he clasped his around mine. "It's really good to meet you. I'm a big fan of yours." His deep-set eyes held my gaze. "I apologize for my late arrival. I got stuck over on the hill." He sat cross-legged on the red-checkered picnic cloth already partaking.

"Was there a crowd?" Vishnu eyed Pythia.

"Nah, not really." Jesus took a bite of a num pang. Crumbles collected in his beard.

"What happened?" Turning one of her rings, Pythia sat next to him.

"Don't sweat it, P." He shot her a loving look. "I'm reeling it back in. That's all." He helped himself to more and turned to me. "I did this thing, and it became a Thang, and pretty soon folks were calling it a miracle. The loaves and fish thing?" He poured himself a drink. "Good stuff, P. Thanks for making the effort." Then back to me, he said, "Maybe I didn't think it through. Probably should've considered how it would threaten Zeus's authority. But we were grieving John the Baptist. We'd been up for like three days, hammering out the details for a kingdom of goodness. If I had to do it again, I might do it differently. But I did what I thought was best at the time. Everybody was hungry." He shrugged. "Maybe I made a mistake. I'm human, after all." He smiled, but this time without the friendly flash of teeth. Looking humbled, he raised his cup. "To the day."

"To the day." We echoed, raising our mugs, toasting.

Pythia frowned. "The loaves and fish again?!" Her hands found their way to her hips. "Honestly! And of all places, too. The very idea that your intention was to embarrass Zeus is ludicrous!"

"I agree." Vishnu mirrored Pythia's mood.

"Who was there?" Pythia picked breadcrumbs out of Jesus's beard. "Right here, a little schmutz," she said, as she motioned above her own lip and watched him take care of the matter. Wiping it away with the back of one of his carpenter's hands, his fingers were visibly calloused.

"P, really, it's all good." He took her hand. "I'm fine."

"Was it Zeus?" Vishnu cast a cross glare across the water.

"Oh, my stars!" Pythia shot up with her fists clenched at her sides. "Zeus never really changes. Just when I think that god has turned over a new leaf, he makes my blood boil all over again. He knows plain well that you never intended such showmanship. Five thousand people were hungry! His ego is beyond frail. Did he make a scene again?"

"Well, P, I might have been a bit ostentatious. I can have a flair for drama. But I'm turning the other cheek, and with equanimity, I might add. This, too, shall pass."

"Why can't he let it go? He takes every opportunity to humiliate you. He is so small-minded." She paced in the emerald grass. "His vengeance will be his demise." She muttered something to herself before yelling, "What in the world is wrong with him?"

Jesus reached again for Pythia's hand seeming to untether her from her consternation. "Sit," he said with authority and pointed to the blanket, waiting until she complied. "Hey, everybody." He called to the rest of us. "Come. Break bread with me." He passed the plate.

"Well, I think a couple of centuries is long enough, don't you, Vishnu?" Pythia asked.

"I completely agree. This has gone on long enough." Vishnu ranted. His ginormous dangly earrings swung wildly before he crossed his arms over his chest and regained composure, all four limbs entwined and resembling some sacred geometry design. "Zeus is without peace. His behavior is destructive and doesn't serve his highest good or the good of others. It is as Buddha said, 'Without peace in the heart, there is no peace in the world. Turning the other cheek is noble, but only—'"

"With equanimity," Jesus added.

"Yes, with equanimity. We are obliged as servants to the kingdom of goodness to lovingly assist a fellow god so he can join in the evolution of consciousness."

"I hear you," Jesus began. "I told him exactly what the Big B said. Trust me. I'm schooled on the whole forgiveness, compassion thing." He laughed, then seeing the others didn't find it funny, he acquiesced to the inevitable conversation. "Okay. Here's how it went down. I was like, 'Look, Zeus, the goal here is not to best the other guy, but to best your previous self for the greatest goodness. Your behavior is mean-spirited, dude, but it doesn't have to be your nature. We're all in this together. Compassion is critical for evolution.'" Grimacing, he helped himself to a load of sticky rice.

"So, how did you leave it with Zeus?" Pythia tried to sound casual.

"Well." He wiped his hands on the hem of his tunic.

"There are napkins." She pointed to the folded cloths.

"Thanks, P. Well, I tried to appeal to the high opinion he holds of himself and took the angle of 'Zeus, I get that you bustin' my chops is an opportunity for me to practice forgiveness, brother. But look, dude, the roots of all goodness lie in the soil of appreciation. So, come on, dude. A little latitude here. Some common decency and respect, please.'"

"And then what happened?" Pythia tempered her anger with her arms folded across her chest.

"Well, let's see. I think he said something like, given the scale of the natural order of things, any one thing is no Thang."

"He did not!" Vishnu flashed such anger his headdress went askew, and when I caught his eye, I motioned silently with my hand to demonstrate that his crown and collar were cockeyed.

"Oh, yes he did, and then he asked all high and mighty like, 'What thing among mortals is not done without my hand?' I tell you, the old god looked like he was going to blow a gasket before he got real fire and brimstone and shouted at me." Jesus crossed his brows until they bore down in heavy judgment. He dropped his voice an octave, imitating Zeus's righteous authority. "'Shut your eyes wide open, so you can see. What greater mistake could there be than judgment? Find your mortal purpose and live with meaning. Connect and serve humanity.' Yada, yada, yada. The god was fired up for sure."

Pythia seethed. "He is a wily one with his pointy reckonings."

"He does have that righteous reputation. Forgiveness evades him," Vishnu said to me. "However, from a great enough perspective, the grief he imparts does serve a purpose. But still, his ways are harsh indeed." Eyeing Jesus, he asked, "How did it conclude?"

"I told him, Zeus, I gotta hold you to this, dude. You are demeaning me at every turn. And this is no little thing. It sets a tone and threatens to corrode our moral ethics. This stuff affects the evolution of humanity."

"Good for you." Pythia nodded a single sharp nod.

"Thanks, P. But I can't say it made any difference. I tried again to introduce the idea of forgiveness and compassion, saying, 'If not for the grace of God, there go I.' But he wasn't feelin' it. So, I said flat out, Zeus, dude, I'll not justify nor excuse behavior that perpetuates cruelty. I'll not allow you to drive me into my own dark side, nor will I abide by your shadow."

Pythia clapped. "Bravo, bravo!"

"Well said," Vishnu chimed in.

"What did he say then?" Pythia leaned in.

"Well," Jesus hesitated before admitting, "I got a little riled myself after that speech, and ... I mighta pushed the old goat."

"Not like the time with the money-changers?" Vishnu looked worried.

"No, no, nothing like that." Jesus dismissed the concern with a wave of his hand. "I said something like, 'So, maybe I took it over the top and you felt disrespected. I've already apologized for any way it's harmed you. I've forgiven myself, and now it's time you've forgiven me.' And then I put a little heat behind it and added, 'Stop raining on my parade, dude!'"

"And then?" I asked.

"He gave me the strawberries. You know?" He clarified by sticking out his tongue and blowing until he made the familiar juvenile sound.

"You mean the raspberries?" I asked.

"Yeah! Then the old god threw a lightning bolt and cast that dark little cloud over me." Jesus pointed above his head and noticing the cloud gone, he said, "Oh, hey! Thanks, P.," and grinned and nodded at Pythia before turning back to me. "Dude," he said, "that god's got issues," and he loaded up on sticky rice.

"Well," Vishnu said, crouching before standing. "On that profound note, I must depart. The day has well begun, and I am of no use this side of the pond. Besides, I am sure Lakshmi is already looking for me."

"Duty calls." Pythia sounded sympathetic. "And isn't it so that someone or something is always in pursuit of us? Such is the business of life."

"So shall it be," he said and turned to me. "My friend, I wish you farewell. I grant you moksha." Pythia and Jesus knelt. Vishnu cupped my hand in one of his and drew me to him. He placed my free hand on his heart and another of his on top of mine. His remaining hands found their places at the back of my heart, behind my skull, and at my brow. "Peace to you." He closed his eyes, and a powerful surge shot through my body. I staggered, but he steadied me as something hot left my body at the places he held. "I leave you peace. Go now. You have surrendered your fear to serve in goodness, and goodness shall prevail." He kissed my forehead and released me.

"As always, your heart is welcome here," Vishnu said to Pythia and kissed both her cheeks before grabbing a sandwich. "These are scrumptious," he said, passing one to me and then taking another; he looked perplexed.

"Something wrong, Vishnu?" Pythia asked.

"It's only that I wish I had another hand," he said, trying to retrieve his discus.

"There are never enough hands, are there?" Pythia helped him.

"Isn't it the truth, dude. Life can be a handful." Jesus rose, then shook my hand and embraced me with a hearty hug. He whispered in my ear. "Thanks for signing up. All the rhetoric aside, even Zeus knows that creating the kingdom of loving goodness is The Thang." He released me and held my forearms. "God speed." He kissed Pythia before calling to Vishnu, "Hey! Wait up. I'll walk with you," and he slipped out of his broken sandals and jogged barefoot, leaving the big stick behind.

49

"Don't you love it here?" I asked Amy, sounding cheerful, hoping we could soon return to being more than just the "friends" we'd become since the big fight. Sweeping my hand from the untamed banks of the creek to the green manicured expanse of our little town's park, each just steps from the other, I thought she might see me as more evolved than I'd behaved. "It's the cusp of wilderness and civilization. You know you can follow the creek all deep into the mountains."

Amy stretched her long legs in giant strides, stepping on the sidewalk cracks while snapping a wad of pink bubble gum. She birthed a large pink balloon from between her lips which burst before she sucked the deflated bubble back into her mouth to chomp. The heels of her boots made a distinct sound as she advanced ahead of me. "So," she said, friendly but guarded, "I've been thinking about what happened between us and all the other things you've been figuring out. So, I wonder, do you believe in God?" She faced me and blew another bubble.

"Do I believe in God? That's a good question?" I said and thought hard, wanting my answer to mean she'd forget what an utter idiot I'd been and love me again.

"I mean, after our parents, *what* is God?" she said. "If we can transcend our desire for attachment, what's the purpose of God?" She plunked onto a bench, nestled in some trees along the creek bank. A well-worn dirt path meandered down to a low spot where people often skipped stones. She patted the bench. "Sit with me?"

"Speaking of gods." I pointed to a father and son fishing in the shallows. Looking relaxed and comfortable near each other, each was absorbed in their own fishing.

We watched, and then, I blurted out, "You know," but stopped myself to gather my composure. "Did I ever tell you about Big Gabe and Little Gabe?" I didn't look her way or give her room to answer. "Thank God he didn't stay around long enough for that to stick."

"Your stepdad?"

I drew my lips tight together, shaking my head. "Maybe because it had been me and my mom for so long, it felt like he ruined something. Or maybe I thought he was there because I'd failed my mom. Or maybe I was just afraid he'd take her away. But whatever, it'd felt like he'd replaced me."

Holding the fly rod, the eight- or nine-year-old boy checked the line for tangles then brought the rod tip over his shoulder. The father gave a sideways glance, stealing a peek at his son.

"Or she abandoned you?" Amy asked.

Using his whole body, the boy slowly twirled the rod in a figure eight motion until the line whirled. Abruptly he stilled his body, the line unrolled into the water.

"Maybe," I said, trying it on while the kid's dad smiled to himself. Then feeling like Amy might be right, I shook it off. "Sorry. I'm babbling. What I wanted to say," I pointed to the fishing duo, "was I wonder what *that* would have been like. But I guess I'll never know."

"Not until you have a child of your own." She reached over and touched my knee. "Then you'll be so curious about your kid's experience that you might miss your own again." She laughed but not like it was funny. "That's what I think, anyway. That I'll be so concerned about doing it differently than my parents that I'll miss the opportunity to just enjoy it."

Then Amy bent forward, scrutinizing something. "Look." She pointed across the water. Spotting the mountain lion across the creek, I fumbled with my phone to call 911. "Hey," Amy called out to the fishermen with her hands cupped around her mouth. "Back away from the water." She articulated each word, "There's a mountain lion across the water at two o'clock," she said, loud and clear. Giving the details to the operator, I grabbed Amy's hand and we climbed to stand on the bench. The father spoke low to his boy, and they slowly stumbled backward, bumping into trees, making their way up the bank. Methodically, Amy and I raised our hands high over our heads and spread our legs, making ourselves big. People collected behind us.

"Move on. She could be across the water in three leaps." I said, my voice steady, never taking my eyes off the big cat. The powerful predator stood frozen in mid-step with her ears back, her head hung low. Even from across the creek, it was easy to see the vigilant animal's eyes were fixed on Amy.

Within minutes, rangers began securing the area, redirecting people to other parts of the park. With the excitement, the lion took off. First trotting just a few steps, then pushing off with her haunches and sprinting with such grace she hardly made a sound disappearing into the woods upstream.

Blowing out from my cheeks, I bent over with my hands on my knees, hoping I wouldn't vomit. "I've never seen a mountain lion that close before, and I've lived here most of my life!"

"That was fricking scary. Come on." Almost giddy but with a pained grimace Amy giggled nervously and grabbed my hand, pulling me. When I resisted, she pleaded, "Please," reminding me of a child and then dragged me through the park, forcing me to make the light and cross the street.

"Stop," I said, on the other side. "Come here." I hugged her and kissed the top of her head. "Are you okay?" I took her face in my hands and kissed her before she could answer.

"Gabe." She pulled back and we both searched the other's face.

I flushed with the hot fear of rejection.

She laughed and I turned away to swipe at the sweat beading above my lip and at my brow. "I just swallowed my gum." she said and yelled, "Oh my God!" Then speaking more to herself than me, she said, "Shake it off." She wiggled. "Come on," she poked me.

I waggled my tongue and waved my arms. I whooped out a cry.

"Ahhhha!" she shouted back to me, and we both laughed before noticing that people were staring.

"We just saw a mountain lion!" I called to the gawkers. "Yeah!" I shouted to their horror. "Over in the park, by the creek." I grabbed Amy. "We're okay, now," I hollered back, waving.

"Maybe we'll see the upside-down piano player. That'd be a good omen."

"We're looking for omens, are we?" I asked, shoving my hands in my pockets and crossing my fingers as we turned onto the bustling outdoor mall.

The garden beds were bright with tulips fluttering in the late spring breeze.

Greeted by the warmth of the sun, we headed west with the mountain range drawing us in. A young busker dressed in a white collared shirt and black pants blew hard on a trombone, high stepping and swinging his arms as he marched in circles.

I reached into my pocket for a few bucks and dropped the bills into his up-side-down, fancy band hat as we made our way out of the crowd the kid was at-tracting. "Hey," I leaned in, "what were we talking about before all that?" I nodded toward the creek.

"God," she said, over her shoulder through the rush of people.

"Ah, right." I trailed behind. "God. Interesting, huh?" I said, catching up. "So, what do you make of you asking about God, and then a meat-eating lion shows up with eyes only for you?" I teased.

She made a disagreeable face. "I wouldn't say she had eyes only for me."

"She was locked on you and nobody but you." We weaved through the crowd.

"Don't look so amazed. If you're saying I was the target of the wrath of God, I don't believe that." Her whole face frowned.

Spying an open bench in front of the courthouse, I drew us to a seat where the contortionist was trying to gather a crowd. "Please, everyone, look at me. I need some attention," the thin elderly man said. "Please gather around while I bend my body, making myself fit into this small, clear acrylic box. Please, every-one, look at me. I need some attention!"

"He's insistent."

"He looks sad. I suppose it's hard to feel whole if you spend your life bend-ing like a pretzel so you can fit in a see-through plastic box. It's weird, but isn't the point of boxing yourself in so that you are safe? What happens when you do that, and you're exposed, too?" she snapped, but then her faced screwed up and she cried.

"Hey? Everything's okay. We're okay." I wanted to touch her, but unsure, I refrained.

"That mountain lion looked right at me like she was saying, how dare you challenge the natural order of things? Like, what right do I have to ask questions?" Out of character, Amy was a mess, swiping at snot with the back of her hand and heaving for breath as she cried. "I've felt like this all my life, like I can't ask why. I can't ask what happened? Like I'm just supposed to accept that my dad's dead, and my sister, oh, I'm blubbering." She burst into deep, heart-wrenching sobs. "And you! You did it, too! Of all people! My God, Gabe, I trusted you with my heart."

"Oh, Amy. Amy, look at me," I said, doing my best to get in front of her face. "Hey, hey, look at me. I know. I understand. I get it." She turned my direction, but her eyes remained downcast.

Risking rejection, I wiped tears from her face, but they kept coming. "Hold on." I stood, then squatted again, wanting to be sure she'd heard me. "I'm just going to walk over to the taco stand and get some napkins. Okay? Amy?" She nodded. "I'll be right back."

I dodged the contortionist, serpentined through the crowd right to the front of the long line, grabbed a stack of napkins, and dashed back to Amy.

"I am so embarrassed." She scanned the crowd. The contortionist was now folded inside the see-through box; a crowd grew, many pointed, but few dropped money into his jar. Amy blew her nose. "I just fell apart. I don't know what's wrong with me."

I sat beside her, taking her hand. "You don't always have to be strong. You can lean on me. I can be here for you. I won't leave you like before ever again."

She leaned against me, resting her head on my shoulder, occasionally blowing her nose. Across the way, two men in baby-blue leisure suits and white shoes with greasy, shoulder-length hair performed, "Saturday in the Park." One at the keyboard, singing his heart out. His shirt was unbuttoned to reveal gold chains and fake chest hair. The other's mustache was askew as he blew on a horn. "People dancing, people laughing, a man selling ice cream, singing Italian songs. Eh cumpari, ci vo sunari. Can you dig it? Yes, I can. And I've been waiting such a long time, for Saturday."

"That's such a ridiculous song," Amy said.

"Yeah."

"Do you know the Italian is fake?" She sounded more like herself again. "It's completely made up."

"Really?"

She nodded. "What do you think is the most ridiculous song ever?" Her lashes were wet, eyes puffy and bloodshot, but she was beautiful. "I've got a hankering for a milkshake," she said like it surprised her.

"Milkshakes? Sure." I took her hand and led her into the crowd. "Let me see, the most ridiculous song of all time would be ..." I set my mouth in a hard line and considered the question as we opened the door to the diner. "How about 'Safety Dance'?"

"Ah, 'Safety Dance.' Yeah. How's it go?" she asked herself, then sang low near my ear. "I say we can act if we want to. If we don't, nobody will, and you can act real rude and totally removed, and I can act like an imbecile. We can dance, we can dance, everybody look at your hands. Safety dance, safety dance, la, da, da, da, da, da."

"That's good, especially the 'La, da, da, da, da,'" I teased, sliding into a booth.

"You missed a 'da.'" She blew her nose and looked smug.

With our order placed, I asked, "So, tell me about God."

She looked around, then leaned across the table. "Do you think it's safe?" sounding half-serious.

I turned to the window. "It's sunny now, but if a lightning bolt strikes and a cloud bursts releasing a deluge of rain, then I think it's fair to consider that you've got a pissed-off god on your back."

"Yeah, well ... ." She looked around again, rubbing her neck before she spoke. "If love is a reflection of God's love for us, then it's biased toward how God loves us. Right?"

"Are you talking about a Christian God?"

"Sure. Let's start with that."

"Okay. Then, in that case, love's a reflection of God's love, and it will be biased toward that god's version of love," I said, feeling confident and at ease with the topic.

"You've studied this?"

"Yeah," I said, and in a split second, I weighed talking more about my recent trip with Pythia against the fragility of our situation. Determining that a conversation that included a blue, four-armed god and Jesus might be pushing it, I stayed with the facts. "I did a timeline for the history of love. Religion was a huge part of it. So yeah. That and a few college classes way back when. The Christian God forgives our sins and wants us to forgive ourselves and others so that we'll evolve spiritually in God's love. If I remember right, that god wants us to use our free will. That's why he forgives us, so we can make mistakes, and learn to build a moral consciousness that sustains humanity."

"So, why the Christian dogma about sacrificing his only begotten son to provide us eternal life?" She fidgeted with an earring. "See. It seems like Christianity says that God's love is forgiving while simultaneously making it conditional. The whole judgment day and, of course, heaven and hell."

"That's the religious part. Not the god part."

"Okay, well, what if you separate god from religion?"

"Like in Buddhism?"

"Well, I guess, but Buddhism is more of an orientation for living than a prescription for salvation. There is no god or gods. Just universal compassion called loving-kindness. It's really conscious living that's guided by a core set of disciplines, values, and directives for living lovingly."

"Now you sound like the know-it-all." From across the booth, I couldn't help but notice Amy's charm, even with a red nose. I leaned in. "But you're right. There is no expectation of sacrifice or conditions for love in Buddhism because there's no attachment to the outcome."

"Non-attachment. Freedom from the continuous grasping at and aversion to the cycle of life and death. Interesting, huh?" she asked, flashing her pale blue eyes, her wet lashes.

"You mean how non-attachment relates to healthy psychological—attachment?" I stammered. Then regaining composure, I cleared my throat and added, "Like the idea of being present or having consciousness to each moment that you are alive," I paused to make good eye contact before continuing, "regardless of its content and without expectation."

But I barely finished before she leaned in. "Like facing a mountain lion without being fixated on a specific outcome, like death," Amy said wide eyed, "or life, for that matter!" The black ram came to my mind and I drew back while she hammered on. "That's some consciousness! The kind that opens your eyes to whatever confrontation you've been avoiding your whole life." She paused thinking, then rolled her eyes and threw up her hands. "Then what? The only thing left is to decide what the hell you're going to do next." She stared at me.

I looked away before I caught myself and then looked back, but only for a second. I lowered my eyes. "I guess Buddhism doesn't really help our conversation concerning God's purpose," I said, scratching my beard trying to seem intellectually stumped, when really, I struggled. Then catching a glimpse of waitstaff balancing two plates of food while scanning the room, I lifted a finger signaling to our table. In that moment I bottled up, not only fear of the black ram, but fear of any hostility Amy might still harbor against me.

Amy leaned away from the table so the server could set big plates of food in front of us. "Yum. Thank you," she said to the person, and then to me, "What about Hinduism?" She sucked on the straw making a noticeable dent in the strawberry shake, its whipped cream top sinking into the glass.

"It's the world's oldest religion with three hundred and thirty million gods and goddesses that are all manifestations of a singular reality, or God," I said as I dipped several fries into a puddle of ketchup but never brought them to my mouth. "Interpretations of Hinduism are diverse, but in general, it encourages its followers to seek religious truth from multiple perspectives." I squeezed a ring of mustard onto the inside of the burger bun and lifted the sandwich. "It emphasizes respect, kindness, and justice," I said taking a bite.

"So, what's the purpose of all those gods?" she said, gobbling her burger.

"Hindus can choose their own paths in pursuit of healing their karma and obtaining spiritual perfection. I guess the gods are like teachers, each with a unique approach."

"That sounds pretty forgiving." She took a healthy gulp of her vanilla shake and then leaned across the table. "Here's where I'm going with this: how do you believe in unconditional love and deliver justice? I mean, there's little difference between justice and revenge."

"Well, I think you can." I wiped my mouth, then indicated to Amy that she had mustard at the corner of her mouth, which she promptly licked. "But it does require compassion, which, as I understand, is the recognition that we are all human and can make mistakes, sometimes big ones. Maybe that's the difference between justice and revenge." I took the opportunity to pause and make eye contact. "Compassion offers forgiveness for our human capacity. So, say you clobber someone over the head with a big rock because you want their pterodactyl leg, and the tribe says, 'We all know how hungry we can get, but we have a duty to protect each other, so you sit outside the cave, and when you're ready to behave civilly, we'd love to have you back.' Something like that." I took another bite, noticing my burger had gone cold.

"Okay, maybe, but I think a pterodactyl leg is hyperbolic. That would be pretty big." She drew up the last of the shake until the straw sucked air.

"But the rest of the story is believable?"

"Sure." She sounded quiet. "Or," she waited until our eyes met, "maybe a better story is one where two people agree that creating a loving space requires trust. And both agree that trust is a super-power, only secured in the face of abandonment. And even if they each fail over and over again, they agree there is a way to be held responsible that respects dignity." She paused.

"Are you saying you forgive me?" My stomach fluttered.

"Of course, I forgive you. You're my friend, Gabe." She looked me dead in the eyes. "Okay? I want to be friends. Can we just be friends?" she asked taking an earring out to rub her lobe. Having found a way to not say outright what she was really saying, she returned the dangle to her ear and flashed me a pleasant smile.

But I knew and nodded. Looking to my plate, my appetite was gone.

"So, Gabe Mendes, I ask you, is that justice or forgiveness?" She loaded several fries with ketchup from the large pool on her plate. "See, I think this justice-judgment thing muddies the water." She carried on like we were friends.

"Good question." I sighed, forcing myself to participate in what was now our agreed reality. "To your point, I think Jesus Christ was crucified by the Romans for claiming to be King of the Jews. But according to Christianity, he was sacrificed by God in the name of forgiveness. Jesus died so we'd be forgiven of our original sin, or humanness. His death and resurrection is like a portal to God's love, which is what gives our lives meaning," I said, feeling some resentment and deciding I'd had enough; I left the last bite of my burger on my plate and never touched my chocolate shake.

"But that doesn't make sense to me. Forgiveness that requires sacrifice is not dignified. And I still don't understand the purpose of the heaven and hell thing. I never did. If God loves us and Jesus died so we could be forgiven, why must we still live in judgment? It seems manipulative." She shoved her plate, it rested just before going over the edge.

"Those are just the rules if you want to play Christian. All religions have tenets." I stacked my plate atop of hers and brought them both from the edge. "But you can believe whatever you wanna believe." I challenged her, noticing I sounded a bit like Pythia.

"Okay." She looked at me long enough that I looked away. "So, we've covered

Buddhism, which is not really a religion, Hinduism, and Christianity. What about Islam?" She crumpled her napkin and tossed it atop the plates.

"Islam is more similar to Christianity." I leaned sideways to retrieve my wallet as the server passed me the check and cleared our plates. "It includes a day of reckoning and requires its followers to be in service to humanity by obedience, devotion, and unconditional submission to their god."

"So, like Christianity, it's sort of the big daddy way of governing moral behavior." She rooted through her bag. "I've got the tip."

"Don't worry about it." I threw some cash under the check. "That'll cover it."

"Thank you." She looked into my eyes before grabbing her bag, then slid out of the booth. "So, what's that leave us with if we're examining the most practiced world religions?"

"Ah, only Judaism." I held the door for her, trying harder to be a good sport. "Judaism is based on the Old Testament. While it proclaims a strong adherence to 'Love thy neighbor as yourself,' there's also 'An eye for an eye.' And, unlike Christianity, there's no built-in mechanism for forgiveness. Judaism's big in the United States, but worldwide its practicing population is small. So we've covered the big ones. Today, Christianity has about two billion adherents, and Islam has over one and a half billion, but projections speculate that Islam will soon grow and match the number of Christians."

"Really?"

"Yep. By mid-century, Islam will supplant Judaism as America's second most popular religion while holding its own worldwide, barely trailing Christianity."

"Wow! Think about that? As a planet, we're moving down Kohlberg's scale of morality and relinquishing our agency to a dogma that deems itself good and opposition to it as bad. Do you think people understand what they're buying into?" she said, concerned.

"Not sure, but what you think about your god will influence your outlook on all aspects of your life and the relationships you nurture, even the relationship you have with yourself. That's why people misunderstand love, they don't even really know what they believe," I said, not wanting to look at her, and waited for the green crosswalk light. We walked west and then waited to cross north before heading up the hill to my house.

After some time, she said, "Did you know that agape in the Greek sense of the word is in decline worldwide. I guess empathy has been on a sharp decline since the seventies. I've always thought the seventies felt sad, like people were grasping for something to hold on to but knew there was nothing left. You can hear it in the songs," she said.

"Like 'All by Myself.'"

"Yeah, and how about 'At Seventeen'? That's a real downer. Or even the television shows. *Mary Tyler Moore.* That show is way depressing! Mary's so sad."

"Maybe that sadness served a purpose. Maybe it provoked people to find something different. Their own motivation to love their neighbor or practice good deeds." We climbed the familiar incline to my house. "Maybe it created an awareness of the human potential for the purpose of evolution." We huffed up the hill.

"New Age religion?" She stopped. "Boy, I gotta sit and catch my breath. I don't know what's wrong with me." From a bench between my place and campus, the students intersected around us on bikes, skates, boards, and foot. "I'm tired just watching them."

"I know. Look at that." I signaled to a kid riding a board and holding a box on his head while being pulled by a big dog. We both laughed. "I don't know if I've ever been that comfortable in the world."

"Youth." She sounded reminiscent. "When you're that young, you don't really believe, or maybe it's more that you can't conceive that anything will really go wrong. Something makes you believe it will be safe to skateboard down a steady decline with a big dog tied to your wrist and a large box on your head. Maybe it's not stupidity. I guess it's trust."

"Whatever you want to call it, it sure promotes some kind of freedom from fear."

A group of under-dressed college students in shorts waited to cross the street. The early May air was damp and cold with a stiff wind at times, and still, the young women wore midriff tops, and one of the young men was shirtless. Several went barefoot. The friends huddled together, crossing the street in our direction. They talked over each other until one of the young women looked pissed and said, "No!" to the kid without a shirt and the others laughed.

"What do you think he said to her?" Amy asked.

"Something dumb."

"Loving life sure encourages exploration." Amy turned to me and slid to the edge of the bench. "Do you know why a baby puts everything in her mouth?"

"No, why does a baby put everything in her mouth?"

"It's not a joke. She does it to learn about the world. These kids are doing the same thing, taking risks to discover more information about the world, trusting that it'll be okay if they do. Is that stupid, or is that a healthy curiosity that facilitates evolution? What kind of god promotes that?"

"I suppose the one that's in favor of evolution." I stood and reached for her hand. "Ready?"

"Do you think the Higgs boson abides by some obligation?" she asked, joining me, ascending the hill. "I mean, if it's facilitating choice within a grand scheme, it would always be calculating the outcome of those choices and thereby offering a counter choice somewhere else that would bring everything back into balance. So, is that forgiveness? Maybe it's love."

"What do you mean?"

"Well, religion can't do that. The dogma of right and wrong, even an eye for an eye, can't do that. It seems that religions like Christianity and Islam are based in Newtonian physics, the idea of cause and effect. Be a good follower, and you shall be rewarded. But Hinduism, Buddhism, and New Age are more about causing an effect. So, what if you believed in the Higgs mechanism, you know, the process that produces *an* effect, and trusts that an intelligence with a natural purpose for evolution has the bigger picture covered? Higgs eliminates conditional considerations because Higgs is the nature of things. Maybe that's God, the thing that promotes the natural course of evolution." Winded, she gasped after every few words. A bearded man resembling Rip Van Winkle with a fully loaded travel pack strapped to his back passed using trekking poles to push himself up the slope. An ice pick dangled from one of his gear loops.

"If that's true," she said, struggling to breathe.

"Slow down," I interjected under my breath, and we stopped on the sidewalk just steps from my house.

She drew in a deep breath and nodded. "Whew. Sorry." Using both hands, she wiped the sweat beading on her cheeks and forehead.

I pointed to the back gate. "Let's sit in the garden."

"Anyway, if that's true," she said, still winded and I opened the gate, "Oh my gosh! This is incredible." She looked at me with her mouth hanging open. "Boy, what a difference spring makes!" She took in the yard. "Gosh, Gabe, look at all the tulips. And you're gonna have so many peonies. Wow! Are those all rose bushes?" She pointed to the thorny row that lined the side of the yard just beyond the giant lilac. "This is absolutely magical. You did all this?" She touched a soft fuzzy bud that was almost ready to open on the bush and then walked to the pond. "Columbine and iris. What colors?" She squatted beside the water. "These fish are big!"

"The columbine is mostly yellow, and the irises are purple. I planted some. My mom helped with the daffodils." I pointed to the few remaining. "And Dally and I planted the tulips. But the roses and peonies were here, and so was the pond. Although, I brought in those big boulders and planted the columbine and wild strawberry."

"Oh my gosh, hotshot. I had no idea."

I blushed, inviting her to sit in one of the Adirondack chairs.

"Who's Dolly?" she asked, settling back into the chair.

"My Ex, Dally."

"Ah. So, she does have a name, Dally?"

"Delilah, but I only knew her as Dally." I nodded. "But go on. What were you saying?"

"What was I saying? Whatever it was, it pales to this place."

"You were saying that maybe God is the thing that promotes the natural order of things. Like a supreme intelligence that lovingly facilitates evolution."

"I just can't get it over this place." She looked at me like I was the garden. "It's stunning." Her voice was soft. "What if God is life? Curious, messy, and ultimately joyful, fun even. Perhaps life and love are unconditional. Maybe interchangeable. It's hard to tease life out of love and love out of life. Don't you think?"

"I know, right! How can you separate life, love, and God? Maybe they're the same, or at least very similar. What did Gandhi say?" Two squirrels raced up the tree trunk, out onto the limb where the bird feeder hung. Amy pointed and smiled while they performed entertaining maneuvers intended to release the mix of seeds meant for the birds. "Where there is love, there is life! That's what he said, and it doesn't matter what you call yourself, Christian, Jew, Hindu, whatever; what matters is your own beliefs."

"And at the heart of that is *your* moral drive."

"And if you don't recognize your own moral drive, you can easily fall asleep at the wheel."

"And not even know it!"

"And let's say your moral compass points you toward believing that everyone has the right to feel loved. I think that everyone should be allowed their human flaws—held accountable, but inevitably loved. You know, forgiveness."

"But there's still the well-worn idea of judgment day, the desire for justice."

"Right." I scratched my beard. "Okay. Well, I think forgiveness is really self-forgiveness. You have to forgive yourself first for being human before you can ever forgive others and then trust that some greater intelligence has a plan that accounts for the offending error."

"I like it." She nodded but then made a face. "But people can get pretty cozy in the illusions of good and bad. Like in those early stages of morality: people make moral choices so they won't get punished; because it benefits them in some way; or to garner good standing. In every one of those stages, they relinquish their moral authority to something outside themselves. I think it will be challenging for those people to own their own transgressions."

"Right. But that's because they're attaching, grasping at safety and reward, essentially to avoid judgment. I'm suggesting that instead of posturing as good for some god, practice living with the obligation to participate in, collaborate with, and create life. Then anything challenging can become an opportunity. Eventually, a person becomes their own goodness in the likeness of a goodness that perpetuates life."

We fell quiet, considering the conversation. One squirrel chased another until the other stopped and chirped at the first. The first took off and the other pursued it. "Do you think they're playing?" I asked.

"I do." We watched from the sturdy chairs. "This is so nice, Gabe. I could sit here all day."

"Amy, earlier when you said that life is curious and messy, and even fun. I think love is those things too. Maybe God is fun, like that kid on the skateboard. Freedom, right? Choices. Like the squirrels."

"Holy shit!" Amy struggled to get out from the comfort of the deep-seated chair and, finally, grabbed the wideset armrests, wrangled her way to the edge of the chair, and turned toward me. "Higgs really is God, and God really is Higgs."

That night, in bed beside Cat, with my computer open, I lingered a moment but decided to take a risk and hit the button that shipped a big bottle of Vitamin C with an enclosed card.

> *Amy,*
> *Take two each night at bedtime.*
> *Your friend,*
> *Hot Shot (also known as Gabe)*

I flipped the thin silver lid shut, set the computer on my nightside table, turned off the lamp, and lay in the dark imagining Amy opening the box.

50

"Wow, Mom. It's weird to see this place empty." I handed her a bag of Werther's while looking around. "You might not be able to find those where you're going," I deviled her.

"Oh, you." She pecked my cheek and led me to my old room, now packed with boxes. "This is your stuff." She opened the flaps and pushed her curly gray hair behind her ears. Then adjusted her glasses while we looked down into the box.

I dug past the Pokémon and baseball cards to find a few beanie babies and a red Power Ranger mask. There were two *Goosebumps* books and the Barenaked Ladies CD without its jewel case. "Did you come across my baseball glove?" I asked, seeing the Transformers and Star Wars figurines sorted into Ziploc bags and labeled with my name. She pulled the mitt from another box and smiled while I tried it on my man-sized hand. "That's not happening, is it?" I joked before I smelled the leather. "What else?"

She passed me a couple of sketchbooks.

I opened one, and the life of a nine-year-old boy spilled out in painfully crafted letters, misspelled words, and hand-drawn pictures of dragons and swords. In the other, I'd been a teen and had drawn a boy whose head was a television that he struggled to pull off, revealing cords and wires that kept him plugged in. Beneath the picture I'd written, *I'm trying too hard to be real, and so are you.*

"That box," my mom said, pointing, "is full of letters and pictures, and other stuff from college. I didn't look through them. I just packed them."

I squatted on my haunches and lifted the lid of one of the shoeboxes. "What! You didn't divvy them up into sub-categories by years and people and label them in plastic bags?" I flashed her a smile.

"Very funny." She rolled her eyes and headed to the kitchen. "We can sit on the deck. I'm leaving that old patio set."

"That'd be nice, mom," I said, noticing the album against one of the boxes. Van Morrison's youthful face. Pensive, from behind a screen of trees, the opacity of the two images merging into a dream. I pulled the vinyl from the cover. Its sleeve was missing. The chorus of "Astral Weeks" played in my head: "If I ventured in the slipstream, between the viaducts of your dream where immobile steel rims crack and the ditch in the back roads stop. Could you find me?"

I smelled the soft cardboard cover.

"I have iced tea, and I know you like these malt vinegar and salt ones," my mom said as I made my way into the kitchen. She showed me the bag of chips before gabbing two subs wrapped in white paper and a couple of bottled teas from the otherwise empty fridge.

"Well, it looks like you're really ready," I said, sitting cattycorner to her on the shaded deck. "But are you?"

"Sorry. I forgot paper plates. These will have to do." She passed me a few napkins as I unwrapped the turkey sub.

"So?" I took a bite.

"I am." She didn't touch her sandwich. "I'm excited but nervous. I've never been very far from you. And you know, it might not be easy to connect sometimes. Most of the area is still without electricity." She warned.

"I'll be fine, Mom."

"Oh, of course, you will. I'm not worried." She waved at me and picked up the sandwich only to return it fully intact to the napkin.

"But promise you'll be safe. I guess it's my turn to worry about you."

"You don't have to worry about me." She winced. "Do you hear me? I don't want you worrying. I can take care of myself. I'm a nurse, for God's sake!" She laughed.

"Don't I know it!"

"Don't ever forget it." She grinned, shaking her head. "Do you know how long I've been saying 'I'm a nurse for God's sake?'"

"A long time!"

"There was a time when I said it almost as a reminder to myself. Sort of like, if I can help the infirm, I certainly ought to be able to help myself. But I did figure out years ago that you'd roll your eyes if I said it, and so since then, I sometimes say it just so," she said, shrugging. "I don't know, so we can connect. I thought in time, you'd say something, but you never have. So, I am telling you now. That's the last time I'm going to remind us both that I am fit to take care of myself. Okay?" She unwrapped her sandwich.

"I think I might miss it." I eyed her over a swig of tea.

"Well, we'll both have to get used to trusting that the other will be just fine. And if one of us isn't fine, then we just have to know, we're gonna be fine once the trouble's over."

"Two years is a long time, Mom. I'm gonna miss you."

"Don't start that, or I'll cry."

"I thought you were a nurse, for God's sake." I leaned back on the chair the way I did as a kid so that only two legs of the chair were on the floor.

"Be careful." She sounded overly cautious.

"Okay. I'll behave myself and act like the gentleman I was raised to be." I lowered the chair and then made a cross-eyed face at her while sticking out the tip of my tongue, trying to get it to reach my nose.

She tsked, mock-scolding me. "You're impossible. You'll be sorry if your face freezes like that. I doubt it'll win Amy over."

"You'd be surprised. Last night Amy made that same face at me, and then, just like you said, her face froze. Just like this." I made the face again. "So, I think she'll be relieved and maybe we'll be like two peas in a pod, again," I said, but all of a sudden felt tired of the game. Pushing up against my mom like a boy didn't solve anything anymore. I shooed a fly from the unopened bag of chips. "I'm sorry you didn't get to meet Amy before you left," I met her eyes. "That's my fault. I messed up."

"You'll work things out, honey," she said and reached to touch my hand, "and then I will meet her. Okay?" She raised her brow. "Listen," she began and scooted her chair closer. Then twisting her body she crossed her forearms onto the table and leaned toward me. "Gabe," she said my name the way a mother does when speaking honestly with her child, "I've realized so much since our conversation about your dad. There were so many things I did and didn't do out of fear and guilt in my life. So much of what I've been afraid of is and always was in the past. I want you to know that I now trust myself in a way I never did before."

I crumpled my dirty napkin, then reached for the bottle to pick at the label.

"Hey." She touched my hand. "Did you hear what I said? You can trust me now because I trust myself. I'm sorry for all the confusion my doubt has caused us both. I regret the ways it's caused you to fear trusting yourself. I know I've made life hard for you in that way. How can a man, let alone a boy, trust himself if his mother can't trust herself?"

The fly beat its wings and buzzed between us. "I'm sorry, Gabe."

"I'm sorry, too, and I want you to know that I'm so glad to be your son." The aerodynamic insect hovering above stalled mid-air between us. "This thing you're doing? Living life as life is and not as life is 'supposed' to be. It's The Thang, mom." The fly lifted and flew off.

"The Thang, huh?" She cocked her head. "Living life as it comes at you and then deciding what you want to do about it."

"Free will, Mom."

"Free will. I like that. I'm gonna remind myself of that when I am feeling like maybe I'm too old to be moving around the world like I'm about to do."

"You'll be fine, Mom. You're a nurse, for God's sake."

That evening in bed, the moon shadows played across the walls bringing a new perspective to my world. Dusky memories of my mom and I dancing around each other challenged me. The two of us trying to quantify love through Newtonian physics. Love as the effect of some cause. A mechanical device cranking out a winner every time. Cupid and his arrow. Falling head over heels, blinded by love, living happily ever after. All as if love was a thing.

But this afternoon had been different. We willingly relinquished our familiar boundaries, and together created a new space that allowed us both to let go of the past and evolve naturally. We'd let down our guard and stopped playing games. Instead, we joined together in our strengths, increased our trust, and found intimacy.

The monochromatic ghost of the tree branch trailed in through the window, casting itself down on the floor, pretending to be the sturdy ash from my backyard. I looked to Cat, fast asleep next to me. Her head turned at an odd angle, her mouth open enough she snored. The lids of her eyes twitched, and her paws paddled as she indulged in a dream. I pulled the sheets back, careful not to disturb her, and swung my legs around to the floor where I sat for a moment, considering whether I felt more inclined to be asleep or awake.

At my desk, I opened my notebook and found the first blank page, nearly at the end. I began writing:

Life is an ouroboros—an infinite cycle, continual and spontaneous: binding particles at the sub-atomical; attracting negative and positive particles for the production of form; creating an illusion of singularity before transmuting the form through decay. My mom and I were doing just that: binding cellularly, attracting aspects of the other to create our relationship, then deconstructing, and redesigning with an intelligence meant for the proliferation of all life. Our blooming love may seem to be a single and particular thing but owes its existence to ever-evolving the laws of nature. Love is evidenced in this process. Without love, all would fall apart and float away.

A refreshing breeze blew through the open window. The cooler evening temperature reduced the concentration of volatile compounds, and the house smelled fresh and sweet, notes of melting snow and thawing earth. I could see the blue light of a neighbor's TV. From not far away, I heard the popping noises of an idling motorcycle, then the fading sound of the dueling pistons as the bike sped off into the distance.

Love is like a ray of light is to the sun. I wrote, feeling the tip of the pen etching the paper. *It is not the sun, but evidence of the sun. The center of one understanding generates the next understanding, each more complex and balanced than the one previous. Love cannot be measured, contained, or even nurtured with expectation. It is not a thing. It cannot be owned or possessed. Love is the intentional creation of a sacred space enacted to deliberately access an infinite plane specific to the purpose of the highest evolution. Or more simply said, love, is the creation of space that allows for change. It's The Thang.*

51

A good couple of hours before dawn, I woke thinking of Amy. I could see her in my mind, pointing to the gray clapboard siding of my house, suggesting that yellow flowers would be a nice contrast. "What happened?" My hands went to my head. The cracked ceiling loomed above reminding me some things never get fixed.

This is your life, Mendes. Did you really think—

"No. Not this. My life is the way I do *this*." My phone alarm sounded, and Nathanial Rateliff & The Night Sweats blasted. I sighed. "Shut up," I snapped, tapping off the fun-spirited, gospel clapping and upbeat singing. How was it possible today was not only my last meeting with Pythia, but that I'd also failed at securing love.

Deaf to the racket, Cat, slept soundly beside me. Dialing back my mood, I stroked her skinny body. I purposely ignored her thinning fur, convincing myself, for just a second, it was only half true she would die. What were the odds, anyway? Maybe it was always fifty-fifty. She stirred and purred but didn't wake. I tugged her tail, then held it until she clumsily wiggled it free and, like old times, flicked it back at me.

Downstairs I filled the bucket and let the sound of the warm rushing water drown my thoughts, and placed the bag of saline inside. Cat looked confused but then made some kind of peace with her surroundings and turned twice in a circle before lying down.

I removed the bag from the bucket of warm water and dried it with a clean, white dishtowel. Then, like some well-practiced technician, I attached the extension tube, careful not to touch the connecting ends, keeping everything sterile. Fixing the needle in place and flushing the air out, I then loosened the clips and clamps. The fluid ran freely from the bag, through the line, and into the needle. Confident that all the air had been released, I reset the clamp, stopping the flow, and hung the bag from the chandelier.

"Okay, my best girl." I grasped the scruff at the back of her neck. I held the barrel of the syringe tight and inserted the needle downwards with the bevel up, piercing her tough skin, feeling the familiar resistance before pushing it all the way in. Queasy at the idea of ever hurting Cat, I licked my lips and engaged the plunger. Then opening the fluid line, I eyed Cat as the flow of electrolytes made its way into her body. In time, I swiftly removed the needle, wiped the site with a gauze pad, and set Cat to the floor while I prepared her breakfast. She brushed against my legs like always.

And so it was. So it had been. So it seemed it was going to be. Just like this. Day in and day out. "We can always have hope," the well-meaning vet had said. Hope? No thanks. I want a real choice.

Out the window, the Flatirons glowed a lacquered vermillion in the morning light, looking ancient. Outside everything was alive and abundant, blooming with brilliant color. In my garden, the verdant sweet woodruff rollicked and consumed the beds in little white flowers. The towering ash tree, last to leaf out, finally showered the back yard with an umbrella of green. Tiny tumbleweeds of cottonseed parachuted and drifted across the airways. Soon enough, those little yellow flowers we'd planted would spill over the window box edges. Of what they'd remind me was yet to be known.

Amy sat out front in her car. She texted with a smug smile, then looked up at my house. Ping! Her text came through. *How about this one? Oh, hot diggity dog ziggety boom what you do to me. It's so new to me, what you do to me.*

I chuckled, more in gratitude for the game than the lyrics. After all, it was a connection to her I still had. My thumbs went at the phone; *I'm too sexy for my shirt, too sexy for my shirt, so sexy it hurts.* I looked up. Amy gathered her big bag and an armful of books. I waited. And the moment the text came through, I knew by the look on her face. I let her set her belongings on the car hood and root through the bag for her phone. She laughed. Then worked the little keyboard and that's when I opened the door.

"Hey," I said, inviting her in, wanting to spend whatever time I could with her before I'd head out with Pythia for our last trip together.

"Why is she meeting you here?" Amy asked, smelling so soapy clean.

Tea tree and honey, I thought, but instead said, "Pythia wants to hike first. I don't know." I shrugged, realizing I hadn't even given it any thought. My mind had been on other things. "Oh!" I made a face. "I forgot. She wants to say goodbye to you."

"You never said that! Does she know we broke up? When will she be here?"

"I see her now." I pointed.

"Oh, Gabe! I'm not prepared for this." She stepped closer to the window, her nose to the glass, spying on Pythia.

Snooping from the window, we witnessed Pythia, strolling leisurely, seeming particularly satisfied. Then she beamed. We looked on as she reached for one of the wispy white cottonwood seeds and greeted it in her cupped hands. Carefully transporting the descendant, she lowered herself onto her haunches. Her green dress puddled around her feet while she presented the progeny. The two cute little neighbor girls filled their cheeks and blew the seed as if it were candles on a cake. Pythia laughed. They clapped, and the high priestess waved goodbye, heading to my door.

Jumping back from the window, Amy hurried to the sofa and sat. Then popped up, "What does she expect? What am I supposed to do?" she asked, practically flying around the room. "Oh, Gabe!" she said, and finally stood behind me.

"Ah, Amy," Pythia said, coming through the door and going straight to her. Taking Amy's face in her hands, Pythia looked into her eyes and said, "Take care of Gabe and take care that he does the same for you. Yes?"

Amy nodded. Her eyes darted my way.

"Pythia, remember? Amy and I, we're—not—you know, I told you."

Pythia held Amy with her eyes a bit longer, then released her, took her hands, squeezed and shook them in her own before letting go. "Oh, here's my girl!" Pythia squatted to scoop up Cat.

"That's astonishing! Cat's not come down on her own in weeks."

Cat sat tall on Pythia's lap, taking in the chin scratches and sweet-nothings Pythia whispered into her ear. "Nothing astonishing at all about good friends saying fare thee well on parting, now is there Cat?"

"I can hear her purring from here!"

"Well, of course, you can," she said to me, loving on Cat. The two adored each other a bit longer until Pythia set Cat to the floor and Cat crossed to Amy. "Well," she said, sighing and placing her hands on her thighs she paused. "I suppose it is time." She stood and smoothed her dress, then turned to Amy and touched her arm. "As I said, yes?"

Amy nodded.

"Well, shall we?" Pythia asked, taking my hand. Her ringed fingers wrapped around mine.

"Well, wait." My hand went for my curls.

"Agape mou, look. I've the proper shoes." She kicked up a foot, revealing an ordinary hiking boot, and the realization washed over me. The significance of her standing before me. Flesh and blood. Alive. Real. I couldn't pretend it wouldn't hurt.

"It is as it is," she said, reading my mind.

52

Pythia and I walked, side by side, down the main trail and across the bridge over the creek. Something about her hiking boots, kicking out from beneath the hem of her dress, made me nervous. I'd wanted to believe this surprise hike was due to her lack of organization, but I knew it wasn't so.

On the trail, dog owners profusely apologized and tugged against their faithful companions who kept veering toward Pythia. But she always stopped and happily patted the pooches, remarking to each attentive pup at her feet, "My, what a beautiful coat you have!" or "Isn't it a glorious day to be a dog?"

"Dogs like you."

"It's the nature of things," she said, matter of fact as we passed the remains of an old stone house I'd never seen before even though I often hiked this trail. "This way." She ducked beneath a low branch and headed off the trail and onto an obscured path. "It's like a secret," she whispered back to me. "Only it's not. It's a surprise. See." The way opened onto a grassy meadow dotted with early blooming wildflowers.

"Is this?" I looked around. "This is Shadow Ridge Canyon. How—" I looked behind me, but the path had vanished. There was only wild foliage.

"Oh, look!" She pointed to a young bear lumbering into the pines. "Can you imagine having so much fun? Feeling so free to be yourself?"

Turning away from the place the bear had been, I looked to Pythia. "How did we get here?"

"The songbirds are lovely, aren't they? Don't you think? Oh, and look." She pointed, shielding her eyes from the morning sun. "A red-tailed hawk. I suppose he's hunting for a snack. You can't blame him. We all have to eat, don't we?"

"Pythia, I'm confused. how did we get here?" I asked, but she plowed ahead with me trailing behind her as we rounded the ridge.

"Oh!" she exclaimed when the Flatirons came into view, oddly still lit in their morning glory. Plopping down on a slab of stone, she patted the smooth rock. "Come. Please sit with me and watch the world turn." Squinting from beneath the dappled shadow of a gigantic spruce, she'd already reclined onto her elbows. I joined in a less relaxed manner perching at the front of the slab. The flat sides of the red rock turned to velvet as the sun climbed into the sky.

"It's nice, isn't it?"

"Yes, it's beautiful. But I still don't—"

"I mean to be outdoors in general. It's nice, isn't it?"

"Yeah." I turned and shrugged. She grinned, waggling her crossed feet.

"Come on. Join me." She waved for me to join her and I scooted back on the giant stone to sit beside her. "In nature, you can feel free to fit in the way you honestly do. Don't you think? There's something quite easy about being outdoors. Natural. Healing. We're all a part of this. We're creatures, too, you know." She smiled. "What?" Her eyes widened, and she reached for my hand. "It's like peeing outdoors, isn't it?"

"Excuse me." I laughed, taking back my hand.

"Don't you quite agree that peeing outdoors is rather liberating?"

"Okay, yeah. I guess. I've never thought about it, but yeah. Though some people might think it's—"

"Crass?" She made a face. "Yes, I know what you mean. But don't you think, here," she indicated to the trees and tall grasses, "it's natural. Not crude or uncivilized, but natural. It's important to know how to be natural, don't you think? To follow your nature and let nature take its course. I don't know. Perhaps I'm barking up the wrong tree."

"You? Barking up the wrong tree?"

"Oh, believe me! I know my nature." She leaned into me. "But do you see what I'm suggesting? Am I wrong?"

"No. I see what you mean. Peeing outside is a rite of passage. It is something we all have done and probably would continue if it weren't schooled out of us."

"You must be considerate, of course. I haven't led you astray, have I? I mean, with the whole business about relieving yourself outdoors? Give it some thought. I think there's something there."

"Okay." I grinned, giving her a sideways look.

"Thank you." She touched my arm. "The greater we open the heart, the greater the heart is open. Shall we? Are you ready?" She stood and held out her hand.

"Oh? You mean? Okay. Yeah." I offered her both my hands.

"No, love." She looked right at me.

I pulled back. I shook my head. "I don't—"

"You know the way. This time," she said and paused, our eyes locked, "it is my turn to follow."

"No, Pythia. Please." I begged as if I were asking for my life. "I, I, I can't!" My eyes darted. "I'm not ready. Please." Not even knowing why I backed away.

"Agape mou."

"I'll explode. I'll come apart. Pythia, I'll die. I can't." I dropped to my knees. The world spun, and I swear I rocketed off, shot into space, my mouth blew wide open. My cheeks flapped against the force. My entire being seized.

"Agape mou." She tapped my shoulder. "Stand up." Smelling like church, she helped me to my feet. "I cannot take you. But you know the way." Her eyes held me. "Yes?" She nodded. "You'll not die. Have faith in yourself. Come now. Take me there."

On shaky legs and rubbing my arm, I stepped past her. The ridge called to me, and I led until we crested the rise and headed toward a clearing. A cottage covered in Virginia creeper stood at its center. Someone had neatly trimmed out the door and windows. A host of sunflowers bowed their heads near the door. The yard was tall wild grasses.

"This is it." I shielded my eyes from the sun. Ignoring my racing heart and burdened breath, I let it draw me in. Flagstones sheltered the roots of dandelions. Traipsing toward the door suddenly I couldn't move. Some force field stopped me dead in my tracks. With my feet magnetized to that very spot, my legs trembled and my fear pressed into profound anxiety. I looked over my shoulder to Pythia.

"You know this place, agape mou. All is fine. You are standing in front of a place you know in your bones, in your heart. A place you thought was missing. That's all, my love. That's all that's happening." Unable to face her, I admitted what

I already knew. I ran my hand through my hair, feeling like something awful was about to happen.

"You are not alone. I have your back." I felt her come closer. "Breathe," she said.

I acquiesced, and on the exhale, made that soft, deflating sound. A calm blue relieved the tension between my shoulder blades. "Okay." I faced the faded red door. I scratched my head, then rubbed my beard. "Can I look in the window first?"

"Would you like to look in the window first?"

I nodded with my back to her.

"It is your life. Feel free."

At the window, I cupped my hand to the dusty pane, and looked through them to search the interior on the other side. Floor to ceiling shelving covered the back wall and my heart pounded. Some fact echoed through my chest. My blood picked it up and carried it to all my cells. Knowledge rose and lingered at the back of my throat. I swallowed hard, accepting a truth. The dusty shelves were filled with pots of all sizes and shapes. Some glazed and finished, some still green. A threadbare oriental rug covered a wide-planked wooden floor, and a man with dark curly hair sat kicking a potter's wheel, throwing a pot.

"What do you want to say?"

Cast beneath the shadow of the tall, showy sunflowers, I turned toward Pythia. "That's my dad. That's him."

"Would you like to meet him?"

Gaping and spellbound, my attention went from her to the window and back to her again. "Please."

53

I nside, my dad turned as I opened the door. He stood, hesitated for a second then untied his muddy apron and crossed the room. A younger version of me, only without a beard, his longer hair tied in a red bandana, his eyes met mine. "Hey, man," he said grabbing my hand to shake it hard, "It's so good to see you. I've been counting the days till you got here." Then he grabbed my elbow, pulling me in, and hugged me until I could feel his heartbeat. He was warm and smelled of pine and leather layered over rich black humus. Generous and strong, he held me like I was something he loved. I heaved against my best effort and hid my head at his shoulder. He held me tight until the emotion subsided, and I pulled back, hearing, for the first time, music coming from a boom box that sat by the wheel.

"I'm sorry." I pinched my nose and cleared my throat. Jackson Browne sang, "Caught between the longing for love and the struggle for the legal tender."

"Hey, man, like, it's totally not a thing. You here is so choice, I can't even say." His eyes were rimmed with tears. "Come on." He motioned to a beat-up sofa with sagging red velvet cushions. "Sit." Crossing the room, he then called over his shoulder, "Cup of tea?" but was already filling a kettle. "I've got peppermint."

"That would be lovely," Pythia said, making herself at home in the studio, sitting in an overstuffed chair near the sofa, her legs already drawn up beneath her.

I sat on the sofa, its springs gave way and I sank into the deep red fabric but quickly maneuvered to the edge, not ready to relax. "Yeah, that'd be cool." I tried to sound the way I wished I felt, and stood to look at the stacks of pottery. Their glazes ranged from soft blues to moss greens, but the most beautiful resembled an aged turquoise finish with undertones of soft browns and striking blue-greens. Those favored artifacts from an archeological dig. "So, what's the little stone dropped in the center of each of your pots about?"

"Here you go. Careful, it's hot," my dad said to Pythia, passing her a cup, then made his way to me. "Oh, that's a feng shui thing. You know?" He gauged my knowledge. "It's a Chinese practice that harmonizes a person with their surroundings. The little stone keeps the vessel from longing for more than its form." He fetched a big bowl from a high shelf. "See? I find these rocks on my walks then pair them with the bowls. Well, really, they pick each other." Unabashed and with his eyes locked on me, he said, "You have your mother's eyes, don't you?" He lingered then to really study me.

A tuxedo kitten brushed against Pythia's legs before leaping into her lap. "Oh, hey, Kitty, you haven't been invited. You okay with that, Pythia?" my dad asked.

"Absolutely. I love cats." Already stroking Kitty, Pythia softly sang along with the music still streaming, "And when the morning light comes streaming in, we'll get up and do it again. Amen."

"Yeah. I'm a cat person, too." He stood holding the mug, grinning from ear to ear, nodding.

"I have this album," I said, realizing that the old album must have been his.

"You do? Ah, I loved that album. Didn't have much music back then, but we had this old record player in the studio. Played that album over and over, along with—"

"Van Morrison and Bob Seger?" I interrupted.

"Oh, man! No way!" He crossed the room to grab a stack of CDs. "Look." He showed me their spines. "The complete collection of both. But my favorite albums will always be—"

"*Astral Weeks* and *Night Moves.*" I finished his sentence.

"This is big-time sick!" He set the music aside. "You're really my flesh and blood. You know things about me that I didn't know you knew. And I know things about you that you don't know I know. But we both know that somewhere deep inside ourselves, this knowledge lives. We can feel it in our bodies; it connects us. That's what I am feeling now." He patted his heart. "Man, I feel connected to you in my heart, in my soul." He looked pained. "This is way real. More than I ever imagined."

The truth of his words made my legs weak and I returned to sit on the sofa. "Listen," he said, passing in front of Pythia making his way between the coffee table and the sofa to sit next to me. "I'm your dad." He nodded, assuring me, looking like the best version of me. The me that would comfort Cat, or Amy, I thought of both wistfully. "And you? You're my son." He took my hand. "You are my son," he said again, helping it sink in. "You are a fine man. And you and me? We've got this gift, this Thang really, that Pythia here arranged." He nodded toward Pythia. "I want to hear about you and your life. The parts that are in your heart." He searched my eyes. "And what can I tell you? What would you like to know from me?"

"Uh, I don't know." I ran my hand through my hair.

"I used to do that." His eyes were sympathetic. "I know what that means when you run your hand through your hair like that." He showed me how he could do it too. "Everything's okay. Even when it feels like it's not, it is. It all works out." He nodded. "Now go ahead. Fire away."

"Well, I, I'm not sure. I guess," I babbled and Pythia stood and crossed the room to poke around the pots. Seeing she was out of earshot, I leaned toward my dad. "How will I know if I'm a good man, a good person?" I asked in a low voice. "What is a good man, a good husband, a good dad? I don't know if I know. What if I don't know?"

He met my eyes. He had a way of making me feel at ease and safe with him. "What I can tell you is that you won't always know, completely that is, what it means to be a good human being. And if you notice that you don't know, that you're unsure? Well, that means you're evolving as a conscious being. Witnessing your life and living it, too. But I know what you're asking. I asked it many times myself." He studied me. Then looked across the room and out the window, The sunflowers bent in the breeze, yellow sunlight flooded the room. "Where's the best place to begin."

His long, thick lashes flashed while his perfectly spaced eyes shifted and blinked. His face was square-shaped, his chin square and strong like mine, though mine dimpled. His cheeks were pocked, and a small white scar near his hairline contrasted his tanned complexion. I wondered if his large ears would look so prominent without the kerchief holding back his curly hair. His hands rested on his clay-stained jeans. His fingers were dry and cracked, the nails worn to the quick, the purple-blue veins on the inside of his wrists noticeable against the pale undersides of his sun-leathered arms. He was beautiful.

He shuffled his feet, situating himself to explain something, and I noticed his work boots were laced only halfway. I wondered if, like me, he preferred them loose. "Well, let me start with being a good human being. Now, understand," he cautioned, raising both hands just off his knees, "this is what I know now. I can't say how good I was at it back then, but I'd like to think I gave it my best." I stared at him. "Okay?" he asked like he was seeking forgiveness. I nodded, wanting to sincerely trust him. He took a breath. "Okay. Practice kindness for yourself first. Then it's easy to show magnanimity to others. But know the difference between generosity and expectation. Do you know what I mean?"

"I do. It can be easy to think in terms of generosity being something that assures some outcome. I think you're saying to appreciate the privilege, the birthright to care for yourself. And once you do that authentically, you can honestly feel big-hearted toward others. Affording yourself such freedom is necessary to care for others."

"Exactly!" He turned to Pythia, who was back on the sofa. Kitty was asleep on her lap. "This is so choice, Pythia. It's to the max. I'm so completely grateful." Turning back to me, he put his hand on my knee. "And you, man? Whew. Woah." He licked his lips, then took the red hanky off his head, running his hand through his hair. "I mean, here you are. Yeah. Here. You. Are. Alive and real." He nodded, really studying me. "We've got the same bones, the same jaw." He touched his own while looking at mine. "You got my mess of hair, too." He laughed. "Does it drive you crazy?" I nodded, laughing, too. Then remembering something, he added, "But the girls like it, right?"

I gave a little smile. "For the most part."

"Your mother told me it made her feel like having fun. I always remembered that because your mom was a heavyweight thinker. Yeah, she was. We were a lot alike in that way, both of us thinking things through, maybe too much. But we tried to figure out how to be responsible *and* have fun. So, to your question, take responsibility. Period." Then he added, "And relinquish judgment. Yeah, be willing to do something with and for those responsibilities. Think stewardship."

"What was it like when you found out you were going to be a dad?"

"Oh, man! I was so psyched! I tell you I was. I wanted to be somebody's daddy, and doing it with your mom? Well, I couldn't have imagined it would get any better than that. I had no family to speak of, just my old man. He was way old school, but decent, you know. My mom died in a car wreck when I was just this high." He showed me he'd been a toddler by lowering his hand to measure about three feet above the floor. "My old man didn't know what to do with a kid. He did his best; he loved me. I always knew that. And you know what else? He loved you, too. Yeah, you loved to visit with him. He'd take you and putter around his garage. He was a good man. But I pretty much had to grow up and take care of myself. Figure this world out on my own."

"I didn't know that. I guess there is so much I don't know. I never even thought about your parents, but I think I remember him. Did he smoke a pipe?"

"He sure did."

"Wow. I remember. And I remember he was special to me. I never remembered he was my grandpa. I don't know why? Isn't that funny? I only wondered about you." I studied him. "That must have been hard, not having a mom."

"Yeah, it was. I mean, it was all I knew. But I knew something was missing even though my pops did the best he could. So, the idea of making my own family meant a lot to me." He looked off. "Boy, I haven't thought about that for a long time. I never knew my dad's family, and my mom's, well I guess you'd say she'd been estranged. There'd been a lot of drama with her folks. They were from the east. I think they thought my old man was some illiterate mountain man. Yeah, I don't know if I ever considered how much my mom's parents were like your mom's. Anybody, or anything for that matter, south or west of New York, was either a hillbilly or flake. Your grandparents thought I was both." He looked sad but took a breath and continued. "But, when it came to being your dad, that didn't matter one bit as far as I was concerned. I thought how someday we'd do the fourteeners. How I'd teach you to fly-fish and backcountry ski. To ride a bike and swim. Throw a pot." He gestured to the wheel. "I imagined all of us camping and hiking out to the falls. No, I'll tell you." He looked right at me. "That day? The day your mom told me, I'd never felt as happy as I did that day, and the days just got better. The day you were born was the best!" His head bobbed. He beamed. "It sure was."

We sat quietly. "So, where was I? Generosity, responsibility. Ah, okay, yeah. Practice inclusivity and curiosity. When in doubt, apply love. Work the muscle of integrity." He tapped his heart. "Mind your manners. Open doors for everyone. Be honest with yourself. Now that one's hard. It can be easy not to want to see something, and there are plenty of people who'll join you if you agree to lie to yourself. But if you're honest with yourself, you can be honest with others, and that makes it possible to encourage others in a meaningful way." He thought again. "Yep, encourage others. Be flexible. It's the only way to grow. Honor dignity while answering to your own agency. Here's a good one. Well, they're all good, but this one is often overlooked: a little self-awareness goes a long way. And I mean that literally. All it takes is a little bit; too much leads to self-absorption," he said like he was letting me in on a secret. "And, welcome the day. It's always full of promise."

"Tell him what you told me." Pythia sat with her legs tucked beneath her. She stretched to touch my dad's arm while doing her best not to disturb Kitty. "Remember? About all boys and, as far as you were concerned, all girls too, having a certain privilege? An enjoyment? You remember." She coaxed.

"Ah, well, it seems sort of silly now, but I was all over it when Pythia and I met. When we talked about the possibility of this meeting. But…" he looked embarrassed. "Now that you're here and you're not a little boy, hell, you're older than I was when I left the world."

"Well, you gotta tell me now. What if I don't know the thing you're talking about? You gotta tell me." I leaned in, my eyes darted between them gauging who I could convince.

"I said that I hoped someone had taught you the joy of peeing outdoors." He full-on blushed.

"Is that what that was all about before?" I asked Pythia. "Wait. The two of you met before? I mean, I guess of course you have, but… I don't know." I turned toward my dad. "You've only existed in my own head for so long that to me, it's like you're only mine. I know that sounds childish."

"Hey, not at all. I hear what you're saying. Pythia and I, oh, hey. Pythia, man. Geez, I've forgotten my manners. I got so caught up, I forgot to thank you for making this happen. Thank you. Really." He gave her his full attention, nodding before returning to me. "Yeah, so we'd only met once to discuss this meeting. I wanted so badly to see you and was so nervous about making a good impression that my enthusiasm got away from me. I ended up saying that thing about peeing outdoors. What I meant was that I hoped someone helped you, reminded you to feel free and connected with being alive in the most fundamental ways. I'm not advocating public indecency or unsanitary conditions, but taking a leak outdoors when circumstances call for it can build humility and respect for the natural course of things. I guess that's what I was thinking." He scratched his head, then smiled at me; his eyes were soft and loving. "Yeah, I'd like to think I have wisdom that is meant specifically for you, aside from the peeing bit. I guess what I hope is that here, together, we can now weave a greater understanding of the meaning and experience of love than we could apart." He turned to Pythia. "Is it still cool? Do we have time?"

54

Outside my dad and I hiked through the tall pines until we found the open mesa. "Check it out." I pointed to a harem of elk grazing. Distinguished by his size and sturdy antlers, the male stood, a watchful guard over the cows and calves until we'd hiked past, before he lowered his head to graze.

"This is one of my favorite places," my dad said stretching his arms out as if to touch it all.

"Mine too!" I turned to him wide-eyed while we traversed stony ground before the wooded approach to the lake. "I make it a practice to get here every now and then, like showing up for church. I kinda just know when it's time to come. It's a touchstone, a talisman of sorts."

"That's funny." He smiled. "We used to bring you here. Your mom would make a lunch, and we'd walk around the lake, you in a pack on my back. We'd talk, making plans. Pretty soon, you were old enough to toddle ahead. The last few times, you were skippin'."

The trail widened, and we proceeded side by side as the breeze blew and the tips of tall pines bent. "You know how kids do that? All that coordination. Such independence." He looked fond. "We'd sit right there and picnic." He pointed to a flat slab jetting out onto the lake. "Sometimes there'd be a local or two, but most times it was just the three of us. It seemed to me that we did that all the time. But I know that's not right." He stopped and thought for a minute. "We probably did it when I taught late-morning classes. Or maybe in the summer? I don't know. I guess it doesn't matter except that it's special to me."

"That's so weird. It's always felt familiar here. I remember coming with Mom. She'd bring a sack lunch, and we'd sit on that rock." I pointed. "I forgot all about that. I guess it's no coincidence that it feels like home here. Though," my eyes dropped, "I don't remember you," and this I said almost to just myself. "But I wish I did." An ancient sadness rose in me. One I'd always thought was just the sensation of being myself. "I'll admit that I imagined you'd show up somewhere, sometime, like at one of my baseball games." I rolled my eyes and scoffed, shaking my head, and picked up my pace, advancing ahead of him as we headed up a hill.

"I never really thought about what I'd say to you," I said, with my back to him once I heard him shadowing me. "Not specifically. Ideas floated around. Like how to be a real man with only a mom to show me." I said, pumping my arms against a growing edginess. "I knew there were things she didn't know. Like the feelings I had about girls. I know she worried too. I think that was a big part of why she remarried." I slowed. "What a disaster that was." I stopped. "It crushed her."

I looked right at my dad but he met my scowl with soft eyes. "It made me think I had to be the man in our lives." I glared at him longer, then shook my head and returned to hiking, talking too loudly and too fast. My dad stayed at my side, unhindered by my animated rant. "The problem with that was that my mom thought she had to be the man in our lives, too! Truth be told, she was better at it than me. Or at least that's what I thought, and that proved very unhelpful!" I labored to breathe.

"It's an unfair question," I said, breathless, dropping my gaze. "And totally one of a child, but I want to know why?" I looked right at him. "Why did you leave? Why weren't you strong enough?" Emotion rose. "Wasn't I worth fighting to stay for?" I choked. "All my life, I've wondered what it could have been like if you were here. I felt you missing in my life. I didn't know how to be alive without you. She didn't either. We were wayward. Lost without you, even broken sometimes, especially in matters of love. And then somehow, I got it in my mind that if you didn't love me enough to stay, why would anyone else?"

He flinched, but I faced him. Agony crept across his face, but I couldn't stop. "Before I met Amy? After my last break-up? I thought it was time to accept my lonely, pathetic life. It seemed like I'd never get it right. That there was something wrong with me for sure. I couldn't figure what the point would be in failing again. It's dangerous to be so vulnerable. You know?" I shrugged, frowning, "And it never stops. It doesn't look good for Amy and me. Cat's dying. Mom's moving. And I gotta find a new job." I dumped on him even though I knew it couldn't possibly be his fault; I couldn't stop. "So, what am I supposed to think. How am I supposed to feel?"

He exhaled, the color drained from his face and he shook his head. "I know. It wasn't fair. It was even cruel, maybe." Then he licked his lips and looked me in the eyes. "But it was never that you weren't worth it. Do you hear me?" He grabbed my arm, pulled me in, and wrapped his arms around me. He kissed the top of my head and I let myself lean into him. He held me, quiet at first, and then said into my ear, "And it wasn't that I wasn't strong enough either. It just wasn't a choice, not really. It was the course of what was to be. It was the nature of things. My time had concluded." He held me tight, then let me go, and we walked on. "I knew it when it happened, but I didn't know it before. If I had, I would've fought tooth and nail against it." He swiped his sleeve across his nose and kicked a stone. "And mostly for you. But once I was there? Once the motorcycle went over, the grid lined up, the doors opened, and I stepped through. I am sorry. I did it before I knew it, and then there was no going back, not really."

"The grid?" I asked, wondering, like a little boy, how my dad's passing could've ever been an option.

"Yeah, it's complicated. Everything has a Thang. You know? A process, an evolution. But once I figured things out on this side, I've been with you ever since." He looked at me like he wanted me to see something important. "I'm what they call The Now Invisible Other." He gave a half-smile. "I can always be with you, just not the same as it was. More like this." He motioned to the space between us, the place that helped define our distinct boundaries.

"With Mom, too?"

"Oh, yeah. She's my best girl." He looked boyish.

"Will she be with you, you know, when she goes?" Then hushed, I asked, "Can I?"

"Hell yeah! You bet I'll be waiting for you both. And Gabe, I got you covered on Cat. Consider it done."

I looked away and pinched the top of my nose, waiting for the excruciating pain to pass. "Is your dad here? Your mom?" I asked, finally composed.

"Yep."

"What about Mom's family?"

"Yeah, sure. But I don't see them much. There's no animosity. We just don't really work together across time. You know? We're not on the same projects, so to speak. We run into each other and maybe might have a gig or two, but we are kind of like, well, oil and vinegar. Not in the way you think, though." He stopped. "We don't mix. Instead, when our vibrations are side by side, they offer choice. Kinda the fork in the road. More like jazz, you know, like how the unexpected creates a unique opportunity for something completely new."

"I can see how that happened for Mom, separating from her family, and falling in love with you. It was her fork, so I guess it was mine, too. Certain things or experiences wouldn't have been significant to me without the loss of you." I shuffled my feet, kicking up dust, understanding how things fit together but at the same time resenting that they did.

"Yeah, in the bigger picture, you can see the beauty of the design. It's only in the minutia that it provides for judgment. You know, like that it's wrong, or bad, or even cruel. It's human to do that, though."

I nodded, understanding what he was saying, yet I was still feeling like a kid without a dad.

"I know. It's not how I wanted it, either."

"What did you want?" I asked, searching his face. "What do you want to tell me?"

"You mean, besides about peeing in the great outdoors?" He tried to be funny but sounded nervous. "Hey, look." He pointed to a long-winged bird sailing across the blue sky, its whiteish underparts a contrast to its blue-gray feathers and sooty head.

"It's a raptor." Shielding our eyes, we watched the peregrine falcon soar and dive.

"There's so much I've wanted to tell you for so long. Pythia suggested a letter might be easier." He dug into his back pocket. "It's not much. I don't want you to be disappointed. It's definitely not mind-blowing, but it's in my hand, and it's from my heart. Take it with you."

"Can I read it now?" I looked at the note, uncertain of what I wanted.

"Not now, and not for any reason other than, when you read it later, it'll be like I'm with you. It's not profound. It's just a letter from your old man."

"What does that mean?" I asked, trying to slow time, bargaining for more knowing full well it was only closing in.

"It means," he began, and then looked to the earth and shuffled his feet. "Everything's okay. It all works out in the end. And in the end, you can always come home. It means I love you. It means you're loved."

55

Pythia and I hiked without speaking, pretending we were comfortable with the inevitable. The sun was past its peak, casting the land with long shadows. Soon we'd part without a plan to meet again. Bittersweet sensations edged in between the great sense of satisfaction in our relationship and the impending heartbreak of it ending. I suspected there was a chance I'd regret not doing or saying something, but at that moment, I only wanted what I already knew so well. To feel Pythia's physical presence, not some watery memory of her.

"Our time, agape mou," she said, tugging at a ring, "has been beyond what I ever imagined. You've helped me become more than I ever knew possible. And I am trying hard—" she laughed nervously and fanned her face with her hands, she crinkled her nose but still didn't face me. "Oh, for the sake of the Gods!" She shook her head and turned toward me. Her eyes were rimmed in tears that she dabbed before they fell. "I am going to miss you." Her shoulders shook, and she hid her face. "I will miss you," she said sniffling.

I hung my head and closed my eyes, squeezing them tightly shut. She cleared her throat. "Will you look at me?" Sounding composed, she waited.

"I can't." I halted, unable to contain my anguish. My jaw gripped, hinging my mouth shut with my teeth stacked against each other, building a defense.

"My love, nothing is separate. Everything is joined in the ongoing equation of love. We shall never really be apart."

I cleared my throat. "I know." My voice was unsteady. "I know that now, but still…" I held my breath, hoping to stave off nausea that was always contained in the false belief of separation, the longing for attachment. "I will miss you sorely and with my entire being," I said and when my voice cracked it came all the way apart.

"Me too. It's been quite a ride," she said.

I glanced sideways at her and reached for her hand. "Thank you for every-thing, Pythia. I really mean it." I couldn't look at her and wished there were more than the words.

She squeezed my hand. "I have something for you." She lifted her necklace over her head, released its clasp, and slid the oak leaf pendant from the chain. "Our warm-hearted friendship, philia really, yes?" I looked at her. I nodded. "This love affords us each inner peace. It shall put our minds at ease as we manage the sweet sorrow of our parting. It bids us trust and fortitude that you and I shall persevere through our farewell and cope with the loss of our companionship. It is the way of teacher and student, is it not?"

"Everything has its season." I grinned, still winning brownie points, gunning for student of the year.

"It is for all of that and more that I bestow to you this golden oak leaf." She pulled a length of black cord from her pocket, slid the medallion onto the silk, then tied the ends in a snake knot. "The oak is an unending repository for the eru-dition of the ages, honored for its endurance and esteemed presence." She passed me the gift. "May you carry it as a reminder of your own perseverance."

"Oh! Pythia, this is yours, from Zeus." I looked at the disc of gold, feeling the weight of the present as I fingered the knot.

"I am aware." She smiled. "Please do me the favor of receiving my offering of gratitude. You have been the finest of teachers."

"Me, a teacher?" I searched her face.

"The finest." She closed my hand around the charm and the setting sunlight cast us in a warm glow.

56

L anding in bed, I opened my eyes. Amy sat on the bedroom chair that no
longer hosted discarded clothing and instead invited people for sitting.
She shifted, leaning forward. "Hey" I said, wrestling to sit up, "You're a welcome
sight." She stood with a doleful air about her. The physical distance between us
was slight, but it felt vast. I pushed myself out of bed. "Hey?" I rushed toward her,
my shoulders edging toward my ears, my brows bending in concern while my
arms reached out, desperate to hold her. "What? What?" I demanded, grabbing
her at the shoulders but she was limp and didn't answer. Her face was blotchy and
red, her eyes bloodshot. When the corners of her mouth turned down, her lower
lip trembled.

"I'm sorry. I'm so sorry." She slouched before me, glossy-eyed, while we stood
with something awful and unspoken between us.

"No!" I shook my head. "No. No!"

Her eyes welled up. Tears streamed down her face. She wiped snot from her
nose and sniffled before wiping her face with both hands. Then, she embraced
me. Dizzy, I pulled away. I held her at her shoulders. I searched her face. "On your
desk," she confessed.

Stretched out and long, Cat was still. Her front paws extended as if she was
flying. I closed my eyes and knelt before her, my hands grasping the desk, holding on. I struggled to breathe, working hard to keep my heart from rising into a
mouthful of sobs, my nostrils flared to the deafening sounds of nothing. Holding
my breath, I pulled the cruel, awful truth closer, dragging the fuzzy pink blanket
weighted with Cat's body until she was before me. "No!" I cried again, witnessing
the deadness of my beloved until the fact of it shook me further.

I cascaded through a torrent of mournful cries and into a chrysalis. Reduced from my physical form to a spill of hot salty tears and snot, I shut my eyes again. Trying to accept the blackness as a strong medicine, I laid my head on the table, hoping to feel supported by the smooth, cool surface. I whimpered, and the terrible silence shattered until all I knew was a world of my own inner vibrations. Bawling, I made a fist, but I couldn't defend myself. There was no beating this back.

Amy's hand trembled on my shoulder until she also dropped to the floor and held me from behind, weeping. Cat was gone. Her body cold and stiff, no longer alive and already obliging to Newtonian physics. I draped the old Spider-Man shirt over her, hoping it carried my scent, and wrapped her in the pink blanket. I asked Amy to sit with her while I got a shovel from the shed and dug a hole near the rose bushes.

The earth gave away easily, and I dug deeper, wanting it to be more challenging than it was, wanting to work up the good sweat Cat deserved. When the growing pile of dark-brown earth amounted to something, I could offer my best friend a soft bed.

On that late-spring eve with the sun setting and the squirrels scampering in the trees, we buried Cat there. Amy dug up a large piece of creeping phlox that bloomed alongside the pond, and we planted the pink carpet over Cat's grave.

When we finished, we sat undisturbed, peaceful even; our emotions lulled into a moment of acceptance. A single magpie landed on the shed's roof. The large bird turned its head, looking curious and dapper in its black and white tuxedo. I remembered such birds poking through the window boxes. "It's odd to see just one, isn't it?" Amy sniffled. "What's that nursery rhyme? One for sorrow, two for joy, three for a girl, four for a boy," she said, and as if summoned, others flew in. "Five for silver, six for gold, seven for a secret never to be told."

The birds continued to collect. "That's way more than seven," I said.

"A flock symbolizes a bridge." Amy reached for my hand. I pulled her close, and she rested her back against my chest; it was more comfortable to breathe with our hearts beating together.

Collecting in a chorus, the high-spirited birds began a raspy chatter that grew into loud melodious carols until some broke into soft warbles and others shrieked high-pitched notes. "Woka-woka, pjuur, queg-queg-queg-queg, pjuur, woka-woka, wheer," they sang, and I knew Cat was already soaring over the moon even though I couldn't see either.

57

Morning and nights were the hardest. Between my job and finding a new career, I attempted to fill the gaping silent hole that once was Cat by busying myself around the house. Weeding the garden beds, vacuuming the sofa and the awful green carpet, fixing a leaky faucet. I even slid the bed aside and set up a ladder in my bedroom to apply thin coats of joint compound with a putty knife to the cracked ceiling. Over the course of a few weeks, I sanded the repaired spot smooth and painted the whole thing white.

Amy called every day at first, checking in, asking, "How are you doing? Can I bring over carry out?" As unfair as it seemed, the days did make up weeks and so on. After all, there were groceries to buy, a toilet to clean. Then one week I called and said, "Supposed to be nice. Would you like to? Okay I'll see you then." After that, she invited me to the wedding of a colleague as her guest. And the trumpeting sound of the Sherwood Forest horn alerted me with greater frequency to texts from my friend, Amy.

And they whirl, and they twirl, and they tango, singing and jinging a jango, floating like the heavens above, looks like Muskrat Love.

OMG! my thumbs fired, including an emoji that was laughing so hard it was crying.

Captain & Tennille? I don't know if I can top that. That is perhaps the all-time, most ridiculous love song lyrics ever.

Are you giving up, hotshot?

Not at all, Amy. Not at all.

58

I searched my mind for any indication of anything that didn't add up, after all, I didn't want to betray Cat. She was a Now Invisible Other, and as far as I knew, Cat had even had a hand in it all. Cat was like that.

"The movers will be here about noon next Saturday if all goes well," Amy said, with a red pen, checking her list. Then, making a face, she said, "I don't know. Did I make the right choice? What do you think? I just don't know."

"Amy, I don't think it's a matter of right or wrong. You picked what you wanted, and I think—"

"Do you think I went overboard? Got carried away. You know I can do that."

I sighed. "Are you worried about me? Because if you are, how many times do I have to tell you that I'm okay with this?"

"I don't know, Gabe." She stood with the tip of her finger at her teeth.

I swept my hand across the room, coming down a few rungs on the ladder. "I love this color!" I said, with a roller in hand.

"It'll be in every room." She cautioned wearing skinny jeans and white T-shirt. "But one color is the only way to keep the charm of your place." Her brow furrowed. "It's a color you gotta love."

"If by charming, you mean it's a shoebox, I agree. Amy, you would know best. I trust you. I think this..." but I had to pause, and searching the can, I found the words I was looking for, "Ah, yes, Gray Owl, is perfect for making the place our home."

She nodded, cramming her hands into her pockets and giving the wall a critical eye said, "It's unadorned, approachable, right? I think it's going to pair beautifully with the sofa. And when we update the kitchen appliances, it'll go nicely with stainless."

"Ahh, yes." I scratched my beard. "I see it now. This space you're creating will revolutionize our lives."

"You're being silly."

"Not at all. I'm only doing what my old man told me. Look and listen with a child's curiosity, he said. Because curiosity is the spice of life, and it's the only way around prejudice or judgment. So really, all I can say about Owl Gray is what I've already said."

"Stop." She shook her head and rolled her eyes. "Why do you call him that?"

"Because it's fun, and it's what he called his dad."

"You never told me that. What else haven't you told me?"

I rolled the last of what was in the paint tray and climbed off the ladder. "He told me," I said, seeing his neat penmanship in my mind. "How it's easier to feel free to follow your own nature and let your partner do the same when you see each other for who you are and not what you think you are supposed to be." I beamed with pride. "He said and couldn't stress it enough—expect the unexpected and accept it as evolution."

"Expect the unexpected and accept it as evolution," she said, and lowered herself to the floor. "That's interesting. Don't you think?" Her slate-blue eyes meet mine.

"He said, trust first. And explained that trust is what you do when you find yourself unsure. But in time," I enjoyed sharing my dad with Amy, "trust is what you do because you are sure that nothing is certain."

Her whole face lit up. "Oh, I like that," she said, looking up at me from where she sat on the floor, her legs outstretched and ankles crossed. "Come sit by me," and she patted the spot next to her.

"He told me that communication is fundamental to honesty, honesty to trust, and trust to intimacy. He said to consider all the information, and if you're afraid, speak up." We sat in a patch of afternoon sun.

"Smart man. Fear always only reinforces the fear, and then all that's left is doubt." She leaned against me.

"Like with Owl Gray? What? I'm curious. And maybe silly. But serious, too. My dad did say that fear divided my mom and him. It isolated them from their own strength and each other's."

"That's sad. Let's not do that. What else?"

"Well," I said, and wanting her to feel him through me, I closed my eyes. "Everything has its own process and unfolds as it is nurtured and allowed to flourish. He told me, patience provides a place to rest, rejuvenate, and evolve. It helps a couple remember that love is not an achievement or an acquisition; it is something you create."

"Just like your formula. Love is the creation of space that allows for change."

I opened my eyes. "You remember that?"

"Of course. What else?" she sounded shy, "Anything else about me?"

"He said to have patience with Amy."

"You're making that up." She laughed. Then in a softer voice, she asked, "Did you tell him about me?"

"Of course, I did." Then stealing my dad's line, I said, "You're my best girl."

59

The days had become longer and brighter, which sometimes seemed un-natural in my grief, but it was true that every ending led to the next chapter. In the wake of the tulips, the white moon-faced peonies already hung heavy over the faded patches of dying pink phlox. Amy cut the bright orange poppies, singed their cut stems and showed off their deep black innards in a sleek white porcelain vase she'd made. I watched from the kitchen table with a cup of coffee while she took seriously the job of situating the vase just right on the coffee table.

"Looks nice with the Owl Gray," I smirked.

"I know, right." She backed away, getting perspective on the scene. "The early roses are blooming, and the Hosta and grasses are coming in." She was in love with the garden. "I don't know, Gabe, but I think the sweet woodruff might take over." She looked so serious, and I knew she was right. The dianthus and primrose would suffer at its proliferation.

"Yeah, you can just pull it by the handfuls." She opened the window. Birds chattered, and I remembered Cat on the window ledge. Her watchful eye. Her predator call.

"Really? Well, I don't want to kill it." I winced at the word.

"You won't. Some things are crazy hardy." I stood to distract myself and found my way out the door barefoot. The robin I'd been watching for days sat devoted on her nest, nestled into the crook of the crabapple, magnificent in full white bloom, each one dotted with a pink center. Beneath the tree, the grass was a mess of red berries. I grabbed the mail, and dodging the sticky mash, I retrieved the paper. The girls across the street played.

"Wanna see our picture?" the little one called Mushkin shouted.

Kneeling with a fat piece of bright green chalk in hand, Mushkin's big sister looked up from her work. "Is Pythia coming over today?"

"Not today, Bubbles," I said, thinking how easy it is to fall in love with Pythia. "But I'd love to see your picture." I crossed the street with coffee and mail in hand, the newspaper snug under my arm.

"See?" Mushkin said. "It's a rainbow."

"Yeah, but we're not finished yet," Bubbles said, returning to her knees to color. "A rainbow is all the colors. When you see a rainbow, you know your dreams can come true, so I'm gonna draw a basket of kittens right here." She pointed to the end.

"She loves kitties," the little one said with a slash of pink chalk on her forehead.

"I do." Bubbles colored. "Is Cat still dead?"

"Yes," I said, but only looked at the chalked walkway.

"Sorry," Bubbles said looking up to me.

"Me too," Mushkin echoed, springing up. "Is Amy going to live with you now?"

I nodded, trying to meet their eyes, ignoring the reference of time in her question.

Then, back to coloring, Bubbles said, "Cat's probably waiting for me to draw this basket of kittens," but instead, she drew Cat sitting atop the rainbow. "There," she said, resting on her knees. "I drew Cat, so all her dreams can come true." With black chalk, she began drawing marks that I recognized as flying birds. "Now she can fly with the birds."

I half-smiled.

Bringing in the mail, I shuffled through it, and on finding a letter from my mom, I refilled my coffee.

Dearest Gabe and darling Amy, the letter began. *I feel settled in and useful;* she wrote and painted a picture of long days and primitive conditions. But ultimately, she said she was quite satisfied, and I knew it was true.

So, you start your new job in August. My son, the Professor of Love. How about that! Are you as excited as I am? And I think the course title is brilliant, The Ethics of Love. Who wouldn't want to take that course? Have you thought much more about writing a book now that you've put together your syllabus? With the university behind you, this could happen. Your dad would be so proud.

I thought of my dad. I conjured the woody scent of him: ancient and sacred, evergreens and leather-bound books, like a collection of Shakespeare.

He always knew that no matter the obstacles, there is always opportunity for healing. When I'd worry about you, he'd say, "Err on the side of loving, and it'll all work out. Follow your nature, Mama." And you know who taught me to understand what your dad had been trying to tell me? You! See what a good professor you already are!

She'd signed it, *Your biggest fan.* I smiled, folding her words back into the envelope. Not so long ago, I might have read that letter to Cat. She would have jumped from the window ledge, walked across my lap, and butted her head against my chin before lying down and rolling over to expose her belly. I would have pulled her tail, and then she would have grabbed my hand with her paws while I tussled the top of her head. Somewhere, while the Earth tipped its north axis in favor of the sun, The Now Invisible Other, known to me as Cat, was purring as she stretched in a spot of sun in the studio of The Now Invisible Other that is my dad. Soon enough, the sun would reciprocate the Earth's bow, shining brightly on the Solanum Lycopersicum vines Amy had planted in pots outback. Soon the plants would convert the light into energy and produce that smooth, sweet, fleshy red fruit that summer is known for.

Sitting there, I could feel myself breaking apart, tearing down the old cellular templates within, ones that intersected with profound and far-reaching patterns outside of myself. I'd inspired change within myself and change within my mom. And my dad, and Cat, and Amy, too. Maybe even Pythia. We'd all reorganized ourselves around the nature of evolution, and we'd done it in the only space that hosts such brave determination for goodness. We'd done it in love. And for the first time since Pythia, since ever, I'd realized it with ease.

60

In the following weeks, a package arrived addressed to me in her familiar scrawl, the return address simply: *Pythia*. A message was paperclipped to a two-inch transcript of our work. I took the note from the clip. Its energetic marks, m's and 'w's, looked like rolling hills and mountain peaks that told their own story.

Day 29 Moon Cycle of the Goddess Hera

My Dearest Agape Mou,

We are delighted that you have agreed to supplant the old mythology of love with your brilliant proof. Love is of the forces of nature, revealed through the Higgs mechanism, and therefore necessary to the evolution of the multiverse. It is evidenced in the natural propensity to create and results in a space sanctioned for the gradual, complex, interconnected physics of all things, and for the greatest good.

Please find access to the backend of www.prophecyoflove.com and the enclosed record of our conversations and research. I believe you will find it thorough. As discussed, your authorship on the topic of love is vital to the subsistence of humanity. Everyone here (including you know who) agrees that your argument is sound in deductive reasoning, but more pertinent it provides knowledge that is applicable and useful to everyday life. Most essential and to the point of our work, it will change the world.

At this time, please consider the matter concerning the black ram gracefully complete.

Fondly yours and in infinite service,
Pythia, High Priestess

Out the window, a bossy Magpie chirped at a squirrel working the lid off the birdfeeder.

I leafed through the transcript, seeing my past self, feeling compassion for the anxious being I was. The whole bit with the lampshade, the fear I felt of Socrates and Diotima, the certainty that I was dying as I separated from Pythia, Trane, and Einstein and joined the cosmic mystery of Higgs. I laughed out loud, feeling affection for the earlier version of myself. "Cat," I said, before catching myself, but imagined showing her the letter anyway. This time I just spoke the words out loud even though I knew she could always hear me. "Cat, old girl, we slew the dragon."

I leafed to the end of my journal and before tucking the letter in. I read my final entry.

With diminishing beliefs, the self cannot indulge the necessary vulnerability that provides for trust in self and others. Such beliefs starve the free will and capitulate all the systems of a living enterprise into atrophy. Such conditions deplete the systems of energy critical to intimacy. Without intimacy, disconnection leads to isolation and greater distortion of the cognitive system. The proper use of free will, aligned with the truth of the nature of all things, promotes an edification that sustains the systems and perpetuates possibilities for aliveness. Feed the free will healthy beliefs despite the experiences of human existence. This is the only way to live a loving life.

61

A steel brush dragged across the tight skin of a drum. Ernie Watts played the sax slow and sexy like he longed for something, like he knew the moon was full while I held Amy in my arms, and we slow-danced around the kitchen. A piano teased playfully in the background.

Our feet shuffled, keeping time across the old linoleum, cracked and broken in places. Then, Charlie Haden and Quartet West turned the number over to an old recording of "Haunted Heart" by Jo Stafford. The warbling strings, the fluttering flutes, and then her breathy falsetto rang on the evening fall breeze. The kitchen curtains stirred in the glow of a sunset. Jo dug down deep, pulling out a range of notes, almost operatic but holding just enough back that I felt wistful.

"In the night, though we're apart, there's a ghost of you within my haunted heart, ghost of you, my lost romance." Jo crooned, sounding romantic and desperate at the same time.

"This is nice." I said and I drew Amy closer with my hand at the small of her back, feeling her breasts firmly at my chest, the swell of her belly beneath my own yearning. The occasional feel of her hip bone as it met mine. Her head rested at my chest, her neck damp with sweat but still smelling sweet as we danced.

"I'm so tired." Her warm breath tickled the side of my neck while our feet kept time. "Can we call it a night?" She rested her head and a hand on my chest.

"Are you sure?" I pulled back to look at her. "It's not even eight o'clock."

She drew me in, took the lead, and steered my feet back into the familiar box step. "Ah-ha."

Jo sang on, "Dreams repeat a sweet but lonely song to me. Dreams are dust. It's you who must belong to me and thrill my haunted heart. Be still my haunted heart."

"Okay," I said, hoping to dance a little longer. "How come?"

She eyed me. We stopped. She stepped onto her toes and placed her lips at my ear. Slowly and deliberately, she whispered. I struggled to understand. My heart hurried, racing to get ahead of her words. Then my brows lifted. I stepped back, open-mouthed, my hands found hers. "Are you kidding me?"

"No." She looked less sure of herself. "Is it okay?"

"Is it okay? It's more than okay! It's, it's…I don't know, it's beyond words. How long have you known? Are you okay? Do you feel okay? How did this happen?"

"Well, the usual way." She laughed, looking gorgeous.

"I mean how, though?"

"Luck? Fate?" She shrugged. "Manufacturer defect?"

"Are you happy?"

She nodded.

"Me too." I laughed and grabbed her. "Me too." I pulled her close.

Made in the USA
Coppell, TX
21 September 2021

62761186R00246